Guardians of the Eagle

Guardians of the Eagle

John D. Messer

Writers Club Press
New York Lincoln Shanghai

Guardians of the Eagle

All Rights Reserved © 2002 by John D. Messer

No part of this book may be reproduced or transmitted in any form or by any means, graphic, electronic, or mechanical, including photocopying, recording, taping, or by any information storage retrieval system, without the written permission of the publisher.

Writers Club Press
an imprint of iUniverse, Inc.

For information address:
iUniverse, Inc.
2021 Pine Lake Road, Suite 100
Lincoln, NE 68512
www.iuniverse.com

All events have been based on facts. Some names and dates have been changed as well as some locations to protect the innocent.

ISBN: 0-595-25687-2 (pbk)
ISBN: 0-595-74199-1 (cloth)

Printed in the United States of America

I DEDICATE THIS BOOK TO

Margaret (Pagendarm) Messer
Because you loved me so, I was never alone.

Contents

Introduction 1
Gonna Join the Navy 3
Boot Camp 41
USS Helena CA-75 83
Portsmouth Naval Hospital 143
USS Belle Grove LSD-2 183
Clinical Laboratory and Blood Bank School 267
Naval Hospital Camp Pendleton, California 303
The Vietnam Saga 325
End of the Story 433

Acknowledgement

The mind conceives the idea of a book long before it's born into reality. I had given some thought to documenting some of the more important events of my military career but would never have undertaken such a project without my son Joe's encouragement. His assurance that he would be available to give me technical support was invaluable in light of my computer illiteracy. Thanks, Joe, for the new keyboard, big screen monitor and your time and effort in making my dream come true.

Nothing of any major significance has occurred in my life in the past forty-four years without the support of my dear wife, Margaret. My obsession with the story has compelled me to eat, sleep, talk and breathe this endeavor over the past few months. I marvel at her patience and understanding when I take on one of my projects. Having her read my humble work and assure me it was worthwhile was the power that drove me to complete this undertaking.

I want to give special thanks to Michelle Rapp for donating her time and expertise in editing my ignoble efforts. As the weeks turned into months, she didn't give up on me or falter. She never attempted to change my style of writing or alter my method of expressing myself. She dutifully made the grammatical changes and pointed out the areas she felt to be vague. Leaving, always, the final wording to me. Thanks Michelle! You're one in a million.

Last, but not least, I want to thank the many friends and family members who read along as I scribbled. Many times, when I felt discouraged, you cheered me on, assuring me my work was credible. Without your support, this enterprise would have never reached fruition.

Introduction

It appears, with rare exception, each generation down through history has had its own war to confront. From sticks and stones, knives, bows and arrows, muskets and cannon balls, to the modern-day supersonic planes and smart weapons, not to mention, the horrific atomic bombs, we look for new ways to kill each other in our never-ending conflicts.

My generation was no different than the tens of thousands who lived before us. I would predict, unless there are some unforeseen drastic changes in human relations, those who follow are doomed to repeat this same, seemingly endless, cycle.

Libraries are full of books about famous people and how they changed the course of history by individual acts of heroism in certain battles. I do not wish, in any way, to diminish these brave men's importance nor their contribution to the betterment of mankind. Men such as these have earned their special places in history and inspire us. But this story is not about them. It's about the ordinary man.

The truth is that most of us who have served our country and fought our nation's wars were not extraordinary. Ninety-nine percent of us were not decorated for heroism or given a special place of honor in our history. Eighty-five percent or more of us were enlisted men and women. We held no great position of power nor were we knighted with impressive titles; we merely washed the dishes, scrubbed the floors, shined the brass, stood the watches, cared for the sick and injured among us and bore the day-to-day grind of military service.

These ordinary men and women were my friends and peers. Within the pages of this book, I have tried to pay homage to those special individuals who had the greatest impact on me and were responsible for the forming of what I refer to as, "my military conscience".

Some of the names, I have changed to protect the individuals and their families. In cases where I used real names, it was to bring honor to that person and to show in what high regard I held them. Other times, I have omitted using their names completely. In most cases, it was because their position was the only thing that the reader needed to know in order to understand the story. On other occasions, it was because our relationship was casual and I had simply forgotten.

The details of the story cover only the first eleven years of my military career, with a short summary. There were many men and women in the last nine years who I held in high regard that I wasn't able to mention. Perhaps, some of them will be disappointed, but I assure you they were no less important to me. I just felt the story had been told and it was time to bring it to an end.

My hope is that, in the coming generations, when the twentieth century and the Vietnam War fade into history, there will be an account by an ordinary man and how he perceived military life of that era.

Gonna Join the Navy

A big, black dog trotted across the rock road toward our house. He stopped and sniffed a tall, green weed with little yellow flowers on it, lifted his leg and made water.

"Where did that old dog come from?" asked my sister Jean, who was six years younger than me. We were sitting in the porch swing in front of the old, faded, wooden farmhouse we had lived in for three years.

"Oh, them sorry bastards from over in town come out here and dump everything off they don't want," I answered.

The dog trotted on over and started up the little incline toward our house.

"Get outta here, damn you!" I yelled, as I stood up and pretended to throw something. He tucked his tail between his legs, lowered his head and moved on past the house in the direction of Fontaine. "If old Pal was still alive, you can bet he wouldn't dare show his face around here," I said to no one in particular.

It was the middle of April, 1956, in the late afternoon.

"Daddy said there is a place in Pocahontas where you can buy a suit for thirteen dollars," commented my sister Jean.

"I ain't wearing no damn thirteen-dollar-suit to have my graduation picture made. Hell, they hang it up in the hall. Can you imagine people looking at me dressed up like that for the next hundred years?"

"Well, daddy said he ain't gonna spend a nickel more. And he can't even give you that until he gets the money he borrowed from the FHA to make a crop. He ain't too interested in spending money on you anyway, especially since you're gonna go off to the Navy and leave him here to work the farm by hisself."

My sisters, eight-year-old Armentia, known to us as Boogie, and five-year-old Cleo, who we called Fuzzy, were sitting on the top of the steps that lead up to the porch. They guided their dolls in rhythm to a yet unknown dance as they listened to our discussion. I watched them for a moment.

"You two get over here and bow down to your king, right now," I said, getting up out of the swing and taking off my belt. I then slammed the floor of the old, wooden porch as hard as I could. I walked toward them trying to look as I imagined a king might look, who had the power of life and death over his subjects.

"We ain't a gonna be your slaves no more, Dick. Mommy said we don't have to do what you say. Besides, Daddy said, if you hit us with that old belt, he'd beat the tar out of you hisself. He don't care how big you think you are!" Cleo declared defiantly.

I slammed the floor again, advancing closer, trying to scare them.

"Come on, Cleo," said Armentia, as she took Cleo's hand pulling her up into a run. They quickly disappeared around the corner of the house giggling.

"Those two are spoiled rotten. When I was Armentia's age, I was a full hand in the field," I said, as I sat back down. Suddenly, I felt defeated.

"Yeah, I know. Things gonna change around here when you go in the Navy," Jean responded. "They gonna be slaves for real then," she added.

"Gonna take a lot of doing before that happens," I laughed.

My home-birth occurred in the northeast part of Greene County, Arkansas on 31 October 1937. My folks were tenant cotton farmers. From where we lived, it was fourteen miles to the nearest town if you headed west and eighteen if you went east. Two miles north of us was the little village called Light. A small restaurant, gas station, general store, cotton gin and a post office were located there. It was the heart of the community during my growing up years. During the war, it had been much larger. At one time, there had been a pool hall, theater, two cotton gins, a white apartment building, several rental houses of various colors and two cafés. The community was now in transition; we had gone from horsepower to mostly tractor power in the eleven short years since the big war. More successful farmers had expanded their operations into two and three hundred acres and had swallowed up the smaller farms. The community population had been reduced considerably. There was no longer a family on each forty-acre parcel of land.

The small, rural community schools had been consolidated and we were bussed fourteen miles to a centrally-located tech school that served students from all over the county. The curriculum consisted of courses to prepare the boys to become future farmers. The girls could take cosmetology or business with their primary course of home economics. I had no intention of living out my life working long, hard days on other people's land. My aptitude and interest in the Agricultural Department's wood and machine shop, where I was often required to put in two hours a day, was non-existent. I was, however, required to complete the course if I intended to graduate. I had become so disgusted and bored that after completing the tenth grade, I dropped out. My mother became distraught at the idea of me not finishing high school. After months of her constant badgering, pushing, pleading, bribing and long tearful prayers, she finally extracted a promise from me that I would go back. The beginning of the semester, the following year, I enrolled once again. I struggled daily with my resentment against a school and teachers that dictated to me what my future would be. I was determined to do the minimum to graduate but nothing else. I couldn't wait to walk free and become my own man.

We were farming what was known to us as the Bush farm. It was approximately ninety acres with sixty of it available for row crop. The rest was low bottomland and sloughs covered in scrub woods of various species. Most of the cultivated land was in cotton. We did grow some soybeans and corn on the poorer parts of the farm. Somehow, we had managed to buy a small, two-row John Deere tractor. We had moved up to what was, for us, a very large farm. The three years we had lived on Mrs. Bush's place things had been quite prosperous for us. I knew, however, that the farm wasn't large enough to support my family and my growing ambitions. I didn't want to follow the masses of young men who had gone to the large industrial cities to become factory workers. No one had ever mentioned going to college, so I never even considered it a possibility. The fact that I was graduating from high school seemed no less than miraculous.

During the war years, most of the younger men in our community had served in the Army. I had been impressed by these men in their uniforms with starched shirts, neat neckties, spit-shined boots and pointed caps that sported shiny buttons with the letters US stamped on them. It appeared to me that they had the admiration of everyone in the community, especially from the beautiful, young women.

There was one uniform that stuck out in my memory more than any of the others. When I was five years old, I remember standing in some now-forgotten place, staring up at this man who stood five times my height. He had a strong handsome face and pearly white teeth that I could see when he laughed and talked. He had a little, white hat casually propped behind a massive head of black wavy hair. One curl hung down just above his right eye. I had never seen anything like the beautiful blouse that he was wearing. It was deep navy blue, almost black. It had three little, white stripes that ran from the V-neck in front to up over his shoulders and around a flap in back that extended down about a foot. Two little, white stars adorned each side of the flap. There was a black, silk neckerchief rolled and tied neatly in front with a square knot just above the V. The blouse had long sleeves that extended down to his wrists. The cuffs had the same little white stripes. The most fascinating of all was his matching trousers. They seemed to have no pockets and hugged his hips snugly in the back. In front, they were held closed with a row of beautiful, black buttons which ran across his abdomen and down each side about eight inches. Etched onto the buttons, were little anchors all perfectly lined up pointing in the same direction. The trouser legs dropped loosely down to just below his knee and then flared out into a bell shape, stopping just above a pair of brightly polished black dress shoes. He took his gleaming white hat off and placed it on my head. I remember it fell down around my ears, almost covering my eyes. The wonder I was feeling must have shown in my face. He smiled down at me and said, "Don't worry, Dick, someday you'll have one of these of your very own." I didn't know it at the time, but my fate had been sealed forever.

A black, hatchback 1949 Chevrolet passed in front of the house traveling at approximately seventy miles an hour on the little, narrow, rock road. The dust and small rocks were being thrown into the air thirty to forty-feet and trailed behind it for a quarter of a mile.

"That's probably the son-of-a-bitch that ran over old Pal and killed him," I lamented, as I watched the dust settle on the one lone rose bush in front of the house. "If I knew for sure it was him, I'd kick his ass."

"But who knows, with all the fools that come up and down this road?" Jean sighed, as she turned and searched my face for some clue of what I might be feeling.

"Yeah, well, there never will be another dog like old Pal. I just feel like something in me died when he did."

Mother came to the door, "Would you grind up some corn and feed the chickens before supper, Dick?" she asked.

"One thing about it, they don't have no damn chickens to feed in the Navy," I answered.

"You'll be wishing you were back home grinding up chicken feed before they get done with you," she said, letting the screen door slam shut as she turned and went back to the kitchen.

In the spring of the year, as far back as I could remember, my mother had ordered a hundred baby chicks from the Sears and Roebuck Catalog. The first week or so, they were kept in one corner of the living room near the wood-burning heating stove. Later, they would be moved out to a more suitable place. Here on the Bush farm, we had an old building just out the back door we called the smokehouse. It was about twelve feet wide and fourteen feet long. We didn't smoke anything in there but it served as a storage shed and combination utility room. Mamma had my daddy put down a piece of plywood in one corner and put boards about twelve inches high all around it to hold in the baby chickens. He had used an old extension cord to improvise a light bulb that dangled about eighteen inches above the box to provide warmth. On an old bench, was a hand grinder that had been bolted in place. Grinding corn for the chickens consisted of going to the barn and getting corn still on the cob. It would be shelled by hand and then put in the opening at the top of this ancient apparatus. A long handle crank turned an auger that crushed the corn. It was a slow and difficult daily chore that I despised. Jean was my constant companion and would always be at my side as I cursed my way through this unpleasant chore. She would often try to turn the handle a few rounds to give me a break. The resistance was so great that she would soon tire and I'd take over again.

Anticipating this chore, I did some heavy sighing and the usual grumbling. We got up from the swing and started walking toward the little, red barn where the corn was stored. The barn was one of two on the farm. This one was on the north side about a hundred yards from the house. The bigger barn was an eighth of a mile away located on a high knoll. Between our house and the larger barn, was a big slough with two to three feet of standing water. As we strolled toward the little red barn, I could see my daddy kicking hay out of the big barn's loft to the white-faced Herefords that he was raising on shares with Mrs. Bush. As we gathered up the corn to carry to the smokehouse, I heard the John Deere tractor start. I followed his journey by the sound as he came toward the house. I knew he would be going around the standing water and follow the old road on the south side to the tractor shed. His day was finished. I knew my mother was also following his trek and, within a half-hour of her hearing the tractor being parked, supper would be served. I felt the urgency of the situation and quickened my pace.

We were soon seated around the kitchen table for the evening meal. My daddy no longer discussed the business of the farm with me nor did he seek my opinion on important matters. The dynamics of the family were changing. We didn't understand it; we sat powerless, unable to stop the wheels that were slowly grinding out our destiny.

Finally, my mamma broke the silence and said, "Dick, when are you gonna find out what day you'll be leaving for your Navy training?" Everyone looked at me and waited. My daddy gave me a quick glance, dropped his head down and pretended not to be listening.

"I've gotta take a test first. The recruiter only comes to Paragould on Thursday. I'll ride the school bus to school next Thursday then hitchhike on into town. I'll need to get you to write a note giving me permission to leave school, though," I answered.

"Okay, but you write the note and I'll sign it. You know more about what it needs to say than I do."

"He may as well sign it, too. Otherwise, the signature won't look like all them other notes he's turned in the past two years," Jean joked.

Armentia threw back her head and cracked up with laughter. Cleo, not quite getting it, looked quickly at her sister. Deciding there must be something really funny going on, she joined in the laughter.

"You girls hush and eat your super," cautioned my mother.

My daddy surveyed the table, giving us notice with his eyes that he was still in charge. We ate in silence. The meal was coming to an end. My mamma went to the old, white china cabinet where two chocolate pies sat cooling. There was an inch and a half topping of slightly browned, beaten egg whites crowning them. She cut one into quarter pieces and served my daddy. The second piece then went to the youngest member of the family, as was our custom.

"When will they be making your picture?" she asked.

"I don't know and I don't care. I don't have a suit to wear to no damn picture-making." I answered belligerently.

She looked at me sadly. "Don't cheat me out of that son. You're going to be the first in the family to graduate from high school. I, at least, want to have a picture of you. With you going off to the Navy and Darrel up there in St. Louis, I just don't know how I'm gonna bear it. I'd think you'd at least want to do that much for me. I just can't believe you want to go off and leave your daddy here alone to make this crop by hisself. I just don't know what you're thinking about. I'd be ashamed if I was you. We wouldn't of come here in the first place and took on this big farm and went in debt for that tractor if we'd known you was gonna up and leave. We thought this was what you wanted," she said.

My daddy looked at me accusingly and held my gaze.

"Mom, I don't want to have my picture made nor go to no damn graduating ceremony. I just want to pick my diploma up and leave for the Navy as soon as I can. All the other people graduating are going on a senior trip to Florida. You know we don't have the money for me to do all of that stuff. Why don't you just leave me alone? Why do you want to put me through all of that? I went back to high school cause you wanted me to. Ain't that enough? I feel as poor as Job's turkey," I explained.

She commenced to weep silently, and after a moment she dried her eyes. "I wish we knowed what it is you're mad at. We've done the best we can by ya. There must be some other poor children in your class that ain't no better off than we are. Why don't you be friends with them? Maybe you'd feel better," her voice trembled with emotion.

My chest tightened and tears rimmed my eyes. How could I make her understand? The mixed emotions of wanting to please her and at the same time rebel against our poverty overwhelmed me.

My daddy had sat quietly listening. He looked at mamma. His eyes darkened and his face became tense. "You'll have your picture made and you'll graduate with all the other kids," his voice had a sound of finality. "You're still under my roof and eating from my table. As long as you're doing that, you'll do what I say," he ordered. A still silence crept into the room. I didn't respond. Jean glanced at me with an embarrassed look, eyes wide, waiting for my reaction. I looked at my mamma. The pain in her face was too much. I looked at my daddy; his gaze didn't waiver. There had been days in the past when I had challenged him. This wouldn't be one of them. My mamma stood up to clear the table. Seeking to diffuse the tension and seize the moment she gave me a soft smile and said, "Tomorrow I'll go up to the scale house at the gin and ask Vance if he'll advance us twenty dollars until the crop loan comes in. I'm sure he won't mind."

The following Tuesday found me seated in the back seat of Mr. Bingham's two-tone green 1949 Chevrolet sedan. My thoughts drifted as I listened, without hearing, to him and my daddy talk as we traveled toward Pocahontas. My daddy had exerted his authority over me and I had submitted. This had warmed him toward me and we had commenced to have a cordial coexistence. I hadn't grown up on the mean streets of Los Angeles, Chicago, or New York. But neither had the lessons of life that Mother Nature had taught me been wasted. I had learned the power of submission from watching my dog Pal. I had observed that, in his prime, when other dogs entered into his domain his tail and ears would go erect and his hair would bristle as he marched toward them with his eyes blazing. Provided they rolled over and exposed their neck in complete surrender, he would straddle them and hold his mouth over their throat for a moment. After an order of dominance had been established, they would often romp and play together. A challenge, on the other hand, would be met with a fury of tooth and claw that would fairly send chills up my spine. My joining the Navy had given enough pain to my mamma. I would walk through this one last humiliation in order to maintain peace in the family.

When I was very young, Mother Nature had taught me another lesson about the use of power. This one I was never to forget. It was quite brutal but, perhaps, one of the most important lessons of my life. This is the way I remember it happening.

I was ten years old and had, for some now-forgotten reason, been hanging around the Faukner store at the bend in a road about a mile and a half north of Light. Seven or eight men between twenty-five and fifty years old were sitting in a circle around the old wood-burning stove that sat near the front door. They whittled on sticks, chewed tobacco, and told bawdy tales for lack of something more exciting to do on those cold winter days. Their conversation was rough and laced with profanity. These were sons of rural Arkansas farmers, grandsons of those who had fought the Civil War, survivors of the Great Depression, and veterans of the Second World War. For most of them, their education had stopped long before finishing the fifth grade. They were born in a time when only a few survived childhood diseases. These were the men Mother Nature had selected to continue our species before the discovery of miracle drugs. They were dressed in old, faded, work clothes of various sizes, shapes, and colors. Some had caps; others wore hats. Their shoes and boots matched perfectly with that particular time and place.

Leroy, a young son of a prominent farmer, had rode up on a spirited two-year-old, black stallion. He dismounted; the men were all watching. Just as Leroy's feet hit the ground, the stallion reared and flailed his hoofs in the air. One rein slipped out of his hand as the stallion circled. The bridle had started to slip; the situation had become dangerous. Three of the men ran out of the store to where the struggle was in progress and grabbed the loose reins, pulling the fighting stallion back under control. Jessie Fears, the oldest of the men, had walked casually to the door and watched with a great deal of interest. He continued to whittle on his stick. He had a heavy beaded scar on his neck that ran from ear to ear. It had been said that, while Jessie was riding the rails during the years of the Great Depression, a fellow had tried to cut his throat while he lay sleeping. Unfortunately, for the would be assassin, Jessie woke up. No one seemed to know what happened to the other feller and I don't remember anyone being brave enough to ever ask.

"That damn stud horse is gonna kill yea one these days, Leroy," he drawled. "I thought you were gonna cut him," he added, leaning out the door as he spit a stream of tobacco juice onto the gravel driveway some eight feet away.

"I wuz, but I've let the son-of-a-bitch get too big," Leroy answered.

The other men gathered around as the stallion snorted and tried to rear. The four men stubbornly held on to the reins.

"Us just cut the son-of-a-bitch right now," one of them said.

I had known these men all of my life. They were my daddy's friends and our neighbors. I suddenly felt fear. For the first time in my life, I was witnessing the power of dominance that God had given man over all living things that mamma had told me about being written in the book of Genesis. A cold chill shimmered up my back.

"By god if you ol' boys ull help me, we'll just do it," Leroy said with a nervous laugh. A quietness settled over the small group. I watched their faces turn dead serious as they considered the proposition.

The silence was soon broken. "Us just get on with it then," someone said.

They all agreed and the frenzy commenced. One of the men went to the back of his pickup truck and took a piece of bailing wire from the floor of the truck's bed. Two of the men grabbed the stallion's head and held it firmly. The bailing wire was looped around his lower lip and twisted into a knot. One rope went around the back legs, pulling them together. Another was put around the front left, just below the knee.

"Us throw the son-of-a-bitch," one of the men commented. The rope on the front leg was then jerked and the powerful stallion went plummeting to the ground. Both front legs where then tied together before the beast could regain his balance. The rope was tightened on the back legs as the hoofs flailed in the air. The front and back legs were then joined and firmly fastened in place. The man in front holding the bailing wire attached to the horses lower lip pulled the stallion's head out straight. The stallion's eyes dilated with fear. Loud, labored AARRUMPHHS rose up out of his barrel chest as he struggled to rise. The big, strong, beautiful, magnificent animal now lay stretched out completely powerless in front of these Masters of the Earth.

"You do the business, Jessie," one of the men commented.

"I'll do it," said the big, red-headed man they called Fats. He took out of his overall pocket, a ten-inch knife, which had a single eight-inch blade. In one single motion he opened the knife and wiped it on his pant's leg and sat down on the side of the horse's rump. He reached in between the huge thighs of the stallion and pulled the scrotum out where he could see it. He then squeezed the skin tight over the testicle. Without hesitation, he sliced through the taunt scrotum. Bright red blood squirted up into his face and streamed down onto his overalls. He reached and pulled out the pink, baseball size testicle. A long white cord followed which he quickly cut with one swift motion. From deep down inside of this helpless creature came a loud, desperate scream. I somehow felt I was in the presence of an ancient evil, which I didn't

quite understand. I was filled with horror to realize that human beings were capable of such things. The men struggled to hold the mighty beast down. Another quick slice and the job was finished.
"Cut 'em loose, and let 'em up," someone commanded.
"That'll quiet the son-of-a-bitch down," another added.

The once-proud stallion now staggered to his feet. Blood ran out of his scrotum and dripped onto the ground as he stood trembling before his master. His ears were drooped in total defeat. In less than five minutes, this proud, regal animal had been reduced to a thousand pounds of quivering flesh. I was not aware of how deeply I had been affected. For a moment I felt separated from all that was good and decent. A great shadow of sadness fell across my soul. My dreams would be filled with the screams of bloody, dying animals for many months to come.

I heard something that pulled me back to the present. Turning toward the front, I listened to my daddy talking to Mr. Bingham.
"How you figure that old Jew sells them suits so cheap, Burl?"
"Hell, he buys them up there in Popular Bluff at one of them factories where they make 'em. They all got a little something wrong with 'em and he probably buys a whole damn ton of 'em for almost nuttin. Jews can do that you know. They're all merchants and know about business. I ain't ever saw one that was a farmer or do any hard work. Have you?"
"No, I ain't" laughed my daddy. "Ain't none in Greene County that I know of either."
"No, that's true. There's a few up here in Randloph County. Some niggers up here, too, I heard."
"Well, they ain't none of them in Greene County either. Last bunch that lived there, they hung 'em. Young nigger boy visiting with 'em from up Chicago way and they just hung him, too."
"Damn poor timing on his part. Wouldn't you say?" laughed Mr. Bingham.

We arrived in Pocahontas and wound our way through the little hill town and parked out in front of a small storefront. A big sign high up on the front of the red brick structure read *GRABERS CLOTHING*. "Well, this looks like the place," commented my daddy. We disembarked and went into the little store. A tired-looking, ageless, balding man stood behind the counter talking to a thirtish, blonde woman. He was dressed in an off-white, threadbare shirt that contrasted with a light brown tie. A tape measure was draped loosely around his neck. He stood, leaning on one leg, listening attentively.

"My daddy worked hard all his life trying to dig a living out of the dirt," the young woman was explaining. "I want him to at least be buried in something decent."

The balding man switched his weight to the other leg as he continued to listen patiently.

"I don't really care what it cost. I've got me a good job up in St. Louis, been working for McDonald Aircraft since high school. I aim to see to it that he's buried right. But if we can get him in a nice suit for less than fifteen dollars I won't have to go way off some place to buy it." she continued in a pleading tone.

"Yes, well, we can do that," the tired-looking man answered. "Just leave the measurements here with me and I'll get the suit over to the funeral home."

"I don't want to pay extra for sewing up pants cuffs. Nobody gonna be a looking down there anyway," she added, as she turned away to leave. Upon seeing us, she gave an embarrassed smile to my daddy and Mr. Bingham. They tipped their hats to her.

"Ma'am," they said, and she was gone. Turning his attention to us, the balding man smiled weakly.

"Poor lady has lost her father," he commented. My daddy and Mr. Bingham acknowledged they had heard by a slight forward movement of their heads. With that, the matter was closed.

"Wanna get my boy a suit for graduation," my daddy informed him.

Coming out from behind the counter, he took several different measurements of my extremities. Turning to my daddy, he happily announced, "I think we have just the thing." Then he disappeared into the back room. He soon returned carrying a gray jacket in his right hand with a pair of matching pants draped over his left arm. Holding the jacket by the shoulders, he indicated for me to slip it on. It was tight across my chest and the sleeves came down about three inches past my wrists.

"Yes, that's perfect," he said, as he pushed here and tugged there.

"Seems a little tight," I commented.

"No, not at all, that's the latest style."

Never owning a suit before, I took him at his word. I soon stood in front of the mirror with the gray trousers on. The pants legs hung down about four inches too long.

"That can easily be remedied," he assured me. Noticing the waist was two sizes too big for me, I pulled on the waistband.

"You'll need a nice belt," he added.

The bill was over fourteen dollars. My daddy, upon receiving his change for the twenty dollars, handed five one-dollar bills to Mr. Bingham. "Much obliged," Mr. Bingham said, making sure my daddy noticed he didn't count it, as he shoved the money deep down into his pocket. "Glad I could help, Johnny."

We were able to get me fixed-up for less than twenty dollars. Of course, I would have to wear the old, blue tie my daddy had bought to wear when his papa died. This same outfit would've cost us at least thirty dollars at Sears and Roebuck. All in all, it was a profitable day. I am happy to report to you that if you go to Greene County Tech High School and walk those hollowed halls, you may see a picture of me hanging there. Perhaps if you look real close right around my eyes, you can see the anger and hostility I was feeling the day they immortalized me.

The following Thursday found me across the street from the high school. A big, black 1949 Hudson came out of the gravel driveway a few feet behind me. The man driving stopped, looked both ways, then he turned right and pulled up on to the narrow two-lane highway and headed east toward Paragould. I stuck out my thumb. He accelerated and glared straight ahead so as not to make eye contact with me. "Son-of-a-bitch," I murmured. "Wish I had your car and you had a wart on your ass and ever time you thought about it the tank would be full of gas." I felt, at least, some better for having cursed him. I knew he didn't think of me as dangerous. He was just a selfish bastard that didn't want some country bumpkin to dirty up his car.

I rode the bus to school, turned my note in at the principal's office and walked out to hitchhike into town. It was now about nine in the morning. The sun was already warm; it promised to be a very hot day. I stood across the road looking northeast up the little hill at the Greene County Tech High School. Looking from left to right, I could see the long gymnasium that was known to us as the Reynolds Field House. It was a newly constructed, yellow, brick building with the wood frame in front, painted white. Next, came the main building where the administration was housed and the majority of the classes were being taught. It was an older, two-story, yellow, brick building that was about twelve hundred feet long. A little farther down the slope were two other buildings. They were smaller and constructed with the same colored brick. I stood watching as two boys entered the first building; they would be going to their agriculture class. A hundred feet on down the walkway a small group of girls were walking toward the Home Economics Department.

I waited impatiently for the next car. Several minutes passed as I strolled back and forth kicking rocks with the toe of my shoe. As I paced, I noticed an old beer can lying behind me in the ditch. I went over and picked it up. The can was a beautiful white color, almost enamel. It had a man dressed like a knight in a red robe and a high, pointed, triangular hat imprinted on it. The words on the can were written and not printed. I thought it to be very sophisticated. I read the message then lifted it to my nose to smell. Not at all unpleasant, but different. Turning it upside down, a few drops ran out. I was tempted to taste it, but better not, God only knows, someone might have pissed in it. Thinking that, I threw it across the road and watched it bounce down the side of the embankment out of sight.

I heard something coming up from the west heading in my direction. I didn't see anything right away. Soon an old, green pickup truck crested the hill and came crawling toward me. As it got closer, I could see it was a pre-World War Two Chevrolet. I held out my thumb as it approached. I heard the clutch go in disengaging the motor. Seemed, for a moment, it gained speed as it went gliding by. The driver gave me a big smile and motioned for me to join him. I started running as fast as I could. I heard the motor whine as he engaged it into a lower gear. I soon caught up, jerked the door open, and hopped in.

"Brakes went out," my benefactor said, smiling over at me.

"Yeah, I noticed," I answered nervously.

"Gotta get these old pigs over to the sale barn," he said, jerking his thumb toward the back of the truck.

I turned and looked at the eight or so big hogs jammed up in the right-hand corner against the cab. The smell of hog manure radiated inside the cab. No doubt about it, I was in the presence of a genuine pig farmer.

"So where you going, boy?" he asked, looking me over closely as he moved his chaw of tobacco to a more secure place deep inside his cheek.

"Going into Paragould to see the Navy recruiter," I answered. He gave me a big, toothy, brown-stained smile and looked back at the road.

"Going in the Navy are you?" he asked.

"Gonna try to," I responded, glancing over at him.

The button on his overalls was open on the side at the waist; he lifted his shirt and commenced to scratch. I didn't see any underwear, just white naked skin with little red blotches.

"I tried to get in the Army once," he commented sadly, looking over at me. "I'd be retiring next year wadn't for these flat feet," he added, lifting up his heavy work shoes to make his point. Little piece of manure fell on the floorboard as I looked down. I spent the next few minutes trying to imagine him in some kind of uniform.

"Well, I'll let you out when I turn off for the sale barn. I magine at Navy feller is downtown somewhere," he said.

"Yeah, down on Pruett street, right next to the Corner Café," I replied.

We traveled happily along the next seven miles chattering about this and that. He was pleased to have a companion and I was happy not to be walking. In about ten minutes, we approached the corner where he would be turning back north to the sale barn.

"Get ready to jump," he prepared me in a tense voice. "I'll try to slow her down."

I put my hand on the door handle and readied myself for the jump. We rounded the corner and just as he straightened up the wheel, I leaped out toward the side of the road. Hitting the loose gravel, I staggered a few feet before regaining my balance. I looked after the truck and gave a big wave. I heard the clutch catch as he moved slowly on down the road. I heard his voice against the wind but was unable to make out his words. He's sure one happy bastard for a dumb shit, I thought to myself. Maybe he knows something the rest of the world doesn't know, I mused.

Facing the increasingly hot sun, I started on my mile and a half walk to Pruett Street. Upon arriving at my destination, I came upon a small door leading into the ancient building that was located between the barbershop and the Corner Café. I pushed the rickety old door open and entered into a narrow, green hallway and followed the steps leading up to the second floor. Turning right, I found an office with, "US NAVY RECRUITER" stenciled in black on the opaque glass that formed the top part of the narrow door. I could see shadows moving in the room. I listened for voices. Upon hearing nothing, I tapped lightly. The door swung open and I was met with a friendly, "Come in, Messer. We've been waiting for you." Two other young men about eighteen or nineteen sat quietly at two of the four desks in the room.

I had talked to the recruiter on several occasions when he had visited at Greene County Tech. I had agreed to come and take the Navy's aptitude and IQ test. Provided I could score high enough, I would be guaranteed a school of my choice. The test turned out to be long and difficult. My grammar studies had been interfered with in the sixth and seventh grade when I was attending Pruett's one-room schoolhouse. The one teacher we had just didn't have time to get to us all and she had relied on Jessie Fear's redheaded daughter to teach us. Unfortunately, the poor thing was not much better off than I was. Never having learned the basics, I struggled through my English classes and, at the end of each year, they would pass me along with a C or D.

I had also taken Algebra in the ninth grade. Our teacher was a gentleman that had lost his leg in the big war. He acted like he belonged in an insane asylum instead of being in front of a class of fourteen and fifteen-year-olds. Two plus two equaling X had never made sense to me in the first place. But about the time I was beginning to think it might be plausible, my teacher was killed in a railroad crossing accident. The rest of the semester was spent trying to figure out if the poor soul had committed suicide. We were passed along to the tenth grade with the assurance we would pick it all up later. Of course, I never did.

The tools and mechanical equipment that appeared on the test I had seen in the workshop at school but had not been interested enough to use them nor had I bothered to learn their names. The exam had a few boxes turned upside down and a few square holes that were to be fitted in round holes that didn't seem to have any rhyme or reason that I could see. Some of the more basic math made a little more sense. I worked, sweat, erased, and cursed my way along until the recruiter stopped me.

The other two young men had long since left. The recruiter took my answer sheet and covered it with a piece of clear plastic with holes in it. He quickly made little red marks on some of the little round holes. Lifting it off, he counted the red marks. Writing a score at the top of the paper, he looked up at me. "Well, you won't have any trouble getting in the Navy," he said with a smile. "You missed the guaranteed-school program by a couple of points. But don't worry about it. You scored plenty high enough to enlist." I watched him gather up the papers to put into his brief case, "The test that really counts is the general classification test you'll take in boot camp. This one doesn't mean that much. It's just to make sure you don't belong in the Army," he added humorously.

I felt a little frustrated at not obtaining a high enough score to be guaranteed a school. No one had really explained to me what would happen if I wasn't assigned to one. I had never even seen the ocean, much less a Big Navy War Ship. All the sailors I had come in contact with were always wearing the beautiful dress blue uniform. I couldn't imagine anyone so elegantly dressed doing anything that was not dignified.

"We need to get you a date for a physical so we can get you inducted," I heard the recruiter say, as he opened a big blue notebook binder. "Let me see. Now, you said you wanted to leave as soon after graduation as possible. Right!" he said as he looked up at me for confirmation. I didn't answer. My heart was racing. "I could get you out of Jonesboro and down to Little Rock on Monday the twenty-seventh. They can do your physical and get you sworn in on the twenty-eighth. All you have to do is give me the word."

He then laid the pen down and turned up the cuffs of his blouse that were bordered with the little white stripes. On the underside, I could see beautiful, embroidered, golden and green dragons with red, fiery tongues sticking out of their mouths. They were sewn on a black, silk background. I stood transfixed, staring at the beautiful artwork.

He picked the pen up, and looked at me. "Well, Messer…" he hesitated. "You want to be a part of my club or not?" he asked, almost accusingly. I still felt confused about the uncertainty of what might be expected of me in the Navy. But I felt the need to prove to the world that I had the courage to do what I had dreamed and talked about for three years. I sensed the recruiter was beginning to doubt my sincerity.

"The twenty-seventh will be fine," I answered.

He smiled and scribbled my name in a block. Standing up, he stuck out his hand. "Congratulations, you've made a wise decision," he proclaimed.

It was still early in the day. I knew the principal was aware that seeing the recruiter wouldn't take up my whole day. I should go back to school but the hell with it. I had just made the most important decision of my life. The test was over and I didn't think Greene County Tech could do much more for me.

The recruiter closed his brief case and came around the desk to the door with his keys in his hands.

"I've got to go over to Walnut Ridge to see someone. Can I give you a ride back to school?"

"No," I said, hesitating, "But you can give me a ride out to Light. You'll have to go through there if you're going to Walnut Ridge."

"Sure," he responded, grasping my shoulder firmly as we started down the stairs.

"I am going to need a ride to Jonesboro on the twenty-seventh. I wrecked my car and I'm afoot. My daddy ain't big on me leaving him at crop time. He sure ain't gonna take no time off to help me get to Jonesboro."

"Don't worry about it. I'll pick you up. Starting on the twenty-seventh, the Navy is going to take care of all your needs for the next four years. We'll run by your house today so I'll know where you live. It'll be early. Gotta get you on that Greyhound for that eight o'clock run into Little Rock."

After telling the family I had a definite date for my departure, we all entered into a new phase of acceptance. April slowly passed into May as I impatiently waited. One day in early May, I was sitting on the porch with Jean, my daddy, and the hired hand, O' Donnel. My daddy had hired him to help make a crop. He looked to me to be about twenty-eight years old. He always dressed in khaki pants, shirt, and a matching baseball cap. This set him a little apart from the other men in the community as they all wore overalls. O'Donnel wore his cap pushed back just a little, showing a full head of black hair. He always seemed to be just on the verge of laughing or at least to be thinking of a very funny story. That seemed strange to me, considering the problem he had had with the local Sheriff.

We had a cross-eyed neighbor by the name of Bo Bo Laderman that lived about two miles away from us over on the river. Now, him being of marrying age and no one in the community showing any real interest in him, he up and ordered a wife out of St. Louis from one of them lonely heart catalogs. Now, the funny thing about her was, when she showed up, she was cross-eyed just like old Bo Bo. The one big difference was he was about six foot, two inches tall and skinny as a rail, as we used to say. But she, on the other hand, was about four foot, nine inches and just about as wide as she was tall. They were indeed a strange sight coming and going up and down the old dirt road to Rachel's store.

Now, what really happened, I never did quite get it all straight in my head as my daddy didn't like to talk about it much in front of the girls. But it seemed one day that O'Donnel, he took a notion he wanted to go over there and do some visiting with old Bo Bo and welcome his new wife. Problem being, when he got there, Bo Bo was nowhere to be found. Well, O'Donnel, I guess, wanted to make the young woman from St. Louis to feel at home. So, he commenced to get real friendly with her. According to all accounts, he got so enthusiastic about his welcoming that they ended up on the bed. Now, right in the middle of all this exchange of good will she looked up from where they were lying and seen old Bo Bo coming into the house. That kind of gave her a fright and not understanding all the customs down in Arkansas, she started to scream. Well, O'Donnel, that scared him and he took off a running. Now, old Bo Bo, thinking something must be bad wrong with old O'Donnel, he took off after him. They finally had to get the Sheriff out there to get it all sorted out. Somehow or another O'Donnel ended up in jail on some kind of an assault charge.

My daddy was never an outlaw or broke any laws, at least that I knew of, other than killing a few squirrels out of season. But, being a Southerner and our people reaching way back before the time of the Civil War, he always kind of favored people being on the wrong side of the law. After the Yankees won the war and sent all them carpetbaggers down south, it just kind of seemed natural to protect the people that were brave enough to try to get even with the son-su-bitches. That's why everyone loved old Jessie James and kind of felt bad when he got himself killed. My daddy said Bonny and Clyde were mean alright, but it sure was a cowardly way them federal men shot them down in an ambush. I guess it's kind of hard to understand if you're not a Southerner. Well, anyway, when my daddy heard that O'Donnel was in jail, he got some fellers together to go see what he could do for him.

Now, one of the fellers he took with him was one of our good friends, a Mr. Calvert Webby. One time Calvert had stole a bunch of cows from a feller who didn't much need them anyway. He drove them up Cache River about 8 miles and met another feller with a truck. They loaded 'em up and hauled them way up to Popular Bluff, clean over in Missouri, and sold them. I never knew how they caught old Calvert but he ended up over there in the Paragould jail where O'Donnel was for a while. Now, Calvert, understanding O'Donnel was a free spirit and how hard jail was on a feller, decided he would go with my daddy to do what he could to help out.

One of our other neighbors went with them, too. He was known to everyone as Old Man Shannon. Now, Old Man Shannon had killed a feller one time with a twelve-gauge shotgun. When you passed his old, silver trailer you could still see the blood right out there on the white gravel where he parked his old, blue pickup truck. The story was that he had a son-in-law who use to get drunk and beat his daughter. One day, the daughter came running over to Old Man Shannon's trailer and told him her husband was after her. "Come on in. He ain't gonna bother you here" he told her and they went on about their business. Well, pretty soon the drunken son-in-law came driving up and went up to the door of the screened in porch that Old Man Shannon had built on the front of his trailer. Now, there wasn't a regular lock on the door. But he had put one of them little old latches on to keep the dog in. Well, when the son-in-law reached inside to undo the latch, Old Man Shannon walked out with his shotgun. "That's far enough," he said and raised it up and backed the hammer down. The son-in-law, being drunk and not thinking real clear, laughed at Old Man Shannon, lifted the latch, and started up on the porch. "If you come any closer, I'll kill yea dead," Old Man Shannon told him. The son-in-law then stepped up onto the porch and that's when he shot him right in the chest. It blew the feller back about six feet, right out on top of them white rocks. They said he laid out there and begged for help a little while before he died. Didn't bother Old Man Shannon none. Later on, he told my daddy wudden notin more'n killing a mad dog, as far as he was concerned. Somebody called the Sheriff and he came out and took Old Man Shannon over to town. They didn't keep him over night, though, and he was back home in time to feed the hogs that evening.

They also took this other neighbor of ours along by the name of Alex Palmer. He had an argument with a feller that everyone said was a big bully. I don't remember him myself but his son was in the third grade with me before they moved away. He must not've taken after his daddy at all, as he was about as a peaceable of an old boy as I ever knew. Anyway, this feller and Alex got in an argument over on this guy's farm about something. He gave Alex a good cussing and decided he was just going to give him a good whooping. Well, old Alex, he took off a running for his place. He jumped the fence and right there where he jumped over laid a handle that had been broke out of an old scoop shovel, one like you use to shovel shelled corn. The feller was right on top of him by that time. Now, according to Alex, he grabbed up the handle and gave him a good whack, just trying to protect himself. He must of hit him a little harder than he intended to, as he died right on the spot. All the men in the community got together and went over there to Paragould and swore this feller that Alex had killed was just plain ornery and it was only a matter of time until someone killed him. Alex just happened to be the one what done it. Well, they did put Alex on trial, finally, but the jury decided the feller really did need killing after all, so they decided to turn Alex loose.

Now, there were some other folks that went to help get old O'Donnel out that had hardly done anything wrong. Like I said, I didn't get all the details about it but my daddy and them fellers signed a bunch of papers about O'Donnel being a good fellow and all, so they let him go. My daddy liked to tease old O'Donnel about being a one-man welcoming committee. At those times, O'Donnel would go ahead and give a whole smile. He'd take his cap off and run his fingers through his long black hair, look down, and smile for the longest. Putting his hat back on, he'd go back to his almost smile and that would put the story to rest, at least, for the moment.

While we are sitting there on the porch talking, I saw a man coming into sight walking south on the gravel road coming from the direction of Light. His head was tilted back as though he was listening for something as he moved along. He carried a walking stick in his hand; he'd tap the grass then the road. He was moving at a pretty good clip and doing a fairly good job at staying over on the side of the road.

"Here comes Old Bill," chuckled O'Donnel. "Whole damn family blind as bats." Bill had heard voices and he turned his head so his right ear would be toward the sound. You could see he was listening intently, as he tapped along. I could see the whites of his unseeing eyes as they darted back and forth.

"Come by and set a spell, Bill," my daddy called out to him. Old Bill stopped and tilted his head directly toward the sound of my daddy's voice.

"Is that you, Johnny Messer?" he asked.

"Yeah, it's me Bill, come on up here a minute," my daddy answered.

Bill appeared to be a little uncertain, as he came slowly forward, feeling his way up the little incline toward our house. His stick soon found the porch.

"What'cha ol' boys doing?" he asked, stopping and listening to see how many people he could hear breathing.

"That you, Dick?" he asked moving his stick up and touching my leg.

"Yeah, I'm here Bill, and Jean is with me," I answered, wanting to relieve him of any anxiety of not knowing who was present.

"How that love potion work I gave you?" he chuckled. Everyone laughed.

The four Ramsey boys had all been born blind to some degree. The one they called Zy could see a little, or so they said. Now, Old Bill was the youngest of the boys and he loved to cut up. It was told around that he had been born with special gifts to compensate for that one handicap the Lord had put on him. Now, Old Bill he took full advantage of this rumor and did what he could to promote it. Everyone said he could tell fortunes and predict the weather better than the fellers on the radio. But his specialty was matchmaking.

I had been on a double date the previous week with my friend Jack Stalkner. He was dating Jeaney Carr and she had a younger sister they called Joyce. Jack had talked me into going along to keep Joyce busy as her folks made him take her with him as a chaperone when he went out with Jeaney. As it turned out, Joyce showed very little interest in me. Seemed she had been enamored with some feller in the Air Force. Adding insult to injury, she didn't seem to be at all impressed with the fact that I would soon be leaving for the Navy.

While the two sisters were having a conference in the bathroom, Jack said to me, "Us go out and get Old Bill to put a spell on these girls. Hell, they say that, after you give that stuff of Bill's to someone, they just can't resist you."

"Old Blind Bill is going to make these girls love us?" I asked.

"Hell, yes. It can't do no harm the way you're getting along with Joyce," he goaded.

Well, he had me there and we were soon headed out to the Walnut Corner Community where the ol' blind Ramsey boys lived. I was sitting in the back seat with my future love as we fairly flew along. We passed where I lived, went another quarter of a mile and turned up an old dirt road going back west. Passing the Ramsey house, I noticed it looked real spooky-like.

"Looks like they are all asleep," I commented.

"They don't have any lighting in that house anywhere," Jack replied.

"Guess they don't need it," I mused.

We went on down the road and came back very slowly and pulled up into their yard. Two black and tan hounds set up a yodel you could have heard all the way to Paragould. After a few minutes of wondering if anyone was home, a trembling voice called out.

"Who is it?"

"Jack Stalkner and Dick Messer," answered Jack.

"What'cha boys want?" the voice asked.

"Bill here?" Jack asked.

The hounds had quieted down but were circling the car, sniffing. Voices from inside the house drifted out into the darkness. I heard Old Bill's stick pecking as he came out the front door and down the steps.

"How you all doing?" he asked and listened for a reply so he could follow the sound of the voice to the car.

"We're fine Bill," Jack answered.

Bill was soon seated in the car with us and we drove down the road a comfortable distance from the house. After parking and introducing the girls, we got down to business. We had explained to Jeaney and Joyce this mysterious power that Bill possessed and had convinced them we should give it a try. They seemed unconvinced but it sure sounded like a lot of fun. Jeaney was already in love with Jack anyway so she was all for it. Joyce, on the other hand, was bored stiff with me and felt it couldn't possibly do any harm. After much laughter and a fortune telling session, we got down to business.

"Bill, have you got any of that love powder?" Jack finally asked.

"Yeah, I got enough for about two doses," he chuckled, rummaging around in his pocket.

Jack turned the dome light on so we could get a look at this magic substance. It was in a little amber colored bottle with about a teaspoon of white powder inside.

"This is hard to get. I have to send off for some of the stuff I make it out of. I can't catch them humming birds and pull their teeth, me being blind and all," he teased.

We all laughed at the thought of old Bill trying to catch a humming bird.

"Seriously, I'll need a couple of dollars," he added.

"No problem Bill," I said handing him the last five dollars I had to my name.

He rubbed the bill between his forefinger and thumb.

"What is it?" he asked.

"A five," I responded.

"I don't have any change," he answered and hesitated a moment.

"I could have guessed as much," I whined.

"I'll get you your dollar back to you, Dick," he assured me.

The business being completed we got down to the instructions of how to use the potion. Bill lowered his voice and became very serious.

"You'll both need to put half of this in a Coca Cola, shake it up real good, and then share it with your intended. After you've drunk it, you'll need to chew two pieces of doublemint chewing gum. Then just wait about a half an hour for it to work," he said.

"That's it?" I asked incredulously.

"Yep, that's it," he replied.

This being a week later, I was feeling very foolish as I sat looking at Old Bill's mischievous smile. I knew my daddy would have killed me on the spot had he known I had given Old Bill my last five dollars for a love potion.

"Yeah Bill, that potion is really something. You ought'a bottle it up and distribute it," I answered.

"Maybe O'Donnel could use it next time he goes off on one of them one-man welcoming committees," chided my daddy. We all laughed heartily. O'Donnel took his cap off and ran his fingers through his hair.

To fully understand some of my neurosis and the things that have driven me in this life, you would need to know the relationship I had with my mamma. She was strong willed and dominant. There were two main concerns that drove her in life. One was to feed, clothe, and nurture us. The other was to insure we didn't lose our souls. One was equally important as the other, as far as she was concerned. Every waking moment of her life was dedicated to trying to bring those two things about. I never questioned my mother's love and devotion to us; therefore, I accepted this as a matter of course as I grew up. My mamma felt it was not only her right, but also her duty, to threaten me with the fires of Hell, as the occasion deemed necessary. When I was seven years old, she thought I was mature enough to know right from wrong and decided it was time I accept Jesus as my personal savior. My dreams were filled with Judgment Day and being marched off to the fires of Hell. Seeing a red sunset as a child, I would think the world was on fire and Jesus was coming for us on a great cloud. I would run to my mamma petrified. She would use these occasions to reinforce her message. I would then be rededicated to the Lord.

When I was about fifteen and a half, I commenced to struggle to have my own identity and to have my own thoughts. That became a great battle of wills between my mamma and me. The more I struggled to break the invisible umbilical cord she had securely wrapped around my neck, the tighter it became. I didn't especially like such a mean old God. It had come to me early on that I was the greatest of all sinners. I couldn't see any possibility, whatsoever, of making it into heaven. I was sure to spend my eternity in Hell and, it being such a terrible place, I often wished I had never been born. That being as it was, I decided if I was going to Hell anyway, I might as well enjoy myself on this earth. But the guilt left me feeling unsettled and angry.

When we moved to the Bush Farm, I took on the roll as an equal partner with my daddy. I was no longer disciplined with the strap and was allowed the same rights and privileges as an adult. To test the limits of my independence, the first thing I did was to announce I would no longer be going to church. My mother knew every emotional button that I possessed and she commenced to push them all. The cord tightened and I struggled to loosen it. Loving my mother more than life itself, I directed my hostility and rebellion outward. An inordinate amount was manifested toward the Baptist Church.

The week before my departure had finally arrived. The reality that I soon would be leaving had finally seeped into my soul. I stayed as close to my family as I could, savoring every precious moment of those last few days of us being together. At times, I had been tempted to call the recruiter and tell him it had all been a mistake. But it would soon pass with the compelling realization that this was my destiny. When someone asked me why I was leaving, I didn't have an answer. It was my first realization that there are forces beyond our control driving us to our distinct destiny. My mamma never gave up the idea that I might change my mind if she could just somehow come up with the right formula, but I was determined to break free from that umbilical cord. I continued to raise my level of resistance as the war of wills waged on. After days of crying, begging, cajoling, and long tearful prayers, she finally accepted that I would be leaving. I was of legal age to join the service and she was helpless to stop me. She then decided to concentrate on saving my soul.

I had been driving the tractor for my daddy and had come to the house for dinner. I had entered by way of the screened-in back porch and walked into the kitchen. My mamma turned upon hearing my footsteps.

"Dick, Brother Marion is here," she advised me.

"Really! On a weekday?"

"Yes, son. I asked him to come down and have a word of prayer with you."

"Goddamn it, Ma, I don't want to see no damn preacher. How many times have I told you that?"

My mamma's face contracted into a sad frown and she looked as though she was about to cry.

"But you were saved when you were younger and I know you still love the Lord. It may be your very last time to rededicate your life to Jesus. I would feel so much better if I knew you were right with Him before you go."

Her voice trembled as she pleaded. Closing her eyes, she lifted her arms up toward heaven and commenced to pray.

"Loosen the bonds of Satan from the shoulders of my poor boy. Deliver him up from the fiery furnace of Hell. This day, O' Lord, I put him into Your hands to protect. Touch his heart at this moment with your Holy Spirit so he may repent and see that the wages of sin are death."

The preacher she had referred to as Brother Marion had taken this opportunity to come into the kitchen and join my mother in prayer. I noticed he was about forty years old and robust. He was dressed in the preacher uniform of the Southern Bible Belt. I stood, unable to move, listening to the two of them. I felt a great pity for my mamma as I watched her shoulders tremble as she cried and prayed. I loved her desperately and wanted to please her these last few hours. At the same time, I felt angry and frustrated. I would have very much liked to have been somewhere else at that moment. This Mr. Marion, whom I had never met, then turned to me.

"Can we go somewhere more private?" he asked.

Without waiting for me to answer, he took me by the arm and forcefully walked me out the back door and into the old smokehouse. Thirty or forty, two to four pound chickens fluttered in all directions as we entered. Smell of chicken manure rose up to my nostrils. Pulling the door behind him, he released me and looked at me with eyes that flamed with righteousness.

"Do you see what your sin is doing to your poor mother?" he asked.

All the pain I was experiencing from watching my mama's suffering now turned to hatred for this man.

"I just want you to lift your hands to the Lord while I lay my hands on your head," he commanded, as he placed both hands on my head.

I recovered my composure as he launched into his prayer. I had had enough. I grabbed his hands and threw them away from me. "The hell with you! I don't need no goddamn fanatical preacher praying over me!" I said, pushing my way past him. I went back into the house, entered my bedroom and sat down on my bed.

I heard Brother Marion enter the kitchen. "I fear he's lost forever, Sister Ocie," he said passing his final judgment on me. A wail like that of a wounded animal came up out of my mamma's throat and pierced my ears and broke my heart.

On the morning of the twenty-seventh, I woke up with the smell of bacon being fried. I could hear the familiar sounds that my mother made in the kitchen as she moved about to cook breakfast. I knew my daddy would be sitting at the table, sipping his coffee. The realization that I had slept my last night under the roof with my family seeped into my soul. I lay quietly listening to the clatter, waiting for them to speak. A train whistled somewhere off in the distance. A feeling of profound loneliness came over me. My daddy's voice pulled me back to the present.

"We have to go on with our lives, Mother. They're all going to grow up and leave us one day, so you better start getting used to the idea."

"I just don't know why he has to go so far away? Lord knows, we may never see him again." I knew by the sound of her voice that she was trying to choke back her tears.

"Where is that great faith you're always talking about?"

"Don't you question my faith, John. Wasn't for the Lord, I wouldn't be able to stand it, shore enough."

"Well, try not to throw one of your conniption fits when he leaves. It'll be hard enough on him without all of that. You'll get him to crying, too. And what'll that Navy feller think about us raising up a big, old, squalling calf like that."

I heard O'Donnel come to the back door and knock lightly.

"JOHNNY!" he called.

"I'll be right there," my daddy answered.

I knew he would be putting on his shoes now. I wondered if he was going to come in and say goodbye. I waited tensely. I was relieved when I heard him walk to the back door and go out. The spring pulled the screen door closed behind him with a bang. I heard him say something to O'Donnel. Laughing heartily, O'Donnel answered but I couldn't make out the words. Their voices soon passed out of hearing range. I heard the old John Deer tractor start with the familiar putt, putt, putt, putt.

The previous Friday night, I had graduated from Greene County Tech. One of our neighbors, a Mrs. Weaver, came and took mamma and me to the ceremony. My daddy felt uncomfortable with the whole thing. Declaring he had nothing decent to wear, he decided to stay home and watch the girls while we attended. I felt uncomfortable and out of place during the whole ceremony. I tried to stay away from my classmates and not engage in conversation. I didn't want to explain why I wasn't going on the senior trip. Mrs. Weaver, at my mamma's insistence, did manage to get me to stand in my cap and gown long enough to take a quick snapshot. I was belligerent and felt angry but really didn't understand why. Much to everyone's relief, we were soon back home. Mamma took the picture of the big St. Bernard dog that had rescued the little girl from drowning out of its frame. It had been hanging in our home as far back as I could remember. After a little adjustment, my diploma fit perfectly. The big St. Bernard picture had been hanging behind the couch. Looking for a more appropriate place to hang my diploma, she looked around the living room. Finally, she decided on the wall opposite the couch. She went to the kitchen, brought back a hammer and a small tack, and mounted it on the wall in the place she had selected. After straightening it up to her liking, she backed away a few feet. "There now, ain't that nice?" she said. My daddy looked at it from where he was sitting but didn't comment.

I knew I had to get up and get ready. The recruiter would be coming for me at seven-thirty. I knew my mother would be waiting for me to come to breakfast. I dressed, took a deep breath, stilled myself the best I could, and went into the kitchen. I looked at mamma frying eggs. The girls were all seated waiting their turn to be served. Armentia and Cleo seemed unconcerned with my leaving and chattered happily with each other. Jean looked as though she was on the verge of tears but was determined to give me her moral support. She looked down at her plate to avoid making eye contact. I was grateful mamma was turned away from me, keeping herself busy. I went to the old wash stand, poured the water out of the water bucket into a wash pan, and prepared to wash my face and shave in the cold water. I looked at myself in the mirror. I hardly recognized myself.

"You'll write and let us know you're alright as soon as you get there won't you, son?" asked mamma.

"First chance I get," I answered as softly as I could.

I finished shaving, washed the soap off my face and sat down. She carried the skillet to my side of the table and lifted two fried eggs out and onto my plate. I was looking down at my eggs but I knew everyone was watching me.

"Your daddy just can't bear to say goodbye to you, son. He loves you but he can't bring himself to tell you. It's just killing him for you to leave us like this," mamma continued. I choked back the emotion. I finished eating quickly and went back into the old bedroom, pretending to be busy. I heard mamma putting the water in the old wash pan as she prepared to wash the dishes. The noise stopped and I felt her presence enter the room. Turning around, I saw her coming toward me with her outstretched arms. I fell into her arms and the floodgate opened and the rain came down. I could feel her whole body convulsing with her grief. I forced back my own tears as I held her firmly against my chest. After an eternity, she held me away.

"You sure you gonna be alright?" she asked.

"I'll be fine, Mamma," I answered.

Picking up the small overnight bag she had given me for graduation, I started for the front porch.

"I'll wait outside in the swing," I added.

From nineteen hundred and thirty-seven when I was born until nineteen hundred and fifty-six when I enlisted in the Navy, the world had changed in almost inconceivable ways. We had come into the age of miracle drugs and atomic power.

In my world, we had gone from kerosene lamps to electric lights. Water was now being pumped out of the ground with an electric pump. TV antennas had appeared on various houses throughout the community. Horsepower to tractor power had changed life on the farm forever. As I sat waiting, my mind drifted and I said good bye to all I once held dear. I could see my childhood dog, and best friend, running and barking as he played with me in the swaying wheat fields. I could see my daddy sitting on his beloved gray mare as she carried him happily across the high water after a severe rain. I could see us all sitting around Grandma and Grandpa Poe's dinner table laughing and talking about a pair of old wild mules we would soon buy. I could see the swaying canopy of the forest where I once looked for the evasive gray squirrel as a boy. It was all passing before me. This was the quiet hour before my birth into a New World.

I saw the dust long before I could see the car. Slowly, the black sedan came into view. It passed the Walnut Corner Church, slowed down, made its approach, and pulled up the little incline in front of our house and stopped.

"You ready, Messer?" came the voice from the car. I stood up, grabbed my little bag, and took one final look around at the old house that had been my home. This was where all the people that I loved lived. I felt the final contraction of Mother Nature as she squeezed me forth into a New World.

Mamma came slowly out onto the front porch trying the best she could to hold back the tears. She had been waiting inside the house to ease the pain of my new birth. We walked arm in arm to where the car of the recruiter sat waiting. Turning to me she gave me one final embrace.

"Always be a good boy, son," she said through her tears. I kissed her wet cheek, stepped into the car, and left my childhood forever.

Boot Camp

"GET OFF THE GRASS! GET OFF THE GRASS! GET OFF THE GRASS! WHAT IS THE MATTER WITH YOU?" he screamed at me. I was now running in circles on a cement slab trying desperately to understand what he was talking about.

We had boarded the plane in Little Rock, Arkansas to fly to San Diego, California at 8:00 P.M. on the evening of May 28, 1956. Some of the more worldly-appearing young fellers said it was called a Jet Prop. They left me with the impression that although we had been in the Navy only a short period of time we had somehow gained a certain measure of sophistication. Not wanting to show my ignorance, I spoke of this Jet with a certain amount of authority and explained to some of the less knowledgeable lads the working of this marvel. Inwardly, however, I felt that somehow there was something profoundly arrogant about man presuming he had a right to fly like the birds of the air. I felt God would punish us sooner or later for encroaching on His domain. This could very well be the moment that He had chosen to do just that. In less than half an hour, I sat petrified watching the clouds as they floated by my window. The stewardess moved up and down the aisle trying to reassure us fourteen new recruits that all was well. I began to realize the wisdom of my mamma's words that one should always be prepared for death.

In spite of my fears, at 2:30 A.M. we landed at the San Diego Airport. That was when I got my first look at what I soon would learn was a Chief Petty Officer. He was a tall, lanky gentleman dressed in khaki trousers, shirt, jacket, and black tie. On the left sleeve of the jacket there were six-inch-long, half-inch-wide, blue stripes sewn on just below the elbow. He wore a khaki hat with a black visor. The hat was shaped very much like the ones Greyhound bus drivers wear. Right in the middle of the visor was a big gold anchor. He seemed to know who we were immediately. "WHO HAS THE ORDERS?" he asked, with a southern drawl.

"I do, sir," answered the one we called Phelps.

The man dressed in the khaki uniform then took the brown manila envelope and ripped it open. After satisfying himself all was in order, he turned on his heels. "FOLLOW ME!" he commanded. The business-like manner in which he conducted himself gave me the feeling that we had somehow entered into a new, unknown world, and it wasn't going to be an easy one.

A big gray bus with U.S. Navy stenciled near the door waited at curbside. After we got on and sat down, the tall feller stepped up onto the first step. He looked at each of us individually before speaking.

"My name is Chief Petty Officer Miller," he finally said, then hesitated for a moment before continuing. "I am probably the last nice son-of-a-bitch you're going to see for a few weeks. But I want to tell you something and I never want you to forget it. You're now men of the United States Navy. If you successfully complete these next few weeks of boot camp, it will be a source of pride for you and your loved ones for the duration of your lifetime. I want to be the first to welcome you aboard. You're now a part of the most powerful Navy that ever existed, serving the greatest nation on the face of this earth. It's going to be a lot of hard work. I want to ask each one of you to give it your very best and do yourself proud." Then, turning to the driver, he said, "Take 'em to the house Charley."

A short time later we were disembarked in front of a building that had a long shed attached to the side. There, waiting for us, was a man dressed in the beautiful uniform that I so admired. Six long, four-foot-high tables ran the full length of the shed. "LISTEN UP," he said. "I WANT YOU ALL TO COME TO THESE TABLES." We moved quickly to the tables. "TAKE THE PENCIL ON THE STRING AND HOLD IT UP WHERE I CAN SEE IT." We all hastily complied. The Chief's words were still ringing in our ears. "NOW, I AM GOING TO PASS OUT A CARD TO EACH OF YOU. ON THE SIDE WHERE IT SAYS ADDRESS, WRITE YOUR PARENT'S OR GUARDIAN'S ADDRESS." He waited patiently. "HOLD DOWN THE CHATTER," he commanded, then, continued. "HOLD UP YOUR PENCIL WHEN YOU'RE FINISHED. NOW ON THE OTHER SIDE, I WANT YOU TO WRITE THE FOLLOWING: DEAR MOTHER (FATHER, GRANDMOTHER, OR WHOEVER YOUR GUARDIAN MIGHT BE), I HAVE ARRIVED SAFELY IN SAN DIEGO. I AM WELL AND BEING CARED FOR. I WILL WRITE AGAIN WHEN MY TRAINING SCHEDULE PERMITS. NOW, PUT YOUR LOVING SON AND SIGN YOUR NAME. WHEN YOU'RE FINISHED, PASS YOUR CARDS TO THE RIGHT AND THEN FORWARD."

The cards were soon completed and turned in. By this time, it was just after 4:00A.M. We had been up for about twenty-four hours. The day before had started at 4:30 A.M. at the Armed Forces Examining Center.

The sailor in charge was speaking again, "NOW LISTEN UP! WE'RE GOING TO GET YOU GIRLS TO BED. THERE IS A DOOR JUST TO MY RIGHT. I WANT YOU TO GO IN THAT DOOR AND FIND THE LADDER ON THE LEFT AND FOLLOW IT. AT THE TOP, TURN BACK LEFT AND YOU'LL ENTER INTO A DORMITORY. FIND A BUNK AND GRAB A WINK WHILE YOU CAN. NOW GET," he ordered.

We soon found the dormitory and individual racks and happily climbed into them. Even though I was exhausted, I stretched out under the gray wool blanket feeling quite content. The sweet smell of mothballs entered my nostrils as I covered my head. At last, I was doing something I wanted to do and being paid for it, too. Not a lot, just over ten cents an hour but, never the less, being paid. A feeling of purpose fell over me as I dozed off. I wasn't quite sure I had been sleeping when the lights came on. Someone had a nightstick in a trashcan, banging it from side to side, making a tremendous noise. "Up and at 'em, up and at 'em, up and at 'em," he kept saying over and over.

"What time is it?" I asked.

"Four-thirty-one!" came the answer.

Suddenly, we were surrounded by dozens of other young men who were wearing civilian clothes. We were made to understand that we were supposed to march to the chow hall some mile and a half away. After much confusion and head shaking by two of our future trainers, we were pointed in a westerly direction and commenced to struggle forward in a very unmilitary-like manner. Dozens of marching companies came flowing down the street in perfect precision. We watched fascinated. A company came marching alongside of us, suddenly, someone called out, "RIGHT OBLIQUE………HUT" and the company did a quick quarter turn and headed right for us. When they were about eight feet from us they all screamed in unison, "YOU'LL BE SORRY." Right when I thought they were going to run over the top of us, someone yelled, "LEFT OBLIQUE……………HUT," and they returned to their previous position, stepping along smartly. They soon left us far behind to contemplate their warning. Nearing the mess hall, the companies had all stopped and individuals peeled off in single file. They hugged the side of the building as they moved forward.

"Is there anyone here from Arkansas?" someone called out. I stepped to the side and looked down the line of people trying to see who had asked. In the process, I had somehow managed to step on the invisible grass. After asking what was the matter with me, the man in charge came rushing over and showed me the line where the sidewalk stopped and the grass started. Noting my confusion, he turned to the gentlemen behind me, "YOU SEE THE GRASS, DON'T YOU?" he demanded to know.

"Yes, sir," came the reply.

Turning to me, "YOU SEE IT NOW, PUKE?" he yelled.

"Yes, sir," I responded. The grass suddenly appeared and I could see it plain as day.

We were given fifteen minutes to eat and fall back into ranks. I was so nervous from my experience with the feller in charge of the grass that I had lost my appetite. The all-metal trays clanked and the mess hall roared with activity. The men serving the food looked at us with an air of superiority mixed with sympathy as we passed silently in front of them holding up our trays. I gulped down a few bites of food, drank my milk, and followed the stream of multicolored clothing back out into the street. We were soon marched back over to the R&O (recruit and outfitting) sheds.

I felt a great need to seek the comfort that comes from having companions. I soon found myself lounging with a group of three others very much like myself. Two of the young men were from Texas and the other one was from Arkansas. There are men that somehow conjure up the idea of certain stereotypes. This is how it was with my friend from Arkansas. He was a couple of inches shorter and a little heavier than I was. He wore big, round, flesh-colored glasses on his little pug nose that sat in the middle of his very round, red face. His hair was brownish to blond and cut very short. He spoke with a slow Southern drawl. He related to the world around him as though, one day, he had just suddenly been born as an adult with the ability to talk. He would focus his magnified eyes on the occurring events around us and react in absolute awe. We found this quite comical. Perhaps it was because we felt like he looked. The Texans just naturally fell into calling him Arkey.

We soon figured out by the gossip, and watching the activity around us, that we were waiting to be assigned to a training company. The dozens or so ahead of us had advised us this would take two or three days. In the meantime, we lay around on the cement floor of the R&O shed like stray dogs.

Long about the middle of the morning, Arkey raised up his head, "I gotta piss," he declared and looked all around.

"Well, they got that building where we slept last night secured for cleaning," declared one of my Texan friends.

"I don't give a good goddamn. When I gotta piss, I gotta piss," replied Arkey, as he started getting to his feet.

I looked toward the entrance of the building that was secured for cleaning and I saw a middle-aged, short, obese sailor. He had a full sleeve of stripes on his left arm and was wearing a white uniform with a little white hat sitting on top of his fiery red hair. "I'll just go ask that sorry son-of-a-bitch," commented Arkey and started walking toward him. The red-headed sailor with all the stripes was watching him out of the corner of his eye.

Arkey made his approach. "Hey..." he commenced.

The redheaded man stopped. Looking stunned, he leaned forward, stuck his head out toward Arkey as far as he could, while at the same time pushing his hat to the back of his head, all in one swift motion. "HEY!" he screamed back at Arkey. We all came scurrying to our feet. Arkey's mouth dropped open. He looked like he was in shock as his mentor continued.

"DON'T YOU EVER SAY HEY TO ME, BOOT, OR ANYONE ELSE AS LONG AS YOU'RE ABOARD THIS TRAINING STATION. THE FIRST THING I WANT TO HEAR COMING OUT OF YOUR MOUTH IS 'SIR'. YOU GOT THAT, BOY?"

"Yes, sir," Arkey answered.

"NOW, GET YOUR UGLY ASS OUT OF MY FACE," the man with all the stripes commanded. Lifting his right hand, he pointed toward the shed where we waited. "GET!" he repeated. Arkey hurried back to the bosom of our small group.

"Did you find out where the head is, Arkey?" one of the Texas teased.

"Hell, no," lamented Arkey. "I'm gonna find me a coffee cup and just piss in that," he said, resuming his old position.

We all laughed until tears ran down our cheeks. Somehow, things didn't seem so bad when you knew there were others that were at least as miserable as you were.

In less than a minute, the door of the building flew open and someone yelled out, "HEAD'S OPEN FOR YOU GIRLS THAT NEED TO PEE."

"About goddamn time," grumbled Arkey, as he headed for the door.

We passed the morning listening to the squawk box call out names and watched people scurrying around from here to there. We made another trip to the chow hall, then back on the cement floor for more speculation about our future. Through the process of elimination, we had discerned that anyone wearing olive green leggings, or duty belt, was still in boot camp. As we lounged in the afternoon heat, we noticed a young man walking about with a nightstick, dressed in the traditional garb of a trainee. The desire to alleviate the fear of the unknown was heavy upon us.

"Let's go over there and talk to that dumb-looking bastard," suggested Arkey. "Maybe he can give us an idea of what to expect," he added.

We all agreed and moved slowly in his direction, trying not to be conspicuous. When we came within a few feet, Arkey engaged him in a conversation.

"About to get out of this shit hole, are you?"

"Soon!"

"What's it been like for you?"

"Agh, not that bad; you get used to it."

"How long you think it'll be before we get our uniforms and get started?"

"About three days. They'll put you in a company and issue you all your gear right away. It'll all be dumped in a big fart sack when you first get it. You'll have to wash it all up and learn how to put it out for junk on the bunk.

"What the hell is junk on the bunk?"

"Oh, it's all your clothes folded and laid out in a certain way. They are going to issue you one of them old Springfield rifles to carry around, too. You'll work out with it three or four hours every afternoon. You'll have classes in the morning starting right after barracks and personnel inspection."

"Will we have inspection every day?"

"Yep, every goddamn day. You'll wash your own clothes and tie them on a big rope that is fastened to a sixty-foot mast pole. After you tie each item on the line exactly a quarter inch apart with a square knot, you'll hoist it up in the air. Some asshole that has nothing else to do will inspect it every morning, and if he sees anything not tied correctly, he'll cut it down and the whole company will get demerits. All the companies are in competition to be the best, and the ones with the least demerits will carry the honor flag and get to go to chow first every day."

"Damn, we gonna learn how to do all of that in nine weeks?"

"No, you're going to learn all that in three days; that's just to get you started. You'll have a week of fire fighting, a week of mess duty, a week of seamanship on the old USS Neversail, go through the gas chamber, and jump off a ninety foot tower into a pool that has been set on fire. They want you to learn how to escape from a sinking ship where there has been an oil spill. You'll be taking exams on all the classes they give you. Make sure you study and pass the test. If you fail one, they'll set your ass back and you'll be delayed graduating."

"Boy, that's a lot of shit. What time you boys get up?"

"We get up at 0430. You'll have to get the bunks all lined up exactly fourteen inches from the bulkhead (wall) and in a perfect straight line. Your peacoat and raincoat will be placed on hangars and tied to the head of your bed with a square knot; your bucket with the scrub brush in it will be tied at the end of your bunk in the same manner. If they are the least bit loose or slack or have any Irish pennants (end of rope, line or tie ties dangling loose) hanging out, they'll cut them down and throw them out in the patio and march the whole company over them."

"How often you get stuck with the guard like your doing now?"

"You'll have at least one or two watches a day. Sometimes it will be at night and sometimes during the day. The night watch cuts your sleep back to about four hours, and that makes it hard to stay awake in class. I don't know if you've seen that big, old, fat First Class Petty Officer marching about twelve assholes around here or not. The son-of-a-bitch looks like he weighs about three hundred pounds. He's the Company Commander of 4013 and it never graduates. You just have to work your way out of there into a company that's on regular T-days (training). We call that the Crumb Company. You don't want to get too many demerits and get your ass stuck in there. I better move along. I'm supposed to be on fire watch. Good luck to you guys."

Arkey gave a big sigh and shook his head from side to side. "Our ass is grass, boys," he said, looking as though he might cry.

I felt a little weak in the knees at the thought of what lay ahead of us. We went back over and lay down on the cement deck (floor), feeling subdued. No one spoke for a while, then the silence was broken. "I don't know about you old boys, but I tell you the idea of looking up that old mule's ass don't sound half as bad as it did a week ago," Arkey commented. We all laughed.

At 1500 the squawk box crackled,

"LISTEN UP! IF YOU HEAR YOUR NAME CALLED, FALL OUT ON THE STREET IN FORMATION."

The names were being read off,

"MESSER, WILLIAMS, JEFFERSON..." I stopped listening after I heard mine and ran for the street. A serious-looking, tall Chief Petty Officer marched briskly up and down in front of us, barking out orders.

"STAND AT ATTENTION!" he ordered, as he turned and walked back down toward the end where I stood. He looked me right in the eyes.

"EYES FRONT!" he commanded. I shuttered, locked my knees, and stared straight ahead.

"DON'T LOCK YOUR KNEES, LADIES, I'LL BE PICKING YOU UP OFF THE DECK. YOU'RE GOVERNMENT PROPERTY NOW, WE DON'T WANT YOU DAMAGED. STAND UP STRAIGHT. GET YOUR MIND OFF THAT LITTLE GIRL BACK HOME. IF THE NAVY WANTED YOU TO HAVE A GIRL, WE WOULD'VE ISSUED YOU ONE," he continued to talk as the ranks filled up. In what seemed like an eternity, we had sixty-seven men lined up in four rows. The Chief stopped his pacing, went to the shed and spoke to someone, and then returned.

"GENTLEMEN, YOU ARE NOW MEMBERS OF COMPANY 248. I AM CHIEF BOATSWAIN MATE CAUSEE. I AM GOING TO BE YOUR COMPANY COMMANDER FOR THE NEXT NINE WEEKS. YOU ARE GOING TO CAUSE ME TO BE VERY HAPPY THE NEXT FEW WEEKS OR I'M GOING TO CAUSE YOU TO BE SORRY YOU WERE EVER BORN. I AM GOING TO BE YOUR MOMMA AND YOUR PAPPA. I WILL PUT YOU TO SLEEP AND I WILL WAKE YOU UP. YOU'RE TO DO EXACTLY WHAT I TELL YOU, WHEN I TELL YOU, AND HOW I TELL YOU, AND NOTHING MORE. IS THAT UNDERSTOOD?" he asked. No one answered.

"I CAN'T HEAR YOU," he added.

"YES, SIR!" we bellowed.

"GOOD!....ATTENTION..." there was a slight shuffle of feet.

"FORWARD...MARCH," he ordered and we clopped forward to the corner of the street.

"COLUMN LEFT.....HUP," he commanded. We came along the backside of the building where the shed was constructed. There was green grass and two big shade trees in the elbow of the building.

"COLUMN LEFT.....HUP," came the order, we turned up onto the grass under the trees.

"MARK TIME......HUP," he commanded. We all stepped up and down going no where.

"STRAIGHTEN IT UP THERE," he directed. We continued to lift our feet up and down.

"GUIDE RIGHT, GODDAMN IT," he yelled. We looked right and much to my surprise the line became straight.

"READY....HALT.......AT EASE..........SIT DOWN. NOW, TELL ME HOW MANY OF YOU GENTLEMEN ARE FROM TEXAS?" he asked.

Fifteen hands that belonged to smiling faces went up. He went around individually and asked them the location of their origin. I had begun to feel left out and was envious of my Texan neighbors.

"HOW MANY OF YOU KNOW THE LONE STAR STATE SONG?" he asked, smiling broadly. The same fifteen hands went back up. "GOOD, LET'S SING IT," he suggested and they raised their voices to the heavens and shouted out their beloved state song. When it was over, he walked back in front of the company. He suddenly took on an air of seriousness as he looked around. "I HATE GODDAMN TEXAS," he proclaimed emphatically, big blue veins appeared on his neck and his face turned red. "THAT'S THE LAST TIME I EVER WANT TO HEAR THAT NAME SPOKEN. IS THAT UNDERSTOOD?" he asked, as he walked among us looking at those who had raised their hand. I somehow started feeling redeemed in my lowly state, of having the sad honor of coming from the Land of Opportunity. I didn't want to hear anymore about Texas myself, as a matter of fact.

I looked around for my two Texan friends and Arkey to see how they had reacted. I realized they had somehow missed the good fortune of being assigned to company 248. A feeling of loneliness and desperation came over me. I heard a train whistle off in the distance.

The Chief soon regained control of himself and resumed his former demeanor. He returned to the front of the company and said, "IN A FEW MINUTES, WE'LL BE GOING TO CHOW. I WANT YOU ALL TO EAT QUICK AS POSSBLE AND FALL BACK IN. WE'LL THEN BE GOING TO THE NAVY EXCHANGE. THERE YOU'LL BE ISSUED A COUPON BOOK WORTH $20.00. YOU'RE TO BUY A BUCKET, WASHING POWDER, SCRUB BRUSH, SOAP, RAZOR, DEODORANT, TOOTHPASTE, SHAVING CREAM, BLACK SHOE POLISH, TWO PADLOCKS, TIE TIES, STENCIL KIT, STATIONERY SUPPLES, A NOTE PAD, AND A PACKAGE OF BALLPOINT PENS. YOU MAY BUY ANY OTHER SUNDRY ITEMS YOU DEEM NECESSARY, BUT NO GEE DUNK. FOR THOSE OF YOU THAT DON'T KNOW WHAT GEE DUNK IS, I SUGGEST YOU FIND OUT. LIGHT 'EM UP IF YOU HAVE 'EM AND SIT AT EASE. I'LL BE BACK IN A MINUTE."

The Chief disappeared around the corner of the building. I looked around at the people who would be my companions for the next nine weeks. I only recognized one of them. He had been on the plane from Little Rock with us. He was a tall, thin, black man. There were six dark-complexioned men in front of me, talking in a musical language I didn't recognize. I noticed the rest of the men in the company were all white. I looked back at the black man. He was sitting quietly, not moving. I smiled at him. I thought I saw him nod, but if he did, it was very slight. His eyes were dark almond brown, almost liquid. His lower chin jutted out in stubborn defiance. Everyone else seemed to be talking to someone. We made eye contact.

I had never known a black person or talked to one. I had seen them in Pocahontas walking down the street. I noticed there were several black ladies preparing sandwiches at the AFES back in Little Rock. But I didn't eat anything I thought they might have prepared, for fear of it making me sick. My grandfather had been the youngest son of an Alabama family whose roots went back to the Great Civil War. My ancestors had been middle-class before the war, but the South's defeat left them destitute. They found themselves competing with the poor blacks for the few resources that the North had overlooked in its path of destruction. I had never been taught to hate blacks, but my Southern upbringing told me they were different. Segregation fostered the idea we were born superior both morally and intellectually. I had no reason to question that. I was a product of my environment. I heard my daddy say many times that my grandpa had told him he never seen a nigger that wouldn't steal.

Those liquid brown eyes held me like a spell. I saw no fear in his face, only resolve. I didn't feel at all threatened, nor the need to turn away, as we looked at each other. The realization came over me that the soul behind those dark eyes had drunk deeply from a cup of suffering that I had never tasted. I suddenly felt inferior to this man who was suppose to have been born to a lower state in life than myself. The playing field we now shared was level. There would be no benefits for my white skin in this New World. White, brown, yellow, and black, we were all destined to suffer the same humiliations. I made my way over to where he sat. I stuck out my hand, "I'm Messer," I said.

"Jefferson," he answered. I liked the feel of his hand. It was warm and strong and filled with confidence. "Watcha tank abut dat chief?" he asked.

"About a son-of a-bitch, I'd say," I answered and smiled. Jefferson nodded his head.

"Got dat rite," he replied.

We finished chow and marched to the PX. We were directed to a window where a nondescript, middle-aged woman had us print, then sign, our names on a lengthy, official-looking form. Then, we raced through the aisles collecting the things that we had been directed to buy.

Afterwards, the Chief took us on a long march to the rear of a building that would be our home for the next several weeks. He climbed the stairs, up to the little four-foot by eight-foot porch attached in front of the door, and faced us. "IT'S BEEN A LONG DAY TODAY, BUT TOMORROW WILL BE EVEN LONGER. INSIDE, YOU WILL FIND BUNKS WITH MATTRESSES. I AM SORRY TO REPORT THERE ARE NO BLANKETS AVAILABLE. TOMORROW YOU'LL BE ISSUED YOUR CLOTHING AND BEDDING. WHEN I GIVE YOU THE WORD, I WANT YOU TO FALL OUT AND FIND YOURSELF A BUNK. THERE ARE TWO LOCKERS ON THE LEFT OF EACH BUNK. THE TOP BUNK GOES WITH THE TOP LOCKER AND THE BOTTOM BUNK TO THE BOTTOM LOCKER. I WANT YOU TO PUT YOUR VALUABLES IN YOUR CORRESPONDING LOCKER AND PADLOCK IT. YOU'RE GONNA HAVE TEN MINUTES TO SHIT, SHAVE, AND SHOWER. WHEN YOU'RE FINISHED, RETURN TO YOUR BUNK. NOW FALL OUT!" he ordered. We all dashed for the door at the same time shoving each other forward. The fourth bunk bottom right was open and I put my ditty bag on top of the mattress. The Chief walked the length of the barracks observing our every move.

"OKAY, HIT THE SHOWERS," he commanded. I grabbed my long white cloth ditty bag and ran to the head. I found a vacant sink and rummaged for my toothpaste and put a nice glob on my brush. It tasted awful. "What the hell brand is this?" I said to myself. I finished with my teeth and grabbed the tube of shaving cream. I smeared it on my face. Damn, it burnt like fire; I scraped it off with my new razor.

"SNAP IT UP," someone yelled. I quickly looked down at the tube to read the name. I sure wouldn't buy this again. The word toothpaste jumped up at me. I looked at the other tube I had used to brush my teeth; yep, shaving cream.

"LET THE NEXT GROUP IN HERE, YOU GUYS HIT THE SHOWER, LET'S KEEP IT MOVING," a voice yelled. I looked at my face in the mirror; it was cherry red and burning. No time to worry about that, I dashed for the shower. In less than fifteen minutes, we were all back lounging on our bunks.

"IS EVERYONE OUT OF THE SHOWER?" asked the Chief.

"YES, SIR," we all bellowed out.

"I NEED FOUR MEN TO STAND TWO HOUR FIRE WATCHES. ANY VOLUNTEERS?" the Chief asked. Ten hands went up. Mine was not among them.

"YOU, YOU, YOU, AND YOU, COME OVER HERE. THE REST OF YOU LADIES GET IN YOUR BUNKS. ONE OTHER THING, THESE FOUR MEN THAT HAVE VOLUNTEERED TO STAND THE WATCH TONIGHT WON'T BE STANDING ANOTHER ONE FOR FIVE DAYS. THAT SHOULD GIVE YOU AN IDEA OF HOW MUCH I VALUE ENTHUSIASM FOR TEAMWORK. NOW, THE REST OF YOU HIT THE SACK. I WANT YOU ALL ASLEEP IN FIVE MINUTES!" he commanded.

The term "June gloom" in San Diego comes from the fact that the sun doesn't break through the overcast until the middle of the morning. This puts a damp chill in the air at night and it becomes quite frigid. Arkansas, on the other hand, doesn't have the marine layer and nighttime temperatures don't fluctuate to any great extent. I was expecting it to be warm and sunny in the Golden State. I had only worn a short-sleeve shirt and a pair of faded jeans when I left for Little Rock. The recruiter had advised me not to take anything with me, as it would all be shipped home anyway. I drew myself up in the fetal position, trying to keep warm as I dozed. My fitful dreams and chattering teeth kept me awake most of the night. I was happy when the lights came on at 0430.

"YOU GOT FIVE MINUTES TO USE THE HEAD AND FALL IN," came the voice of Chief Causee.

"Don't that son-of-bitch ever sleep?" someone mumbled. I welcomed the opportunity to be moving.

In less than five minutes, the last of the company was coming together and standing at attention in front of the little porch. Chief Causee watched us with a blank expression as we quieted down under his watchful eye.

"LISTEN UP!" he commanded, then hesitated. "WE ARE GOING TO MARCH OVER TO THE CHOW HALL FOR BREAKFAST. I WANT YOU TO EAT IN FIFTEEN MINUTES AND FALL IN RANKS. THE FIRST THING ON THE AGENDA THIS MORNING IS THE BARBER SHOP. IT OPENS AT SEVEN AND WE ARE GOING TO BE STANDING THERE WAITING WHEN THE DOORS OPEN. ANY QUESTION?" Silence. "LEFT......FACE!" We made an uncoordinated turn to the left. "FORWARD........MARCH!" he ordered.

We shuffled awkwardly along through the darkness. I could hear the training center coming to life in the early morning. Lights were coming on almost simultaneously and men were running about in all directions. I could determine we were housed in H-shaped barracks that were constructed in long rows that faced each other in the back. They were painted the same tan to beige color as all of the other buildings aboard the Naval Training Center. There was one company on each end of the barracks on the bottom floor and also on each end of the top. The passageway that connected the H was where cleaning lockers, small offices and the heads were located. The area where we were now marching was the alleyway between the buildings in back. As we shuffled along, I could see the cement slabs on each side of us where the clothes were to be washed.

We passed underneath sixty-foot-high mast-like poles that held eight lines of clothing. The thick, rope-like lines were attached at the top of the pole, then ran down toward the ground, and secured to a five-foot high post. The short posts were painted white at the top and navy gray on the bottom. They stood like silent sentinels, holding on tightly to their assigned lines; white clothing flapped gently in the early morning breeze. The sound of the uneven steps could be heard as we clopped along. We came out of the alley and into an open space.

"COLUMN RIGHT........HUP," Chief Causee barked. We turned right bumping into each other. "GET IN STEP, GODDAMIT!" the Chief ordered. As we plodded along, rows and rows of uniformed men in blue stretched out in front of us. Sharp cadence calls cut through the morning air. I wondered if this motley-looking group, dressed in our rainbow of colors, would ever be able to move as though we were one entity. Somehow, this all felt very familiar to me. The thought came to me, "Have I been here before?"

Seven in the morning found us standing in front of the barbershop. "NOW LISTEN UP…WE'RE GOING TO PEEL OFF IN SETS OF FIVE FROM THE RIGHT WHEN I GIVE THE WORD. GET IN THE BARBER'S CHAIR AND KEEP YOUR MOUTH SHUT. WHEN THE APRON IS PULLED OFF, THAT'S YOUR SIGNAL TO GET BACK HERE DOUBLE TIME," instructed the Chief. He then disappeared inside the barbershop. We could see him talking to someone.

"We going to have to pay these assholes for scalping us?" a voice asked.

"Shut up before you get us in trouble," someone snapped. We could see the Chief as he came to the door. He stopped and was talking again. Suddenly, the door flew open.

"FIRST FIVE...LET'S GO," he yelled. The first group ran for the door. Less than twenty seconds passed.

"NEXT FIVE," the Chief called out. Men were running out as others hurried in. In fifteen minutes, it was all over. We now stood like sheared sheep in front of our company commander. Humiliation hung in the air. The first step, of giving up our individuality, had been taken. Knowing smiles played around the lips of men as they came marching by. The Chief returned to the front of the company.

"WE ARE NOW GOING FOR CLOTHING AND BEDDING ISSUE. RIGHT...FACE...FORWARD...MARCH," he commanded. We faced right and unceremoniously staggered forward. In a half-hour, we came to a long, one-story building.

"READY...HALT," the Chief ordered. A young sailor sat on the banister of a raised platform in front of the structure. When we came to a halt, he stood up. The Chief went to where he was standing. In a few minutes he returned.

"STAND AT EASE AND LISTEN CAREFULLY TO WHAT YOU'RE GOING TO BE INSTRUCTED TO DO," he said, then turned back to the sailor and nodded. The young sailor then came forward.

"WHEN I GIVE YOU THE WORD, I WANT YOU TO START FROM MY RIGHT IN SINGLE FILE AND PASS THROUGH THE DOOR ON MY LEFT. THE FIRST THING YOU'RE GOING TO RECEIVE IS A SEA BAG. YOU'RE TO OPEN IT UP AND TAKE THE STRAP OF THE BAG AND FASTEN IT AROUND YOUR NECK. HOLDING IT OPEN, YOU'RE TO PROCEED TO THE NEXT ISSUE STATION. THERE WILL BE SOMEONE AT EACH LOCATION. YOU WILL BE ISSUED ONE OR MORE ARTICLES OF CLOTHING BY THIS INDIVIDUAL. WHEN YOU STEP IN FRONT OF HIM, GIVE HIM

YOUR SIZE. ONCE YOU'RE FITTED, MOVE ALONG. WHEN YOU COME OUT THIS DOOR ON YOUR LEFT, YOU WILL HAVE A FULL ISSUE. ARE THERE ANY QUESTIONS?" hesitating after his final question he turned to the Chief. "When you're ready, Chief," he said.

The Chief walked back in front of us. "NOW LISTEN UP, MEN. AMONG OTHER THINGS, YOU'RE GOING TO BE ISSUED TWO PAIR OF DRESS SHOES AND ONE PAIR OF BOONDOCKERS. YOU'RE GOING TO BE WEARING THEM BOONERS SIXTEEN HOURS A DAY FOR THE NEXT NINE WEEKS. TAKE THE TIME TO MAKE SURE THEY FIT. LEAVE THEM ABOUT A HALF SIZE BIGGER THAN YOU THINK IS NECESSARY AT THE END OF THE TOE. I AM GOING TO BE IN THE AREA WHERE THEY WILL BE ISSUED. I WANT EACH ONE OF YOU TO SIT DOWN, PUT THEM ON, AND LACE THEM UP. GETTING SHOES THAT AREN'T TOO TIGHT OR ONES THAT WON'T GIVE YOU BLISTERS IS THE MOST IMPORTANT THING THAT'S GOING TO HAPPEN TO YOU TODAY," he looked at us for a moment to satisfy himself he had been understood, then added, "NOW LET'S MOVE IT."

Pandemonium commenced. We entered the building and moved rapidly down the line. We were issued seven sets of underwear, six pair of socks, four white hats, three sets of dungarees, three white uniforms, two undress blue uniforms, one dress blue uniform, peacoat, raincoat, flat hat, jersey sweater, pair of gloves, white belt, blue belt, two pair of dress shoes, one pair of boondockers, three pair of heavy socks, and two mattress covers. Our tailors stood between cardboard boxes stacked to the ceiling. A little board two-feet long and six-inches wide, lay across the top of two boxes at waist level. This identified the individual's issue stations. The attendant would look us up and down, go to one of the big boxes and count out the articles required, return, and dump them in our seabags. No conversation was required. Chief Causee stood in front of where the shoes were being issued. He insisted that shoes be tried, and exchanged when necessary, until he was satisfied that all of us had shoes that we could march to hell and back in if it became necessary. We moved along until we came to the exit. There, two blankets were heaped upon the already overflowing bags. Weighted down, we fell back into ranks and waited. The young sailor who had given us our instructions on how to receive our clothing issue appeared once again on the platform to give us instructions.

"NOW LISTEN UP....I WANT YOU TO OPEN RANKS AND SPREAD OUT ONE BLANKET ON EACH SIDE OF YOU." We moved hastily to do as he had ordered.

"NOW, I WANT YOU TO DUMP ALL YOUR CLOTHING ON THE BLANKET TO YOUR LEFT. I AM GOING TO CALL OUT THE NAME AND NUMBER OF EACH ARTICLE OF CLOTHING YOU SHOULD HAVE. I WANT YOU TO HOLD IT UP WHERE I CAN SEE IT. WHEN I GIVE YOU THE WORD, YOU'RE TO PUT THE ITEMS ON THE BLANKET TO YOUR RIGHT. UNDERSTOOD?...OKAY!

The procedure then started. "HOLD UP THREE DUNGAREE SHIRTS. EVERYONE HAVE THREE DUNGAREE SHIRTS?" he asked. The routine went forward. "HOLD UP TWO PAIR OF DRESS SHOES," he continued. "EVERYONE HAVE 2 PAIR OF SHOES?" he asked.

"SIR!"

"YES?"

"I HAVE TWO LEFT SHOES, SIR," There was a moment's hesitation.

"WHAT'S THE OTHER TWO?"

A long, dead silence followed. Finally the voice answered, "Two right shoes, sir."

"GET UP HERE BOY AND LET ME SEE YOU." The bald-headed recruit ran forward and stood at attention in front of the young sailor.

"WHERE YOU FROM, SHITHEAD?"
"New Mexico, sir."
"EVERYONE FROM NEW MEXICO AS SMART AS YOU ARE, BOY?"
"I don't know, sir."
"YOU DON'T KNOW. YOU DON'T KNOW MUCH OF ANYTHING DO YOU? GET BACK TO YOUR GEAR!" he commanded. "HOLD UP FOUR WHITE JUMPERS," the inventory continued.

After the inventory was completed, we were ordered to put all of our clothes into one of the six-foot-long mattress covers. We were then ushered into the adjacent building. There, we cut stencils for our name, rank, and serial number that we used to mark each piece of clothing. We used white or black ink, depending on the color of the item. When we were finished, Chief Causee climbed upon one of the tables.

"WE ARE NOW GOING TO PUT ON OUR DUNAGAREE UNIFORM. YOU'RE TO FIND A SKIVVY SHIRT, SKIVVY DRAWERS, DUNGAREE SHIRT, DUNGAREE TROUSERS, BLUE BELT, PAIR OF BLACK SOCKS, BOONDOCKERS, AND A WHITE HAT. I WANT YOU TO TAKE OFF ALL YOUR CIVILAIN CLOTHES AND PLACE THEM ON THE TABLE IN FRONT OF YOU. THEN YOU'RE TO DRESS IN THE FOREMENTIONED ITEMS," he ordered.

Two of the sailors previously working the clothing issue stations walked among us passing out small cardboard boxes and felt tip marking pens.

"WHEN YOU'RE DRESSED, I WANT YOU TO PUT YOUR CIVILIAN CLOTHING IN THE BOX WE'VE PROVIDED, AND PUT THE ADDRESS OF WHERE YOU WANT TO SEND THEM," directed Chief Causee as he moved among us. "NOW, WHEN YOU HAVE YOUR CIVILIAN CLOTHES PACKED, I

WANT YOU TO STACK THEM HERE ON THIS TABLE IN FRONT OF ME," he moved and took the box from the recruit nearest him and placed it on the table. "I THEN WANT YOU TO PUT ALL YOUR CLOTHING BACK IN YOUR FART SACK, PLACE IT OVER YOUR LEFT SHOULDER AND FALL OUT IN FRONT OF THE BUILDING. LET'S MOVE IT. WE'VE STILL GOT A LONG DAY AHEAD OF US," he continued.

I had no idea that such a thing as dungarees existed. All the sailors I had seen had always been dressed in the beautiful dress blue or white uniform. Standing at attention, weighted down, with this long, heavy sack draped over my shoulders in my brand new dungarees, I was hit with a sudden wave of depression. Chief Causee brought us to attention and marched us back to our barracks. Once in the barracks, with our clothing dumped on our mattresses, Chief Causee called us to attention. He then went to the center of the barracks, where the two long picnic tables were located, and sat down.

"YOU MEN ALL GATHER AROUND ME HERE," he ordered. We all formed a circle and listened. "YOU CAN SEE, BY THAT BIG LUMP OF SHIT YOU'VE BEEN CARRYING AROUND, THAT IT'S GOING TO TAKE SOME DOING TO GET ALL OF YOUR CLOTHING IN THE STORAGE PLACE PROVIDED, SO PAY ATTENTION TO WHAT I AM GOING TO SHOW YOU. THESE LOCKERS ARE ONLY THIRTY INCHES HIGH, THIRTY INCHES WIDE, AND THIRTY INCHES DEEP. I'M GOING TO TEACH YOU HOW TO FOLD YOUR THINGS WHERE THEY WILL FIT INSIDE. WHEN YOU GET OUT IN THE FLEET, YOU'RE GOING TO HAVE THIS VERY SAME SIZE LOCKER, SO THIS IS NOT JUST SOME BULLSHIT DRILL THAT SOMEONE HAS DREAMED UP. CUMELLA, BRING YOUR GEAR OVER HERE," he said, standing up.

A recruit I had not seen before brought his gear to the table. Chief Causee directed him to pour it out on the table. The next hour and a half was spent learning how to fold clothing in a manner that would minimize space and prevent wrinkling. The clothes were then laid out on our bed in a manner in which the stenciled name could be read by anyone standing at the end of the bunk. We would do this same layout every Friday for the next nine weeks, at our weekly junk on the bunk inspections. Next, we stored it in the lockers, as Chief Causee directed. It was snug, but it did fit. The two little drawers on the bottom left were used for personal items, and valuables. Only our peacoats and raincoats remained to be stored. These were promptly placed onto hangers and tied at the head of our bunks in a square knot. There were to be no Irish Pennants dangling loose. The buckets containing the scrub brushes were now fastened at the foot in a like manner.

"FALL IN THE PATIO," ordered Chief Causee.

We were soon assembled at attention. He stood before us on the little porch.

"MEN, AFTER CHOW, WE ARE GOING TO GO TO THE ARMORY. THERE, YOU WILL BE ISSUED LEGGINGS, DUTY BELTS, AND YOUR PIECES (RIFLES). WE'LL RETURN HERE AND LOCK DOWN YOUR PIECES UNTIL WE NEED THEM. THE REST OF THE AFTERNOON WILL BE SPENT TRAINING IN CLOSE ORDER DRILL. AFTER EVENING CHOW, YOU'LL CHANGE INTO ANOTHER UNIFORM EXACTLY LIKE THE ONE YOU HAVE ON AND WASH THE CLOTHES YOU'RE NOW WEARING. I"LL BE SHOWING YOU HOW TO TIE THE CLOTHES ON THE LINE. THE CLOTHESLINE WILL BE INSPECTED BY MYSELF AS WELL AS A FORMAL INSPECTOR ON A DAILY BASIS. YOU'RE NEVER TO HAVE IN YOUR POSSESION ANY DIRTY CLOTHING WHATSOEVER. IT'LL BE EITHER STORED IN YOUR LOCKER, HANGING ON THAT LINE, OR YOU'LL BE WEARING IT. TOMORROW IS SATURDAY AND I'LL BE SELECTING THE

APPRENTICE CHIEF PETTY OFFICER AND THE REST OF THE ACTING PETTY OFFICERS FOR MY COMPANY STAFF. I WILL BE LOOKING FOR MEN THAT HAVE HAD SOME PRIOR MILITARY TRAINING OR HAVE GONE TO A MILITARY SCHOOL. I NEED MEN WITH EXPERIENCE, SO IF YOU'RE NOT SELECTED, DON'T TAKE IT PERSONAL. IN THE MORNING, YOU'LL BE WORKING ON GETTING THIS BARRACKS SCRUBBED FROM TOP TO BOTTOM. I WANT THIS DECK CLEAN ENOUGH THAT THE COMMANDING OFFICER HIMSELF WOULDN'T BE AFRAID TO EAT OFF OF IT. ONCE YOU'VE BROUGHT IT UP TO STANDARD, IT'S TO BE KEPT THAT WAY UNTIL THE DAY YOU GRADUATE. WHEN I'VE CHOSEN THE COMPANY STAFF AND YOU HAVE THIS PLACE IN 4.0 CONDITION, WE'LL DO SOME MORE WORK ON OUR CLOSE ORDER DRILL. MONDAY WILL BE NUMBER ONE OF YOUR 45 T-DAYS. ARE THERE ANY QUESTIONS?" he asked.

"Sir, how long will we be wearing dungarees?" came a voice from somewhere behind me.

"THE FIRST 15-T DAYS ARE YOUR PRIMARY PHASE OF TRAINING AND THE REQUIRED UNIFORM WILL BE DUNGAREES. THOSE OF YOU THAT SUCCESSFULLY COMPLETE THIS FIRST STAGE WILL THEN BE ALLOWED TO WEAR UNDRESS BLUES OR WHITES, DEPENDING ON THE UNIFORM OF THE DAY." Upon answering the question he turned and looked at Cumella.

"CUMELLA, THINK YOU CAN GET THIS RAGGEDY-LOOKING BUNCH OVER TO THE CHOW HALL?" he asked.

"YES, SIR!" came the response.

Wasn't much doubt in our minds who was going to be our Apprentice Chief Petty Officer.

Friday afternoon, we received our pieces, duty belts, and leggings. The weekend was spent cleaning, polishing, waxing, shining bright work, washing clothes, writing letters, shining shoes and getting acquainted. The men in the company were a cross-section from all over the country. We had eight men who had turned eighteen in an orphanage in Alexandria, Louisiana. They had lived their lives in institutions and took to the military regimentation like ducks to water. They seemed happy and cheerful and were not at all affected by the scourge of homesickness that had overtaken me and the majority of my fellow comrades. We had six men from Puerto Rico who jabbered constantly among themselves, in what I soon came to understand was Spanish. They had collected at the rear of the barracks, and any attempt to separate them was met with, "I don't a spak a de Inglish." They seemed to perform as expected when left alone, so we largely ignored them. There were three men from Northern California who had obviously been encouraged to join the Navy by the local judge in their area; these would prove to be our problem children. There were the Chief's friends from Texas, Jefferson from Memphis, three Mexican-Americans from New Mexico, and several other men from different parts of the country. There was one other gentleman and myself from Arkansas, making up a total of sixty-seven men.

The Navy Boot Camp's purpose was to prepare us to live in a world the majority of us knew nothing about. Keeping our bodies, clothing, and living area clean was a top priority. Not fighting or stealing from each other was essential to maintaining good order. Working as a team, while at the same time performing our individual duties, was going to be necessary if we were to be successful as a company. Chief Causee had his work cut out for him. The first thing he would do was tear us down as individuals and rebuild us as a team. Monday morning, at 0430, the lights came on.

"HIT THE DECK, LET'S GO, LET'S GO. SHIT, SHAVE, SHOWER, GET DRESSED, AND TEND YOUR BUNKS.

YOU'VE GOT FIFTEN MINUTES TO GET YOURSELF AND THE BARRACKS READY FOR INSPECTION. THIS IS YOUR FIRST T-DAY SO LET'S MAKE IT A GOOD ONE," the Chief ordered as he walked past my bunk. I hit the deck, in bare feet, running. We were soon assembled in the patio facing Chief Causee on the porch. The newly-appointed acting Petty Officers had assumed their rolls. Cumella stood in front of the company as our new apprentice CPO. Chief Causee waited for us to settle down.

"AFTER CHOW, I WANT YOU TO GET YOUR ASSES BACK HERE AS SOON AS POSSIBLE. I WANT THIS BARRACKS SQUARED AWAY. CHECK YOUR PEACOATS, RAINCOATS, AND SCRUB BUCKETS THAT THEY ARE NOT SLACK AND HAVE NO IRISH PENNANTS. I WANT FOUR MEN ASSIGNED TO LET DOWN THE CLOTHES LINE AND EVERY PIECE OF CLOTHING CHECKED TO MAKE SURE THEY'RE TIED CORRECTLY," he said looking at our new recruit CPO. Cumella made eye contact acknowledging he understood and would comply. Chief Causee turned back to us, looking at his watch. It was a little after five.

"I WANT YOU ALL BACK HERE AND ASSEMBLED AT SEVEN. YOU'RE TO HAVE YOUR NOTEBOOKS AND PENS TUCKED IN YOUR BELT IN THE BACK WHERE I CAN'T SEE THEM. YOU'LL BE ATTENDING CLASSES THIS MORNING. TAKE GOOD NOTES SO YOU CAN STUDY. IF YOU FAIL ONE TEST, YOU WILL BE SENT TO REMEDIAL STUDY IN THE EVENING UNTIL YOU MAKE IT UP. IF YOU FAIL A SECOND ONE YOU'LL DEFINITELY BE SET BACK," he then turned back to Cumella and nodded his head. We started the one and a half-mile march to the mess hall.

"ATT......HUT........RIGHT............FACE.......FORWARD.......MARCH! HUP.........HUP........HUP," called out Cumella in the early morning twilight. "GET IN STEP, LADIES," he added in his almost deep voice.

Two thousand recruits were now in some phase of training at the Naval Training Center. The company carrying the honor flag for the week was fed first, then according to seniority of T-days. We waited impatiently at the rear as row after row of recruits moved slowly along in front of us. Once we were inside and had received our chow, the clock on the wall was pointing at six-thirty. We gulped down the food and rushed back into ranks. The rapid march back, a quick head call, and we fell in ranks and waited for the Chief's orders.

"I WANT TWO MEN ASSIGNED TO THE HEAD AND FOUR TO THE DORM. I WANT EVERYTHING IN 4.0 CONDITION. THIS WILL BE YOUR LAST OPPORTUNITY TO GET THINGS IN ORDER," the Chief told Cumela. "HAVE THE REST OF THE MEN STAND AT EASE," he added.

"YES, SIR," responded Cumella. Turning to the newly assigned squad leaders, "GIVE ME A MAN FROM EACH SQUAD AND HAVE THEM TAKE THEIR SHOES OFF AT THE DOOR," he ordered.

I heard my name called and ran forward. "MESSER, CHECK AND MAKE SURE THE FART SACKS ARE ALL TIGHT ENOUGH TO FLIP A COIN AND THAT THE BLANKETS ARE ALL FOLDED AND LINED UP. I DON'T WANT ANY LOOSE TIE TIES OR IRISH PENANTS WHERE THE COATS AND BUCKETS ARE TIED," commanded Cumella.

I worked my way down the row of bunks making sure the blankets were the same distance from the foot and the flaps were turned back on each one. I walked from the head of one bunk to the other, checking the peacoats and raincoats individually. Then I went to the foot and walked from bunk to bunk checking the buckets and ensuring the brushes were inside and turned with the bristles up. I found one brush turned down and several Irish Pennants hanging loose; I quickly corrected them. I took a quarter and tossed it onto each mattress, ensuring it was taut enough to flip over. One man was on his hands and knees crawling from bunk to bunk looking for fuzzballs that seem to collect from nowhere. Another man was measuring the distance of the bunks from the bulkhead with a ruler, as he lined them up with precision. Finishing our individual tasks, we moved toward the door. Two men were now on the buffer. One buffing and the other holding up the cord so as not to make a smudge on the glowing deck. As I put on my shoes, I watched them lift the buffer so as not to roll the wheels and carry it to the gear locker.

    Rejoining the company, I saw four men working on each clothesline, frantically measuring and tucking,
"FALL 'EM IN," ordered Chief Causee. "YOU'VE HAD ALL GODDAMN WEEKEND AND HALF THE MORNING. IF YOU DON'T HAVE IT BY NOW, YOU NEVER WILL," he commented. We fell in ranks rapidly.
"COVER DOWN, COVER DOWN......ATT......HUT." ordered Cumella.
"LET ME HAVE YOUR ATTENTION," the Chief ordered, "WE ARE NOW GOING TO REGIMENTAL HEADQUARTERS FOR COLORS (raising of the flag). RIGHT AFTERWARDS, YOU'RE GOING TO BE INSPECTED. THE INSPECTOR WILL APPROACH THE COMPANY AND CUMELLA WILL PRESENT THE COMPANY. HE'LL THEN TURN TO THE COMPANY AND ORDER UNCOVER. AT THAT POINT YOU'RE TO PUT YOUR HAND ON THE SIDE OF YOUR COVER (HAT). LISTEN UP AND WHEN HE SAYS READY...TWO, YOU'RE TO REMOVE YOUR COVER SMARTLY WITH YOUR RIGHT HAND AND HOLD IT DIRECTLY IN FRONT OF YOU WITH THE INSIDE SEAM FACING THE INSPECTOR. YOU'RE THEN TO TAKE YOUR LEFT HAND REACH UP AND GET THE SEAM OF YOUR SKIVVY SHIRT AND TURN IT OUT WITH THE SEAM FACING THE INSPECTOR. GOD HELP

YOUR ASS IF THERE IS ANY GREASE OR GRIME ON THOSE SEAMS."

There is something awe-inspiring about standing in ranks at attention with thousands of men all focused on not moving a muscle. The feeling of oneness and power is overwhelming. The bugle sounds attention, cars stop, individuals snap to attention and salute. Companies are called to attention as commanders render honors and the bugle plays. The feeling of belonging to something greater than oneself is all-consuming. Somewhere inside this united spirit, one understands the natural law of the greatest good for the greatest number. I have always felt pride at those special times, even in my darkest hours. The need for man to sacrifice himself to a higher calling while losing his own life is somehow understood.

Old Glory traveled slowly up the flagpole. The silent breeze lifted her folds; she unfurled and flapped softly in the early morning sunlight. The bugle stopped and the training center roared back to life. In less than five minutes, a Chief I had never seen before approached our company; he carried a clipboard in his left hand. He exchanged a few words with Chief Causee and then went to the first squad. He started slowly down the first row of men inspecting each individual from head to toe. He viewed the cover, the skivvy shirt, the leggings, the belt buckle and its location, shoes, cleanliness of the uniform, and the closeness of the shave. He would occasionally stop, ask a question, write a note, and move on. Upon reaching the last man, he turned and walked slowly behind them, checking them from the rear. I was in the second squad, third man from the right. He finished the first squad, turned, and started down the line of men in which I was standing. I could hear my heart beat. He was directly in front of me. I felt his eyes move down to my cover, my shoes, my skivvy shirt. My hands trembled. I knew he was looking at my eyes. I was locked in a hundred-yard stare. After what seemed like an eternity, he moved on to the next man. A great relief came over me. I breathed easily but I felt weak. I heard him speaking to one of the three men from Northern California. I saw Chief Causee glance in their direction; a grim look crossed his face.

After the inspection and another long march, we entered a classroom to have our first military lecture. The need to learn military ranks of both enlisted and officer was the number one priority. Class commenced at 0900 and proceeded until 1130 hours, at which time we were reassembled and marched back to the barracks. Upon our approach to the patio area, I could see something white in front of our barracks. It was a mattress.

"SOMEONE DIDN'T GET THEIR MATTRESS SQUARED AWAY," I heard Chief Causee comment, "MARCH THE COMPANY OVER THE TOP OF THE GODDAMN THING." I felt indignation that someone could have been so negligent. I came down hard on the mattress with my left boondocker. Looking down as I regained my balance, I saw the stenciled name, MESSER. J.D. 349 73 43. My breath caught.

"It's that damn Messer's," I heard someone say. We came to a halt and did a right face. The Chief took his position on the porch. I could see the clothesline and a pile of white clothing that had been cut from the line and had been dumped on the dirty patio deck. Chief Causee held in his hands two sheets of paper that were the results of the morning's inspections. His face was serious.

"WELL, YOU'VE FLUNKED THE BARRACKS AND THE CLOTHESLINE INSPECTION AND YOU GOT BARELY A PASSING GRADE ON PERSONNEL INSPECTION. WE'VE GOT A HELL'VA LOT OF WORK TO DO. LET'S GET THAT MATTRESS AND THOSE CLOTHES THAT HAVE BEEN CUT DOWN UP OFF THE DECK AND STORED. TAKE TEN MINUTES TO MAKE A HEAD CALL AND FALL IN FOR CHOW. AT 1230, I WANT YOU REASSEMBLED HERE WITH YOUR PIECES," he ordered.

After reassembling at twelve-thirty, we were marched to a large asphalt space covering about four acres. We were halted in front of a platform where a loud speaker was mounted. Chief Causee climbed the stairs to the platform but did not turn on the speaker. He faced us.

"LISTEN UP," he commenced, "MEN, THIS IS CALLED THE GRINDER. HERE, YOU'RE GOING TO LEARN TO MARCH AND DO CLOSE ORDER DRILL. WE ARE GOING TO WORK AT THIS UNTIL YOU MOVE AND THINK AS ONE. FROM THIS DAY FORWARD, WE ARE GOING TO BE PREPARING FOR YOU TO PASS IN REVIEW. WE'LL BE HERE MOST EVERY AFTERNOON FOR FOUR HOURS. I AM GOING TO TURN YOU INTO THE BEST GODDAMN MARCHING COMPANY IN THIS REGIMENT. I DON'T GIVE A RAT'S ASS ABOUT ANY PENNANT AND ALL THAT ASS-KISSING POLITICAL BULLSHIT THAT GOES ON AROUND HERE. WHAT I WANT IS THAT, WHEN YOU LEAVE HERE, YOU BE THE BEST GODDAMN SAILOR THAT'S POSSIBLE FOR YOU TO BECOME. I AM GOING TO GIVE YOU EVERYTHING I HAVE AND I WANT YOU TO GIVE ME EVERYTHING YOU'VE GOT. AMERICA WON THE SECOND WORLD WAR; WE QUIT DURING THE KOREAN WAR. I CAN ONLY IMAGINE WHAT WILL HAPPEN IN THE NEXT ONE IF EACH AND EVERY MAN IN THE ARMED SERVICES IS NOT PROPERLY TRAINED. NOW, MY JOB IS TO TRAIN THIS COMPANY AND I WANT YOU TO KNOW I TAKE THAT PRETTY GODDAMN SERIOUS. IF YOU WORK WITH ME, BY GOD, YOU'LL BE READY TO PERFORM YOUR DUTY WHEN YOU GRADUATE. IF YOU DON'T WORK WITH ME, I GUARANTEE YOUR ASSES WILL BE MARCHING AROUND HERE WITH THAT BIG FAT SON-OF-A-BITCH CARRYING THAT LITTLE SILLY FLAG WITH 4013 WRITTEN ON IT. CUMELLA, LET'S GET THESE ARMS STACKED AND WE'LL GET STARTED WORK-

ING ON CLOSE ORDER DRILL. MY GOD, MAN, THESE MEN LOOK LIKE A BUNCH OF DAMN OLD LADIES OUT FOR AN EVENING STROLL."

After two hours of intense close order drill, we retrieved our pieces. The sixteen-count manual was practiced until we could have performed it in our sleep. After evening chow, the buckets were untied from the bunks and the washing of the clothes commenced. The scrub brushes were used with an ample amount of soap, paying special attention to the inside seams of the hats and skivvy shirts. Seven that evening found us pulling the big rope loaded down with wet clothing high into the air and securing it to the white and gray post. Each of us was assigned a cleaning station either in the dormitory part of the barracks, the passageway leading to the head, or the head itself. Everything was scrubbed and cleaned until it glistened. The bright work in the head shown like a new silver dollar. The porcelain sinks and toilet bowls gleamed from so much attention. Two were left open for service; all the others were roped off. These would be attended to before our departure for colors the following morning. The floors were swabbed, waxed, and buffed to a high gloss. Every nook and cranny was dusted and re-dusted with damp rags. Nine in the evening found us tidying up our individual areas. Shoes were shined, belt buckles were polished, lockers were straightened up, and scrub buckets were tied back in place and the brushes were placed inside.

A watch list had been posted for the two watch requirements we were responsible for. The fire watch inside the barracks required only the carrying of a nightstick attached to a duty belt. The security watch in the patio was to be patrolled carrying a piece. I had been assigned the 2400 until 0200 fire watch. The Navy requires that all watches be relieved fifteen minutes before the hour. This meant I was to be woke up at 2330 to dress for my watch. It seemed I had just lay down when I felt someone shaking me. "Come on, Messer, it's time for you to get dressed for your watch," I heard someone say. Only the fear of being court-martialed kept me moving for the next two hours. Tumbling back in bed at 0200 it seemed only seconds until the lights came on at 0430.

The next day was a repeat of the day before. The classroom of the morning was warm and I nodded off. The man behind me punched me with his finger. I jerked awake to see the instructor glaring at me.

"STAND IN THE BACK IF YOU NEED TO. NO ONE SLEEPS IN MY CLASS," he ordered.

"Yes, Sir," I answered and went to the back of the room.

The four hours on the grinder that afternoon seemed like an eternity. My feet were heavy and my movements sluggish. I was out of step and just couldn't get my body to follow my mind.

"HALT THE COMPANY," ordered Chief Causee. He walked over directly in front of me. "BETTER GET YOUR MIND OFF THAT LITTLE GIRL IN ARKANSAS, MESSER, AND PAY ATTENTION TO WHAT'S GOING ON HERE," he said.

"I had the 0001 to 0200 last night, sir," I responded.

Chief Causee's face turned black and filled with rage.

"DON'T YOU EVER GIVE ME SOME LAME ASS EXCUSE FOR POOR PERFORMANCE. EVERY MAN IN THIS COMPANY HAS THE SAME DUTIES AND RESPONSIBILITY THAT YOU DO. WHEN YOU JOIN THE FLEET AND YOU'RE STANDING A LOOKOUT WATCH, EVERY MAN'S LIFE ON THAT SHIP COULD DEPEND ON YOU. WHEN THE SHARKS ARE EATING YOUR EYEBALLS OUT ON THE BOTTOM OF THE OCEAN, YOU GOING TO GIVE SOME CHICKEN SHIT EXCUSE ABOUT HOW YOU DIDN'T FEEL WELL? YOU CAN EITHER HACK IT HERE OR GO OVER TO 4013 UNTIL YOU'RE UP TO SPEED," he was screaming by this time. He stuck his face about four inches from mine. I looked into his eyes and they were coals of fire. "DO YOU UNDERSTAND ME, BOY?" he asked.

"YES, SIR!" I answered. Walking back in front of the company, Chief Causee turned toward us.
"NOW LET'S GET THIS RIGHT," he said.

The following morning at seven, Chief Causee had taken up his position on the porch.
"NOW, MEN LISTEN UP. THIS MORNING AT NINE WE ARE GOING TO GO OVER TO THE EDUCATIONAL BUILDING. THERE, YOU'RE GOING TO BE GIVEN A CLASSIFICATION TEST. THE RESULTS OF THAT TEST WILL BECOME A PERMANENT PART OF YOUR PERSONEL RECORD. BUT MORE IMPORTANT THAN THAT, IT'S GOING TO BE THE DECIDING FACTOR OF WHAT JOB YOU WILL BE DOING IN THE NAVY. NOW, IT'S GOING TO BE WARM IN THERE AND THE TEST TAKES ABOUT THREE HOURS, BUT IT'S IMPERTIVE THAT YOU STAY AWAKE AND GIVE THIS YOUR VERY BEST SHOT." He stopped talking and looked all around. "NOW, IF YOU ENLISTED AS A HSSR AND HAVE BEEN GUARANTEED AN "A" SCHOOL (formal technical school to train in a particular field), DON'T MAKE THE MISTAKE OF THINKING IT DOESN'T MATTER THAT MUCH. AND FOR THOSE OF YOU THAT HAVEN'T BEEN GUARANTEED AN "A" SCHOOL IT'S EVEN MORE IMPORTANT IF YOU EVER HOPE TO DO ANYTHING WORTHWHILE IN THE NAVY," he added.

After morning colors, we were soon in the educational building. The test was long and difficult, commencing with the elementary and ending in college calculus. Different aptitude tests for different skills were administered to aid in the Navy's eternal search for special talent. Three weeks later, the test scores would be posted in the passageway just outside of Chief Causee's office. The average score was one hundred for combined General Classification and Arithmetic. I would make one hundred and two, much higher than many of those who had been guaranteed an "A" school. My hopes heightened that I would not be sent directly aboard ship without any technical training. I had now become aware that those who did not complete an "A" school faced a very uncertain future.

The long hard days from 0430 in the morning until 2200 at night droned on and on. Hours and hours on the grinder were slowly molding us into the precision marching machine that, just a short time ago, would have been hard to imagine. Most of our waking moments were spent performing activities as a unit. There wasn't a great deal of time to develop individual relationships. The true character of men becomes obvious when they're under pressure and, very soon, our three Northern California shipmates had left us. One was sent to 4013 for more intensive training and the other two were set back for failing exams. One poor recruit was awakened every hour around the clock to help with his bed wetting, all to no avail. One day, he disappeared and I never heard of him again. One of the Texans climbed the fence in the middle of the night and left behind his duty belt and nightstick. "WE DON'T NEED SLIMY SHIT LIKE THAT," was Chief Causee's only mention of the incident and it was soon forgotten.

On a Sunday night at the end of our sixth week, about 0100 I heard a noise that woke me from a sound sleep. I wasn't quite sure what it was. Then someone called out.

"I HEAR SOMEONE MOVING AROUND, BUT I DON'T SEE ANYONE. IS THAT YOU, JEFFERSON?" Several men chuckled in the darkness.

"FUCK YOU, WHITE MUTHER-FUCKERS," answered Jefferson. More chuckling! Then I heard feet running in the direction of the head, and someone yelled.

"MY GOD, SOMEONE HELP ME HERE." The voice sounded urgent. I leaped onto the deck and ran toward the voice. Two men had entered the head in front of me. At first I couldn't figure out what the commotion was all about. Someone was holding a man in the air and the two men in front of me had begun to help hold him up.

"UNDO THE BUCKLE, UNDO THE BUCKLE," someone ordered. By that time I had grabbed the man and was helping to lift him. He was a dead weight and motionless as we pushed his limp body up as high as we could. His face was purple and he wasn't breathing. One of the men undid the buckle of the belt that had been wrapped around his neck and tied to the upper frame of the commode stall.

"LET HIM DOWN," someone commanded and we lowered the lifeless body to the floor. Cumella had entered just as we had lowered him to the deck.

"I'LL CALL SICK BAY," he shouted and ran for Chief Causee's office. I looked back down at the man's purple, contorted face, his eyelids fluttered.

"He's alive," someone said. I could see his lips had commenced to turn pink. In less than three minutes, the ambulance had arrived with two corpsmen. They took one look at the scene.

"Anyone know what happened here?" one of the men asked.

"Looks like he tried to hang himself," the other man answered.

They lifted the lifeless body onto the stretcher. "Don't touch anything here until NIS arrives," one of them ordered as he grabbed the front of the stretcher; they headed for the front door. We were ordered back to bed and the lights were soon turned off. Sometime in the early morning, I dozed off into a restless sleep.

Soon after the suicide attempt, I had one of my most traumatic experiences of boot camp. Chief Causee had advised us to buy an extra white hat to wear when we were washing clothes. I had bought my scrub hat at the end of our primary phase and wore it daily for the next four weeks while washing my clothes. I took great pride in the fact that I had never washed it. Upon completing the sixth week of our training, we were marched to morning chow then allowed to straggle back. We would then form up at seven in front of the porch for daily instructions from Chief Causee. Afterwards, we would attend to the last minute details preparing for clothesline and barracks inspections then march to Regimental Headquarters. It became my habit to wear my scrub hat to morning chow and change just before we departed for colors.

I had finished morning chow and was strolling back to the barracks with my bunkmate, Sanchez. Suddenly, one of the Texans from our company came running toward us. "Company 248 is to fall in for inspection in front of Regimental Headquarters and not go back to the barracks," he blurted out as he continued on his way, looking for the rest of the company.

Suddenly, my heart skipped a beat. There was no doubt in my mind, if an inspector saw my filthy scrub hat, I would be going to 4013. It would make little difference if I were in the middle of my seventh week. This filthy cover just wouldn't be acceptable. I found myself in formation, waiting for colors. We were running neck to neck with company 249 for the honor pennant that week. I stood frozen with fear. Sanchez understood the gravity of my situation; he had ended up directly in front of me in formation that morning. Leaning back and talking out the side of his mouth.

"Messer, watch, and when the inspector passes me in the back and gets down to the end and turns back left toward the next squad, we'll quick switch covers," he said.

"Okay," I quickly agreed.

Everyone on each side of us had heard our conversation. My heart was pounding as the inspector passed in front of me. He moved slowly along checking each man as he went. When he made his turn at the end of the line, I jerked my hat off and passed it forward to Sanchez. He had taken his hat off and turned to take mine. In the confusion, my cover tumbled out of Sanchez's hand. He knew it was too late to recover it so he snapped back to attention. My hat lay on the ground at his side. The inspector had turned just as the cover went plummeting to the ground. Looking at Sanchez standing there coverless he turned and said, "THIS COMPANY IS MOVING AROUND TOO MUCH TO BE INSPECTED. I'M FLUNKING THE WHOLE COMPANY." With that, he made an abrupt about face and left.

My terror was now mixed with shame. Not only had I caused the company to fail inspection, but also disgraced my best friend, Sanchez. I saw Chief Causee coming out of the corner of my eye.

"GET THEM OVER TO CLASS, CUMELLA," he ordered. We were soon seated in the classroom.

"Goddamn you, Messer, you've done it now. You may as well pack your shit. It's over for you in this company," chastised Cumella. Men glared at me from all sides. Chief Causee entered the room and went to the podium.

"WHAT HAPPENED OUT THERE?" he asked.

"Messer tried to switch hats with Sanchez," answered Cumella.

Chief Causee glared at me; I had already accepted the fact I would be sent to 4013.

"THAT WAS MORE ABOUT POLITICS OUT THERE THIS MORNING THAN ANYTHING ELSE," Chief Causee commented. "NEVER THE LESS, YOU ALWAYS HAVE TO BE READY FOR INSPECTION AND I HOPE YOU'VE ALL LEARNED THE IMPORTANCE OF ALWAYS BEING PREPARED," he added. Then, he focused on me, "MESSER, ONE MORE STUNT LIKE THAT AND YOU WON'T BE GRADUATING WITH COMPANY 248. I CAN GUARANTEE YOU THAT," he declared.

"YES, SIR," I responded, a wave of relief washed over me.

Shortly after my experience with trying to pass off my scrub hat, I had another memorable experience. We were once again gathered in the patio listening to Chief Causee. "STAND AT EASE AND LIS-

TEN UP," he said, and waited for the shuffling to subside. "YOUR ORDERS ARE IN AND THEY ARE POSTED ON THE BULLETIN BOARD. I DON'T WANT YOU ALL PUSHING IN THERE TO READ IT AT THE SAME TIME. I WANT YOU TO PASS IN SINGLE FILE FROM THE RIGHT. YOUR NAMES ARE POSTED IN ALPHABETICAL ORDER. READ IT AND DOUBLE TIME BACK OUT HERE. OKAY, SINGLE FILE, FROM THE RIGHT....HUT." he commanded.

My heart had jumped up into my throat when I heard that our orders were posted. I felt confident, since I had done pretty well on my classification test, that I would be assigned to an "A" school. After what seemed like an eternity, I found myself following behind one of the Texans, "GREAT," he yelled thrusting his fist in the air. "NORMAN, OKLAHOMA," he continued with a smile on his face. I ran my eye down the first page, then the second page, continuing down the third to about the middle of the page. There I found my name, it read: MESSER JOHN D. 349 73 43 USS HELENA CA 75, LONG BEACH, CALIF. I stood almost paralyzed unable to move.

"LET'S GO, MESSER," someone yelled behind me. My legs felt like lead weights as I forced myself to run back to my position in ranks. Happy chatter all around me did little to lift the feeling of impending doom that had suddenly overtaken me. I had never fully accepted that there was a possibility that this would happen. I was now looking at three years and nine months of uncertainty. I couldn't have been more despondent if I had been sentenced to a penitentiary for the same period of time. My childhood impression of the US Navy uniform had been the primary purpose for me choosing the Navy as a military service. I had never in my life seen an ocean or a ship of any kind. My idea of what the Navy was all about was sheer romantic fantasy. Eight weeks of classes on seamanship, fire fighting, biological and chemical warfare, sound powered telephones, first-aid, and uniform code of military justice had sobered me considerable. That was not to mention a week on mess duty, leaping off of a ninety-foot tower with a life jacket, and receiving thirteen immunizations. I had slowly awakened to the fact that this was no daydream and nothing happened here without a lot of hard work and study.

On the thirty-sixth T-day, I stood at the foot of my bunk wearing the beautiful dress blue uniform that I had so coveted. As we stood motionless, a Chinese tailor from the city of San Diego moved from man to man making white marks on the cuffs of our blouses and pants. I wasn't permitted to see myself in the mirror but somehow it seemed right. I felt snug and warm. Regardless of where I was to serve, I was going to be a sailor in the greatest Navy, in the greatest nation, in the whole wide world. No one could take that away from me if I could get through the next ten T-days.

On graduation day, I stood at attention with my company, and two thousand other men, under the hot August sun in San Diego, California. My chest was swollen with pride as I listened to one dignitary after another speak of our promising future. I was never to see or hear from the majority of these men who had shared this time and space with me. We were strangers who had come together, only to complete a common struggle, and then be separated forever. I could smell the odor of mothballs from my dress blues and see the company flag fluttering as we waited. Although it had only been nine weeks, it seemed like a lifetime ago since Arkey, the Texans, and myself had lay under the R & O shed waiting to be assigned to a training company. I had gone through a complete metamorphous both physically and emotionally. I would never be the same again.

We returned to our barracks as a company one last time. Chief Causee stood misty-eyed in front of us at his familiar place on the little porch. We looked at the man who had put us to bed and got us up in the morning for nine long weeks. He had celebrated our triumphs and suffered our failures. The ribbons on his chest told us he was a great warrior and had fought the fierce Imperial Japanese Navy in many campaigns. We knew this had come at great sacrifice to himself and to all of those who had fought in WWII. In our training, he had chosen, over and over, principal before politics and personal gain. He had pushed us to heights we didn't know we were capable of reaching just nine short weeks before. Although I had only known him a short time, his leadership qualities had a profound effect on my career. We quieted down as he prepared to speak.

"I WANT TO CONGRATULATE YOU MEN ON A JOB WELL DONE. YOU'VE SUCCESSFULLY COMPLETED THE FIRST STEP IN YOUR NAVAL CAREER. THE THING I WANT YOU TO REMEMBER IS TO BE THE BEST GODDAMN SAILORS THAT YOU'RE CAPABLE OF BEING. NOW, GET YOUR RAGGED ASSES IN THERE AND PACK UP YOUR SHIT AND GET THE HELL OUT OF MY SIGHT," he ordered with a smile. A cheer went up as white hats sailed into the air.

USS *Helena* CA-75

We waited in front of Regimental Headquarters for the Greyhound Bus that would take us to downtown San Diego. From there, we would all go our separate ways. I felt a light breeze blowing and the two ends of my neckerchief fluttered up into my face. I looked down at the two small stripes on my left arm with a great deal of pride. I was no longer a boot recruit but a seaman apprentice. I could see the companies marching in the distance and hear the cadence calls as they floated across the compound. The eternal presence of the straggling line of people still in civilian clothes passed in front of us. Suddenly, a warm feeling flooded me that I would continue to experience down through the many years that I was destined to wear the uniform of the American Blue Jacket. My trousers fit me snug around my hips and the blouse held me in a warm grasp. It gave me a comfortable, secure feeling that perhaps I had known in my mother's womb. I felt content standing with my stuffed, padlocked seabag sitting in front of me.

"Why don't you just come home with me, Messer?" Sanchez interrupted my thoughts. "My mother would be thrilled and you could meet my sister, Rosa. What do you say?"

"No, I better go on to Arkansas and see my family. Who knows when I'll ever get back there? Besides, my mother would have a fit if I didn't come home. I've told you she took my joining the Navy pretty hard. She would never understand me not coming home."

"Yeah, I know what you mean. Looks like we are going to have about fifteen of us going as far as Santa Fe together."

"Yeah, all the guys from Alexandria, Louisiana, that bunch from Texas, Jefferson, and myself will be going all the way to Dallas together." Jefferson dragged his seabag over and joined us as we waited.

"Well, looks like we finally gonna get outta dis shit hole," commented Jefferson.

"Sure does," laughed Sanchez, grabbing his hand and pumping it up and down. "And I made it out of here without going to 4013. No thanks to Messer." Jefferson laughed heartily and shook his head from side to side. I heard the groan of the big, heavy bus behind us. I turned and watched a black cloud of exhaust smoke follow the silver and blue bus as it approached where we stood.

Within the hour after arriving at San Diego, we had boarded a bus and were traveling east on Highway Eight. The huge Greyhound was state-of-the-art for that era. It looked to be about sixty feet long and had steps leading up to a four-foot elevation in the back where several seats and the bathroom were located. The seats tilted back and the headrests could be adjusted up and down. The first of what would seem like a thousand fifteen-minute stops was made at Yuma, Arizona. I was anxious to disembark and see this place I had so often heard mentioned in the movies. Sanchez and I stepped off the bus; we were greeted with a temperature of a hundred and seventeen degrees Fahrenheit. A hot wind was blowing across the desert. Sanchez and I walked about ten steps outside of the bus station. Across the street, was a drawing of a red and white cocktail glass on a huge, plate-glass window. Loud, honky-tonk music drifted out into the street. In front of the bar, stood a dark-complexioned man about twenty-five years old with long, black hair. He was dressed in heavy, orange and earth-colored clothing; a blanket was draped over his left arm. I assumed this was an Indian and looked at him longer than would have been considered polite by any standard.

"Best get your ugly asses back on that bus before you get hurt, swab jockeys," he commented.

"Hijo de puta," answered Sanchez.

"Fuck you, wetback," came the answer.

"Let's go, Sanchez," I said and took his arm and pulled him back toward the bus.

The big Greyhound soon moved back out on the highway and droned on through the night. Sooner than I was ready, we came to Santa Fe, New Mexico. Separation from a kindred soul who has shared a common hardship with me has never been easy. It's made doubly hard when you know that in all probability you will never see each other again. And so it was, this man who was willing to risk his own well being in order to save me went out of my life forever. As the bus traveled on through the night, I was left alone in the darkness to contemplate what makes noble men. Why do seemingly ordinary men, when faced with tremendous adversity, rise to the occasion, while others fall like tall wheat before a strong wind? What characteristic do certain men have that allows them to risk sacrificing themselves for others? This I would ponder all the years of my military service. I came to understand that this could not be predicted until the hour was at hand.

All that night, we traveled east from El Paso toward Dallas, Texas. On the following day, traveling between these two great cities, we arrived at a small town seemingly in the middle of nowhere. The driver pulled slowly off the highway traveled a couple of blocks, made a left, and entered into the parking lot of a small eating establishment.

"Let's grab a bite and stretch our legs," the driver announced as he jerked the door open and hopped off.

I looked toward the back to see who was awake. The familiar faces of company 248 filed slowly down the aisle and exited the bus with the other passengers. Jefferson brought up the back of the line. I rose and followed him off and into the small diner. The café had a row of twenty or so stools in front of a long counter. I could see the black and white signs on the green bathroom doors in the back. An average-size, thirtysome-year-old waitress with reddish-blond hair stood chewing gum at the far end of the counter. Upon seeing Jefferson, she frowned. A fiftyish-looking man with a long, handlebar mustache appeared behind the window that joined the kitchen. He leaned on the small pass-through platform and watched us passively as he twirled one end of his mustache. The waitress poured a cup of coffee and carried it to our driver. She said something to him I couldn't make out. He shrugged his shoulders but didn't answer. She turned and walked back to the middle of the counter. "I know you boys just came from California but you're in Texas now and it's against the law to serve colored in a white restaurant," she said, acidly. "One of you can order him something to take out, if you want to, and he can eat it on the bus. But I'm not going to serve any of you until he leaves."

Jefferson had been with us for nine weeks. He had marched every step we had taken and suffered every hardship and indignation that we had. We'd long ago stopped thinking of him as any different from ourselves; we had been trained to think as a team, what happened to him, happened to us. All of us from company 248 now present were native Southerners. But this was about more than where you were from. Something inside of us cried out at such injustice. How could you ask a man to die for his country, then refuse to serve him something to eat?

Jefferson sat stone-faced not moving. The waitress turned her back to us, picked up a dishrag, and started wiping down around the coffeepot that was located near the door to the kitchen. I could feel the tension mounting. The man in the kitchen glared at us, as he continued to twirl his mustache, waiting for our reaction. We all looked at one another.

"Goddamn it, he is with us," said the big Texan we called Mullinak. "If he can eat and sleep with us in the Navy by-god you can serve him a hamburger in this shithouse." The rest of us sat silently, not moving. The waitress looked at the driver.

"Get these guys out of here right now," she ordered, as she reached for the phone and dialed.

"Let's go, boys," the driver said rising and taking a long sip from his cup of coffee.

"No, goddamn it, we ain't leaving until we get something to eat," exclaimed one of the men from Alexandria, Louisiana.

The police station must not have been more than a couple of blocks away. I saw the flashing lights before I heard the sirens. As the police cars came swooping into the parking lot, Jefferson jumped up off the stool and kicked it hard. With that he turned, walked out, and got on the bus. Four policemen came rushing through the door.

"WHAT THE HELL IS GOING ON IN HERE, MARYLOU?" asked the big man in charge.

"They brought a nigger in here and wanted me to serve him," she said, matter-of-factly, shrugging her shoulders. He turned toward where we were all still sitting.

"LET'S GO, BOYS," he ordered, tapping the counter with his nightstick.

One by one, we walked back out to the bus. The driver sat anxiously waiting with the motor running. As soon as the last man got on the bottom step of the bus, he slammed the door closed and moved out into the street and headed for the interstate.

Jefferson had been sitting about two seats in front of the steps that led up to the second deck. Upon reentering the bus, he grabbed his overnight bag and moved to the upper level and took a seat in the very back. His eyes were angry and his face was filled with pain and humiliation. I tried to make eye contact with him but he looked away. I felt guilty and confused; it was my first experience with racial hatred. I knew that, collectively, we were all a part of what had happened to our shipmate on that fateful day, but at the time I didn't understand it. Jefferson, unbeknownst to me, had also received orders to the USS Helena. I would see him from time to time in the coming months. But the gulf between the two races in those days was just too wide; we would never speak again.

With our stopping every two hours and the taking on and letting off of passengers, we averaged, roughly, forty miles an hour. Thirty-eight hours after leaving San Diego, we arrived in Dallas, Texas. From there, we went our own separate ways. The older model bus I had transferred to would take me to Little Rock. I made my way two-thirds of the way toward the back and took a seat. There were only a few people on board. Seated directly behind me, was a soldier from Fort Chaffee, Arkansas. He had received some disturbing news from his girlfriend telling him she was in love with another man. The Army had refused to give him leave to go home, so he had decided to go anyway.

"The Army will probably put me in the stockade when I get back. But I don't give a damn. I have to go home and get this all straightened out with Molly." he explained, as we bounced along. I nodded in agreement. I was happy to have run into a traveling companion who was in the military. Soon, we came to a small town by the name of Searcy. We got off the bus together and went inside the station to the food counter and sat down. In a couple of minutes, my friend spied a jukebox in the corner; digging in his pocket, he found a quarter.

"You heard Elvis's new songs?" he asked.

"No, I haven't heard anything the past nine weeks. Only thing I have heard Elvis sing was 'That's Alright Mama'."

"Well, you got a treat coming. Take a listen to this." He made his way to the jukebox and made six selections. I heard the beat of the drum as the music started. "YOU AN'T NOTHING BUT A HOUND DOG," Elvis shrilled. The adrenaline poured into my blood stream as I listened. I felt elated and energized.

"DAMN" I said.

"Listen to this next one," he answered. First came the music with the verse followed by the refrain.

"DON'T BE CRUEEEEL TO A HEART THAT'S TRUE," crooned Elvis. Each record played three times. The nine short weeks I had been in boot camp a whole new movement in music had occurred. Up until that moment, I had preferred country. But there was something about this new sound that really gave me a thrill. Little did I know I was hearing the birth of a new era in music that would soon be known as rock and roll.

The few short days of leave I had spent with my family were soon over and I found myself on the way to the Naval Station at Long Beach, California. I had been ordered to check in at the receiving station where I would be directed to the Helena. I boarded a Greyhound out of Jonesboro and two days later I was in Los Angeles. Upon arrival, I transferred to another bus that was to take me to Long Beach. It seemed we were never going to get out of Los Angeles. It made sense to me that if we were ever going to reach Long Beach we would first need to leave the city limits of Los Angeles. Two hours passed and we were still in the city. We had made a short stop at a place called Compton. Never having been off the farm or out of the state of Arkansas before joining the Navy, this all seemed very confusing to me. I assumed Compton was a part of Los Angeles. "LONG BEACH!" I heard the driver call out, much to my surprise. By now, it was about one in the afternoon. I recovered my seabag and walked out in front of the bus station onto a very busy boulevard. Having no idea whatsoever where the Naval Station might be, I looked around for someone who might be able to help me. I then saw a young sailor walking up the street.

"Pardon me, but could you tell me how to get to the Naval Station?" I asked him as soon as he was in hearing range.

"Sure," he answered, stopping and looking back in the direction he had just come from. "Do you see that little park over there?" he asked, pointing across the street.

"Yes," I said and nodded.

"There's a bus running from the Naval Station about every half-hour. It will go around the park and make a stop at that bench you see on the far side. Just look on the front and make sure it says Terminal Island, otherwise you might end up in Whittier," he chuckled. "What ship are you going aboard?" he asked, looking at my two stripes and brand new seabag.

"The Helena," I responded.

"You're in luck. She's in port for a few days undergoing some repairs," he said over his shoulder, as he continued on his way.

A short time later, I disembarked in front of the Naval Station. The gate guard looked at my orders briefly, "No need to check in at the receiving station. She is tied up at pier nine. She's that big cruiser with number 75 painted on her bow," he said. The hot August sun beat down on me as I struggled along block after block with the heavy seabag slung over my shoulder. Butterflies fluttered in my stomach as I passed row after row of ships tied up at various piers. I could hear voices over the sound of electrical sanders and other noisy equipment as I moved along.

Then, I saw her, wallowing lazily in and out against the pier. Four long hawser lines (ropes) located at different intervals were draped around the bits on the pier that were holding her fast. I could see several boards lashed with ropes dangling over her side with sailors wearing orange lifejackets seated on them, painting. I could hear them laughing and talking as I approached. One of the men nodded toward me. "Fresh meat," he commented, and they all laughed.

Arriving at her bow, I looked down her full length. She had to be at least two football fields long, I thought. There was a gangplank forward about a third of the way down from her bow and another one a little farther on. A big crane was working on the pier, lifting things on and off of the fantail (the aft part of a ship). I could hear the constant ringing of bells as she moved up and down the track. Suddenly, a black official-looking car passed alongside of me and stopped just before reaching the gangplank. A young sailor dressed in whites exited the car and opened the back door of the sedan where an Admiral sat waiting to step out. I heard what I would later learn was the shrill from a Boatswain Pipe (whistle) coming from the top of the gangplank. I then saw several sailors dressed in whites running to line up on each side of the quarterdeck. I dropped my seabag, came to attention, and saluted. The Admiral casually returned my salute and entered onto the gangplank to make his ascent. I stood glued to the pier, watching the Admiral. Halfway up, he turned and saluted in the direction where the flag was flying. As he stepped onboard, another shrill sound from the Boatswain's Pipe brought a salute from the sailors.

I soon recovered from the shock of having seen a real Admiral and proceeded to the next gangplank where I could see enlisted men coming and going. I had learned in boot camp that upon boarding a ship I was to salute the flag that always flew at the fantail. Then, I was to step aboard and salute the Officer of the Deck and request permission to come onboard. The gangplank went up a few feet along her side, then made a right angle, taking you directly onto the quarterdeck. A young sailor, dressed in whites and wearing a duty belt, stood watching me as I made my laborious approach. Reaching the top of the gangplank, I dropped my seabag and rendered a salute aft where I could now see the colors flying. A young lieutenant holding an eighteen-inch spyglass faced me squarely as I stepped onboard. With my heart pounding, I saluted. "Permission to come aboard, sir," I requested.

"Permission granted," the lieutenant responded, returning my salute.

"Just checking aboard, sailor?" he asked.

"Yes sir!"

"Messenger, show this man down to the Personnel Office and double time back up here." he ordered.

"Aye, Aye, sir," replied the sailor wearing the duty belt.

"Come with me," he said smiling. He led me forward a few feet to a ladder that descended down to the lower deck. Once we were out of sight and sound of the OOD (Officer of the Deck) he turned to me, "Hey, when you get down to personnel, they are probably going to assign you to one of the deck divisions. Ask them to put you in First. We got it a little better than the Second does." He started down the steep ladder in front of me. "Be careful here and don't slip; these ladders take some getting used to." Reaching back, he got the bottom of my seabag and helped me carry it down the ladder. I felt comforted by my companion's simple act of kindness.

"I got it," I said, coming to the bottom of the ladder.

"Where you from?"

"Alabama! Everybody calls me Slim." I could see why. My new acquaintance was slender, almost frail, and stood a good six foot, two inches.

"I'm Messer from Arkansas. My Daddy was born in Alabama."

"Hey, alright! Small world ain't it?" As we chatted, we wound our way down a narrow passageway. Descending another ladder, we came into a sleeping compartment. Racks five high were suspended on chains in double rows, on each side of the passageway, completely filling the compartment. I could hear the low humming sound of a vent blowing somewhere within. We doubled back to the left and almost immediately came to an office with a half door open at the top. I dropped my seabag and stuck out my hand to Slim.

"Thanks!" I exclaimed. He grabbed my hand and shook it vigorously.

"I guess I better get back up there," he said, as he turned and dashed for the ladder.

There was a man in front of me talking to the Yeomen (administrative worker) in attendance. The Yeomen had a half smile on his face as he listened. He seemed somewhat attentive and occasionally would shrug his shoulders and give a short answer. Finally, he said, "I gotta check this new guy in. Come on back down later and I'll see what I can do." He then reached his hand out and I handed him my big manila envelope. "Come on in and I'll send you around with these new guys to get you checked in. That shouldn't take more than an hour. The Personnel Officer should be here by then and he'll assign you to your divisions." We were given slips of paper with the names of the different departments to go to. One of the junior rated Yeomen was assigned to lead us through the bowels of the ship to the designated places.

Neither movies, books, nor Boot Camp had prepared me for what I encountered. The Helena was 673 ½ feet long and 71 feet wide at the beam, displacing 13,600 tons of water. She carried 2,500 tons of fuel when topped off. Her armament consisted of nine eight-inch guns mounted on three turrets, two forward and one aft. She had four-twin 40 millimeter and four 20-millimeter guns mounted at various sites. Below the main deck, on the fantail, was a state of the art Regulus Missile. It was designed to be fired from a surface ship then be picked up by a submarine that would then direct it electronically to its target.

The USS Helena was a world unto herself. She had a thousand-man crew that came from all walks of life and several different countries. The educational level was no less varied. It ran from Annapolis graduates with doctorates to the recent boot camp graduate such as myself. The expertise required for navigating, communicating, and caring for her special weapons was enormous. The men in the service departments who provided everyday health and comfort to the crew numbered in the hundreds.

We left the Personnel Office and started walking forward on the third deck, which was mostly berthing compartments. We walked the equivalent length of two football fields without leaving the berthing compartments. The Yeoman led us all the way forward to sickbay to check in our health records. Then, we started working our way back to the Personnel Office stopping at different places indicated on our check-in sheet. Each stop required the filling out of various cards and papers and getting initials on our check-in sheet. I never at any time had the slightest idea where we were or how I might find my way back to any of these places. I was completely lost as we wandered around climbing up and down steel ladders. An hour later found us back at the Personnel Office.

The Yeoman who had initially taken my record was seated at a desk talking to a lieutenant. The Lieutenant was reading someone's record. The Yeoman seemed to be explaining something to him. The Lieutenant would nod his head from time to time as he listened, continuing to read. Noticing that we had returned, the Lieutenant stood up, "Which one of you is Messer?" he asked, looking us up and down. I noticed his uniform looked new. He was a couple of inches shorter than I was and on the plump side. He had clear, friendly, blue eyes and light blond hair.

"That's me, sir," I responded.

"Well, let me shake your hand," he said, as he reached out, grabbed my hand, and pumped it up and down.

"They finally sent us someone that has a classification group higher than a four," he continued. I was surprised and at first thought he was making some kind of a joke at my expense. The Yeoman was smiling, which only reinforced the idea that they were making fun of me. I knew that my general classification and arithmetic scores had hardly put me in the genius category.

"Let's put him in "Fox" Division. The fire control people will be glad to get him," the Lieutenant continued. I wasn't too crazy about fire-fighting, but I had somehow gotten the idea it was a step above the First or Second divisions that Slim had mentioned.

"Take a seat here and I'll give "Fox" Division a call," the yeoman commented.

The Personnel Office fairly hummed with activity. The typewriters clattered, the phones rang constantly, and a steady stream of people appeared at the door with their own individual problems. In about fifteen minutes, a heavy-set, Third Class Petty Officer appeared at the door. I noticed he wore thick, black, horned-rim glasses that magnified his eyes. His protruding stomach pushed against his waistband, causing the blouse to ride up, exposing the top row of buttons on his trousers. Upon seeing him, the Yeoman, who had invited me to sit down, stood up.

"Got a new man for you," the Yeoman commented, looking at the heavy set Petty Officer. He then motioned for me to come forward. I joined them and stood listening.

"This is Seaman Apprentice Messer. Messer, this PO3 Hitman," he said. PO3 Hitman offered me his limp hand and moved it up and down slightly once or twice before removing it. He avoided all eye contact with me. "He'll take care of you," the Yeoman informed me.

"Let's go," said PO3 Hitman and he turned and started for the steel ladder. I had recovered my seabag and struggled along behind him. There would be no help this time as there had been with Slim. "Right now, I want to get you down to our compartment and assign you a bunk and find you an empty locker. Someone might have to give up one of their extra ones," he commented, looking a little irritated.

We climbed the ladder, went forward through a couple of hatches, and wound our way around small groups of men cleaning the passageways. Soon, we climbed down another ladder to a berthing compartment. We then went forward a few feet, passing some hanging racks then doubled back to the right and stopped at the first row. The ones that were not being slept in had been lifted up and fastened to the overhead with a chain so as to give more deck space. PO3 Hitman undid the chain and the racks fell horizontally into place. I could see there was about an eighteen-inch space between the bottom of each rack and the two and a half-inch thick mattress below. All the mattresses were covered with fart sacks except the one on the very bottom.

"Looks like this one's open," observed PO3 Hitman. At the end of the double row of racks, I could see the aluminum lockers were built one on top of the other, four high and two wide. I laid my seabag on my rack and it immediately fell to the deck. The rack's outer frame was made of aluminum-like tubing about ¾ of an inch in diameter. They were three and a half feet wide and six feet long. A piece of canvas with metal eyeholes spaced about four inches apart made up the supporting bottom part of the rack. The canvas was lashed to the tubing by passing a small piece of marlin (thick string) through the eye and around the tubing until it was completely enclosed. The aluminum tubing fastened in the back onto metal stanchions both at the foot and head of the rack. The front ends were held into place by chains that were connected, one to the other, and evenly spaced. One of the links was missing from the chain at the foot of my rack. This threw it out of balance, and it floated crazily around in the air.

PO3 Hitman had found me a locker, too. It was being used to store cleaning gear and bright work polish.

"You can get this cleaned out and it'll be okay," he commented. Going over to a row of lockers, he took keys that were attached to the dog tag chain around his neck and opened up two lockers. "Rank has its privileges," he said, taking out pieces of clothing and moving them about. "Most of us Petty Officers that have been on board for awhile have two lockers," he added. I took the bright work polish and the steel brush and assorted cleaning gear out of my assigned locker and started wiping it out. I had a lot of work to do before it would be ready to receive my few worldly possessions. "It's almost time for liberty and I need to start getting ready to get out of here. Let me show you where the mess hall is located. Then, you can come back down and get squared away. Tomorrow morning, you can make quarters and I'll introduce you to PO1 Jansen. He's our leading Petty Officer," PO3 Hitman continued with my indoctrination.

"You know, I don't want to sound stupid but just exactly what is it that you do here in "Fox" Division?" I asked, looking at PO3 Hitman. I thought he was going to have a cardiac infarction. He gave me an incredulous look and became very red in the face.

"Didn't you ask to be put in the electronics field?"

"No, not really."

"Well, there's about a hundred deck apes (seaman that work the decks) that would give their asses to be in this division. If you don't work out, you can bet you'll be trading places with one of them before too long. We control all the electronics that have to do with firing the big eight-inch guns."

The galley was one deck up and three hatches forward. Once I had my orientation to the mess deck, PO3 Hitman showed me to the shower. It was only one compartment away. Returning to my free-floating rack, I unpacked my seabag and started preparing myself for the following day.

The next morning, at exactly six o'clock, I was awakened with the sound of a bugle blowing reveille. I was surprised to see the compartment was about three-quarters full of men. Crude jokes and laughter floated through the berthing space as they moved about. I noticed several men returning from the shower with towels draped around their middle. They were getting dressed in undress blues. I quickly showered, shaved and dressed as the others.

The man who slept directly above me was dressing within a foot or two of where I was standing. I noticed he was short of stature and medium build. He looked about twenty-two and wore the standard navy issue black, horned-rim glasses. He smiled at me from time to time as he chatted gaily with his shipmates but we didn't exchange any kind of a greeting. I found my way back to the mess deck, ate quickly, and returned to the compartment. I shined my shoes and inspected my rack to make sure it was made up properly. More men were now in the compartment. Several had returned from liberty wearing dress blues and were now busy changing. I listened to their conversations about their wives and families and deduced that the majority of them were married and were living ashore with their spouses.

I noticed a PO1 had come into the compartment and went to one of the lockers just around the corner from where I was standing. He, too, was changing out of his dress blues. He looked to be several years older than most of the men and towered over six feet tall with broad shoulders and a thick chest. He wore standard navy glasses and appeared to be the serious type. I noticed the men deferred to him in a very respectful manner. PO3 Hitman had come over to where I was standing and was giving me my instructions for the day, "When they sound quarters, we'll go top side for muster, Messer. Just follow me and I'll show you where to go. After quarters I'll take you to the shop to meet PO1 Jansen," he said, looking toward the big man that I had been watching.

"Is that him?" I asked.

"You'll meet him soon enough. You don't talk to him, anyway, until you're properly introduced and then only when he asks you a question. Understand?"

"I understand," I responded feeling somewhat confused.

At 0730 hours, a bugle blew and "Fox" Division's thirty-eight men fell into ranks at a designated place on the main deck. A Chief stood with PO1 Jansen in front of the division with two commissioned officers. One of the officers was a Lieutenant Commander and the other a

Lieutenant Junior Grade. PO1 Jansen took a report from assigned section leaders as to the number of men present, absent, on leave, on watch, or otherwise accounted for. He turned to the Chief, saluted, and gave him the combined numbers he had received from the section leaders. Then, the Chief turned to the Lieutenant Commander and relayed the same information to him.

At 0745 hours, another bugle sounded and the Lieutenant Commander went with all of the other officers to report to the Executive Officer. There, they received special orders that later would be passed down to the individual divisions. While the Executive Officer briefed the Division Officers, the Chief read the POD (plan of the day) and gave the divisions their instructions for the day. A few minutes later, the Division Officer returned. At 0755 hours, the bugle sounded the call to prepare for the rendering of honor to colors. We were then called to attention while the Petty Officers and Officers not in ranks faced the direction of where the flag would be raised.

At exactly 0800 hours, the bugle played colors. While the flag was being hoisted on the fantail, the men not in ranks gave a hand salute. A second later, another bugle call and the boatswain blared out, "Turn to, commence ship's work." The ship suddenly came alive with the sounds of electric sanders, jack hammers, and the bell from the crane as it started to move back and forth on the track. I followed PO3 Hitman down a ladder and we wound our way through the passageway of the first deck soon coming up on a small shop. Several men were inside laughing and talking as we made our approach. I felt out of place as I entered the shop behind PO3 Hitman. PO1 Jansen had taken note of our entry and waited for PO3 Hitman to introduce me.

"Got a new boot striker. His name is Messer," he said, looking at PO1 Jansen. The shop became very quiet. PO1 Jansen did not offer his hand but looked solemnly at me over the top of his glasses.

"So, want to be a Fire Control Tech. do you?" he asked.

"I think so, sir."

"Don't say, sir, to me goddamn it. Hell, my parents were married."

Laughter filled the shop.

"Well, you better do more than think, Messer, if you want to be a Fire Control Tech. It's going to require a lot of study on your part. If you show aptitude and work hard, we'll try to get you to "A" school in a few months. How does that sound?"

"Fine, sir! Oh, sorry!"

"Damn! Get him up to Bohmhodt in the forward director, Hitman. We're getting underway Monday for a few days and I want to get him with one of the non-rates to prepare him for the 1-JV watch he'll be standing on the bridge."

Nodding his head, PO3 Hitman opened the door and led me out of the shop. We went topside to the starboard side, angled aft a few feet, and started climbing ladders to the super structure. After climbing three winding ladders, we came to a large opening and entered into a circular space. A young sailor in his early twenties with brown hair and a pleasant face was bent over sweeping dust into a dustpan with a foxtail (short handle broom). PO3 Hitman presented me to PO3 Bohmhodt and, after exchanging a few pleasantries with him, he departed.

Bohnholdt turned and looked at me and smiled amicably. "Looks like you're going to be working with me for a while. Let me show you around. We take care of the forward director here. That's the thing on top of that space behind you that looks like a big radar screen. It tracks targets for the big eight-inch guns. We locate a target and calculate the distance and the speed it's traveling. Then put the information in this computer here." He walked over to a big console with a dozen dials that had a large screen on top. "Then we push this button and the guns lock on the objective automatically and the gunners can then fire at will," he explained, as we walked around. "You'll be learning how to check out the director to see if it's functioning correctly. Later on, you'll learn how to work and repair all of this gear," he added, waving his arms around in a big circle.

I must have looked overwhelmed.

"What's the matter?"

"I've never been very mechanically-inclined."

"You'll learn. Half of the guys here in the division have never been to F. T. School. You'll learn by working here with me. I expect you to get a training manual from I&E (Indoctrination and Education) and study when you're just lying around not doing anything. That's the way I learned. Old Hitman learned that way, too. He never went to school. It took him three years to make PO3, but he made it. You can see he's pretty damn proud of himself. Stay out of his way, if you can. He likes to hard-ass the new guys until they prove themselves," he added.

Bohmholdt, in a few hours, was able to determine my educational background and life experience. He could see I felt lost and insecure in this New World I had found myself in. For whatever reason, he decided to try to teach me as much as possible by sharing his experiences.

"Messer, there is no other authority in the modern world like that of a Commanding Officer of a United States Naval Vessel," he said, as we worked. "He has the full responsibility for the mission of his ship. With that responsibility, comes his authority. He is the absolute ruler over everyone under his command. The discipline required on a Man of War is unlike any other you'll ever encounter or hear about. The chain of command starts with the Captain and comes right on down through the ranks to the lowest man. Everyone of us knows exactly where we stand in the pecking order. We know who we're senior to and who's senior to us by a quick look at the rank one is wearing on their sleeve or collar. The Old Man (Commanding Officer) will put you on piss and punk (bread and water) for three days for being disrespectful to any superior. You always have to keep in mind that our safety and efficiency depends on our being able to trust each other. We work under the concept that if the lowest-rated seaman on lookout falls asleep and misses the sighting of an enemy submarine, we could all die. Our primary mission is to wage war. There is no room in the military to question if an order makes sense or not. You just have to do what you're goddamn well told and keep you mouth shut. If you do that, you'll get along and everyone will respect you. If you don't want to do those basic things, hell, you may as well throw yourself overboard right now."

I listened to Bohmholdt attentively as he continued on through the morning with my indoctrination. "The thing that's hard to understand, coming in from civilian life, is how each individual's responsibility affects the whole crew. For example, if the Old Man is asleep and one of his officers runs the ship aground, the Old Man is responsible. The officer will be held accountable for his action, of course, but the Captain will go right down the tube with him. Another example, if you're working for me and I send you to do a job and you half-ass it, that reflects on me. In civilian life, we'd just fire you. Here, I can't get rid of you. It hurts us both and reflects on my leadership," he said.

I was extremely excited the following Monday as the Helena prepared to get underway and the special sea and anchor detail was set. Hundreds of crewmembers throughout the ship went to vital stations to perform functions that assured we would safely exit the harbor. Those not participating in this function donned the uniform of the day and manned the rail. I stood at parade rest watching the city of Long Beach fade from view as we sailed out to sea. Soon, we cleared the harbor. "Secure the special sea and anchor detail and commence ship's work," piped the Boatswain Mate of the watch over the 1MC system. I followed Bohmholdt up to the director.

"Like porkchops, Messer?" he asked.

"Yeah! Why?"

"Well, the first day out the stew burners always serve up greasy shit so when you boots get seasick, it'll slide up easy when you puke." he chuckled. He might be my mentor but I had still had my dues to pay.

After lunch, PO3 Hitman summoned me to the F.T. shop. There, posted on the small bulletin board, was the watch list for the 1-JV watch that he had so tediously made out for the non-rated men. I would be standing the mid-watch with a young seaman by the name of Blackey. He would be training me in my duties. I was awakened by a messenger at 2330 and told to report to the bridge. At 2345, I was standing in total darkness just outside of the bridge with four other men that were also preparing to take over their assigned watches. The Boatswain Mate of the watch soon appeared carrying his flashlight and inspected us for clean uniforms, shined shoes and haircuts. The message was clear; no one was allowed to go on the bridge of the Helena unless they conformed to the strictest of military standards.

I had met Blackey on one other occasion. He hadn't been rude but had seemed totally indifferent. I had never been up that high in the Helena's super structure before. I followed Blackey forward onto the bridge where he took a set of sound-powered phones from a seaman that was presently on watch. They greeted each other and chatted briefly. Blackey then took the headphones and put them on. We now stood looking out through a huge plate glass window. It was absolutely breath taking. The Helena was cutting through the water at thirty-two knots. I looked down onto the forward main deck at the two big turrets that held the three big eight-inch guns. As my eyes followed the clean lines on each side, I could see the green running lights to starboard and the red to port, reflecting up into the darkness. The wooden decks gleamed in the moonlight.

There was a great deal of activity on the bridge. This was the Helena's control center. The Officer of the Deck was in command. There were two officers and four enlisted men on the bridge, not including Blackey and myself. I noticed a man in a huge swivel chair keenly observing the activity going on around him. I could see the insignia on his collar was that of an eagle. I judged from his rugged features and the gray hair sticking out from under his hat that he was about fifty years old. He sat quietly, looking quite content. He said something to the Officer of the Deck that I didn't understand. "Aye, aye, Captain," came the response. I looked at him again. So, this was the Old Man. He looked calm, and regal, much like I imagined a king would look sitting on a throne.

The 1-JV watch was relatively simple, according to Blackey. Your headphones connected you to CIC (Combat Information Center) and plotting. When they picked up a surface moving contact on radar, they notified you of its position. Also, you could look at the radar screen on the bridge and see a little white dot that would blip when the arc of light hit it. These contacts were identified by the phonetic alphabet as Skunk Alpha, Skunk Bravo, Skunk Charlie, Skunk Delta etc. until you worked your way through the alphabet. If there were more contacts than there were letters in the alphabet, you would revert to Skunk Alpha Alpha, Skunk Bravo Bravo, Skunk Charlie Charlie etc. and continue on repeating that process as many times as was necessary. The non-moving surface contacts were identified in the same manner but the word skunk did not precede them. To the right of where Blackey was standing, was a big piece of Plexiglas mounted on the bulkhead. All the contacts had been written on it with a red grease pencil. Each time there was a significant change, Blackey would wipe off the old position and write the new one. Each time he did this, he would notify the Officer of the Deck. "Alpha contact now bearing 180 degrees, sir," he would report. "Very well," would come the reply. And so it went for the next four hours. "Nothing to this," Blackey assured me, "Unless you're up here when coming into some port like Hong Kong; then you can have as many as two-hundred contacts," he commented casually. I looked forward and watched the bow rise and fall. My heart skipped a beat. Just twelve weeks ago, I had been a civilian.

I had a short class in boot camp on sound-powered phones. I remembered they didn't have batteries to power them but were powered as the name implied. I also had remembered enough of the phonetic alphabet to pass my test but little more. Blackey allowed me to listen to CIC give bearings a couple of times, but somehow I just couldn't quite make out what they were saying. I would then ask them to repeat it. This reflected on Blackey and after a short time he would take the phones back. And so it went every twelve hours for the next three days.

On the fourth day, my name appeared alone. I felt a little insecure. I went and asked PO3 Hitman to give me a couple of more days and to possibly assign me to someone else to teach me the procedure. "Blackey said you're ready. Hell, man, you've already had more time than most people get," PO3 Hitman responded. Not having an alternative, I reported to the bridge at the appointed hour. I relieved the watch and put on the phones. I looked down at the dozen or more contacts on the Plexiglas. The phones cracked and I heard a voice. I didn't make out what they had said.
"Repeat," I requested. It was repeated, but I still didn't get it. I could see surface craft off our port bow and assumed this was the contact that had changed its position. I could see there was no danger of colliding. I decided to ignore it. Occasionally, I thought I understood and I would write it down, but most of the time I just didn't understand what had been said. I was in a panic. I knew I was not performing adequately but I stood powerless, unable to tell the Officer of the Deck I was incompetent.

About an hour later, the Officer of the Deck looked through his field glasses at an approaching vessel.

"What was the last reported position on that Kilo contact?" he asked. I looked at the Plexiglas. I had no Kilo contact written down. He had become aware early on that I was having problems and had become anxious about my performance. Noting I had hesitated, he looked down at the Plexiglas. Giving me an incredulous look, he turned to the Boatswain Mate of the watch. "Let's get someone up here that's qualified on this 1-JV," he ordered. I stood petrified, waiting. In less than ten minutes, one of the other non-rated men from "Fox" Division showed up on the bridge.

"I'll take over now, Messer," he said, and reached for the phones. I broke out in a cold sweat as I took them off and passed them to him. "PO3 Hitman wants to see you in the F.T. shop," he added, putting the phones over his ears.

I climbed slowly down out of the super structure and headed toward the shop with a heavy heart. Bohmholdt's words, "Our safety and efficiency depends on us being able to trust each other," rang in my ears. Blackey had failed in training me properly. Of that, there was no doubt. I also knew PO3 Hitman had the responsibility to make sure I was qualified before putting me on watch alone. But I knew the greater responsibility of what happened lay squarely on my own shoulders. By ignoring the contacts and not telling the OOD of the watch what was gong on, I had put my ship in harms way. I knew that, under other circumstances, I could have been responsible for a major disaster.

Upon reaching the shop, I noticed the door was closed, but I could hear people talking. I turned the knob and pushed the door open. PO3 Hitman and a couple of the other men were inside. Upon my entering, they stopped talking. Before I could gain my composure, the hulking frame of PO1 Jansen slammed through the door. His face was red and filled with rage. Bohmholdts warning, "If I send you on a job and you half-ass it up it reflects on me," now had a whole new meaning.

"What the hell happened up there?" he asked, looking at PO3 Hitman. PO3 Hitman's face turned red and he looked embarrassed, but didn't answer. "Never mind, I'll get back to you later," he said. Then he turned to me. "Messer, you'll stand fours hours on and four off until I tell you otherwise. You're going to learn how to stand that watch and you're going to stand it correctly. Do you understand?"

"Yes sir!"

"And don't say sir to me, goddamn it!"

My humiliation and shame was complete. I didn't answer. The next five days at sea were a nightmare. Although I was standing four on and four off, I was expected to work during regular working hours. The mid-watch runs from 0001 until 0400 hours. Traditionally, the person standing this watch is allowed to sleep in an extra half-hour. On the fifth morning, I had come off of the mid-watch and was taking advantage of the few extra minutes I was allotted. Being totally exhausted, I had failed to get up at 0630, as regulations required. Why no one had bothered to wake me, I couldn't be certain. Suddenly, I woke to a roar of someone's voice. PO1 Jansen had returned from morning chow. He had started down the ladder in front and just to the left, of where I was sleeping. Stopping half way down the ladder, he saw I was still in the rack. His initial roar had awakened me and I looked toward where he was standing.

"IF YOU'RE NOT OUT OF THAT RACK BY THE TIME I GET TO THE BOTTOM OF THIS LADDER I'M GOING TO BOUNCE YOUR HEAD OFF THE DECK," he bellowed, then fairly ran down the ladder taking two rungs with each step. I was folding my blanket by the time his foot hit the deck of our compartment.

In a few days, I was standing the 1-JV watch alone. However, the long hours and stress had apparently pulled my immune system down. In a short time, I had developed a terrible chest cold. The constant hacking all night had become a source of irritation to my shipmates. At

Bohmholdt's insistence, I soon found my way to Sickbay. A long line had formed in front of the door marked SICK CALL 0900-1130 and 1300-1600. I waited patiently with my shipmates for the door to open. At exactly 0900, the door opened. The line moved slowly forward and around 1000 I found myself in front of a PO3 Hospital Corpsman. He was slight of frame and short of stature. His voice trembled as he took my medical history and wrote down my complaint. I could smell the faint odor of alcohol. He smiled slightly from time to time and made a genuine attempt to be cordial. In the middle of our interview, he crossed the passageway and went inside of what looked like a hospital ward. When he opened the door, I could see big steel bunks holding eight-inch mattresses covered with beautiful blue bedspreads. This was a whole other world; my interest peaked. The PO3 came back and took my temperature and listened to my chest. Satisfying himself that I had nothing more than a simple cold he reached into a drawer and retrieved some cough syrup and two packets of cold tablets.

"So, how does one become a hospital corpsman?" I asked. He looked at the lip of my chart.

"You non-designated?" he asked.

"Yes, they got me in "Fox" Division but I am not interested in electronics."

"Hey, you know we always have, three or so, non-designated strikers working here on the ward. Carrying chow to the patients and cleaning up and things like that. One of our strikers just left for Hospital Corps School. If you're interested, put a chit in through your Division Officer. You look like the kind of guy we could use. By the way, my name is Pugh, PO3 Pugh," he said, sticking out his hand.

"Nice to meet you, Petty Officer Pugh. I'll check into it and thanks!" I said, grabbing his hand.

Returning to my workstation at 1300 hours I approached PO3 Bohmhodt. "You know, Petty Officer Bohmhodt, I am not cut out for this electronic stuff. I really like working for you, but I could be here four years and I still wouldn't understand what the hell is going on," I explained.

"You know, I kind of agree with you, Messer. What do you think you'd like to do?"

"Well, I went to sick call and met one of the corpsmen. He seems like a really nice guy. He told me there was an opening for a striker in "H" Division."

"Messer, if you want to strike for corpsman, put in a request. I'll talk to PO1 Jansen. You know you'll have to make seaman before you transfer. It's just not the policy of the division to let anyone transfer until they have shown some initiative on their own. I don't think you'll have any trouble with the written exam. The problem is the practical factors you'll be tested on. The boatswain mates will be the ones to check you off on that. I have to tell you, they don't think any non-designated striker should be promoted to seaman until they put some time in the deck gang. I'll see what I can do for you, but it's not going to be easy."

The Helena was the flagship of the seventh fleet when she was deployed to the Western Pacific. She was a model of what a US Navy ship should be. She gleamed with paint and polish. The conduct and discipline of her crew was exemplary. This was a world where one could be confined for three days on bread and water for the slightest infraction. The thousand-man crew of the Helena was a cross section of people from all walks of American life. Probably, the people aboard were no better or worse than the general society of that era. I soon came to understand that there were two distinct forces of power on the Helena. First and foremost was the official one laid out by the Navy Department. The Uniform Code of Military Justice dictated the legal guidelines as to how this power was to be enforced and was backed by the US Government. The second came from the unwritten law that just seems to naturally develop when you have a large number of men working and living together. The leaders of this second force had little to do with the holding of rank. Their power came from charisma and their ability to exercise ones will over others. This can be as simple as knowing someone in another division and one's willingness to return favors, or as complicated as conspiracy. There was a slush fund that loaned money at the rate of 960% if calculated on an annual basis. Five dollars for seven to be paid on payday was the going rate. The rumor was that the funds didn't belong to the lender but to some higher-ranking official. There were dark warriors who lived in corners and shadows of the Helena where threats and intimidation were the norm.

The written seaman's test was officially administered by a lieutenant that had graduated from the Naval Academy and was controlled down to the last piece of scrap paper. But the dark warriors had somehow obtained a copy of the questions and answers. Their willingness to share this with a selected few often had more to do with being advanced than any other one factor.

Jellison was an unusual character who rarely talked to anyone in "Fox" Division. His friends came from other parts of the ship and they seemed equally as strange.

"Stay away from Jellison. He's bad news," warned Bohmholdt.

"Why is that?"

"Someday the NIS (Naval Investigative Service) will come for him and take that whole damn bunch of dopers off of here," he warned.

Of all the people who had stood the 1-JV watch with me, Jellison had been the kindest and most helpful. He cared little of what CIC might think of our performance. His main concern was that I become qualified. "Don't worry. Just do your best. If you have a problem, tell the Officer of the Deck. This is his responsibility," he instructed, as we stood hour after hour on the bridge. Little by little, I began to relax and in a very short while I became quite proficient. As time went on, I came to understand that Jellison was one of the leaders of the dark warriors.

Jellison knew I had gotten a raw deal by not being properly trained and for this reason he took a special interest in me. The word had gone out that I was not to be hassled. I became aware of this one day when PO3 Bohmholdt had sent me to the paint locker to get a special mixture of paint. On my arrival, the attendant ignored me for several minutes. Finally, he took my request, read it, and handed it back to me.

"We're closing up. You'll have to come back at 1300," he said. His assistant was bent over mixing and pouring paint. He had looked over at me when the attendant had said I would have to return.

"That's one of Jellison's boys," he commented. The attendant stopped and looked at me as if seeing me for the first time. He then reached to retrieve the request.

"May as well save you a trip back down here," he said.

Jellison was later kicked out of the "Fox" Division into the deck gang, but his influence didn't diminish with the dark warriors. Three days before I was to do my practical factors, I was lying in my rack reading. Suddenly, I became aware of someone's presence standing next to me. Looking up, I saw Jellison standing, watching me.

"Hey, what's up?" I asked. He casually handed me a magazine. I could see there was something folded inside.

"Take a look at it before your exam," he murmured in almost a whisper.

"Thanks!" I said, looking around the compartment. Then, he was gone. Later, I went up to the crew's library and opened the magazine. Folded neatly inside, were several sheets of paper. The top one was a completed practical factor sheet for seaman with my name printed neatly across the top. Underneath the practical factors, were three papers stapled together that had all the questions and answers that would later appear on my written exam. A few days later the Lieutenant who had graduated from the Academy bumped into me on the mess deck. "Oh, Messer, I just graded your exam for seaman. You'll be promoted the first of next month. Congratulations!" he said.

I had been in "Fox" Division several weeks when I was assigned to compartment cleaning and felt quite at home cleaning, painting, and taking care of the laundry. My hours were normal working hours and I wasn't required to stand watches, much to my relief. PO3 Bohmhodt had taken my request, for transfer to PO1 Jansen.

"What do you hear on my request to transfer?" I would ask him from time to time.

"That big bastard Jansen still has it. Best not to bug him," he would respond.

"I wonder if I could just stay on compartment cleaning indefinitely?" I asked PO3 Bohmholdt one day. He shook his head from side to side and laughed.

"You're about a dumb shit, Messer. Is that why you came into the Navy, so you could haul other people's nasty shit around and clean up after them?"

"No, but I don't want to work the deck and I'll sure as hell never make a Fire Control Technician. This is about the best I've had it."

"No, Messer, you're just like a lot of folks in the Navy. You just haven't found your place yet. You know, Old Hard Ass Jansen use to be a Boatswain Mate. But he will be retiring soon and wanted to learn something he could use in civilian life. He's about as fucked-up as you are if you want to know the truth. He's not a bad guy really, just spent most of his life working the deck. He'll probably kick my ass, but I'll ask him about your request first chance I get."

Three days later, after my conversation with Bohmhodt, I was alone in the compartment, sweeping the deck. I heard the squeak of the chain that acted as the guardrail on the port ladder. I looked up to see PO1 Jansen descending. He rarely came to the compartment during working hours unless there was a problem. Feeling a sense of anxiety I studied his face as he approached me.

"Get your cover, Messer. You got an interview with Chief Martin in "H" division," he said. My heart jumped into my throat, as I went to get my hat. The sickbay was at the other end of the ship on the same level. I followed him on the long trek through the different berthing compartments. Finally, we came to the passageway where the bulkheads were painted a medical green. We walked a few feet past where I had gone to sickcall a few weeks before and stopped in front of an office marked MEDICAL RECORDS. PO1 Jansen knocked on the door. In a few seconds, the door was opened by a slender young corpsman. He looked us up and down and smiled at PO1 Jansen.

"How can I help you?" he asked.

"Here to see Chief Martin," PO1 Jansen replied. The corpsman invited us in. The office was small with three desks. Two of them were side by side in the back and the other one was up front. The corpsman who asked us to come in obviously had been working in the back at the desk that was now empty. Opposite of where he had been, was another corpsman busy typing. At the front desk, sat a slender Chief Petty Officer about 35 years old. Upon our entry, he stood and shook hands with PO1 Jansen and offered him a seat. I remained standing.

"This is the man I was telling you about," PO1 Jansen said, nodding toward me. "Messer, this is Chief Martin. Me and the Chief go back a long way," he said. The Chief took my hand and gave me a warm handshake. I liked him instantly and the tension I had been feeling started to drain away. "You see the way he's dressed and his personal appearance. I just now took him out of the compartment where he was cleaning. What you see is what you get," commented Jansen. Chief Martin had a folder in front of him and I could see it was my personnel file.

"Well, his scores look good and, I agree with you, he looks like the kid next door," the Chief commented, smiling up at me, he leaned back in his chair. "Why don't you go on back to your work station,

Messer. PO1 Jansen will let you know what we decide," continued the Chief. Then, turning to PO1 Jansen, "How about some coffee, Jansen?" he asked.

I left the office and walked by the sickcall room hoping to see PO3 Pugh. The door was closed. I made my way back to the compartment. I could hardly contain my anxiety as I finished out the morning routine. I had hoped Jansen would let me know something soon. I knew he had probably left sickbay and went to chow in the First Class Mess. There would have to be an emergency before I dared look for him in there. I waited impatiently.

When 1300 came, I returned to work. At 1430, I heard the squeak of the ladder as PO1 Jansen's big frame came bounding down. I studied his face to see if I could get an indication of how the interview had gone. PO1 Jansen showed no emotion as he walked over to his locker and unlocked it. "Messer, pack up all your shit and report to "H" Division," he said, without smiling as he fumbled around inside his locker. I was elated, but speechless. I knew PO1 Jansen had gone to bat for me but, somehow, I felt it would be inappropriate to tell him thanks. He then turned and looked at me for a moment. "I told the Chief you were a good man, Messer, don't let me down, goddamn you," he said. Having found what he was looking for, he closed his locker, turned and climbed the ladder. I wasted no time in packing. I don't remember ever seeing PO1 Jansen again.

I struggled through the passageways, stepping through hatches, toward "H" Division with my heavy seabag slung over my shoulder. I wasn't quite sure where I should go, so I stopped at the sickcall room. The door was closed. I knocked lightly and waited. Someone, I had never seen before, opened the door. He looked rather surprised to see me standing there with my seabag draped over my shoulder. He turned his head a little sideways, as if to say, "What is this?" while holding my gaze.

"I was told to report to "H" Division," I said.

"You must be the new striker. I heard you were coming." he answered, as he stepped out and pulled the door closed behind him. "Come with me." We crossed the passageway to the compartment where I had seen the big mattresses when I had made my visit to sick-call. He opened the door halfway and looked inside.

"Is Walt here?" he asked.

"He'll be back in a minute," someone yelled back. Walking into the big room, he indicated for me to follow him. "PO2 Henning will be coming back soon and take care of you," he said smiling. "I have to get back to work," he added, leaving me standing awkwardly inside the big room.

Immediately inside the door, was the head. Just past the head, the bulkhead doubled back to the left, opening up into a huge ward. I could see a short stocky man, sitting just around the corner at a small desk, reading something. He didn't acknowledge that he was aware of my presence. After an uncomfortable moment, I dropped my seabag and stood nervously waiting. In a few minutes a tall, handsome fellow who looked about twenty-three years old entered the room. Upon seeing me, he gave a warm smile and stuck out his hand. He looked very much like Rock Hudson, I thought.

"You Messer?" he asked.

"Yes, I am. PO1 Jansen told me to report here to "H" Division. Chief Martin had interviewed me and…"

"Yeah, I know. I've been expecting you, Messer. Let me show you to the living compartment and you can get your gear put away. Take your time and when you're all squared away come on back here to the ward." he said, as he lead me back up the passageway and into the Marine detachment's compartment. Halfway through their compartment, a passageway led off to the right and into a far corner on the port side. There, we encountered three rows of single racks, four high. Along the bulkhead were 24 lockers. "Take whichever rack you want here, Messer. We all sleep on the ward, unless it's full of patients. Looks like you got your choice of lockers. Take any two that don't have a lock on them," he instructed.

I picked out two lockers that were side by side. I unpacked, placing my blues in one locker and my whites in another. I was beginning to feel better about my world. Maybe, at last, I had found my niche. I quickly stored my gear and reported back to PO2 Henning.

"WOW! That was fast," commented PO2 Henning when I arrived back at the ward. The stocky man was still siting at the desk, reading. "Campbell get your lazy ass up and let Messer sit down," he ordered. Giving me a look of total disdain, the stocky man stood up, sighed heavily, and walked out the door. "Messer, have a seat and let me fill you in on how it all works around here. You'll be working with me here on the ward. Here in the Medical Department we have an operating room, pharmacy, laboratory, isolation ward, sickcall room, and a record office. Our staff consists of a Surgeon, Chief Martin, ten corpsmen, and two strikers. The two strikers flunked out of Corps School and we're trying to get their dumb asses reassigned back there. They are both pretty good guys but they're E-3's, just like you, so if they give you any shit just let me know. You'll be cleaning, making beds, and carrying chow to our in-patients. I'll be teaching you simple procedures like how to take temperatures, blood pressures, and respirations. I also want to teach you how to give injections. We usually have four to ten men with gonorrhea under treatment all the time. They receive two injections of penicillin a day and we administer them here on the ward. That's just kind of a general idea of what's going on. I'll be explaining things as they come up. Do you have any questions?"

I must have looked confused. PO2 Henning gave me a long look, and then he smiled. "We don't get too excited down here, Messer. Just hang around with me and little by little, you'll get the idea. Every fourth day will be your duty day and you'll be required to take over here on the ward from 1630 until 0800 the following morning. Don't worry about it. We won't ask you to do something you don't know how to do. There will always be a Petty Officer, or designated corpsman, in charge of your section," he said.

Now may be a good time to explain what designated and non-designated strikers are. A non-designated striker is an E-3 or below that has never completed an "A" School or passed a rating exam for E-4. A designated striker, on the other hand, would have accomplished one or the other. There are ratings, such as Hospital Corpsman and Dental Technician that require completing an "A" school before one can become designated or take an exam for Petty Officer. In the mid and late fifties, the Petty Officer ranks were: PO3 (E-4), PO2 (E-5), PO1 (E-6), and CPO (E-7). The rating badge of an Eagle on the left arm easily identified Petty Officers (often referred to as a crow). In the fleet, a non-rated man never spoke to anyone above the rank of E-5 unless spoken to first. To approach a Chief Petty Officer, without having consulted with one of the other senior Petty Officers first, would have been unthinkable.

Our Surgeon was a Lieutenant Commander by the name of Smyth from Michigan. He had been in the Navy Reserve and had opted to come onto active duty for two years. Other than that, I knew very little about him. In those days, I stood in awe of Commissioned Officers. As far as I was concerned, they were another species.

Little by little, I came to know all the enlisted men in the Medical Department. Chief Martin was a father figure to all of us and we adored him. He had that unusual characteristic of making men want to do their very best. He treated us with dignity and respect. He knew that protocol dictated that he not be social with the men below the rank of E-5, but he had a way of making each of us feel special no matter what our rank. When encountering me on the ward, he would nod his head, smile, and say, "How you getting along, Messer?"

"I am fine, Chief," I'd respond, feeling about ten feet tall.

There was PO2 Wilson, from Texas, who worked in the Pharmacy and performed the laboratory procedures. He was pleasant and a hard worker but didn't seem to have a need to be close to anyone.

Hank Minot was a Hospitalman (E-3) from New Jersey. He was the one who had invited PO1 Jansen and I into the office for my interview with Chief Martin. He had served a hitch in the Navy previously and held the rank of PO2. He had a wife and five children and had recently reentered the Navy after being a civilian for a couple of years. Hank could type eighty words a minute and was a whiz in medical records. He was Chief Martin's right-hand man. Hank always had a grin on his face and his penetrating gray eyes fairly danced when he talked.

PO2 Fredricks was our Operating Room Technician. He had feminine characteristics that made the rest of us feel a little uncomfortable. He and PO3 Rogers worked together and seemed to have a very good working relationship. They stayed away from the rest of us during off duty hours but could normally be found in the Operating Room. When it came to patient care that required intensive care, the Surgeon always looked to PO2 Fredricks. We respected him for his professional ability but didn't really consider him to be one of the boys.

In a very short time, PO2 Henning became my mentor. The society in the military of those days didn't permit us to say we were friends. He trained me as though I was his younger brother. He scolded, protected, instructed, and corrected me, as we worked. To say that I admired him would be an understatement.

PO3 Cruz worked with PO3 Pugh in sickcall and often helped us out on the ward, if the patient load was heavy. PO2 Henning and PO3 Cruz were on a first name basis. The difference in their rank rarely came up; however, there were times when PO3 Cruz would order me around. When this did occur, PO2 Henning would very diplomatically say, "I'll take care of it, Jake." PO3 Cruz would be cool with me for a while following one of those incidents. I was of the opinion he resented my relationship with PO2 Henning more than anything else, so I tried to tread lightly when he was around. As time passed, it ceased to be an issue. No doubt my life would have been totally different had I been assigned to work for PO3 Cruz.

Then there was Harpo and Campbell, the two "A" school dropouts. It seemed their one ambition in life was to demonstrate that I was somehow their junior. Problem being, I had made seaman before either of them and, in fact, outranked them both. They, on the other hand, had completed several weeks of formal training at Hospital Corps School. They both felt, somehow, that should make them senior to me.

One day, when PO2 Henning had been called away to a petty officers' meeting, Campbell and I had been left to attend the ward. We had been instructed to clean the head, as well as swab, wax, and buff the ward deck. The head and shower on the ward required considerable cleaning as it was used by both patients and corpsmen. We had finished with the ward and I was wrapping the cord around the buffer to put it away.

"Messer, get the head!" ordered Campbell. This was the first time we had been left alone to work together. I'm sure PO2 Henning never expected that two of the lowest-rated men in the medical department would be concerned about who was senior. But I knew if I complied with Campbell's order, I would be setting precedence. I didn't respond for a couple of minutes, but after thinking it over, I thought it was time to settle this once and for all.

"Campbell, I have more time in grade than you do, so I want you to clean the head," I ordered.

"That's not going to happen, Messer. I am giving you an order as a Corpsman to clean that head." PO2 Henning had come back into the ward just in time to hear the last few words Campbell had said.

"What's going on here?" he asked.

"I have given Messer an order to clean the head," Campbell explained.

"Campbell, you aren't a designated Corpsman and Messer has time in grade on you. I suggest you get your lazy ass in there and clean it yourself."

Harpo had come onto the ward and stood listening as the scenario unfolded. He looked from me to Campbell. The significance of what had happened had not escaped him. I had, for the first time since entering the Navy, asserted my will over another by the merit of my rank. It wouldn't be the last time in my career, but I don't remember ever feeling so satisfied with myself.

I had been in "H" Division a little over a month and we were tied up at pier nine in Long Beach. It was now the early part of January 1957. I was busy swabbing the deck when suddenly PO3 Pugh hurried through the door, grinning from ear to ear.

"McGlaughlin just checked aboard," he said, shaking his head from side to side. I had no idea who McGlaughlin might be.

"That son-of-a-bitch 'Mac' on board here right now?" asked PO2 Henning. At that moment, the door burst open and the room vibrated with energy. I looked up and saw this young sailor, about twenty years old with blond hair, rushing toward PO2 Henning grinning from ear to ear with his hand outstretched. PO2 Henning had been sitting, talking to PO3 Pugh. He jumped up and grabbed our new arrival's hand, shook it and gave him a big bear hug.

"Mac, where have you been, you sorry ass?" he asked, as he smiled broadly and slapped him on the back. I could see that McGlauglin was quite a bit shorter than PO2 Henning but more muscular.

"They locked my ass up down in Juarez, Mexico. Walt, I was coming back off leave and when I got to El Paso, Texas, I decided to go down there with a couple of guys," McGlauglin explained.

He gave me a curious look, smiled and kept talking. PO3 Pugh stood with the grin frozen on his face as though he was watching a comedy act. I could see McGlauglin had Irish features with a large wide nose that had obviously been broken several times.

"Yeah, we were drinking down there in some club. I was talking to this broad when this damn soldier came in, walked over to my table and said, 'It's time for you to move along, Swabbie.' You know how it is, one thing led to another and we went at it. Next thing I knew, everyone in the damn place was fighting, broads and all. Problem was, some asshole threw a bottle through the big plate glass window in front of the place. Before I could get the hell out of there, about twenty cops showed up. They hauled our asses off to jail and booked us for assault, disturbing the peace, and destroying private property," he explained. Everyone was laughing by this time and I was completely captivated by McGlauglin's story.

"Anyone have a cigarette?" he asked, slapping his blouse pocket.

"Here you go," PO3 Pugh said, shaking out one of his Winston Cigarettes. McGlaughlin took the cigarette, put it in his mouth, and slapped his pockets again, indicating he didn't have a match either. PO3 Pugh gave him a light.

"You know, down there in the Juarez Jail, the guards would come by every four hours and throw ten to twelve cigarettes for about twenty-five of us prisoners. First couple of days, about all I got was a sniff from some greaser's second-hand smoke. But after a while, I was down there fighting like a dog for a bone just like everyone else," laughed Mcglaughlin.

"How long did they keep you, Mac?" asked PO2 Henning.

"Nine days. We went in front of the judge on the third day. The soldier, that started all that shit in the first place, paid for his part of the damages and they let him walk. I didn't have enough money to pay mine, so I had to have him call Mom and ask her to wire it to me. I had to stay in there another six days," McGlauglin continued to explain.

Chief Martin walked into the ward and shook hands with McGlaughlin. "Glad you're back, Mac. We've been carrying you as AOL (absent over leave) for a few days. I am going to try to get this all straightened out at pre-mast with the Executive Officer. Meanwhile, I want you to work here on the ward with Henning and Messer and stay out of trouble," he said. He then looked at all of us but didn't smile. We knew the party was over and it was time to get back to work.

After everyone left, PO2 Henning turned toward where I was standing.

"Hey Mac, this is our new striker, Messer. Messer, this is McGlaughlin," he said. McGaughlin gave me a quick smile.

"Just call me Mac," he interjected and we shook hands. In the days that followed, I came to know Mac quite well. His father had wanted him to be a boxer and trained him from early childhood to be aggressive. Mac had gone on to become a golden glove contender in his early teens. When Mac was at his peak, his father died suddenly of a heart attack. He had a hard time getting past that and drifted aimlessly for a couple of years. Finally, he ended up in front of a juvenile judge and was given a choice of either going to jail or entering the Navy.

"Yeah, that old juvenile judge we had in South Boston was about the best recruiting tool the Navy had," Mac would laughingly tell us.

Mac was barely twenty-one and I had turned nineteen in October of the previous year. We got along fairly well and in a short time started going on liberty together. Mac felt that it was his duty to try to teach me the ways of the world. It was obvious to him that, me being from a farm in Arkansas, I had a lot to learn.

"The first thing we have to do is get you over to the Fleet Locker Club and open you an account so you can buy yourself a couple hundred dollars worth of rags," he insisted.

"I don't know, Mac. We're going on a cruise to WESPAC in April. I don't want to be paying for something I can't use."

"I can't be going around with you in uniform. Hell, all the babes will know we're swabbies. No chick with any class would even talk to us. No, you need to get yourself at least a couple of outfits. We'll go over there Saturday and I'll talk to Al; we'll get you fixed up."

Soon, I had a locker rented and a bill for a couple hundred dollars. My total month's salary was $110.00 and now a third of that was going to the Locker Club. The lockers were above a retail and liquor store that joined a big recreation room that had a television, a couple of couches, and a few odd chairs. When we were broke, we'd just hang out there. Mac, being such good friends with Al, made arrangements for us to buy beer and put it on our account.

Long Beach was a fascinating city in the 1950's. The Locker Club was three blocks from what was known to us as The Pike. It was like a huge state fair that never closed. It was two miles long and had every conceivable ride available, including the longest and highest roller coaster in the State of California. The Lido ballroom was one of the main attractions and it featured an orchestra every Friday and Saturday night. Hundreds of young people flocked to the Pike from the surrounding area every weekend. Sailors, pretending not to be sailors, and young women, looking for sailors while pretending not to be interested, were all part of the enchantment. One of the things that made the Pike accessible was what we called the PE or Red Car. It was an electric trolley that went from the steps leading down to the Pike on Long Beach Boulevard all the way to downtown Los Angeles.

Mac and I would start our liberty in the Locker Club. We'd drink a few beers and then go cruise the Pike. If nothing interesting turned up, we'd head back to the lounge. One Thursday night, in late February, we had filled up on beer and were on one of our regular reconnaissance missions. We were passing one of the open-air grills when I looked inside and saw two young women with coal black hair. They were dressed exactly alike. They were wearing black, tight fitting sweaters with black and white zebra stripe slacks. Mac had punched me in the ribs with his elbow as we strolled by. We walked a few feet, making sure we were out of their sight, then Mac stopped and looked at me.

"Did you see that?" he asked.

"What?" I asked, pretending not to know what he was talking about.

"Don't be a clown," he said pretending to slap me. "Let's go talk to them."

Our two young friends' names were Jan and June. They were very happy to have met us and we hit it off right away. It seemed their husbands had, just that day, been sent to state prison for armed robbery. They had held up a liquor store in Santa Monica. The cops had suspected that Jan drove the getaway car, but her husband had confessed to being the driver so the charges were dropped. After a couple of dates going to the movies at the Roxy Theater, we decided we should do something more exciting with these worldly, young ladies. "Maybe we could go down to Tijuana, Mexico," Jan suggested. Mac and I would be getting paid Friday, so we decided the up coming weekend would be an ideal time. Mac and I had changed out of our civilian clothes back into uniform and Jan and June were walking us to the bus stop to catch the bus back to the Naval Station.

"John, I love that beige shirt you have that has those vertically-running, gold threads woven into the material. Could you loan that to me for our trip this Saturday?" June asked, very sweetly. That was my favorite shirt and I was going to be paying for it for a very long time. I hesitated.

"Please," she insisted.

"Well, okay," I finally agreed, "I'll pick it up and bring it with me when we come by for you Saturday morning."

"No, it's better you give me your locker key and I'll just pick it up myself so I'll be dressed and ready to go when you guys arrive."

"How am I going to get my key back to get dressed?"

"Don't worry, hon. I'll give it to Al to hold for you."

"But no women are allowed to go upstairs to the locker room."

"I'll just tell Al you are going to loan me the shirt and he can send one of the employees up there for me. I'll explain to him the one I want. Come on! Aren't I your girl?"

I felt a little uneasy with the whole thing, but I didn't want to do anything to spoil the trip. I gave her the key.

Mac and I were fairly excited about our plans for the weekend. We had duty that Friday night and chatted endlessly about our coming adventure. Saturday morning at 0900, we were dressed and ready to go when the Boatswain Mate of the watch blew liberty call. Reaching the club, I went to the counter to get my key. Al was sitting at the desk doing some paper work.

"Hey, Al! Can you give me the key to my locker?" Al stopped, took off his glasses and looked up at me.

"What key?" he asked. I turned and looked at Mac.

"Ah, it's okay, Messer. Al, can you open Messers's locker with the master? We're in a hurry; we're taking our girls to TJ," Mac explained. I had begun to get an uneasy feeling. Al rummaged through his desk for his key. We climbed the stairs and went to my locker. Al opened it up and we looked inside. The locker was completely bare. Mac and I looked at each other. Under other circumstances, we might have laughed. But we knew our dream weekend had just come to a sudden end. Mac's face had a look of anguish as he shook his head from side to side.

"Those bitches," he muttered. Al shrugged his shoulders,

"Cost you five dollars for another key. I'll put it on your tab," he said, as he locked up my locker. "If you want to get out of that monkey suit, you better come on down and get yourself a couple of things."

Jan and June lived in the Seaside Hotel right on the beach a couple of blocks east of the Pike. They shared one room on the second floor and it was against the law, as well as the hotel rules, to have guests. We had met them in the lobby on occasion and knew it was a requirement that they turn in their key each time they left the hotel.

"Let's go see if the bitches are home," Mac proposed.

"The manager isn't going to let us up there, Mac."

"Bastard can at least ring the room," he answered, as we walked out the door of the club and headed for the hotel. The front door of the Seaside faced the beach and opened up onto a wind-blown, sandy sidewalk. Pushing the door open we entered into a small vestibule that had stairs leading up about eight feet to the first level. Immediately at the head of the stairs, on the left-hand side, was a desk where a balding, frail, fortish-looking clerk sat in attendance, reading the paper.

"Would you ring 207?" Mac asked.

"Jan and June left early this morning with a couple of Marines if that's who you're looking for," responded the clerk, without looking up. Mac and I looked at each other.

"How you know they were Marines?" Mac asked.

The clerk lowered the paper and looked at Mac, "Because they were wearing firemen uniforms," he said sarcastically and turned back to his paper. Mac's face turned crimson red.

"How'd you like me to kick the shit out of you?" Mac asked.

"How'd you like for me to call the Shore Patrol and have your swabby ass thrown in jail?" Mac looked at me and I knew he was very close to going over the counter after him.

"Come on, Mac." I said. Taking his arm, I pulled him toward the stairs. The clerk glared at us defiantly.

"Asshole," Mac muttered, as we turned and headed for the street.

Mac and I returned to the locker club feeling more dejected than angry. It was getting along toward 1100 when we reached the club. We bought a couple of six packs of Olympia beer and commenced to drown our troubles. The more we drank, the more unjust it seemed. We had been lied to, stood up, and robbed. But, worst of all, we had been dumped for a couple of Marines. By three in the afternoon, we were polishing off the last of our fourth six pack.

"Messer, your clothes have to be up there in that damn room somewhere," Mac said.

"Probably are, except for my shirt June wanted to wear."

"Who knows? Maybe them damn Marines are all decked out in those fancy sweaters you're so crazy about." I shrugged my shoulders and we had another beer.

"Why don't we just go back up to that damn hotel and check things out? Maybe the bitches are back by now," Mac suggested.

My thinking was a little foggy but it seemed like a pretty good idea. Couldn't do any harm to take a look. A few minutes later we arrived at the hotel. Things seemed quiet. A few people were scattered up and down the beach sunning themselves in the late afternoon sun. Mac eased the door open and started quietly up the stairs. I followed a few feet behind him. When he got to the top of the stairs, he slowly peered around the corner. He then motioned for me to join him and disappeared out of my field of vision. When I arrived at the top of the stairs, Mac was behind the counter looking in the slots where the keys were kept. The clerk had his back to us and was watching television about fourteen feet from where we were. Quick as a flash, Mac had found the key to 207 and had jumped back over the counter. We tiptoed up the stairs to the second deck and found the room. After fumbling around a few minutes, Mac got the door open and we went inside.

"Let's look for your clothes," Mac murmured. He then opened the closet and I started going through the dresser drawers. We found nothing that belonged to me. Mac discovered a suitcase in the closet that was locked. "Maybe they got some of your shit in here," he said, as he stomped in the sides. He encountered a few odds and ends including an eight by twelve-inch picture of someone in uniform. "Must be one of their husbands," he said smashing the photo with the heel of his shoe. On the dresser was a beauty kit that contained a pair of scissors. Mac smiled at me, picked up the scissors and went back to the closet. Taking dresses down off the hangars he started cutting them in half.

"The bitches gonna pay for robbing you, Messer," he chuckled sardonically, as he worked his way through the closet.

"Mac, let's get the hell out of here before someone catches us up here and has us arrested for breaking and entering," I said, feeling really scared. By that time, Mac had started cutting up the underwear he had found in the drawers. I was now in a total panic. Mac was in a frenzy and there was no stopping him. He ripped the sheets off the bed and cut them in half. When virtually everything in the room of value was destroyed, I finally managed to drag Mac out the door. We tiptoed back down the stairs. The clerk was still watching television. Mac hopped back over the counter and replaced the key. We were now in full flight to make our escape. About the time we hit the second or third step on our way down, the door opened. I looked up to see Jan and June with two of the biggest Marines I had ever seen in my life. We didn't slow down as we pounded down the stairs past them,

"Hi, Mac! Hi, John!" they called out pleasantly.

"Hi, Jan! Hi, June!" we responded and hit the sidewalk running.

Mac and I caught the Red Car for Los Angeles. We spent a very uncomfortable weekend trying to drink enough beer to keep us from worrying about spending the next six months in the brig. I was sure that, when we returned to the Helena, the police would be waiting for us. That was not to be. Why? I am not sure, but we speculated that it had something to do with Jan and June not wanting to have anything further to do with the Long Beach Police Department.

On the tenth of April, we got underway for our scheduled cruise to the Western Pacific. I was very excited, as we sailed out of the harbor. I had heard the older crewmembers talk about the fantastic liberty in Japan and Hong Kong and I was anxious to see it for myself. In six days, we would be arriving in Pearl Harbor. Mac had been on shore duty for three years before coming aboard the Helena and he was as excited as I was. There were only a couple of patients to care for on the ward and they were ambulatory. After a couple of days at sea, PO2 Henning sent Mac to work with PO3 Cruz in sickcall. I was swabbing the deck and PO2 Henning was sitting at the desk making chart entries. He had stopped working and sat watching me. "You know, I worry about you hanging out with McGlauglin, Messer," he said, after a moment of silence. I knew what he was talking about. I, too, had become concerned about some of Mac's behavior. Just the week before, when Mac and I were in the Locker Club, he had decided that I was drunk and needed to go back to the ship. I refused to go and, after a slight scuffle, he called the Shore Patrol for assistance. After interviewing us, they decided Mac was the problem and took him into custody. This had been a real source of embarrassment to Mac and he was determined to prove it had all been a mistake. I wasn't sure how much PO2 Henning was aware of, so I decided to play dumb.

"Why?" I asked.

"Well, for one thing he drinks too much. It's not so much how much he drinks as how he acts afterwards. I am going to put you two in opposite duty sections when we leave Pearl."

"Can I say something?"

"No, you can't. This is non-negotiable. You can go on liberty with him in Pearl, if you want to, but it will be the last time. Hank is working on a letter to send to the Bureau of Naval Personnel requesting that you be assigned to Hospital Corps School. This is your chance to turn your career around. I don't want you to do anything to screw that up. In fact, I am putting you in my liberty section. I'm going to watch out for your dumb ass until your orders come in."

I was relieved and deeply moved by P02 Henning's remarks and tears rimmed my eyes. The words had sounded rough and in the form of military authority. But I knew that within the framework of the military society, in which we lived and worked, that this was as close as he could come to telling me he really cared about me.

Upon our arrival in Pearl Harbor, all hands manned the rail in dress whites as we made our approach. There are few views in the world that I have ever seen that equal that of the Hawaiian Islands. Coming in from the open sea to these fabulous islands, it looks like paradise. One can see low clouds encircling lush, green mountains. They seemed to have just risen up out of the ocean floor. The dazzling blue sky is reflected in the water, changing to a pale green, as you enter the harbor. The atmosphere gives you a warm welcome as the swaying palms and tropical plants come slowly into view. We came alongside the same piers where the great battle ships of the Second World War had been tied when they were bombed by the Japanese only seventeen years earlier. In less than five years, the American Fleet had been rebuilt into the most powerful Navy the world had ever known. As I watched the boatswains mates secure the big hawser lines to the pier, my chest filled with pride.

Mac knew this was to be our last liberty together, so we decided to make the most of it. As soon as the gangplank was lowered, we were on our way to the Enlisted Men's Club. There, we sat laughing and talking the afternoon away. The tropical weather seemed to intensify the effect of alcohol. By five that evening, we were reeling drunk and should've returned to the Helena for the evening meal and a nap. But, that never even crossed our minds. Instead, we decided to take a taxi to Hotel Street in downtown Honolulu where we had heard the action was.

Hotel Street was one of those places that you'll find in all major seaport cities of the world. The streets were lined with cheap bars, hotels, gyp joints, and tattoo parlors. Sailors and women of questionable character seemed to be everywhere. Mac and I found a place to our liking in an upstairs club called the Circus Room. We had gone to the bar, sat down, and ordered a beer. In a short time, four sailors came to the door and looked inside. The one that appeared to be the leader looked at me, "THERE HE IS," he yelled, and flew at me in a rage. I saw him coming and leaped down off the barstool to protect myself. He managed to give me a glancing blow but I quickly recovered my balance. Mac had jumped off his stool when I did. Before I could recover, he hit my attacker, knocking him back onto a small table that went crashing to the floor. By that time, the other three had joined in the melee. Then, I heard a shrill whistle and, before I could figure out what happened, we were surrounded by what was called the HASP (Hawaiian Armed Service Police). These folks didn't play around and in seconds we were all being held in full nelsons. Well, it seemed all of the bartenders on Hotel Street had these little whistles to blow when there was a problem. It appeared there were about as many HASPS as there were sailors on the streets that night and their sole function was to maintain order. To say they were very good at what the did, would be an understatement. After a few minutes of discussion with the bartender, they arrested the four and took them away.

As the evening progressed, Mac and I became less and less rational and sought to find even a seedier place. We had walked down a side street and found a little beer bar. Strings of multi-colored beads hung down in the doorway. I remember the rattling sound they made as we pushed them aside to enter. A middle-aged, Oriental-looking lady was tending bar.

"Messer, I don't want you to drink anymore," Mac suddenly announced, just as we seated ourselves.

"The hell you say!" I responded. I wouldn't have been shocked by anything that Mac might have said at that point.

"Yeah, PO2 Henning is worried about you getting yourself into trouble this cruise and, frankly, so am I. I'll just have one more drink and then I'll take your boot ass back to the ship." Mac ordered a beer for himself and a Coke for me. I didn't resist. I knew he was still feeling a little resentment about the night the Shore Patrol had taken him into custody. I sipped my drink and nibbled from a bowl of cashews. I was thinking, maybe, the best thing would be for us to get on back to the Helena. Suddenly, Mac got up, carried his beer to the other end of the bar, and called the barmaid over. The place was small so I could hear the conversation.

"You see that guy down there?" he asked pointing toward me.

She turned and looked at me. "Yeah, what about him?" she questioned, looking like she regretted ever seeing either one of us.

"He killed a Taxi Driver and stuffed him into the trunk of his own cab. I'll keep him here and you go call the police." She looked back toward where I was sitting and I could see the look on her face. I knew one way or another the HASP was going to be coming for us. Maybe not for murder, but certainly for being out of our minds drunk. I dived for the door and took off running down the street. I knew Mac would be right behind me. Almost immediately, I heard a shrill whistle blow. I was sure it was the Oriental bartender's whistle and dived into the nearest door. I could hear what I imagined was the HASP running behind me, coming closer. An Oriental-looking tattoo artist had been watching the scenario unfold.

"I'll put you in private booth and hook you up good tattoo. If they ask me, I tell them you be here long time," he said. I could hear them getting closer with each passing second.

"Let's do it," I agreed.

A short time later, I boarded a bus and returned to Pearl Harbor and made my way back on board the Helena. I knew PO2 Henning would be on the ward and I didn't want him to see me inebriated, so I went to my assigned bunk in the compartment. The next morning, at the sound of reveille, I woke up with pain radiating from my left upper arm. Looking down, I saw the tattoo and the memories of the night before came flooding back. I was overcome with remorse and shame but it was too late. I dressed and went to the ward to assume my duties, trying to pretend nothing had happened. Quarters sounded and everyone not on duty went to muster. A few minutes later, I heard the sound of the men coming down the ladder to go to their workstations. PO2 Henning pushed through the door a little more forceful than was normal. "Where is that shithead McGlaughlin?" he asked, letting the door slam close behind him.

"He wasn't at quarters?" I asked, trying to act innocent.

"Would I be asking you if he was? Weren't you two together last night?"

"Yeah, but we separated about ten."

"Goddamn you, Messer. Tell me what happened."

"Well, he got all crazy and shit and was trying to get me arrested."

"That crazy fuck. Chief Martin went out on a limb for him once but you can bet your ass he won't do it again. Now you know what I was talking about the other day, don't you?"

I was sick with a hangover and tried to stay busy as the morning passed. I had been angry with Mac but I knew he had just been drunk.

Little by little, my concern for him overcame my anger as I waited to hear of his fate. I figured the HASP had probably just hauled him off to the drunk tank and he would be returned to the ship by noon. At 1300 hours, the phone rang. PO2 Henning answered it. "Yes, sir," he said. "Yes, sir," he repeated. His face became very grim as he looked over at me and continued to listen. After what seemed like an hour, he hung up.

"Well, don't look like Mac will be making this trip with us," he said. I had stopped my cleaning when the phone rang. My heart had jumped into my throat.

"What happened?" I asked, dreading to hear the answer.

"The Hawaiian police have him on some kind of grand theft charge. Go pack his shit up and I'll see if I can get you assigned to take it to him. Maybe you can find out what happened."

About 1330 the Yeoman and I were in the Helena's carryall with the duty driver headed for downtown Honolulu. Soon, we arrived at a long, single-story, white building in the middle of a huge, asphalt parking lot. Fifteen or so olive, drab vehicles with HASP stenciled on the side were parked out front. We exited the carryall and went inside. There was a large, army green desk just inside the door where the duty Sergeant was sitting. Behind him, about eight feet, was a steel wire partition that ran from the deck to the ceiling and extended across the whole width of the room. A locked door in the center led back to where the prisoners were being held. I could see Mac sitting on a bunk with his head in his hands about two cells back. The Sergeant had looked up when we first came in. I sat Mac's seabag down and the Yeoman handed him some papers.

"What's all this?" he asked, taking the records.

"Records on McGlaughlin that you folks requested," the Yeoman answered.

After some formalities of signing papers, I asked if I might be allowed a few words with Mac. The Sergeant was the amicable sort and agreed to let me talk to Mac for a few minutes. The Yeoman and the Driver opted to wait in the carryall. The Sergeant unlocked the door and led me back to Mac's cage. Mac stood up, reached out, and grabbed my hand. His face was contorted in fear and looked like he was on the verge of tears. His hair had been shaved off and I noticed that his scalp was black with some kind of grease or oil.

"Mac, what happened?" I asked. He sat back down on the bunk and his shoulders slumped forward.

"They said I broke into some kind of a boathouse and stole a boat. I must have got into the damn thing and got it started and drove it around until it ran out of gas. They said they found me passed out about fifteen feet away from the boat. My white jumper blouse was in the boat along with my wallet and ID Card," he sighed. "I'm in deep shit here, Messer."

"What's that shit in your hair, Mac?" I asked.

"When I woke up in here I had this black crap all over me. One of the guards said I broke into a five-gallon can of grease. Apparently I rubbed it all over my body. I must have thought they wouldn't be able to see me in the dark. Who in the hell knows?" he added and smiled meekly.

"Time's up. You'll have to go now," the guard called, coming over and unlocking the door. I stood up, shook Mac's hand, walked to the door, and looked back where he was standing. His face was filled with agony and despair. He tried forcing a smile but it wouldn't come. I gave a final wave and hurried out the door.

We were to be in Pearl for a total of five days. After my experience on Hotel Street with Mac, I had lost my desire to see any more of the Island. PO2 Henning knew I was suffering from guilt over what had happened and tried to cheer me up.

"Tomorrow is the last day here in Honolulu, Messer. What do you say you and I take that four-hour tour and see some of the sights?"

"No, I saw all I wanted to see of Honolulu. Besides, I pretty well blew what money I had that first night."

"Well, at least you got that tattoo to remind you of what a great time you had," he teased.

"Yeah, I got something I just as soon forget about."

"You know, Messer, it's kind of funny when you think about it. If you go to any big seaport city in the world and wander around you can always find the seedy part of town where all the low-lifes hang out. And, of course, there is always one place that is a little bit bigger shithole than all the others. Once you're there know what you'll find?"

"No! What?"

"A drunk ass sailor, talking to this old, fat-ass, toothless barmaid, who no one in his right mind would be caught dead with. Now, he could just as well be uptown in some classy lounge where the ladies are, but no, he is down there in the shit rolling around with the hogs. You ever wonder about that?" he asked, studying my reaction. I knew PO2 Henning was trying to teach me something about life.

"No, I guess I never did," I answered.

"Well, isn't that kind of what you and Mac did?" I didn't answer. "But tomorrow, you and I are going to see the other side of life," he said and smiled over at me.

"Okay!" I laughed.

After our tour, I had to admit Waikiki beach, with her miles of beautiful white sand shining in the tropical sun, was indeed a long way from the tattoo parlor on Hotel Street.

On May 28, 1957, exactly one year to the day after I had joined the Navy, the Helena arrived in Yokosuka, Japan. It was one of the most exciting days of my life. It was thrilling for me to think that we had tied up at the same pier where only a few short years before the Japanese Navy had made repairs on her great battleships. My adrenaline was pumping as the eight of us from "H" Division requested permission to go ashore. We walked the mile or so to the front gate, turned right, and headed for Club Alliance (enlisted men's club) two blocks away. The smell of open sewers left an impression on me that I would forever identify with being in the Orient. The sound of horns and engines from small cars filled the air. Hotels and bars were everywhere. Upon arriving at the Club Alliance, we went to the dining area and hurriedly ate. We then rushed to exchange our money to yen and headed out into the city.

Upon leaving the club, we turned right and started walking in the opposite direction from which we had come. We walked several minutes taking in the sights, sounds, and smells. Occasionally, we would stop at a vending stand and look at the many coffee cups, cigarette lighters, ball caps, and small toys that seem to be everywhere. We soon came upon a white, two-story hotel. Over the entrance, in English, it proudly displayed a sign that said, "New Shima Hotel and Bar." It looked inviting so, after some discussion among ourselves, we decided to go inside.

As we walked through the door, we came into an open, dimly-lighted room. On the far side, was a long bar that ran the full length of the wall. On each end of the bar, was an open space to allow the bartender to go in and out. On the left-hand side of the entrance, an older woman was sitting on a stool. When she saw us come in, she got up and came toward us smiling and nodding her head, almost bowing. She indicated with both arms for us to have a seat. As my eyes adjusted to the darkness, I could see a young Japanese girl sitting at a table to the left of where we had entered. In front of her a couple of feet, was the staircase that led up to the second floor of the hotel. The older woman said something to her in Japanese and she disappeared. The older woman came to our table and we all ordered beer. In a few minutes, the Japanese girl who had gone upstairs returned. Then, one by one, the room started to fill up with beautiful young Japanese women. I estimated the oldest to be, maybe, twenty-two and the youngest around eighteen.

"You reckon all these girls are prostitutes?" PO3 Pugh asked, looking at PO2 Henning.

"I doubt it. Hell, they are just kids," replied PO2 Henning.

None of the young ladies made any attempt to come near our table. They seemed shy and withdrawn. We weren't quite sure what to make of the situation so we finished our beer and ordered another round from the older woman. "Sailor man want talk to girl?" she asked, rather casually as she set our beer in front of us. We smiled at each other and moved uncomfortably in our seats. She laughed at us teasingly and spoke to the girls in Japanese. Several of the girls walked timidly to our table and joined us. In a short time, we were all laughing and talking like we had known each other forever.

The rate of exchange was eighteen hundred-yen for five American dollars. A hundred yen would take you anywhere in the city by taxi. A fifth of Kentucky Bourbon could be bought at the club for $1.25. A quart of beer in the local bars cost seventy-yen. Ice and table service for the whole evening was three hundred. For the first time in my life, I seemed to have enough money.

The New Shima became a regular hangout for "H" Division. Soon, we called the older lady "Mamason" and knew all the girls by their first names. I had met Fumiko the first night we were there and we soon became very good friends. At first, the language barrier was a problem but, little by little, we hammered out a vocabulary that enabled us to communicate. Our time together was somewhat limited as only Petty Officers were allowed overnight liberty. Non-rated had what we referred to as "Cinderella Liberty," meaning we were due back on board at midnight.

The Helena became the flagship of the Seventh Fleet upon our arrival in Yokosuka. There was a great amount of tension between the Nationalist and Chinese Communists at that time. We spent considerable amount of time in waters off of Taiwan and sailed in and out of Hong Kong on a regular basis. But, the majority of our port time was spent in Yokosuka and the corpsmen from "H" Division could always be found at the New Shima.

We had returned to Yokosuka in the middle of July and quickly made our way to the New Shima. All the regular girls seemed to be there with the exception of Fumiko. I was very disappointed and nagged at Mamason to please tell me where she was. "She go home. Maybe, never no come back," she informed me.

I had actually received a letter from Fumiko in Hong Kong and she had told me she would be waiting for me when we returned. I just couldn't believe she would leave without giving me some kind of a message. I continued to return to the New Shima in hopes of seeing her. I would invariably get drunk, become very depressed, and mope around. Everyone was having a great time, as usual, but I just couldn't seem to join in the fun. I continued to beg Mamason to please tell me where Fumiko had gone. I knew there was some kind of an explanation if I could just get her to tell me.

It was two days before we were to make another voyage into the Taiwan waters and I had gone with PO2 Henning to the New Shima. We had sat down and ordered a drink. Mamason came to my side of the table and was setting the drinks down. "Fumiko come soon, talk you," she said, very quietly looking at me with a great deal of compassion.

I waited very impatiently for her arrival. After what seemed like an eternity, I finally saw her slip through the side door. She wasn't wearing western style clothes that she worked in but was in a traditional-style, blue and white print, Japanese Kimono. She didn't join us at the table, but instead went up the stairs. Mamason had returned to her usual perch on the barstool. When she saw Fumiko she looked at me and motioned with her head for me to follow her. I quickly excused myself and wound my way up the stairs. I found her sitting quietly on the bed in her room. She was looking down at her hands and did not look up right away. She seemed sad and withdrawn.

"What is it, Fumiko? Where have you been, baby?" I asked.

"Please, sit," she said, moving her legs to give me room and patting the bed. "You nice man, John-son. I like you so much. I have tell you something." I sat down quietly without responding. She didn't say anything right away. After a few minutes, she took a deep breath. "When war finish, my family very poor. Many brothers and uncles die. My father, he very old man and my family no having nothing to eat." She hesitated and looked at me with tears in her eyes. I listened intently and a sad foreboding entered my soul. "One day, rich man come to my house and asked my Papason if he sell me for much money. My Papason never no talk me. But my Mamason, she tell me I have to go with man to save family. She say me, 'I so sorry, but you never no come back here,' then we cry together. I don't understand that time, but later man who buy me, he say everything me. I have to work here as prostitute for seven years to pay for money he give my Papason. I no get pay, but I can keep tip from customer."

"Damn! Have all the girls here been sold into prostitution?"

"Yes, everyone same same."

"Now I know why everyone looks so young and innocent."

"John-son, about six months before you come my seven years finish. I meet nice American boy here. He on ship, too. We marry and someday I go States. I know you mad me now, but when he go, I bored. I come here to see friends sometime and, then, I meet you. I so sorry you like me too much. But you good man, I no likey you suffer."

"Fumiko, you love this American Sailor?"

"He very nice man. No very handsome like you, but very nice. Japanese man, no marry girl, she no virgin. Prostitute girl no have happy life. Maybe little business or marry American boy, she can do. Love not important for me."

I was devastated by what I had heard, but I understood. I knew this tender soul had endured years of suffering and had been ostracized from her family. My heart was broken for her, but I was from another world and I didn't want to cause her any more pain. "Come, we drink together," she said, and so it was.

Down through the corridor of my years, from time to time as I have sat quietly alone remembering my youth, she has come to me. A long, long, time ago in a very far off place, I sat with her and she tried to heal my aching heart. I remember her with fondness. When the evening ended she went from me and I never saw nor heard from her again.

On the early morning of the fifteenth, I was making an empty bed in the back of the ward when I heard Hank Minot rush through the door. "Where is that goddamn Messer?" he asked PO2 Henning. I looked up from where I had been kneeling and saw PO2 Henning pointing at me. "Get your ass over here, Messer," Minot ordered. I knew something had happened. I climbed out from between the racks, stepping over the linen on the floor, and walked over to the desk where Hank was standing. PO2 Henning was sitting at the desk watching the scenario unfold.
"Now what?" I asked.
"Pack your shit up. You're off of here in thirty minutes. You've got orders to Hospital Corps School in San Diego. You'll be going to the Naval Station and they'll get you a flight out to Treasure Island. Hurry your ass up. We're getting underway in less than two hours," he said, smiling broadly.

I had never suspected that I would be leaving the Helena before the cruise was over. I had been aboard just over a year and had found a happy, safe place with some of the finest men I had ever known. I felt closer to Walt Henning than I did my own brother. I was having mixed emotions as I went to the compartment to pack my seabag.

I returned to the ward to get some odds and ends. I had gone to the locker in the back of the ward where I had stored a few things and started packing. The men started drifting into the ward and gathered around the desk, waiting to say goodbye. Suddenly, the realization that I was leaving and would never see them again overcame me. PO2 Whining came over and helped me with the last of my things. Soon, I had it all packed and was ready to go. I carried my seabag over to the desk and set it down. I shook hands all around, putting off saying goodbye to PO2 Henning until last. He grabbed my hand and embraced me. I was trying, with little success, to hold back the sobs and regain my composure; after a few seconds, he pushed me away. "Come on kid, this is what we have been waiting for, isn't it? And you better be honor man of your class. If you aren't, I'm coming down there to San Diego and kick your ass when we get back," he said, trying to sound lighthearted. Fighting back the tears, I found my way to the gangplank and requested permission to go ashore.

Portsmouth Naval Hospital

Eight to twelve inches of snow was on the ground when I arrived at the Naval Hospital in Portsmouth, Virginia. My teeth chattered and the cold wind cut through my peacoat like a knife. I got out of the taxi in front of the gate and the guard directed me to the Personnel Office straight up the street a half-mile. It was now the eighth of January, 1958. I had left San Diego on the fifteenth of December and spent a couple of weeks with my family in Arkansas. When I received my orders to proceed to the East Coast, I was less than enthusiastic. The thought of leaving California saddened me.

I had arrived at Hospital Corps School in San Diego the latter part of August the previous year. The school was at the backside of the old Balboa Naval Hospital compound. This part of Southern California is truly one of the garden spots of the world. The warm weather, tropical plants, and swaying palms give one the feeling of being in paradise. As you came out the front gate, turned right, and walked a few blocks, you would arrive at the famous San Diego Zoo, located in the center of Balboa Park. The opposite direction would take you to downtown San Diego. There, one could take a bus to one of the many beaches in the area. Mexico was only a few miles to the south if one was feeling adventurous.

A short time after arriving, our company formed and we started classes. At our orientation, the Commanding Officer informed us we would be completing the equivalent of a two-year Pre-Med course in just 16 weeks. Classes were eight hours a day, five days a week. We were assigned to a port and starboard duty status that ensured we would be on board every other day for our studies.

There were thirty-five students who started in my class; twenty-seven would graduate. Two of my fellow classmates were in the Naval Reserves and were members of the San Francisco Police Department. We got along well and I did most of my studying with them. One of my fellow students had also come from the fleet. He had been in the Navy for four years and had agreed to reenlist for Corps School. He was appointed our Company Adjutant and became known to us all as Daisy.

The pressure of a Navy "A" School is hard to imagine if one has never experienced it. A two-hour class every other day in a community college or university is one thing. But to receive information eight hours a day, five days a week as fast as it can be given, is quite another. Our classes consisted of Anatomy, Physiology, First Aid, Nursing Procedures, Dietary Principles, Preventive Medicine, Pharmacology, Toxicology, Chemistry, Nuclear, Chemical and Biological War Defense, and Laboratory Procedures. In the Pharmacology class, the Metric, Avoirdupois, and Apothecary systems of weights and measures were studied ad infinitum. Most nights, long after the lights were out, we sat huddled around a small table studying with flashlights.

I never really learned how to study in high school and the first few weeks were difficult. Failing three exams, or having one's average fall below seventy percent, got you a fast set of orders to the fleet. I knew I had been lucky to escape the deck and the hot engine rooms of the Helena on my first sea duty assignment. I figured my chances of doing so again were practically zero. My two police friends both had completed two-year degrees at a local community colleges. They had developed good study habits and I soon adapted myself to their methods. The first exam or two, my grades came back in the low seventies. Not only was that embarrassing, it also frightened me. I renewed my efforts. Slowly, I worked my way up into the top twenty-five percent of the class.

Daisy and I had been drawn together because of our past experience in the fleet. He was a handsome, blue-eyed blond and wore his hair in a crew cut. He was an inch or two shorter than myself and tended toward the stocky side. He had an easygoing disposition and was popular with the students and staff alike.

The first week or so I had met a young lady while on liberty by the name of Ruthey Gentile. She was full of fun and laughter. When I was on duty, she would come to the base and just hang out. On one occasion, she brought her younger sister, Gina. I knew from the stories Ruthey had told me about Gina, that she had a wild streak. Daisy met her the night of her visit and became completely infatuated with her. I warned him to be careful and related some of the stories I had heard. This only served to increase his interest. He hounded me until I finally asked Gina to go out with us on a double date.

Four weeks into the course, Daisy re-enlisted and received his re-enlistment bonus. He and Gina immediately went on a wild weekend and she somehow convinced him to buy her a car. I was seeing Ruthey on a regular basis by this time and had the unfortunate experience of seeing the whole scenario unfold. A short time later, Gina dropped Daisy and went to San Francisco with another sailor for a weekend. Daisy became distraught and started to drink; his grades plummeted. We all became very concerned about him, as he flunked one exam after another. No amount of counseling or consoling could get him back on track. In a very short period of time, our company adjutant had orders to a destroyer. Perhaps, I learned a more valuable lesson from observing what happened to my friend than I did in my classes. I knew the six years Daisy had given the Navy to become a corpsman was now all for nothing. I could only speculate as to what his future might be. Knowing that, linked with knowing that Walt Henning would be checking on me when the Helena returned, became my motivation. I completed the course with a respectable grade point average of 84.3.

As I started up the snow-covered sidewalk at the Portsmouth Naval Hospital, I could see a large, tall, dome-like structure at the end of the street. Two long wings, six floors high, jutted out toward me on each side. The rose-colored, brick building on my left was relatively new and looked to be about three stories high. I could see long, white outbuildings scattered throughout the compound. As I trudged forward, the gray, leafless trees on each side of the sidewalk waved at me with their barren branches. I soon arrived at the Personnel Office. It was located in one of the many typical-looking outbuildings. I found the entrance door on the east side with two feet of snow drifted up against it. I couldn't get it to budge. After much pulling and tugging, I finally managed to pry it open. Sitting just inside the door, was a much-amused PO2 who had been observing me. Once inside, I dropped my bags, looked at him and waited. After a moment's hesitation, he grabbed his cup and went to the coffeepot. Upon his return, he reached out his hand toward me.

"Just checking in?" he asked.

"Yeah!" I answered, and handed him the brown, sealed, manila envelope that contained my orders. He ripped it open.

"Just got out of Corps School, huh? San Diego! Damn! How did you end up in Shit City?" he asked, as he continued flipping through my record.

"Just lucky, I guess," I answered, shrugging my shoulders.

"I'd give six months pay just to be anywhere on the West Coast," he continued. I didn't answer.

"Messer, I'm going to send you down to the BEQ (Bachelor Enlisted Quarters). Did you see that reddish brick building as you came in the gate?" I nodded.

"Take this check-in sheet with you and get HM2 Wilson to sign it and bring it back with you in the morning at 0800. We have a half-dozen other new corpsmen that will be checking in with you. Lieutenant Commander Angelina will be taking you around for orientation tomorrow. Hang on while I type you out a chow pass and liberty card."

I put the liberty card and chow pass in my wallet, shouldered my seabag, and walked back up the street to the BEQ. It set well back off the street a respectable distance among a dozen or so barren trees. Must be nice here in the summer, I thought, as I followed the curved sidewalk to the front door. Pushing the door open, I came into a big dormitory where a dozen or so men about my age were lounging. A couple of them looked at me curiously but didn't say anything. To my left, I could see a small office with a couple of men in uniform moving around. A little black sign was mounted over the door with the lettering: MASTER AT ARMS SHACK.

The office was no more than twelve feet long by nine feet wide and looked crowded with a desk and couple of chairs. The man sitting behind the desk seemed to take up half of the office space. He appeared to weigh a minimum of two hundred and seventy pounds. His huge, slightly-balding head looked like it was sitting directly on top of his shoulders. His powerful barrel chest moved heavily up and down as he painstakingly wrote in a long, green logbook. His hand holding the pen looked like a big beefy ham. He smiled at his frail companion who was standing by the desk observing him. His huge teeth caught my attention. They were powerful and spaced well apart. I remember thinking they looked like they had been driven into his gums with a hammer. He said something I didn't quite understand to the smaller man. The big fellow had a deep, whiskey voice and his laugh sounded raspy. His nametag identified him as HM3 Coons. He had three long, red hash marks on the lower left sleeve of his undress blues. Each hash mark indicated four years of service. With that kind of a promotion history, he was either dumb as hell or had been in some very serious trouble. I suspected the latter.

In contrast, the other man couldn't have been more than five feet, four inches tall. He was frail and had an indistinguishable weakness about him. His identification tag read HM2 Wilson. He was wearing four hashmarks. "Another rate grabber," I said to myself. HM2 Wilson was the senior petty officer assigned to the BEQ, but it was obvious the HM3 ran the place. I had stopped at the half door and stood waiting. HM3 Coons looked up at me with big, menacing, gray eyes.

"What do you want, boy?" he asked.

"Just checking in, sir." He handed me a big thick notebook filled with instructions.

"These are the BEQ Regulations. Read these through and, when you're finished, I'll need you to sign a form that states you understand them." I glanced through them quickly, signed the form and handed it back to him.

I was assigned to the second floor, "B" dormitory, and given two sheets and a blanket. I made my way up the stairs to my assigned space. Two side-by-side, seven-foot-high, five-feet-wide, dark green lockers, spaced every eight feet, divided the dormitory into cubes. Each space had a bunk bed and a small writing table with a desk lamp. Some of the men had hung up curtains at the entrance of their areas to give them more privacy. I opened my big, double-door locker and put my clothes away. I was delighted to see it was adequate to hold my uniforms and the few civilian clothes I owned. Turning to the bunk beds, I noticed the bottom was occupied. I put my sheets on the mattress of the top bunk. The overhead blower was on and the warm air made me feel cozy.

I had just finished my bed and jumped down on the deck when I sensed a movement to my left. I looked over and saw a young sailor, about nineteen, had entered and was busy opening the other locker.

He was about five foot, ten inches tall with a slender build. He took off his peacoat and hung it inside. I noticed he was strikingly handsome with a head of black, wavy hair and olive skin. His almond-colored eyes smiled at me as he turned to introduce himself.

"I'm Rick Sandaval," he said shyly.

"John Messer," I said, grabbing his hand.

"Welcome aboard, John. Just checking in?"

"Yeah, just got out of Corps School."

"You'll be working the wards then. I've been here about three months. I work down on the old C-units on a Med. Ward. Have any idea where they'll put you?"

"No, I'm suppose to check-in with some other people tomorrow. I understand a LCDR. Angelena will be taking us around."

"Yeah, she is in charge of training new corpsmen. She's okay. You'll like her. You'll be checking in and taking a couple of written exams. You'll probably have the weekend off. I'll be going home to Connecticut to see my Mom and younger sister this weekend. You'll have the place to yourself. Have you been to chow?"

"No, I don't even know where the chow hall is located."

"I'm going to kick back here a half hour, then I'll show you where it is if you want."

The next morning at 0800, I reported to the Petty Officer at the Personnel Office. There were two other corpsmen and a corpswave sitting in front of his desk. Within five minutes, another corpswave and a corpsman joined us. "Looks like we're all here," commented the Petty Officer, as he stood up and handed us each a check-in sheet. "Put your name, rank, and serial number across the top," he ordered. We silently filled out the long, white paper and waited. At 0815, a tall, thin woman came into the office. She looked to be about forty and her hair was streaked with gray. She smiled politely at the Petty Officer, as she neared his desk.

"How many we got this morning, Miller?" she asked, politely.

"Six today, Commander," he answered and stood up. She gave us all a glancing smile.

"The first thing I want to do is to get you over to I & E for a little test. It's painless and it will help me determine what subjects you're weak in. It'll cover all the subjects you had in Corps School. Any subject you make less than seventy percent on will require a few classes," she announced, smiling happily at us all.

We slugged our way through the ice and snow a few blocks to one of the many old, white buildings and climbed the stairs to a classroom. There, we were greeted by another PO2 in his early twenties. After a short discussion with LCDR Angelena, he led us into an adjoining room. "Have a seat," he ordered, and we quickly sat down. He distributed a booklet and an answer sheet to each of us.

"Open the booklet to the first page and commence when you're ready," he instructed, glancing up at the clock.

For the next hour and a half, we poured over the exam book. I had just finished the last question and looked up when the PO2 called, "Time." He quickly gathered up the booklets and answer sheets. "Just keep your seats. I'll have these graded for you in a minute," he declared. We all looked at each other expectantly. LCDR Angelena came into the room and chatted amicably with us as we waited. In a few minutes, the PO2 returned with our test sheets and passed them out.

"Who's Messer?" he asked. I raised my hand. "Congratulations, you're the only one that passed them all," he commented. LCDR Angelena smiled at me but somehow I got the feeling she wasn't all that pleased. After making the rounds to Medical Records, Disbursing Office, Chaplains Office, and Special Services, we ended up in LCDR Angelena's private classroom.

"Have a seat," she invited and handed out three typed pages of medical procedures. "These are all of the practical things you'll need to learn. I'll expect you to have the senior corpsman who checks you off on these things initial it beside the procedure. When you have finished everything on all three pages, return it to me. It'll become part of your permanent training record." I flipped through the pages quickly feeling a little overwhelmed.

"Now, let's talk a little about the Corps that makes up the Medical Department in their order of importance. First we have medical officers who have completed medical school and are the Navy's physicians that make up the medical corps. That school can either be here or in another country that has an approved curriculum. Next, we have the Nurse Corps. All of their members are also commissioned officers. They are required to have completed an approved course of nursing and have a current license. They will have either completed a three-year or four-year program. On the administrative side, we have the Medical Service Corps. They, too, are commissioned officers filling specific rolls. They may or may not have a degree, depending on their function. Often times corpsmen or corpswaves with the rank of E-6 or above are selected to become MSC officers. Last, but not least, we have the Hospital Corps, which makes up about 80% of the personnel in the Navy's Medical Department. That, of course, is what you're all members of. Are there any questions up to this point?" We looked around at each other but none of us were inclined to say anything.

After a moment's hesitation, she continued. "Let's talk about the career pattern of the average hospital corpsman. You all have completed four months of basic Hospital Corps School and are now ready to go into your next phase of training. You will be working on the wards where you will receive specific instructions for various procedures. All new hospital corpsmen and corpswaves are required to do a minimum of six months ward duty. Some of you will go on to become senior corpsmen. The backbone of patient care in the Navy is its hospital corpsmen and corpswaves. Now, when you complete your six months, you'll have the opportunity to request a "C" School and become one of the many technicians made up from the Hospital Corps. Your six months on the ward is going to be both rewarding, and demanding. We work on what we call an AM and PM system. Ward corpsmen work one week of AMs and then one of PMs. The PM week starts with a clean up in the barracks at 0900 and is done again at 1300. At 1430 there's a muster in the main lobby, just outside of the messing facility in the main hospital, for roll call and inspection. From 1500 until 2300 you'll work your assigned ward. Every other night, you'll have the duty from 2300 until the following morning at 0700. On your duty nights, there are times you'll be assigned special two-hour watches on critically ill patients. Now, the weekend is when it becomes a little challenging for you. The AM crew is off the weekend. That means the PM crew works from 1500 until 2300 on Friday night and then reports back at 0700 the following morning and works until 2300 that night. On Sunday, they work from 0700 until 2100. That's a pretty grueling eighteen hours. You'll be happy to hear that during your AM week you'll only work from 0700 until 1500, Monday through Friday. You won't have any duty days and will be off the following weekend. Now, in reference to nights, that will depend on the need of each individual ward. Normally, you can expect to do a tour of nights about twice during your six months of ward duty." LCDR Angelena hesitated and looked at us individually. "Any questions?" she asked. I raised my hand.

"Yes, Messer!"

"I was wondering. The Saturday you work sixteen hours, is it possible to have a two hour special watch before coming back Sunday for the fourteen hour day?"

"Yes, it is. Any other questions?" We sat quietly.

"Very well! You're all going to be off this weekend, but before you go, I have your assignments." I listened as she read off our names.

"Messer, you're to report to LCDR Smith at 1430 on Monday. She's located on the second floor of the main hospital."

The following Monday started my career working the wards. I mustered in the barracks at 0900 for the daily clean up as LCDR Angelena had directed. Two other men and myself were assigned to the head next to the dormitory where I berthed. The work, itself, went fairly fast but we had to wait for PO3 Coons to give us his blessing before we could leave our assigned space. He, apparently, enjoyed the power play and it was 1000 before we were secured. We mustered again at 1300 and repeated the process. I then took a shower, shined my shoes, and dressed in a crisp white uniform. At 1430, all the ward corpsmen were mustered inside the main hospital for roll call and personnel inspection. Afterwards, the Master-At-Arms directed me to LCDR Smith's office. "It's at the back of ward 20 on the right. You can't miss it," he informed me.

I found the ward a few feet to the right of the elevator and proceeded toward the rear. At the very back, on the right hand side, I found the office. As I approached, I could see someone who I assumed was LCDR Smith. She was busy filling out papers of some sort. I estimated her to be in her early forties. She was impeccably dressed in a starched, white uniform. On her head, neatly pinned in place, was a white nurse's cap with gold stripes designating her rank. On the right-hand side of her collar, she wore a gold oak leaf indicating her rank of LCDR. On the left side, she wore a gold leaf that was a little longer. This designated her as a Nurse Corps officer. Her blondish hair was cut short and was well up off of her collar. She was of medium height and her build, although not heavy, had taken on a middle-age look. I stopped and knocked gently on the side of the door facing. She laid her pen down, almost ceremoniously, and looked up. "Come in," she ordered. I approached her desk and assumed the parade rest position. "Sit down, please," she invited in a commanding tone, and nodded at a chair that sat to the right of her desk. I sat down at attention and waited. I could see she had my personnel record open and, obviously, had been reading it. "I see here you were aboard ship for a year before you went to Corps School." Her voice was cold and official. I found myself wondering how long it had been since this woman had rendered any patient care. Judging by her age and rank, I calculated she had probably been on active duty when the Second World War started. I sensed her heart belonged to another time.

"Yes, ma'am."

"I'll expect more out of you than I do the other young corpsmen, Messer."

"I'll do my best, ma'am."

"Good," she closed my record. "I'm going to assign you to ward 20 and 21. That's the ward you just passed through to get here. You're to report to LCDR Foster. Any questions?"

"No, ma'am."

"Very well," she said. Glancing at the clock to her left, she wrote something on a long form attached to my record.

"That'll be all then. You'll find LCDR Foster on the ward. Give her this form," she directed, as she handed me the paper she had been writing on.

When I had walked through the ward to get to LCDR Smith's office, I had not really taken a good look at what was going on. Now that I knew this was going to be my workstation, it suddenly came alive. I came out of the office onto the ward, turned left, and walked toward the desk. It was located on my left, just to the right of the main entrance. I could see three uniformed nurses busy doing some type of paper work. One was older and wore the rank of LCDR on her cap. I assumed this was LCDR Foster. The other two were younger, probably in their early twenties. I noted one was an Ensign and the other a LTJG (Lieutenant Junior Grade). The ward was long and filled with patients, beds, and bedside lockers. I saw an adjoining glassed-in salon on my right that was apparently used when there was an overflow of patients. As I walked toward the desk, I passed four men sitting at a small table playing cards. They gave me a passing glance as they laughed and argued good naturedly with each other. I estimated that there were at least thirty to forty patients on the ward. Many were in bed. Some were hooked up to overhead frames with complicated-looking devices. Several sat next to their beds either reading, conversing, or just idly looking off into space. They were all dressed in the ward uniform of light blue pajamas. Some were wearing, over their pajamas, a lighter colored, blue robe with white pinstripes that ran vertically. Half way down the ward, on my right-hand side was an older man who had lost his legs. His big, owl-like eyes followed my trek down the aisle.

I approached who I assumed to be LCDR Foster. She was bent over the desk, absorbed in her work. I was sure she was aware of my presence, so I waited. After a pause, she looked up.

"LCDR Foster?" I asked.

"Yes!" she responded, and looked at the long form I was holding. "Oh, you're the new Corpsman. I knew you were coming. The PM shift will be here in a couple of minutes. When they get here, I'll be giving a ward report to the charge nurse. You'll need to listen, too. I'll introduce you as soon as I'm finished."

The two younger nurses seemed to be unaware of my existence. As I stood waiting, I took a good look around. The sudden realization that I was going to be working with some very seriously ill patients overwhelmed me. The feeling of incompetence and insecurity made butterflies flutter in my stomach.

A young nurse and two corpsmen walked onto the ward at exactly 1445. I had seen one of the corpsmen at the PM muster. The other, I didn't recognize. I looked at the nurse I was going to be working for. The first thing I noticed was her hair. It was the color of reddish-gold cornsilk and curled up on the ends. Her skin was light and smooth with no freckles. She looked like she was a little over five feet tall, healthy, and not at all on the thin side. I moved to the front of the desk and waited for the report to begin. The redheaded nurse looked at me and gave me a dazzling smile. A pleasant, comfortable feeling came over me, and my butterflies settled down. LCDR Foster droned on with the report. Finally, she finished and turned to me. "This is our new Corpsman, Hospitalman Messer. Messer this is LTJG Pagendarm. She'll be working with you this evening," she introduced. LTJG Pagendarm smiled at me again and I nodded. I wasn't quite sure what to do, so I waited. After the initial commotion was over, I approached LTJG Pagendarm.

"I have no idea what I'm supposed to do," I declared, with a great deal of trepidation.

"Don't worry! I'm sure things will be just fine. I haven't been working orthopedics that long myself. But we'll teach you everything you need to know," she said, and smiled reassuringly. I felt a warm fondness stir inside me.

Portsmouth Naval Hospital served thousands of active duty and retired military personnel and their families in the surrounding areas. Dozens of ships were home ported in Norfolk, right across the river. In addition, Marines were airlifted from Camp Lejune, North Carolina and Airmen came in from the Langley Airforce Base. A good number of our patients came to us on the PM shift from motorcycle and automobile accidents. It was not uncommon to have as many as six new admissions on any given day. They normally arrived either from the Emergency Room or Surgery. Each new admission required a tremendous amount of nursing and tons of paper work. The more seriously ill patients resided on ward 20. Orthopedic problems are not resolved overnight and often require months of hospitalization. Ward 21 was the sleeper ward and held forty or so rehabilitation patients that were waiting for old wounds to heal or to be discharged.

The one Nurse Corps officer and the two hospital corpsmen that worked the PM shift had little time for chitchat. It was a dash from the time we went on duty until we were relieved. Treatments, giving medications, receiving and admitting new patients, PM care, and charting made for a never-ending cycle.

The AM shift was another world. LCDR Foster, two other nurses, and three corpsmen made up the day crew. One of the three corpsmen was a Hospitalman by the name of Brown. He was the Senior Corpsman and worked straight days from 0800 until 1630. LCDR Foster was a frail, hardened-looking, wizened, older woman in her early fifties. She had been in the Navy during the Second World War but had left shortly after it was over. Eventually, her love for the Navy and the fast pace of military life brought her back on active duty with a reserve commission. She ran a tight ship and delighted in dressing down a troublemaker. Any new arrival who mistook her sex for weakness was in for a big surprise. The patients who were long term residents of the ward had occasionally made that mistake. These same folks would later delight at her wrath when it was directed toward someone else.

LCDR Foster adopted certain corpsmen as pets and treated them as though they were her sons. With these individuals, she was either blind to their imperfections, or chose to ignore them. My first few weeks on AMs, I was responsible for direct patient care. This meant I made the beds, gave bed-baths, emptied bedpans, gave fresh water, and shaved the patients when it was necessary. LCDR Foster insisted that all the patients confined to their beds have their feet rubbed down daily with cocoa butter. Each morning, after completing this process, we would walk from patient to patient and she would inspect them head to toe.

I soon came to love my work and ward 20 and 21. I respected and admired LCDR Foster and delighted in the presence of LTJG Pagendarm. LCDR Foster had insinuated on many occasions that when Hospitalman Brown received his orders, I would, in all probability, be moved up to senior corpsman. With that in mind, I doubled my efforts.

The Navy, when feasible, tries to recognize any civilian training that her personnel may have. Often times, commissions or special designations, are granted when certain guidelines are met. It's an eternal struggle to keep qualified people in certain fields due to the dire need and the rapid turnover. Many times, personnel are assigned to tasks they are barely qualified to do or have been inadequately trained for. In a short period of time, I was drawing blood for laboratory procedures, passing out medications, giving injections, catheterizing, and performing clinical and surgical procedures. In civilian life, this would most certainly have required more than four months of formal training.

The first patient I catheterized was a poor airman by the name of Shaw from the Langley Airforce Base. I carried the Catherization Tray to his bedside along with the Handbook of the Hospital Corps. Upon my approach to his bed, he looked at me nervously.
"What'cha doing wi dat, man?"
"Sorry, Shaw, but I have to catheterize you."
"You ever do dis befoe, man?"
"No, but it don't look that hard. I've seen it done several times." Poor Shaw was at my mercy. I had him lay down and commenced the procedure. After each step, I would read the instructions and continue on to the next. He soon began to cry softly.
"Someday, someone gonna do dis to you and I hope you remember dis day." he proclaimed through his tears. Somehow, we got through it without any real problem. I would have preferred one of the nurses to assist me. But in those days females weren't allowed to do such things when male corpsmen were available. I've been catheterized several times since that infamous day and I would like for Shaw, wherever he may be, to know that his curse is still upon me. I never experience this

procedure that I don't hear his soft whimpers and hear his words of damnation.

Emptying bedpans has never been one of my most favorite tasks. On an open military ward you get to carry the pan down the aisle in front of the patients and past the desk where the nurses are busy with their never ending cycle of paper work. At one time or another, everyone who has ever endeavored to do nursing care has had, or will have, their opportunity to render this service to his fellow man. On one busy afternoon, I was rushing to try to complete my nursing duties when I was summoned to help one of our patients off the bedpan. I rushed to his side, lifted him off, covered it, and carried it to the hopper room. The hopper was a contraption that flushed, washed, and rinsed the pan. It had a very convenient foot pedal that you pushed at the various stages during the procedure. I had finished the flush and hit the pedal for wash. Unfortunately, I had hit the lever to open the hopper by mistake. It was in mid-cycle of flush and still retained a good amount of fecal material. When the hopper lid opened, it blew the material into my face and the upper part of my white uniform. I didn't have to announce to anyone what had happened. The odor accompanied me to the desk where LTJG Pagendarm, through fits of laughter, gave me permission to return to my quarters for a quick shower and a change of clothes.

As the days passed, I became increasingly fond of LTJG Pagendarm. The weeks we were assigned the same shift became a joy for me. I had illusions that maybe somehow we could spend an evening together doing something of a social nature. One late PM shift as we were finishing up, I decided to make my play.
"I'd sure like to have a beer. Wouldn't you?" I said to her, as I replaced the last of my charts I had been working on.
"Not really, I prefer champagne," she replied I felt like I had had the wind knocked out of me. I knew I had made a complete fool of myself

for even thinking such a thing. I decided to put the idea out of my mind forever. After all, it was against Navy Regs. for a commissioned officer to fraternize with an enlisted men.

The first time I saw LTJG Pagendarm in civilian clothes was at the base theater. I had gone with Rick, my cube mate, to see the movie "Airplane" with Dana Andrews. Just before the movie, I glanced toward the balcony and saw her looking back at me. She smiled and her hand went up in a friendly gesture. I waved back. There was a tall, slender woman sitting next to her. She had seen me wave and leaned over and said something to LTJG Pagendarm.

"Who's the tall, good-looking chick with Pagendarm?" I asked Rick. He turned and looked up into the balcony.

"That's LTJG Weiss. Don't ask her where she's from unless you want the chamber of commerce version about the great state of California," he chuckled. I wasn't exactly out with LTJG Pagendarm, but at least we were sharing the same space. "Well, she's not drinking champagne tonight," I said to myself. I decided what I needed was a more direct approach. I would bide my time and when the occasion presented itself, I would try again. I fixed on the idea to feign a little anger about her rejecting my favorite drink. I knew she was a compassionate, caring person, and sooner or later she would ask me what was the matter. Then I would spring my trap. It wasn't long in coming. The following day when I wasn't my usual talkative self she became concerned.

"Are you okay, Messer? I notice you're quiet."

"I'm alright!"

"Did something happen to you?"

"You know you're an officer and I can't really tell you how I feel personally."

"Sure you can. It'll be our little secret."

"I don't know."

"C'mon, what is it?"

"Well, the other night when I asked you if you wouldn't like to have a beer and you said you only drink champagne,"
"Yes!"
"I had hoped we could go have a beer together." I held my breath. I waited for the answer that would tell me if she was interested. I studied her reaction. She seemed almost embarrassed and didn't say anything. It looked like I had my answer, but I still wasn't sure.

A couple of weeks passed and we had one of those nights on the ward where none of us even had time to stop and eat. At 2330, we had finished our charting and were walking to the elevator together.
"So, how about that beer," I asked.
"I could go for that. We'll take my car if you want to."
"That would be nice since I don't have one." We both laughed.
"Where can I pick you up?"
"I'll meet you just outside the front gate." I was very excited and rushed to the BEQ to shower and dress.
"Rick, wake up."
"What is it?"
"I finally asked Pagendarm out, and we're going to get a beer. Do you have a couple of bucks I could borrow?"
"Sorry, man! I really don't."
"Well, it's going to have to be one beer. I have a total of seventy-five cents. I'll worry about that later."
"Let her pay for it, man. The nurses got all the damn money."

I had been waiting less than five minutes when I saw a car coming from the direction of the nurse's parking lot. The car slowed down at the gate and the light shone in on the driver. There was no mistaking that red hair. Her car was a two-tone, blue and white, 1957 Chevrolet Belair. She came to a stop as she approached me and smiled. My heart skipped a beat as I opened the door. This was too good to be true. Me going out with a beautiful red head in a new car, not to mention she was a commissioned officer.

"Well, I see you made it," I said, as I climbed into the car.

"Did you think I wouldn't?"

"I wasn't sure, but I'm glad you did."

"Where to?"

"There is a little place down on Front Street where we can get a beer." I said as I looked at my watch. It was just after midnight. Finding the bar and seating ourselves, we both ordered a draft beer. The waitress brought us our drink and I gave her two of my three-quarters.

"So, what should I call you? I can't call you LTJG or Miss Pagendarm."

"Why don't we just drop the endarm and call me Peg. In fact, when we are working, why don't you just call me Miss Peg instead of LTJG Pagendarm?"

"Okay by me, Peg."

I was so happy I was feeling giddy. She was dressed in a black sweater and a green skirt that hung down past her knees. I could see her red hair glistening in the light when she moved, as we laughed and talked. Her green eyes fascinated me. I loved her smooth, pearly white teeth that seemed forever to be smiling. I felt special warmth with this woman that I had never felt with anyone. Her acceptance of my thoughts and ideas gave me confidence and made me feel eight-feet-tall. I had never been happier. We chatted gaily with each other and soon the beer was gone. She looked at me.

"Want another?" she asked. The beer had relaxed me and it no longer seemed to matter if I was broke.

"I only have a quarter," I laughed.

"Don't worry about it. I have some money," she said and reached in her purse, pulled out her wallet and put a five-dollar bill on the table. I shrugged my shoulders and gave her an embarrassed smile.

Over the next few weeks, we became inseparable. We talked endless hours of every conceivable thing under the heavens. For the first time in my life, I loved, trusted, and respected someone more than I did my mother. She became the first person I ever gave my total confidence to. I knew that no matter what I said, or did, she was going to be at my side and support me. In a short time, the only thing that seemed to matter was that we be together. I had found my soul mate.

It's hard to imagine how two people could have been more different. Peg was from a middle-class industrialist family on the West Coast. I was from an impoverished, poorly-educated family from Arkansas. She was Catholic. I was a fallen-away Baptist who was at war with all religions. She had graduated from an all girls' parochial high school and had a degree in nursing. I had barely finished public high school. She was an officer. I was enlisted. She was twenty-four. I was twenty. She was mature and stable. I was neurotic and already had begun to show signs of early alcoholism. She was cultured and refined. I had never really been out to dinner in a nice restaurant and barely knew which end of a fork to eat with. She loved classical music and the opera. I liked country music and rock 'n' roll. But somehow none of that seemed to matter. I became her understudy and little by little she began to teach me about another world.

Both Peg and I lived in military quarters and could not visit with each other aboard the hospital compound. Although we spent a lot of time in movies, restaurants, and on the beach, the majority of our time together was spent in her car.

Having no family or home to go to, friendship with others became especially important. The majority of men on the East Coast were from big cities like New York City, Philadelphia and Pittsburgh, Pennsylvania, and Cincinnati, Ohio. I found these men to be totally different from those from the Midwest and California. They were a tougher, more aggressive bunch. There was a pair from Philadelphia by the name of Childs and Miniski who shared a cube directly across from where Rick and I berthed. Their greatest delight in life was to cruise the bars in downtown Portsmouth and find some poor unsuspecting soul, pick a fight, and beat them senseless. There was a big six-foot, two-hundred-pound man from Georgia by the name of Crane who liked to hang out with them. They detested him but, for some unknown reason, they tolerated his presence. From time to time, they would take him on liberty with them. One day, I was lying quietly on my rack reading a magazine when I overheard them talking.

"Minsk," Childs said.

"Yeah," answered Miniski.

"You think you could take Ol' Crane out with one punch?"

"Damn straight," he snickered. "I tell you what, I'll bet you five dollars I can."

"Done deal. Let's shake on it." I listened, horrified. I knew Crane practically worshipped them. I lay quiet hoping they wouldn't become aware of my presence. In a few minutes, I heard Crane coming up the stairs.

"CHIL! MINSK!" he called out.

"Yeah," one of them answered.

I heard him enter their cube.

"What's up, dudes?" he asked.

"This!" answered Miniski and I heard a loud smack. A prolonged silence followed. Apparently, Crane hadn't gone down.

"What the hell was that for," Crane asked. Miniski and Childs both laughed.

"Oh, it wasn't anything," Childs replied lightly. "Miniski just owes me five dollars. Let's go get a beer." I heard a locker close and listened as they all three left together. "Sick ass bunch," I said to myself, and made a mental note to stay away from them.

Brown, the Senior Corpsman on 20 and 21, had a friend from his hometown of New York City by the name of Moreno. He was tall, dark, and had typical Italian features. He tended to the lean side, probably not weighing more than a hundred and sixty pounds. His eyes were the most captivating part of his character. They were dark, almost black, piercing, and would hold you like a spell. He would often come to the ward at the end of the workday and wait for Brown. There was always uneasiness when he was about. It was hard for me to imagine him as a patriotic, military man.

Moreno felt it was his duty to watch out for Brownie, as he called him, or anyone that Brown might consider to be his friend. I had been assigned a tour of nights and had moved into the assigned quarters, which was an old outbuilding away from the main BEQ. The Master-At-Arms (MAA) who ran the quarters had taken a special dislike to me and had repeatedly called me back to re-do my cleaning assignment. I found it to be a little irritating but of no major significance. I knew in thirty days I would be returning to the regular BEQ. One evening about 1900, I had decided to go to the club for a sandwich and beer. I had placed my order and was sitting at the bar waiting when I heard someone call my name. I turned and looked toward the back of the club and saw Moreno and Brown sitting at a table. Brown motioned for me to come over. I made my way to their table.

"So, Mess! How is it going?" Brown twanged in his New York accent, as I took my seat.

"Not that bad, but I won't cry when this tour of nights is over," I answered. In a few minutes, I noticed the night MAA from the BEQ had come into the club.

"You see that asshole over there?" I asked. They both looked at the MAA.

"Yeah! What about him?" Brown asked, seemingly unconcerned.

"He's been giving me a hard time for some damn reason."

I saw Brown and Moreno give each other a knowing look but didn't really give it a second thought. In a few minutes, the MAA walked past us to the head. A little while later, he came out and was walking past our table. Suddenly, Brown jumped up from the table knocking his chair back and grabbed the MAA by the shirt and slammed him back on the table. His face was beet red and he was biting his lower lip as he straddled him. At the same time Moreno had leaped up, reached in his pocket, and pulled out a ten-inch switchblade. He grabbed the MAA by the hair and pulled his head back and laid the blade against his neck.

"I hear you been giving my man here some shit," Brown said through his pursed lips. I could see blood running down the blade of the knife and onto the MAA's shirt. I looked at Moreno. The look on his face petrified me. I knew he desperately wanted a reason to cut his throat.

"I haven't done anything to him," the MAA whined.

"Shut up, you lying prick. If you so much as look at him cross-eyed the rest of the time he's on nights, we'll kill your stinking ass. Do you understand?" Brown asked, giving him an extra shake of the collar.

"Yeah, yeah, I understand." Brown slowly released him. Moreno glared at the MAA menacingly. The poor man stood erect, straightened his shirt, never looking at either Brown or Moreno, and slunk out the door in total humiliation. The commotion had attracted the attention of everyone, but no one intervened. I felt ashamed and embarrassed.

"I better go and get a little sleep," I commented.

"Yeah, go ahead, Mess and if that turd bothers you again, let us know," commented Brown.

The following morning I did my cleaning assignment. This time, apparently, it was satisfactory. I saw the MAA a few times after that but he avoided making eye contact with me. I felt ashamed for having been an unwitting participant in such a cowardly act. To resolve conflict in such a manner, went against everything I believed in or had ever been taught. From that day on, I kept my distance from Brown and Moreno. Although the Uniform Code of Military Justice governed us, raw power, fear, and intimidation were all very much a part of our daily lives.

Margie Weiss and Ann Mullins had gone through nurses training with Peg in Oakland, California. They joined the Navy together under the buddy system and all three received the rank of LTJG in the Navy Reserve. This guaranteed their being stationed together upon completion of their Indoctrination. Rick had pointed Margie out to me in the theater the night we had gone to see the movie, "Airport." A few days later, I was walking back to the BEQ from the hospital when I found myself walking with her and a corpsman by the name of Wayne Paige. Margie was tall, slender, and had light brown hair. Her face was angelic and there was a countenance of peace about her that I found charming. Her voice was soft and gentle, almost musical. I didn't know Paige that well but I felt uneasy around him. Later, Peg told me that Margie was dating him from time to time. I wasn't really that thrilled with the news. I thought Margie was too classy for Paige.

There was a fellow by the name of Jack Christian who berthed on the second floor with me and we got along well. Jack was from West Virginia and had a southern background very much like my own. He was six-foot, two and weighed about two hundred and twenty pounds. Jack had worked on the EENT ward with Margie a couple of weeks when he had first checked on board. They really didn't have the opportunity to get acquainted before Jack was recruited into the psychiatric service. Peg had mentioned to me they had worked together and that Margie had been quite attracted to him. Jack had a quick smile and a ready laugh. I thought this was just the kind of guy Margie needed. I decided I would get to know him better with the idea of us maybe becoming a foursome.

One day I mentioned to Jack I was dating Margie's friend and asked him if he would be interested in double-dating. He agreed that would be a great idea. Now, what I didn't know, and Jack didn't bother to tell me, was that he had made an anonymous call to the nurses quarters and asked Margie if she would ever consider going out with an enlisted man. She, of course, recognized his voice and assured him that she would. That fueled his confidence and he asked her for a date and she accepted. I suppose Jack never gave the fraternization issue a great deal of thought as he had the audacity to call for her at the nurse's quarters. Never having been there before, he wandered into the wrong entrance. Soon, he happened onto a lady who, apparently, had just left the shower. She was dressed in a robe and had a towel wrapped around her head. Now, Jack had never seen this lady before so he had no idea who she was. She stopped and looked him up and down and must have thought he was a businessman from the surrounding area.

"Yes, can I help you?" she asked.

"I hope so, I'm here to pick up Miss Weiss," he responded. With that she sent the maid to inform LTJG Weiss that she had a visitor. Upon learning that CDR Ericson, the Director of Nurses, had sent word that her date had arrived Margie came close to having an apoplexy. We didn't know it at the time but, in the not too distant future, CDR Ericson was destined to become head of the Navy Nurse Corps.

Now, I liked Jack a lot, but I found the NP Corpsmen to be a little strange and quite clannish. I had, on occasion, heard them expounding on the psychiatric diagnosis of some of my fellow corpsmen. I suspected they had nice little rooms picked out for all of us. I noticed, too, it was not a good idea to walk up behind one of them if they didn't know you were there. Taking these little oddities into consideration, I felt an obligation to make sure that Jack treated Margie with the proper amount of respect. I decided to take him aside for a little talk.

"Jack, Margie is a beautiful, kind, well-educated lady from a good family. You treat her right and she'll always be there for you. Who in the hell knows? You might even marry her someday." He looked at me and nodded his head in agreement.

"I'll do it, John," he answered. It was my one and only successful attempt at matchmaking. I'm happy to report that these some forty years later they are still happily married and that all eight of their beautiful children have earned college degrees. I don't know if I merit any credit for any of that, but it makes me feel good to think maybe I do.

I don't remember the first time I saw David Paul Bierley. I just kind of became aware of him one day. He was another big guy who stood well over six-two and weighed in at about two and a quarter. David was known to everyone as the Moose. He had gone out a couple of times with a young nurse by the name of Phyllis Plinger. Things, apparently, hadn't gone all that well as she never went out with him again. That, however, didn't keep him from being head-over-heels in love with her. He knew Peg and I had been dating and, I suppose, thought I must have been privy to some information he didn't have. He would follow me around and pick my brain as to what I thought he should do. Not wanting to be selfish with all of my knowledge about women, I gladly shared a few of my secrets. I'm very sorry to report it did very little good. Nevertheless, we soon became the best of friends. When I wasn't working or with Peg, you could usually find me hanging out with the Moose in one of the many local honky-tonks in downtown Portsmouth.

I remember very well the night I realized I was in love. I had gotten off the PM shift and Peg was coming onto night duty. We had agreed to rendezvous and say hello just outside of the main hospital in front of Patient Affairs. It was a cool spring evening and she was wearing her navy blue sweater over her white work uniform. I had exited the hospital and walked a few feet when I saw her walking toward me. There was a full moon out and it cast a white light on her golden hair. I watched her glide toward me. I had never seen anyone so beautiful and I knew, at that moment, I loved her. When we drew near she smiled, reached out, and took my hand. I kissed her gently in the dark. From that moment on our destiny was forever linked.

The need for enlisted men and officers not to fraternize is obvious. If one is dating a Commissioned Officer who is in charge and working for them, it doesn't take a lot of imagination to see the conflict of interest. In those days, the majority of the nurses who staffed the military hospitals were on their first tour of duty. Their average age ran between twenty-two and twenty-six. The corpsmen out numbered the nurses about ten to one and their average age ran between nineteen and twenty-two. Human nature being what it is, sparks flew. The Navy needs to keep her nurses and recruit new ones. For this reason, a great deal of fraternization is tolerated in Navy hospitals that wouldn't be in other military settings.

At first, Peg and I made somewhat of an effort to conceal the fact we were dating. But as time went on, we became more blatant about our relationship. One AM, LCDR Foster called me aside.
"Messer, you know it's not really a great idea for an enlisted man to be dating an Officer," she commented. I looked at her but felt it better not to respond.
"These nurses have all completed nursing colleges and are prepared to go out and earn good salaries. Most corpsmen aren't sufficiently prepared to give these girls what they want in life. It's a recipe for disaster," LCDR Foster continued. I knew she was fulfilling her duty to counsel me.
"Yes, ma'am," I answered.

When a corpsman or corpswave was reassigned, LCDR Smith called them to her office and personally gave them the news. In mid March, on a Friday afternoon, LCDR Foster informed me that I was to report to LCDR Smith's office at the end of my shift. I had an ominous feeling that this was not going to be good news. At 1505, I made my way to her office, knocked on the side of her open door, and waited. I could see her writing in some kind of a logbook.

"Come in, Messer," she said and laid her pen down.

I made my way to the front of her desk and stood at parade rest. This time she didn't invite me to sit down.

"Messer, you know we only have five corpsmen for all three shifts on the Sick Officers Quarters. I have to pull experienced corpsmen from other parts of the surgical wing to cover their night shifts. You've been on ward 20 and 21 about three months now so I feel you're more than qualified." I stood listening, stunned. I had expected a reprimand for dating Peg but I wasn't expecting this. LCDR Foster had continued to train me to take over as senior corpsman. No one else had been considered, as far as I knew. I felt the blood drain out of my face.

"You'll be off this weekend but I want you to report to SOQ-2 for one week of indoctrination this coming Monday at 1445. Then, the following week, you'll be going on nights," she continued. She picked up her pen and looked down at what she had been working on. "That'll be all?" she concluded.

"Yes, ma'am!" I responded. I went back to 20 and 21 almost in a daze and found LCDR Foster.

"LCDR Foster, could I talk to you, please?" I asked. I knew she could get this straightened out if she would just explain to LCDR Smith that she had selected me to be Brown's replacement.

"Yes, wait for me in the treatment room, Messer." In a few minutes, she came into the treatment room and closed the door.

"What is it, Messer?"

"Commander, did you know LCDR Smith was transferring me to SOQ-2 for nights?"

"Yes, well, I just found out this morning," she said timidly. I looked at her face and it told me the whole story. I was remembering her counseling session.

"But, I thought I was going to replace Brown."

"Messer, things change. We're in the Navy and we all have to do as we are told. LCDR Smith has the final say on ward assignments. I can only make recommendations. I'm sure you'll do fine over there. I better get back out to the desk. Good luck to you over there." she said, turned and opened the door. I followed her out and took one last look at the ward. It seemed nothing had changed since the first day I arrived. The patients were still playing cards at the same little table. There were some I wanted to say goodbye to but that would have to wait.

The following Monday found me at my new work assignment. SOQ-2 had fourteen rooms for retired and active duty officers. Half of the rooms were private and the other half were semi-private. The nurses were more involved with patient care on SOQ than on the enlisted wards. I found it almost boring after being on a fast paced ward like 20 and 21. I made a smooth transition to nights and things went relatively well for a few days. At night, there was only one corpsman assigned to each ward. The charge nurse floated between eight wards and in general kept us on our toes and made sure we stayed awake.

There were a few nurses who dated corpsmen and other enlisted men. I knew most of them personally and felt quite comfortable when we worked together. The charge nurse who was on nights had married one of my old patients from ward 20. She was nearing the end of the expiration of her contract with the Navy and couldn't wait to get out. Her manner of relating to the corpsmen in her charge was pretty informal. She knew Peg and I were dating and she would often come by to chat and pass some time. One night we had finished checking on the patients, and had walked back to the little galley that was on the ward.

"Got anything to eat in here, Messer?" she asked as she opened the door to the refrigerator.

"I haven't had a chance to look," I replied and looked over her shoulder inside. There staring up at us was a watermelon that had been cut in half. It was at least two-feet long and barely fit in the refrigerator at an angle. The heart was a blood red rosette, surrounded by little black and white seeds. Reaching in a drawer of one of the cabinets she took out a small teaspoon and lifted out a good size piece.

"I don't think they're going to miss that little bit," she said and quickly put it in her mouth.

Now, had I given a little thought back to my days on the Helena, perhaps, I would've viewed this event a little differently. But, being around Medical Officers who had completed two weeks of military indoctrination and nurses who had had six, I'm sorry to report my military bearing had become somewhat lax. I really never gave it a great deal of thought at the time and went on about my business. The following evening, I reported to SOQ-2 for my night shift and was informed by the charge nurse that one of the patients wanted to see me in the galley. I went to the galley and noticed the door was closed. That was unusual, as ward policy required the door always to be open. I pushed it open and saw Commander Allison, one of my retired patients standing there. His lips were pursed in a straight line and I could see he was angry.

"Yes, Commander!" I said.

He reached over and pulled the refrigerator door open. I looked down at the mutilated heart of his melon.

"You know, Messer, I was going to share this melon with the patients and staff here on the ward. But, now look at it. The pastor from my church drove sixty miles to bring this to me. I have to tell you, Messer, I'm very disappointed in you. All the other nurses and corpsmen on this ward have been exemplary in their duties with me." He stood there holding the door open looking at me waiting for an explanation.

"What do you have to say for yourself?"

"I didn't do that to your melon, Commander," I responded. He slammed the refrigerator shut and looked at me with his cold, steel-blue eyes.

"You'll apologize by-god or I'll see you go to the brig." he threatened. I was innocent and I had no intention of apologizing for something I didn't do.

"Sorry, Commander, but I'm not responsible," I answered with a great deal of self-righteous indignation. I knew he thought I was lying and that I was the biggest slime ball in the whole U. S. Navy. I also knew there wasn't anyway he was going to believe me no matter what I did. He reached into the refrigerator, picked up what was left of his melon and handed it to me.

"Here, eat the whole damn thing since you wanted it so bad. I hope you enjoy it," he said, and stomped down the hall to his room.

News travels fast at a military command. By the following afternoon, there wasn't a man or woman on board that didn't know who I was. Little did I know that my troubles had just started.

About a week later, I had finished my rounds and completed my charting. It was about two in the morning and things were quiet. I had found Hemmingway's novel *The Old Man and The Sea* in the linen closet and had started reading it. I had pulled the bottom drawer of the desk out to prop up my feet. This had positioned my back to the entrance. I don't know how long I had been there when I heard a noise. I turned around quickly, and there, about five feet from where I was sitting, I saw two monsters crawling through the door toward me. They had huge heads and their skin was covered with green scales that looked very much like that of a crocodile's skin. An involuntary scream escape me and I jumped up on the chair I had been sitting in. I had left the charts out after my last entry and, before I realized what I was doing, I hurled them at my intruders. I hit one of them squarely over the eye and opened about a three-inch laceration; the blood poured out onto the floor. Suddenly, the monster I had hit stood erect. Then, the strangest thing occurred. It changed into HN Childs. Then the other monster magically transformed into HN Miniski.

"What the hell is wrong with you, Messer? You crazy?" asked Childs, grabbing his bleeding forehead.

Recognizing who they were gave me a whole new kind of fear. I grabbed some 4 X 4 gauze and applied pressure to his wound.

"We should just take you out, Messer," commented Miniski as he tried to decide what was the most macho way of handling the matter. The smell of alcohol radiating from them did little to quell my fears. I later learned they had been drinking and had sneaked over into the officer's swimming pool and took a little dip in their underwear. Upon leaving the pool, they had wrestled on the fresh cut grass before deciding to crawl down the passageway of SOQ to have some fun with me.

"I'm sorry but you guys scared the hell out of me," I explained. Lights were going on in the patient's rooms and Commander Allison came down to the nurse's desk to investigate.

My ruination was complete. At the end of my tour on nights, I was transferred to the old C-units. The C-units consisted of five wards that were in the old outbuildings. Most of the patients were retired, and had chronic medical conditions of one sort or another. I soon found myself on C-3 doing another tour of nights. It seemed my reputation had preceded me. The nurses, in one form or another, let me know they knew who I was. I allied myself with my patients and did my best to care for their needs. They weren't stupid. They knew about Peg and me and were very much aware I was out of favor with the powers that were.

I had been working nights on C-3 for about a week when the Ensign that worked the PM shift said she wanted to talk to me.

"Messer, I have some great news."

"Wonderful! I could use some good news."

"Well, it's no longer required to chart temperatures, pulses, and respirations on class IV and V patients."

"That is good news." Naval hospitals of those days had five classes of patients. I, II, III, IV, and, V. Class I, being the most serious was confined to absolute bed rest. Class II was confined to bed rest with bathroom privileges. Class III was ambulatory but confined to the ward. Class IV and V, were assigned to rehabilitation or waiting for a discharge. So this new policy of not charting TPRs on IV and V class patients made perfect sense to me. The night corpsman, having more time than the AM and PM, crew had been assigned this responsibility. It took a considerable amount of time, so I gladly discontinued the chore.

Five days after I had been informed of the change in procedure, I reported to the ward and took over my duties. I noticed a patient by the name of Phelps was still awake when I came on duty but didn't pay much attention to him. Once the PM crew left he got up and came to the desk.

"Messer, the PM nurse is out for your ass." That kind of surprised me and I stopped and looked at him.

"Why do you say that, Phelps?"

"Listen, when she came on this afternoon I heard the AM nurse tell her you hadn't been charting TPRs. She said she had directed you every day this week to do the charting. She said she would leave you a direct order in writing this time. And if you didn't carry out her order, she'd take you up on charges to the Commanding Officer. She said she had already discussed it with Commander Wolfgang and they were both in agreement. With that, Phelps flipped up the top card of the nurse's cardex and showed me the order that had been hidden behind the very top card. It was a written direct order to chart all class IV and V patients no later than 0700 the following morning. My heart skipped a beat. I knew I was unpopular, but I had no idea that there were commissioned officers who hated me enough to commit perjury to have me court martialed. I kissed Phelps on the cheek.

"Don't ever tell the bitch I told you," he pleaded.

"Don't worry, Phelps. You've saved my ass, and I won't forget it." I charted furiously all through the night. The early morning light found me making my last entry. Upon being relieved by the day crew, I took the direct order I had been written and went to see CDR Wolfgang, director of the C-units. I showed her the card and explained to her what had happened. I expected her to be outraged at such an act by one of her officers but in fact that wasn't what happened.

In the Navy the old saying, "we take care of our own" is a tradition that runs deep in all the Corps. The Commander informed me I had brought this on myself and that several of the nurses had been intimidated by my attitude. I knew this was going to be the end of this particular situation. I neatly folded the card under her watchful eye and placed it in my wallet. "I have a witness to everything I told you," I said, as I replaced my wallet in my pocket. I was a Hospitalman in a desperate battle for survival with a full commander but justice stood fairly in my corner. The courage and conviction that comes from knowing you're right is an awesome power. That little bit of knowledge would serve me well in the years that followed.

I don't remember asking Peg to marry me. I think we just kind of talked about it in a general way and kind of decided it would be the sensible thing to do since neither of us could imagine life without the other. Although we were worlds apart, the only real problem was religion. I had no personal knowledge about the Catholic Church but my mother had told me that they believed babies went to hell if they weren't baptized and that Catholics paid their priest to forgive them of their sins. That left them free to do pretty much as they pleased as long as they paid up once in awhile. I didn't think that was anyway for civilized people to act, so I told Peg she'd have to drop her religion. I didn't expect a lot of resistance as she had pretty well given in to me on everything else. I couldn't have been more wrong.

"If you want to marry me, Dick, you'll have to take marriage instructions from a Catholic Priest and sign a paper agreeing to let me practice my faith."

"Well, you can forget that. I'm not going to ask you to sign a paper to let me practice my faith, so why should I have too?"

"The Catholic Faith is different. We're required to agree to bring up our children in the Church in order to receive the Sacrament of Matrimony. You don't have to convert to Catholicism, but you do have to allow me to bring our children up as Catholics."

"The hell with that. We'll just get married by the Justice of the Peace." We were driving to our favorite restaurant for dinner and she didn't respond right away and I thought the matter closed.

"Dick, I really want to marry you, but I'm afraid I can't if you really feel that way."

"That's fine with me. We'll have dinner and you can drop me off at the BEQ." When I didn't hear from her for several days, I decided I'd call her.

"Hey, how you doing? I really am missing you. Are you ready to forget all that nonsense about me having to sign papers with the Pope?"

"I love you, baby, but that's one thing I can't do. I'm so sorry. It's probably better we don't talk anymore."

"Fine!"

After several days of soul searching I decided that since I didn't practice any religion anyway, perhaps it would be better to teach a child the Catholic Faith rather than none at all. Having settled that with myself, I called Peg.

"I've been thinking about this religion thing. I want to ask you about birth control. How are we going to handle that?"

"Well, my old civilian doctor, Sadie, told me I would probably not be able to have any children. But if you are worried about it, we can use the rhythm method."

"Is it effective?"

"Very effective. Don't worry, I know you want to go to school and get an education before we have children. We'll be careful. I can work while you go to school and we'll have our family later."

I suppose the nursing staff at Portsmouth Naval Hospital had given up on me. They assigned me to C-6, which was a sleeper ward. All the patients were class V and were assigned to rehab and were allowed to go on liberty daily. I went to work at 0700 and secured my watch at 1500. I was on my own. I didn't report to anyone nor did anyone bother to check on me. I felt like Br'er Rabbit in the briar patch.

I could write a whole book on our wedding and the preparations that went into it and never even mention the scandal it caused in both of our families. I think it will suffice to say we were married in the little Catholic Chapel aboard the hospital compound on the seventh day of June 1958 at 1700 on a Saturday afternoon. The Moose was my best man and Margie Weiss was the maid of honor. We rented an apartment about four blocks from the main gate of the Naval Hospital at 819 Webster Ave. Peg was pulled off the military wards and assigned to the delivery room where all her patients were dependents. I continued in service to my country overseeing a ward full of empty beds.

Those were, perhaps, the happiest days of our married life. We rushed home the days Peg was on AMs and basked in each other's presence and our love for one another. I doubt if any two people were ever happier. When she was on PMs, the evening dragged by, but once she came home, it would soon be forgotten.

My neighbor across the hall was a PO2 who worked in the personnel office at the Naval Hospital. We had met coming and going and had become quite friendly. He knew Peg was a nurse at the hospital and that the command wasn't exactly thrilled with us. One evening, in the early part of July, I had just gotten home and turned the TV on when I heard a knock. I opened the door to find my neighbor looking at me rather anxiously.

"Messer, your name has come down from the nursing staff to send you out on the first blank draft." he explained.

"What the hell is a blank draft?" I asked.

"Well, we get blank orders in to send non-rated men to different locations as the need arises. The command uses it's own discretion on whom to send. That way they get rid of personnel they consider undesirable. I just wanted to let you know what to expect," he warned.

I broke the news to Peg and we prepared ourselves for the coming separation. Less than a week later, our neighbor returned and knocked on the door again.

"Oh, hi! More good news for me?" I laughed.

"Messer, we got fifteen blank orders in to fill and three of them are for the dispensary here at the shipyard in Portsmouth. I can give you one of the billets if you want me to. It'll be fun to stick it to those bitches for a change," he chuckled.

"Damn right, I want you to. Thanks! Come in and let's have a beer. Peg will be home in a few minutes. She's going to love you for this."

Within the week, I checked aboard the Shipyard in Portsmouth and reported to the dispensary for duty. It would be one of those duty stations that I had dreamed about. It served the active duty military as well as the civilian shipyard workers. There I was rotated through the Treatment Room, Operating Room, X-Ray Department, Laboratory,

EKG, Audio Booth and the Physical Exam Room. It turned out to be one of my greatest learning experiences.

My greatest delight came when I returned to the hospital and paraded around the compound announcing to friend and foe alike of my new duty station that was only three miles down the road. Being out of reach, while at the same time remaining visible to those who would crush me, gave me a sweet feeling of invincibility. Only now, in retrospect, can I appreciate the dangerous path that I once danced upon.

The next rating period, I was promoted to PO3 and in early May, 1960, I was released from active duty. Peg had been wrong about not being able to have children. John Darrel was born on April 16, 1959, and Theresa Ann on April 9, 1960. I was now unemployed with a wife and two children. My life had changed considerably in four short years. It seemed like only yesterday when I had sat on the old porch of my family home and waited for the black sedan to come and take me away.

USS Belle Grove LSD-2

Frances Marie Korte was born in Saint Helena, California on November 10, 1894. She graduated from San Francisco State College in 1920 and married John F. Pagendarm in 1922. John's first wife had died in childbirth and left him with four boys. Frances unflinchingly took on the job of helping him raise his sons. Later, they had three children of their own. Harold C. was born in 1925, Frances M. in 1926, and Margaret A. (known to us here as Peg) in 1933.

When Frances married John, he had a successful machine shop in San Francisco. As his sons completed Saint Ignatius' all boys' Catholic High School, they joined their father in his shop. Through the years of the Second World War, and on into the late forties, the shop became quite successful. John's creative nature had led him to invent and patent several items that were considered to be of major importance. The most significant was a machine that folded the outer package of frozen food containers. The notoriety and profit from this propelled him, and his four older sons, firmly into middle class America.

Frances, who became known as Marian, earned a degree in education. After much soul searching, she decided to seek a religious life and become a Catholic Nun. In 1948, she joined the Dominican Order of Preachers. Harold served in the Second World War and later went to Santa Clara College, courtesy of the GI bill. He earned a degree in mechanical engineering. Peg, as we already know, had graduated from Providence Nursing College in 1953.

These many years later, I can only speculate as to what my mother-in-law "Frances" might have felt when she learned that her baby daughter was marrying a twenty-year-old, enlisted man, from Arkansas who had barely finished high school. Like all good mothers, she wanted her daughter to marry well. It's certainly understandable that she didn't want her to marry beneath herself. She felt the solution to this unfortunate incident would be for me to pull myself up in the world. I would need to go to college and earn a degree so that I could properly provide for my growing family. She would baby sit, Peg would work, and I would get an education.

Upon discharge from the Navy, I traveled to Oakland, California with my young family. We moved into the Pagendarm family home where Peg had been born. Peg immediately went to work at Providence Hospital in downtown Oakland where she had earned her degree in nursing. I had decided to enroll at Saint Mary's Catholic College in nearby Moraga. I took the entrance exam and was scheduled to start the fall semester.

In the mean time, I took a job at Sunshine Biscuit Company working the three to eleven shift. The union scale for non-skill workers was $1.99 an hour. My job consisted of catching cookies in a large sixty-gallon container after they had passed through the hot ovens on a conveyor belt. The work was hard, hot, and monotonous.

My first check after paying taxes and union dues was $62.31. I didn't have to be an accountant to know that would just about cover our food cost. Many of my older coworkers had been working at Sunshine Biscuit for several years and never held another job. The very thought that this could happen to me caused me to break out in a cold sweat.

On the first day of July, I had arrived home from work a little before Peg. I went to the attic, which we were using as our living room, turned on the television and waited for her. A short time later, I heard her making her way up the three flights of stairs. I watched expectantly as she came into view.

"Hi, Babe! How was your evening?" I asked.

"It was okay. But I need to talk to you," she said and took a seat on the couch. I could see she was troubled. I turned the TV off and sat down on the coffee table in front of her.

"What is it, Honey?" A long moment of silence followed as she studied my face.

"I think I'm pregnant," she finally said and sat motionless, waiting for my reaction. I went numb. A feeling of impending doom washed over me. The vision of three children and us living indefinitely with my mother-in-law flashed through my mind.

"What are we going to do?" I asked, as I tried to regain my composure.

"I don't know," she answered. I was still awake the following morning when the pale, orange light made its unwelcome entrance into our bedroom. I couldn't have been any more depressed had I been thrown into the sea with a great weight around my neck. How was I going to take care of a family of five?

Frances was sixty-five years old and had advanced diabetes. Needless to say, her general health was not that good. I never knew how she reacted when Peg gave her the news that she was expecting. In retrospect, I think she must have felt as desperate as we did.

Up until that moment, I had never considered making the Navy a career. The cold reality that Peg was not going to be able to work while I went to college forced me to take a more realistic look at my situation. I knew that my present earnings were inadequate to provide even a basic living. Frances had already done more than I had a right to expect. The responsibility of my family was rightfully mine.

I decided to call the Navy Recruiter and inquire as to the possibility of going to the Navy's Clinical Laboratory and Blood Bank School. The Oaknoll Naval Hospital was about five miles from where we were living. The school was fourteen months long and held the record as the longest school available to Navy enlisted men at that time. Completion of the course would qualify me to obtain a California License as a Medical Technologist. However, I would need to finish the course in the next eighteen months. The State of California was in the process of passing a law that would mandate a bachelor's degree as a prerequisite for licensing. The recruiter informed me there had been another corpsman who had requested this school as a reenlistment incentive. But at the last minute, he had changed his mind.

"Come on over anytime before you've been out more than ninety days, and I'll submit a request that your name be substituted for his," he advised me. I hadn't completely decided that was what I wanted to do at that point. Having a few days before I had to make the final decision, I decided to think it over.

The following Tuesday, I had slept late and Peg came into our room.

"Hurry up and get dressed. One of the girls that use to rent a room from Mom while completing her master's degree is coming for lunch."

"Should I dress in my good clothes or just put on my work uniform?"

"Your uniform will be fine." I showered, shaved, dressed, and went down stairs. A rich aroma from the roasting leg of lamb permeated the house. My mouth watered. Frances was setting the table with her best china. I could see the long-stem crystal glasses adorning the table. My young son was hanging on to grandma's leg as she puttered from the breakfast nook to the kitchen. I scooped him up and went into the living room and sat down. In a few minutes, I heard Peg come down the stairs and go into the kitchen.

"Why don't you fix Dick a plate and have him eat in the foyer?" I heard Frances tell her.

So, I was to eat out behind the kitchen like a servant. At that moment, I understood how she felt about presenting a man dressed in a white Sunshine Biscuit uniform as her son-in-law to a sophisticated lady with a master's degree. My self-esteem plummeted. Here I was living in my mother-in-law's home with a pregnant wife, two children and working in a cookie factory? Tears rimmed my eyes. Not wanting anyone to see my pain, I left early for work. Upon arrival, I went to the Personnel Office. Just inside the office door, I encountered my supervisor sitting casually on the desk of one of the female employees. They were chatting gaily and seemed to be enjoying my discomfort at having to wait until they acknowledged me. I had had enough rejection for one day.

"EXCUSE ME! I would like to hand in my resignation and collect my wages," I said, with as much dignity as I was capable of at that moment. The supervisor stood up and gave me a surprised look.

"You pass those two men that just walked out of here?" he asked.

"You mean those two that looked like they slept in the dumpster?"

"Yeah, well, there has been a steady stream of people coming in here all week looking for work. You better give this some thought before you up and walk off the job."

"Thanks! I already have; I've decided to reenlist in the Navy." He looked at the lady. Her eyes moved from him to me, but her face was expressionless. He turned back to me.

"Well, I can't say I blame you. You can pick up your check next Tuesday at the cashier's window. I wish you the best; you're a good worker."

"Thanks! I'm sorry to be leaving on such short notice, but I don't think I was cut out for factory work."

On my way home, I stopped at the Firefly Bar for a beer and tried to get my thoughts in order. I also wanted to make sure that the lunch guest would be gone when I got home. I stayed longer than I intended; upon my arrival at the house, it was dark and quiet. I tiptoed upstairs to our living room and waited. About eleven-thirty, I heard the front door softly close. I made my way down the stairs and found Peg in the kitchen making a sandwich.

"Can we talk?" I asked.

"Sure! What is it, Hon?"

"Babe, I've decided to go back in the Navy." Peg stopped and gave me a stunned look.

"You've done what?" I sat down at the dining room table.

"Come over here and sit down. I need to talk to you a minute. I have to accept who and what I am. I'm not a Pagendarm, a machinist, or an engineer. The only thing I've ever done is to serve in the Navy. I know PO-3 is not much, but at least it's something. I'm going to go back in the Navy and try to make some kind of a life for us. It looks to me like that's about the only thing available to me right now. We'll never be rich but we won't starve. From now on, I'm going to be my own man. Whatever I have, or do, will be of my own making. It's the only way I can live with any dignity. I would like for you to go with me, but I want you to be sure you can be satisfied with what I can provide. If you rather stay here with your folks I'll understand. It's up to you." Peg reached across the table and took my hand.

"Of course, I'll go with you. I took you for better or worse. You're my husband and whatever you provide for us I'll take it and do the best I can. We'll make our own life in the Navy. I kind of miss it, anyway."

The next morning, I called the recruiter.

"I'm not sure you remember me, but my name is Messer. We had talked about submitting my name to replace the corpsman that changed his mind about going to Laboratory and Blood Bank School?" I heard him shuffling papers.

"Let's see…HM3 right?"

"Yeah!"

"I got some bad news for you, buddy. The dude changed his mind again and accepted the orders."

"Damn!"

"Yeah, I know. Look, why don't you come on down and let's get your paper work going? We'll swear you in and I'll put you back on two weeks leave until your orders come down."

"You think there is a possibility I might still be assigned here at Oaknoll?"

"We can try. But we'll have to get you reenlisted before the nineteenth if you want to retain your rank. You'll just have to take your chances."

The next day I reenlisted and went on leave. Ten days later, the recruiter called.

"Messer, your orders are in. You're going to the USS Belle Grove. It's home ported down in Long Beach. You're to report aboard no later than the fifteenth of September. Congratulations! I know it's not what you wanted, but you can request Lab. School when you're up for shore duty."

On the fifteenth of September, I arrived in Long Beach. I was excited, as I had fond memories of my days aboard the Helena. Walking down the familiar steps from Longbeach Boulevard to the Pike, the familiar sound of the huge organ that played incessantly reached my ears. I strolled between the many concession stands and honky tonks, heading toward Magnolia Street with my seabag thrown over my shoulder. It felt good to be back in uniform. I had added a hash mark (denotes four years of service) to my left sleeve. I had called the receiving station the night before and had been told the Belle Grove was anchored in the Long Beach Harbor. I was directed to go to the Magnolia Street Landing where I could catch a liberty launch. I walked up the stairs, out of the Pike, and onto Magnolia Street. I turned left and headed toward the boat landing about two blocks away. Up ahead, I heard the engine of a motor launch as the engineer cut the power back to enable the Coxswain to make the landing ramp. As I came closer, I could see several ships anchored in the hazy distance. No doubt, one of them was the Belle Grove, but I had no idea which one it might be. I subconsciously scanned the horizon looking for the Helena. I wondered where the old crew was by now? "Scattered to the four winds no doubt," I said to myself. A feeling of nostalgia came over me.

Coming to the end of the landing, I joined a dozen other sailors. I noticed little blue and white patches about three inches long and a third of an inch wide were sewn on the right shoulder of their dress blues. This was something new since I'd left the fleet. On closer examination, I could see it was the name of a ship. I started looking for someone with a Belle Grove Patch. Standing with his foot on a bench, where two other sailors were seated, was a big, rough-looking, blondish redheaded fellow. Trying not to be conspicuous, I glanced sideways at his ship's patch; it read USS Belle Grove LSD-2. He caught my eye and looked down at my rating badge, then at my seabag.

"What ship you going aboard, Doc?" he asked.

"The Belle Grove," I responded.

"I'm MM2 Studenbordt," he said extending his hand. "I got some bad news for you, Doc," he said smiling at the others.

"So soon? And what might that be?" I asked.

"The whole damn Medical Department is on restriction for drinking up the medicinal alcohol." I was trying to be cool but I must have looked shocked.

"But I don't think they did it," he laughed, and looked at his two companions. They both chuckled and looked up at me for the first time.

"U.S.S. BELLE GROVE DEPARTING," came over the 1-MC.

"Let me help you with that, Doc," said Studenbordt, grabbing my seabag like it was a feather. He trotted down the clanky ladder and climbed into the motor launch that bobbled up and down against the mooring. There were six or seven men already in the boat. Two others came running down the ramp as the boat hook prepared to cast off the line. Studenbordt dropped my seabag and turned to me. "There you go," he said. I nodded and pulled the bag in front of me. The noise from the motor and the sudden lurch caused me to stagger. A young fireman, dressed in dungarees with a white hat propped on the back of his head, sat nonchalantly on the boat housing.

"Better hang on, Doc," he said, giving a big smile as he looked down at the caduceus on my rating badge. "Matthew is about a crazy bastard," he added, looking at the Coxswain.

"Square that goddamn hat, Ridings," the big red-faced seaman responded. The young fireman grabbed his hat, playfully feigning fear. I couldn't discern any real change of the hat's position after he put it back on. I got the feeling I had just entered into a very different kind of navy than what I had expected.

When there are more ships than piers, the commanding officers are designated anchorage spaces according to their seniority. Considering the distance we were traveling, I thought the CO of the Belle Grove must be about the most junior skipper in the whole damn fleet. We passed several ships at anchor as we continued toward a big gray hulk in the far distance. Soon, the Coxswain cut the engine and swung the launch expertly along side the gangplank where we disembarked. Studenbordt once again grabbed my seabag and started up the ladder ahead of me. I wobbled along behind trying to keep my balance. I was surprised to see the OOD (officer of the deck) was a PO1 instead of a commissioned officer. Studenbordt dropped my seabag, rendered a hand salute aft to where the colors were flying, then turned to the

OOD and requested permission to come aboard. I followed his example.

The USS Belle Grove's commanding officer was CDR Sam J. Gilliland. She was built in Oakland, California and commissioned on August 9, 1943. Her name had been taken from President Madison's home in Belle Grove, Virginia. She was 457 feet long and 72 feet at the beam, displacing 4,500 tons. She had two five-cylinder, Skinner Uniflow, reciprocating engines. They were driven by two Babcock and Wilcox "D" style, saturated steam boilers. One was located in the starboard engine room and the other in the port. She could steam at 15-16 knots and carried a crew of 330 men and 18 officers, when at full compliment. She was part of the Pacific Fleet's mighty Amphibious Force that had delivered marines to the great battles of Okinawa, Guadalcanal, and Iwo Jima during the Second World War. The LSD tacked on the end of her name stood for Landing Ship Dock. The welldeck was 44 feet wide and 396 feet long, being just 61 feet short of her overall length. There were 36 ballast tanks located along the keels that could be pumped full of water. This lowered her sufficiently enough that 7000 tons of salt water could be flooded into her welldeck. This permitted amphibious landing craft to enter by sea. Once they were on board, the ballast tanks could be pumped out. She would then rise, and the salt water would drain away. Her sole mission was to deliver landing crafts and their crews to the many hot spots around the world.

I was expecting to enter back into the spit and polish navy of the Helena. There was as much difference between the Helena and the Belle Grove as there is between a race and plow horse. I wouldn't say she was ugly, but she certainly wasn't built for beauty.

After giving me permission to come aboard, the OOD motioned for me to stand to one side. I pulled my seabag well back out of everyone's way. When the last man had clamored on board the OOD took a bullhorn and held it to his mouth.

"Coxswain, make Magnolia Street landing and return to the ship immediately," he barked.

"Aye, aye, sir," came the reply.

I heard the loud reverberation of the motor and watched as the boat swung out in a big arc and headed back in the direction of the landing. The OOD then turned to me.

"Welcome aboard, Doc. I'll give a call down to sickbay and get one of the corpsmen to come get you checked in," he said as he turned, picked up the phone, and dialed. "Hey, this is the OOD. Can one of you pecker checkers come up and get your new man?" he asked in a gleeful tone. He chuckled to himself as he hung up. "They'll be up in a minute." Taking my record, he wrote my name, date, and the time in the ship's logbook.

A short time later, a medium-built man about four inches shorter than myself appeared. I estimated him to be about twenty-five years old. He had on dungarees and a blue baseball cap. He looked at my seabag and walked toward me. "Ready?" he asked, without introducing himself. I nodded, picked up my bag, and followed him.

A good portion of the Belle Grove's main deck was enclosed. We entered almost immediately into a passageway that ran alongside of the big welldeck on the port side. We followed it down a few feet, made a left onto a narrow, steel, walkway that ran up above the welldeck. I could hear men working down below. Looking in the direction of the noise, I took in the size of the cavity hulled out below us. We stopped about halfway across the walkway at the entrance to a large office. Several men were busy talking, typing and filing. A frail PO2 came to the half door and looked at my companion.

"What can I do for you, Meeker?" he asked, looking at my companion.

"New man," Meeker answered, nodding his head at me. The frail man then took my record, read the name on my envelope and stuck out his hand.

"I'm YN2 Yeager. Welcome to the good, old Two Can Do," he said, and pumped my hand up and down. "Why don't you go on to sickbay and get your gear squared away. When you're ready, come on back down and we'll get you checked in."

"Great! Thanks, Yeager," I said and turned back to Meeker. He lead me back up the walkway and turned left into a passageway. This led us into a berthing compartment and we wound our way around a maze of men and bunks. We soon came to a head and went through to the other side and out into another passageway. Then we turned right, went a few feet, and came to a door. Meeker opened the door. I followed him into a small medical ward that looked about eight feet wide and fourteen feet long. The bulkhead and overhead were painted a pea green and the deck was covered with white tile. As we continued on, I noticed on my right, a hospital bunk that had a big six-inch mattress with a light blue cover. To my left, were eight standard, aluminum-colored, shipboard lockers, standing four high and two wide. A wooden laundry hamper painted the same color as the bulkhead stood between a stainless steel refrigerator and the lockers. Just beyond the refrigerator, were two more hospital bunks on both sides of the small passageway. As we walked through the ward, I felt a cool breeze blowing. I looked to my right and saw an open porthole over the top bunk at about eye level.

Stepping through the hatch, we entered into a treatment room that was about twelve by fourteen feet. This deck was covered in black tile, which struck me as strange. Later, I learned it was antimagnetic to prevent an explosion in case ether was used as an anesthetic. Four or five feet in front of the hatch, was an examination table. It was covered with one of the same blue covers that were on the bunks in the ward. A frail, bald-headed man, wearing glasses was sitting next to the table. Upon our entry, he stood up and forced a smile. He looked middle-aged and was of medium build with a very ruddy complexion.

"This is the new head cleaner," Meeker commented, and nodded his head toward me. He then went to the other side of the table and sat down.

"I'm HM1 Mahan. Welcome aboard," he said as he stood up, took my hand and shook it limply. I took a quick look around the room. There were stainless steel cabinets with several drawers and a dressing table along the bulkhead directly in front of me. On my left, was a small stainless steel table with instrument trays sitting on white towels. Just past the table, was a door leading back into an office space. Along the bulkhead in front of the dressing table were a sink and water closet mounted over a large steel safe that was painted a battleship gray. To the left of the sink, from where I was standing, was a half-size stainless steel refrigerator. Just beyond the refrigerator, a door led out into a berthing compartment. I was brought back to reality by the sound of HM1 Mahan's voice.

"We'll get you a bunk and locker here on the ward. We don't have a doctor on the Belle Grove so we try not to keep patients on the ward. Sometimes when we have troops on aboard we might have one or two, but we have six bunks." he said as he led me back toward the ward. "You can have this rack here," he commented, pointing to the bottom bunk on his right. "There are three empty lockers, so take anything that don't have a lock on it," he said and opened one of the empty lockers. "When you get finished, I'll tell you a little bit about what to expect," he continued.

The back door where I had entered was suddenly jerked open. A heavy-set PO2 about my height stepped through the hatch. He was wearing thick, black, horned-rim glasses that magnified his eyes. He was dressed in dungarees and wearing a blue baseball cap. He was chewing on a six-inch, cotton-tip, applicator stick. In his right hand he had a paperback book. His index finger was marking the page. Something must have amused him, as he wore a broad smile on his round face. "Mahan, you ain't never gonna believe what that goddamn Miles just said," he chuckled. Shaking his head from side to side, he continued on into the treatment room. I watched him as he sat down and threw his leg upon the treatment table. He then opened the book and started to read. PO1 Mahan gave him a look of disgust but didn't say anything. I smelled the faint odor of alcohol as PO1 Mahan turned back toward me.

"He's being transferred in a few days. Meeker was transferred over from the Carter Hall to replace him," he explained. I glanced back at the table where the two were sitting. "It's about time for chow. I'm going over to the First Class Mess and eat. Meeker will show you the way to the mess hall. I'll see you back here at 1300," he said, turned, and left through the ward's backdoor.

I opened up the two lockers and started stowing my gear. I saw Meeker out of the corner of my eye as he stood up. He scratched his head vigorously. A nervous habit I would grow to detest in the coming months. He then came into the ward and jumped up on the top rack that was right under the porthole. He hung his shoes off the edge of the rack and lay back on the pillow. "We'll wait until 1230 when the line is down and then we'll grab a bite," he commented. A few seconds later the other PO2 stood up, stepped through the hatch and into the ward. Never taking his eyes off his book, he laid down on the rack directly across from Meeker. He continued chewing on the wooden applicator stick. Occasionally, he would turn his head and spit on the deck.

We were all back in sickbay by 1300. I stood leaning against the sink in front of the treatment table. Mahan had resumed his seat on the left-hand side, and Meeker was seated opposite him. The big PO2 had missed chow. If he had moved at all, it wasn't apparent. He had chewed the applicator stick down to a splinter. His constant spitting continued. Mahan looked back at where he was lying and shook his head. Meeker smiled, scratched his head and threw his leg upon the table. I started feeling uncomfortable and totally out of place.

I listened as Mahan explained what my duties would be. "Messer, the TO (table of organization) for a LSD only calls for three corpsmen. I'm going to assign you to sickcall. Meeker will be taking care of supplies and I'll take care of the records. Sickcall starts at 0800 and 1300 and runs until all the patients have been seen. You, being the junior man, will be expected to do the daily clean up. We'll give you a hand on field day." He stopped talking; I felt his eyes searching my face. I tried not to show what I was feeling. "Thursday is laundry day. Meeker will show you where the ship's laundry room is located and give you a hand if you need it," he continued. I looked at Meeker. He was locked in a thousand-yard stare. "It has to go down right after morning quarters. They'll call when it's finished and you can pick it up," he continued. I could hear the line forming for sickcall just outside the door. "We have thirty-two first aid boxes scattered throughout the ship. They'll need to be inventoried monthly. Every time one of these little shits wants a box of Band-Aids to take home he breaks into one of them. We seal them after making sure they are up to snuff. If the seals aren't broke you won't need to worry about them. We have two battle stations that have to be kept up to IOL (items on the list) too. But I hear the vermin gathering for sickcall so we'll get into all that later. Meeker, why don't you hangout here and show him where everything is?" he asked. With that, he opened the door. I could see four or five sailors leaning against the bulkhead waiting. Mahan walked past them and disappeared down the passageway. I turned and looked at Meeker. He didn't move.

The first few days I found it troubling that my fellow corpsmen had so little interest in treating patients. But, in the end, it became my salvation. The crewmembers could have cared less about supplies or monthly reports. They were looking for someone to render them medical treatment when they were sick, injured or emotionally upset. I was now challenged to put all the things I had previously learned to work. In a few weeks, I became comfortable caring for my shipmates. Little by little, I gained their confidence. For all practical purposes, I was their family physician. It was a rewarding experience and I felt needed and appreciated. I don't think anyone ever gave much thought to my rank. To them I was just Doc. My patients were all young men between the ages of eighteen and forty. The usual cuts, scrapes, burns, colds, earaches, body lice, venereal diseases and hangovers made up the majority of their complaints. The more complicated cases I would refer to a doctor at the Naval Station.

HM1 Mahan had joined the navy in 1943 at the age of seventeen. He had served as a corpsman aboard one of the big battleships that had been attacked by the Japanese kamikaze pilots. He still carried the well-worn sicklist of the people killed or injured on that infamous day in his wallet. Perhaps, he had been affected in a way we can never understand. He was highly intelligent and quite knowledgeable but had absolutely no interest in using either of these qualities. The only time I ever saw him when he seemed comfortable was when he was drinking or drunk. His leadership consisted of pouting and slamming out the door when he was displeased.

Meeker had been in the Navy for seven years. He had been married and had two children. A couple of years prior, his wife had met and fallen in love with an attorney while he was serving aboard the USS Carter Hall. She sued Meeker for divorce and had been awarded child support and alimony. His anger and bitterness was bone deep. It contaminated everything and everyone around him and ate away his life force like cancer. He talked constantly of murdering his ex-wife and her lover. His contribution to the safety and welfare of the Belle Grove's crew was minimal at best.

The second week I was on board, we were scheduled for an amphibious operation off the coast of California. The first day out was uneventful. I found it exciting to be at sea again after three years. Mahan seemed agitated and stayed in his bunk most of the first day. I tried to ignore him and went about my duties. The second day out, right after sickcall, he went into the office and filled out a request form for a liter of ethyl alcohol. "I'm going to get the custodian to issue this," he said and walked out the front door. Meeker had resumed his favorite seat at the treatment table. I glanced over at him for his reaction. He was locked in his normal mindless stare but a slight, knowing smile played around his lips. In a few moments a tall, handsome Lieutenant, about thirty years old, came into sickbay. He went over to the safe, knelt down, turned the combination lock a few rounds, and opened the door. He took the requisition that Mahan had filled out and made an entry in a logbook. Upon completing his administrative task, he reached in, took out a silver-colored, metal can, and handed it to Mahan. I noticed it had large black letters on both sides. Mahan placed it nonchalantly on the treatment cart.

Navy regulations required that an inventory board control alcohol and narcotics aboard naval vessels in the absence of a medical officer. The board was responsible to do a monthly inventory and appoint a custodian. The custodian was responsible to issue the items to the senior medical department representative upon his request. Once issued, the item would be entered into a working stock logbook and put into a smaller safe. It then became the responsibility of the medical personnel to account for its use.

Once the custodian had left, Mayan opened the can and sloshed three fingers of the white liquid into a coffee cup. He then took a sip and seemed to relax. As he continued to drink, his demeanor changed. His face soon became cherry red and he commenced to laugh and joke. "I signed this off to use as a cold sterilizing agent," he said to me, and lifted up the lid to one of the long trays where the surgical instruments were soaking in a colorless liquid. "But we use Benzalkonium Chloride," he continued and smiled over at Meeker. "I can tell you one thing, if there was alcohol in here I'd be sucking it out with a straw," he added and laughed hysterically as he replaced the top back on the tray.

Mahan had compromised his leadership position and made us all co-conspirators. It was obvious that this pleased Meeker. He could do pretty much as he pleased and Mahan dared not say anything. I was appalled by the situation, but being the junior man, I felt powerless to do anything about it. The investigation of the Medical Department's mishandling of controlled substance had concluded the day before I had arrived. I knew if I told the wrong person and they covered it up my life would be a living hell from that point on. I found it hard to believe that Mahan's actions weren't common knowledge to the officers and crew alike. I decided the best thing for me to do was to keep my mouth shut. I knew there was a good possibility that Mahan would not only destroy his own naval career but ours as well.

Mahan continued to drink throughout the day and far into the night. The following morning he refused to get up. It was a requirement that a corpsman be on duty in sickbay at all times, therefore, no one paid any attention when he didn't show up for quarters the next morning. Right after muster, I went below and started preparing for morning sickcall. I noticed the empty ethanol container was in the trashcan under the sink. I was somewhat amazed, as one quart of ethyl alcohol is equivalent to a half gallon of hundred proof liquor. Upon securing from sickcall, I swept and swabbed the treatment room and the ward. Mahan was in his rack still dressed in his dungarees. He appeared to be sleeping. The head was part of my cleaning responsibility. It was located just outside the back door of the ward. I had just entered and started to work when I heard the door to the ward slam and a click. I reached and tried to turn the knob. Mahan had locked me out. Apparently, I had disturbed his sleep. I was forced to return by way of the office. Carrying my cleaning gear, I returned to the treatment room and started washing out the swab. Meeker had resumed his post at the treatment table. "How long did you say you're going to be on this shit bucket?" he asked with a smirk. I didn't answer.

The crew aboard the Belle Grove was a cross section of mid America, with a little more emphasis on minorities. In those days, the steward mates were little more than servants to the officers. They cleaned their rooms, made their beds, prepared their meals and when imposed upon, shined their shoes. Their ranks were filled with Afro-Americans and Filipinos. The undeniable leader of the Afro-Americans on the BG was a PO1 Steward Mate by the name of Charlie Miles. Charlie was about as wide as he was tall. His feet slapped the deck when he walked and I could hear him coming long before I saw his familiar swagger. He was loud, gregarious, and fun loving. His experience working with difficult officers, resentful Filipinos, angry Afro-Americans, and prejudiced whites had honed Charlie's skills as a negotiator. Often times, he would accompany one of the blacks to sickbay for one reason or another. Sometimes it was because they were too embarrassed, or scared to come alone. Other times, it was because they felt like they hadn't been treated fairly. On those occasions, I went to great lengths to explain my reasoning for doing what I had done. Once I had gained Charlie's confidence, most of the others accepted me, and I became known as the main man in sickbay.

In those days, and I understand it remains so today, the Filipinos could join the American military. A good percentage of them seemed to prefer the Navy. Providing they were aboard ship on the West Coast there was a good chance it would be going to the Philippines at periodic intervals. At that time in our history, they were only permitted to enlist in the Navy with the understanding they would serve as stewards. They were, however, afforded the opportunity to transfer to other rates upon meeting certain requirements. It would have been hard to identify any one particular person as their leader, but they did stick together. The stewards prepared the officer's food as well as their own. The smell of cooked rice, onions, and garlic would often times permeate the passageways. On these occasions, the Filipinos who had managed to transfer to other rates would beat a steady path to the officer's mess to beg for a handout of "Gili Gili" (Traditional Filipino goulash dish made from many different kinds of meats).

Life aboard ship is a community unto itself. The personnel who cook, do the payroll, give shots, issue supplies, and keep service records are important folks in a shipboard sailor's life. Being in a key position to provide one of these services puts one in an enviable position. Each and every crewmember strives to have a contact with someone in these sectors. Provided you don't know anyone yourself, it's a good idea to have a close friend that does. The social dynamics of life aboard ship are truly unique. There's a certain camaraderie that comes from sharing a common destiny and being interdependent on each other. The military chain of command is the backbone that brings order and discipline. But the good ol' boy system brings with it the feeling of warmth and humanity.

The first of October, Peg and I made arrangements for her to join me. The price of apartments was exorbitant in Long Beach. Peg found a two-bedroom apartment in neighboring Wilmington for seventy-five dollars a month. The complex was in the older part of the city and was occupied by low-income families. Peg has always had a talent for turning the ordinary into something special. In a short time, our humble apartment became a comfortable home.

Peg's life was a lonely one and money was tight. My full take-home pay was three hundred and three dollars a month. I had made out her monthly allotment for two hundred and seventy-five dollars. I kept twenty-eight a month for my own health and welfare items. After Peg paid the rent, utilities, and made a fifty-dollar a month car payment, there wasn't much left. Being pregnant and without child-care, she started looking for a job that she could do at home. One Sunday, she found an advertisement by a company in Glendale looking for someone to address envelopes. Soon, she was gainfully employed. Each Monday she would drive to Glendale, some twenty miles away, and pick up a thousand envelopes and return home. The following Monday she would return them and pick up her check for seventeen dollars and another box of envelopes.

The BG required that one corpsman be on duty at all times. We ran a three-section watch, which meant I stayed aboard overnight every third day. Our operating schedule was a busy one and most weeks we were out on training exercises Monday through Friday.

In the latter part of October, one Thursday evening, I was sitting in the treatment room reading a magazine. We had been to sea for four days and had returned to Long Beach for the weekend. Most of the crew was on liberty and things were quiet. Someone knocked on the door.
"It's open," I called out and laid my magazine down. A tall, handsome, Second Class Petty Officer came in. He was dressed in an impeccable dress blue uniform. His skin was smooth and his hair dark and wavy. He walked to the opposite side of the table where I was sitting and stopped.

"How can I help you?" I asked. I could almost hear his brain clicking as his intelligent eyes sized me up. His face had a sad, lonely look. I could see he was extremely depressed.

"I'm not feeling too well, Doc?" he said.

"What seems to be the trouble?" I asked, and went to where he was standing, took his wrist and started counting his pulse. It was beating rapidly. He obviously wasn't drunk at the moment, but I suspected he had been on a drinking binge.

"I don't think I've ever seen you before," I remarked.

"My name is Maurice Karst; I just checked on board. I got out of the Navy for a few days and just recently reenlisted."

"Been celebrating?"

"A little," he replied and lowered his head while I counted his pulse. When I dropped his wrist, he raised his eyes and looked at me.

"I just reenlisted myself. This old mud-boat takes a little getting used to. Why don't you get a good night's sleep and if you still feel bad in the morning, come on back to see me." He stared off into the distance. I suspected he was having doubts about his career decision.

"Okay, Doc," he looked at me and offered his hand. I took it and we shook vigorously.

"Nice to meet you, Maurice. Everything is going to be alright."

"Thanks, Doc!" he said and nodded his head in agreement. I had the feeling he just needed to talk to someone and know that he wasn't alone. I was slowly coming to understand that was what most of my patients needed. The next morning I went through the chow line, filled my tray, and went over on the mess deck. I noticed Petty Officer Karst was chatting happily with one of the men from the damage control division. I went over and joined them.

"How you feeling?" I asked, looking into a clear set of hazel eyes.

"I'm feeling a damn site better than I was yesterday," he chuckled. I shook my head and we exchanged knowing looks.

Christmas passed and the New Year brought us into 1961. The first of March, the Belle Grove was scheduled for a three-week operation. Our baby was due the first week of April. My brother-in-law Hal, would be driving Peg's mother down the weekend of the tenth. I figured with any luck, I would be back in port before the baby arrived.

Seven days into the operation the word came down that it had been canceled. It seemed the Communists were trying to prevent their government from entering into a national coalition with the United States in some place called Laos. President John F. Kennedy had ordered military forces into neighboring Thailand. This was to symbolize the American Commitment to the Thai and South Vietnam Government. We were to proceed to Pearl Harbor with the amphibious task group. Upon our arrival, the ships started loading on marines and equipment. The Belle Grove took on four big Marine Amphibious Tractors and their crews. We immediately set sail for the setting sun. On the morning of the thirteenth, I had just finished sickcall and was swabbing the deck in the treatment room. I had latched the door open so as to increase the airflow. I was standing at the sink rinsing out my swab when out of the corner of my eye I saw a head pop through the door.

"Doc Messer," I turned and looked at RM3 Jones from the Radio Shack. He had a clipboard in his hand.

"Hey, what's up, Jonsey?" I asked.

"Got a message for you, Doc," he said and handed me a piece of flimsy paper. My heart skipped a beat. "Just sign here next to the red X," he added, handing me the clipboard.

I read:
Baby girl 6 lb. and 5 oz
Born 13 Mar 1961 at 0004
Mother and baby doing well
RM3 Jones hadn't said anything until he was sure I had read the message. I'm sure relief must have flooded my face. When I looked up, he was smiling.

"Congratulations, Doc," he said and offered me his hand. "First one?"

"Third!"

Mary Jean had arrived three weeks early. Hal drove Frances down and had stayed to visit. Peg had asked him to take her to Saturday evening confession at the local Catholic Church. In the middle of her confession, she suddenly said, "Father, you'll have to excuse me, my water just broke." What effect this had on Hal, I can't be sure. I do know that he was so nervous that he forgot to leave her overnight bag at the hospital that evening. Having to return to work the following Monday, he assured himself Peg and the baby were fine, and left town with the bag still in his car. Five days later, Peg made her barefoot trip home in a taxi wearing a hospital gown, carrying our new baby girl wrapped in a hospital blanket.

Meanwhile, I was on my way to an unknown destination. There was no way of communicating to her that the BG wouldn't be returning as scheduled. She would learn the day I was due back, the ship's location had been classified. When a ship gets underway, it seems to burst into life as it throbs with energy and activity. Men work, sweat, laugh, and curse on every deck and in every nook, crack and cranny. The vibrating, creaking and groaning of the ship's metal as she plows through the water brings a tranquil feeling of security to her crew. The men have a sense of mission and purpose as they fulfill their individual tasks. All the normal functions that one participates in when ashore become faint memories. The ever-present sound of the boatswain's whistle tells you when to wake, work, sweep, dump trash, eat and go to bed. The constant ringing of bells reminds one of the hour. The galley crew is forever cooking, cleaning, swabbing, washing and securing as the ship's crew pass through her mess decks three times a day. The men gather there between meals to complain, gossip, lie, drink coffee, smoke, argue, boast, joke and speculate on their destination.

Often times, after I finished sickcall I would prowl the Belle Grove's many decks just to visit and socialize. I would stop in the galley and do the daily-required sanitary inspection. I did more sampling, tasting, and laughing than I did inspecting. One of my favorite cooks was CS2 Robert L. Hansen. He spent so much time in sickbay visiting that his chief referred to him as the Hospitalman Cook.

As I strolled about, I would stop and chat with all of my favorite personalities in the different shops and offices. They would call to me cheerfully as I passed through their workspaces. There was Weatherman, Boling, and Armstrong supervising the deck gang. Teutekin worked in disbursing, Yeager and Golz in personnel. Romero and The Catfish (Maurice Karst) were in the shipfitter's shop. Murphy was assigned to the machine shop. Smith and Dixon worked in the small engine repair shop. Down in the engine rooms was a multitude of men that beat a steady path to my door from working in such an adverse environment. The conditions below decks were so horrendous I wondered how they survived. The metal handrails on the ladders leading down to their spaces were so hot I could barely touch them. They would laugh at me as they stood under the hot spot cooling blowers, dripping sweat onto the metal grated deck. The superstructure where the skivvy wavers (Signalman) worked was equally fascinating to me. I would watch them as they hoisted their many colored flags and talked in a language that only they could understand. I would finish my tour in the Captain's Pantry with John D. Rockett the Captain's private steward. I was always curious as to what the Old Man might be having for dinner. From there, I would go to the Officers Mess and inspect the food preparation area. I could only speculate as to the truth of their jokes about rubbing their penises on, and spitting in, the food of the officers that had in some way offended them. But if I were a betting man, I'd take odds that a good portion of their tales was true.

In the evening, the treatment table in sickbay would be covered with a large piece of plywood and converted into a card table. Pinochle or poker games would often times last far into the night. Those that didn't play would gather to laugh, talk, and give advice. Taps was at 2200 hours but sickbay was located behind closed doors and was a place of refuge. The room would be filled with cigarette smoke and a faint odor of Mahan's homemade cocktail.

Twelve days after leaving Pearl Harbor, the task group arrived at Okinawa to take on fresh stores. The marines had fought a fierce eighty-two day battle to capture the sixty by twenty-mile island from the Japanese during the Second World War. For this reason, plus its strategic location, the American military was reluctant to give up the island and retained control of her until 1972. It was considered then, and remains so today, the stepping stone to the Orient. One end of the island was known as Red Beach due to the bloody battle at the time of the invasion. The area where we were now located had faced little resistance and was referred to as White Beach. Little villages, with bars and houses of prostitution, were located all along the main road en route to the other end of the island where the big Navy base was located. The names were two difficult to remember so we referred to them as Village One, Two, Three and Four. Within a stone's throw of the White Beach boat dock, was an EM (enlisted men) club.

We were to be at White Beach for a couple of days. Each liberty section would have at least one day ashore. I went topside to take a look around the harbor. Big, gray amphibious ships surrounded us. I saw the big signalman they called Dixon leaning on the lifeline. I went over and joined him.

"Dixon, how many ships in this task group?" I asked.

"I think, about twenty," he replied.

"Looks like it's going to be a little crowded on the beach tonight," I remarked.

"Sure as hell ain't enough women in the villas to go around," he said and smiled over at me. "You know how sailors and marines are. If there aren't enough broads to keep them busy, they're going to beat the hell out of each other. They'll call White Beach, Red Beach after tonight," he laughed.

I was fortunate enough to be in the section that had liberty the first day. But, due to finances, I had decided to confine my liberty to drinking twenty-five-cent beer at the EM club. It was 1500 before the gangplank was put into place. Dozens of sailors and marines had lined up and stood waiting to catch the one liberty launch we had available. Liberty boats are loaded according to RHIP (rank has it's privileges). Being an E-4, I decided to wait until after evening chow, rather than stand in line for several hours.

Being in the same department with Meeker and both of us having limited funds, we decided to go to the EM club together. It was approximately 1800 hours when we arrived. We took a seat near the window, sipped our beer, and watched the steady stream of boats come and go from the landing dock. Around 2100 hours, I noticed there were more people gathering to return to their ships than there were boats available to take them. I watched, as the crowd steadily grew over the next hour. By 2200, about two thousand people had collected.

"Meeker, look at the damn people out there," I said.

"Jesus Christ, we better get our asses out there or we won't never get back," he said, and started picking up his change. We downed our beer and headed for the dock. As we approached, I saw the Shore Patrol trying to break up a fight. Then another broke out and then another. The Shore Patrols were thumping heads with their nightsticks. Everywhere I looked, I saw marines and sailors fighting with each other. The brawls were breaking out like brush fires. There were never less than three altercations going on at any one time. The Shore Patrol would quell one clash only to have two more to deal with.

I could see seventy or eighty Belle Grove sailors waiting on the landing dock. We picked our way through the crowd trying to get close to the loading ramp. The pushing, shoving, kicking, and punching prohibited us from making much of a headway. Soon, I heard the sound of a large motor and I looked seaward and saw a huge LCM (landing craft for putting marines on the beach) coming into view. APA-208 was stenciled on her side. "There's one of Talledega's LCMs," I said to Meeker.

The officer in charge of the landing dock was frantic. In spite of his efforts to maintain order, the crowd was rapidly turning into an uncontrollable mob. Upon arrival of the big LCM, the Talladega sailors were quickly ordered on board. The Officer noted that there was still ample space left in the LCM. Wanting to get as many men off the landing ramp as possible, he quickly filled the boat with Belle Grove sailors.

"Make the Talladega first, then the Belle Grove, and return here immediately," he ordered. Meeker and I had been too far back to make it into the LCM. The craft had no sooner left when the Belle Grove launch arrived and we clamored on board. Meeker had climbed upon the boat housing to get away from the crowd.

"Get your ass down from there, Meeker," ordered the Coxswain.

"Fuck you," said Meeker. The Coxswain cut the engine and the boat drifted dead in the water.

"We aren't going anywhere until you get down from there." The men stopped talking and started looking to see who was the senior man in the boat.

"Do what you're told right now, Meeker," SK1 Doresch ordered. Meeker looked sullenly around the boat for a minute then hopped down. I thought that was the end of it but I was badly mistaken. Upon arrival in sickbay, Meeker went to the file cabinet where the health records were kept. He found the coxswains medical record, walked over to the porthole and threw it out.

"What the hell you doing, Meeker?" I asked.

"We'll see how he likes taking his shots over again," he answered. Then, he turned to me. "If you ever say anything about this to anyone, I'll cut your goddamn throat while you're sleeping," he threatened. I knew if I said anything to anyone that it would be my word against his. I abhorred his action, but once again found myself in a no-win situation.

The next morning about seven, someone knocked on the door. I thought, perhaps, it was an emergency since it was about an hour before sickcall was due to start. I opened the door and MM3 Grant walked in. His dress blue uniform was in rags and his face, neck and arms were black and blue. He walked over and sat down on the stool next to the treatment table.

"What the hell happened to you?" I asked. Before he had time to respond, MM2 Studenbordt walked in and sat down on the opposite side of the table. His right eye was swollen completely shut, and the white piping on his dress blue jumper was blood stained. Grant looked at Studenbordt. "Huh, huh, huh," he laughed and his whole upper torso heaved up and down. I took a handful of alcohol sponges out of the canister and started cleaning Grant's wounds.

"Doc, did you know that goddamn Shore Patrol Officer put all of our asses in that LCM with them assholes from the Talladega?" asked Studenbordt.

"Huh, huh, huh," laughed Grant.

"Yeah, I know. Meeker and I missed it by a hair," I replied, as I continued working on Grant. I could see several other men with cuts and bruises lining up outside the sickbay door.

"Well, about halfway to the Talledega a goddamn riot broke out in the boat. I was minding my own business when this skinny little son-of-a-bitch ran the full length of the LCM and jumped on my chest like a little spider. I hit him right on top of the head and he went out like a light. Then, all hell broke loose," Studenbordt continued to explain.

"Huh, huh, huh, huh," Grant laughed, remembering the ordeal.

"I tell you, Doc, it was really something. Every goddamn person in that boat was fighting. The coxswain made the gangplank but we just kept kicking ass. The OOD got on the bullhorn and ordered everyone to come on board. Things kind of broke up and the Talladega sailors started up the ladder. I thought that was going to be the end of it but the OOD kept yelling, 'All of you, get up here.' I told everyone to just ignore the asshole and not look up. We started milling around in circles. Finally he told one of the marines, 'Go down there and march them up here.' 'Why don't you do it yourself, my big, brave leader?' the marine asked him."

"Huh, huh, huh, huh," Grant continued with his ridiculous laugh.

"Damn, then what happened?' I asked, thinking how lucky we'd been not to have made it into the boat.

"Well, after about fifteen minutes they sent for a marine fire team. The OOD ordered them to lock and load their weapons. Rounds slamming into the chamber of them old M-1 Rifles makes kind of a convincing sound. We decided it was time to give it up," chuckled Studenbordt.

"Huh, huh, huh, huh," laughed Grant.

"They kept us standing at attention there on the quarter-deck from 2300 last night until 0600 this morning," continued Studenbordt. Having cleaned and treated Grant's wounds, I went to work on Studenbordt.

"So, now what?" I asked.

"The OOD wrote us up for mutiny and the Commanding Officer on the Talladega wants us court-martialed," he answered.

"Holy shit," I replied.

"Huh, huh, huh, huh," went Grant.

At 0800 hours that same morning, the Captain held Captains Mast on the twenty-four Belle Grove Sailors that were charged. He dismissed all charges after giving them a good dressing down. The Uniform Code of Military Justice doesn't permit that one be charged for the same crime twice. There was no way the Old Man was going to wait for a directive from the Captain on the Talledega ordering him to court martial his men. Nineteen of them were from the engineering divisions and we would need our Mutineers to get us underway.

The next day we set sail for parts unknown. Liberty in foreign ports is mostly centered around drinking, whoring and fighting. I don't ever remember any dignitaries or nice families from the local communities coming on board and inviting us over for dinner. You can be relatively certain that no one I knew would have accepted anyway. Stories of the events at the last liberty port would be told and retold. A good deal of the things that happened were outlandish enough but became even more so as they were embellished.

We, of course, had our natural storytellers. The Catfish became notorious for his descriptive narrations. He had the tone of voice and the facial expressions down to an art form. Upon completing his tale, he would hold his mouth open in an idiotic grin, shrug his shoulders, arch his eyebrows and look around at his audience. Once the hysterical laughter began, he would laugh as long and hard as the rest of us. Descriptions like, "I was so nervous I couldn't have taken a poop in a bathtub," and "My heart was pounding like a baby robins butt," became classics.

Catfish was a two fisted drinker and had his share of adventures. He had quickly learned as a young sailor that one needed to be perceptive if he was to survive. He was a keen observer and developed some rather unique survival skills. One of which was to pretend he was asleep after a couple of drinks. When everyone else became roaring drunk, he would miraculously come out of his stupor. This, of course, would put him at great advantage when dealing with the evil ones. Some of our more worldly shipmates would often times find themselves out maneuvered when battling for the hand of a fair lady. There was also the matter of the bill that had to be dealt with as the evening progressed. Once on board, the war of rivalry previously waged on the beach would soon be forgotten. At that point, the accounting of what had happened would become more important than the actual occurrence. Catfish had a warm sensitive side and cared deeply for his shipmates. Over time, he became one of my best friends. We spent many long nights talking into the wee hours of the morning.

At sea, one of the big events in the evening was the movie of the day. When the weather was fair, we would have the showing on the weather deck. Foul weather would find us in the shipfitters shop. There, we would cluster to laugh and talk of the day's events. The camaraderie that we shared gave meaning to our lives and was the single most important factor that enabled us to endure the long, difficult months that we were separated from our loved ones.

We lived by the orders of CINCPAC (Commander in Chief, Pacific Command) and his directives governed every aspect of our lives. One of the primary concerns of those days was controlling VD (Venereal Diseases). I had a stack of instructions on how the program was to be conducted. One of the requirements was to show certain training films to every crewmember on board. The movies were old and outdated. Apparently, the primary purpose of the films was to modify any promiscuous behavior that one might be contemplating by scaring them half to death. Graphic pictures of grotesque body parts were a big part of the subject matter. The older men were immune to such tactics, but seemed to enjoy adding to the fear of the younger sailors. I would follow the movie with a fifteen-minute common sense lecture stressing the importance of good hygiene and the use of condoms. The graphics would often times make the greater impression. Those that were about to make their first foreign liberty port would shake their heads and vow abstinence. Experience taught me the truth of the old cliché, "The road to hell is paved with good intentions."

One of the biggest problems I had was trying to convince my shipmates not to go to the bathroom and examine themselves fifteen times a day. "Look, if you start squeezing your nose every half hour, it's going to swell up, too." I would warn them over and over. CINCPAC directed that all hands have a short arm inspection at periodic intervals while deployed outside the Continental United States. What possible better time could there be for this unholy task than payday? I would station myself just outside the hatch of the compartment where the crew was to pick up their money. As they stepped through the hatch, I would instruct them on the unpleasant procedure at hand. Wanting to ensure that I suffered in their humiliation, they would refer to me as the Pecker Checker.

We had a cook from Montana and we just naturally fell into calling him Monty. He was pleasant enough but tended to be on the worrisome side. We had been out of Okinawa less than a day when he found his way to sickcall.

"Doc, I think I got it."

"Got what, Monty?" I asked.

"You know, the creeping crud."

"No, Monty. It takes three to five days to develop any symptoms. Don't worry about it. You'll know soon enough. Just check your skivvies in the morning for a yellow discharge and if you see something suspicious come on back and I'll take a specimen for analysis." Monty would seem to be reassured for the moment. But each time he went to the bathroom to urinate he was sure he felt something burning. A week passed, and he continued to return to sickbay two or three times a day. Each time I would dutifully examine him and reassure him that he was fine. He insisted he could feel a burning sensation and it was getting worse by the hour. I was sure he was irritating himself in his vigorous self-examination.

Finally, in desperation, I treated him for a urinary tract infection in the hopes that it would give him some peace of mind. I decided to treat him with Pyridium. It's a relatively harmless drug and specific for mild bladder infections. The only side effect is that it turns your urine a bright red to orange. I treated Monty at morning sickcall and he returned to his duties in the galley. About ten in the morning, I heard the back door to the ward burst open. I looked up and saw Monty rushing toward me with his penis in his hand. Tears were streaming down his cheeks.

"I told you, Doc; I told you, Doc," he repeated over and over as he entered the treatment room.

"What is it now, Monty?" I asked, feeling exasperated.

"I'm pissing pure blood, Doc," he responded and burst into tears. I knew it was an oversight not to have explained that one little minor characteristic of Pyridium. I tried very hard not to smile as I took his blood pressure and calmed him down. I explained to him why his urine had changed color.

"You sure ought to have told me about that, Doc." he lamented.

"Yeah, I know. I know, Monty. I'm sorry about that." I answered.

"It was just wrong what you did, Doc," he continued, as he recomposed himself and dried his eyes.

"You're right. You're right," I agreed.

In time, Monty saw the humor in the whole affair. A few weeks later he gave one of his pills to a mess cook and told him if he had VD his urine would turn red. I locked the Pyridium in the Narcotic Locker and never used it again. Enough was enough.

Over time, I learned that each rating had it's own occupational hazard. The men that worked down in the hole (Engine and Boiler rooms) sweat profusely and it ran down into their ears. They would come to sickbay with their ear canals swollen almost closed and in excruciating pain. I cut small pieces of gauze, soaked them in boric acid, and packed it in their ears. I would then give them a small 1-oz bottle of the solution and instruct them to keep the gauze wet. In twenty-four hours, they would experience what seemed like a miraculous cure. The eternal acne and dehydration was much harder to combat. The deck gangs kept me in practice suturing up their lacerations and treating their many scrapes, cuts and bruises. The cooks and mess-cooks managed to send me a good burn case about once a week.

Treating dental problems was normally restricted to gum disease and replacing fillings that had fallen out. I became proficient at putting Zinc Oxide with a little Eugenol (oily local antiseptic used to relieve pain) and stirring cotton fibers into the concoction until I had a nice paste. I would clean and dry the cavity and then pack it with the mixture. I would have them grind their teeth before the paste hardened and scrape away the excess. The fillings were never meant to be anything more than a temporary measure. I always advised them to make dental sickcall as soon as a support activity became available. However, going on liberty was often their first priority. Consequently, several of my shipmates retained the old fillings for years.

The crew's faith in my ability to heal, often times left me feeling humble and totally inadequate. I had been forced by necessity to memorize a good portion of the Handbook of the Hospital Corps. I pretty well knew what I was capable of doing and tried not to cross over the line. But, on occasion, it was impossible not to do things that would have been questionable under normal circumstances.

The fourth day out from Okinawa, at about 1500, one of the marine sergeants who was accompanying the AMTRACS showed up at sickbay. I had secured from sickcall a little earlier and was rather surprised to see him. He was holding his jaw and had a pained expression on his face.

"Doc, I have a tooth that's killing me," he moaned.

"Come on in and let's take a look," I replied. I directed him to sit in the chair next to the treatment table and tilt his head back. "Okay, open your mouth and show me the one that hurts," I told him. He touched one of the large molars on the lower right side.

"Doc, can't you just pull the goddamn thing?"

"Well, I don't pull teeth. But, I'm sure we can get you comfortable." I could see a black cavity in the middle of the tooth. I took a dental tool and probed the area. He winced with pain when I touched it. I could see it had extended down into the root of the tooth and concluded that the nerve was being affected. I cleaned it out and packed a piece of cotton with Eugenol in the cavity. I then gave him a couple of aspirins and sent him on his way.

Two hours later, he was back. I could see my treatment had done very little to alleviate his pain, but there wasn't much more I could do. I considered giving him some morphine but I wouldn't be able to keep him on it indefinitely.

"Please Doc, you've got to pull this damn tooth," he lamented. I had him sit back down and open his mouth and I took another look.

"I never pulled a tooth before. I'm afraid I'll break the damn thing off."

"Doc, I can't stand this pain. I can't eat or sleep. You got to get that tooth out of there." I continued to examine his mouth. I knew I had to do something. The tooth didn't really look infected; that was to my advantage. We had a book on dental emergencies in the office. I retrieved it and started reading. There was an area on teeth extractions that was quite explicit. I could block the whole lower jaw by injecting

Novocain in the back of the mouth just above the wisdom tooth. I took another look at my patient. He gave me a look of desperation. That convinced me.

"Okay, Sarg. Let's get you over here in this chair where the back is a little higher," I directed him, patting the back of the chair. He gave me a hopeful look and changed seats. I laid all the equipment out on a white towel that I had put on the treatment table. "Let's get your head back," I instructed. He laid his head on the back of the chair. "Okay, open up," I continued. He quickly complied. I picked out an area that most resembled the picture I had been looking at. I injected the Novocain and waited five minutes. I then opened his mouth and touched his gum on the lower right. "Feel that?" I asked, touching his gum with a small dental probe.

"Don't feel a thing, Doc," he answered. Meeker had got out of his bunk and came into the treatment room and stood watching.

"You're going to be in a world of shit if you break that off," he commented sarcastically. I did my best to ignore him. I didn't need any negative input at that point. I had already decided that I was going to take the tooth out one way or another. I took the extractors and slipped the lip of the instrument over the tooth and down to the gum. I then squeezed the handles down tight. Having a firm grip on the tooth, I then rotated my wrist inward. I felt the tooth loosen and come free. I took it out of his mouth and laid it on the towel in front of my patient. He tried to smile, but his lower lip was completely numb. The blood and saliva ran out of his mouth and slid down his chin.

"Damn that feels great, Doc."

"Good!" I said and gave him a pat on the shoulder. I was feeling pretty good about how well things had gone, but I knew that there was still danger of him developing a dry socket. I cleaned the cavity good with hydrogen peroxide and packed it with a small cotton ball. "Leave that cotton in there overnight and come on back to see me in the morning," I advised him.

Fortunately for us both, it healed without any problem. Over the next few days, I saw him from time to time chatting with his comrades. He would give me a big smile, "There's the Corpsman I was telling you about," he would say and nod his head in my direction. "Pull any teeth today, Doc?" he would call out. I would shake my head, and smile back.

The sixth day out we steamed into the Gulf of Thailand. We now knew we were to go up the Chao Phraya River some twenty-six miles to the city of Bangkok. There we would off-load the AMTRACKS and their crews. Hopefully, we would then return to the States and resume our previous operating schedule. Coming into the Gulf from the open sea, the water became rough and the Belle Grove commenced to rock, roll, and pitch from side to side.

The first class petty officers (E-6) took their meals from the crew's galley but had a small messing area set aside where they all gathered to eat, drink coffee, socialize, and pass the time. The only things the area afforded them, that the crew's mess deck didn't have, were a refrigerator and a Mr. Coffee maker. The most important thing, of course, was being separated from the E-5's and below. Most of them retained the title of Division Leading Petty Officer and it was important not to fraternize with the junior-rated men. They were considered the privileged class of those who still wore the white hat. This was their private domain. They were little less than the chief petty officers who lived just up the passageway. Everyone knew you didn't go into the CPO quarters unless you had official business. We all abided by the military pecking order and took a certain amount of comfort in knowing where we stood.

As we entered into the Gulf, I was busy cleaning up after morning sickcall. I had just swabbed the head, stepped out in the passageway and turned to go into the ward when I heard an ungodly noise.

"OH LORD NO, MY GOD NO, OH LORD PLEASE NO, JESUS, SAVE ME, O LORDEY, LORDEY, MY GOD HAVE MERCY ON ME, MERCY, DAMN." I looked up and saw Charlie Miles running toward me with his head thrown back and his arms flailing wildly in the air. As you remember, Miles was one of the most respected and loved petty officers on the Belle Grove. He was also notorious for his antics and when he thought the crew needed a morale boost he could be pretty original. I naturally assumed Miles was putting on one of his performances and didn't pay much attention to him at first, but I did notice he had a wild look in his eyes.

"What are you up to, Charlie?" I asked, and looked at him suspiciously. When he got within a couple of feet of me, he turned and started back up the passageway. Then I saw the steam coming off his clothes. I ran and touched his back. He felt hot. Two other first class petty officers came running into the passageway.

"The hot water from the top part of the coffee maker spilled over on him when we took that big roll," one of them blurted out.

I could see he had been burned from the top of his neck, across his back and down to his upper buttocks. I reached out and grabbed his arm. "CHARLIE, WE'VE GOT TO GET THOSE CLOTHES OFF OF YOU," I yelled. He threw me back against the bulkhead with such force it knocked the breath out of me. He then ran back in the other direction, all the time crying and whimpering. I recovered and ran to the treatment room and grabbed a pair of bandage scissors. Three other first class had joined us.

"GRAB HIM AND HOLD HIM," I pleaded. Two of them tried to hold him by his arms, but he quickly broke free and ran back up the passageway.

"HELP THEM!" I cried. They all ran after Charlie and were finally able to restrain him. I started cutting the clothes away. For once, thank God, HM1 Mahan was sober. He was at my side instantly. He grabbed Charlie's right arm and injected him with a ¼ grain of Morphine.

"WE HAVE TO TREAT THE PAIN BEFORE HE GOES INTO SHOCK!" he exclaimed. I nodded in agreement. We walked Charlie toward the treatment room as I cut away the last of his clothing. I could feel his big body trembling in agony.

"PUT YOUR HANDS ON THE TABLE AND LEAN FORWARD," Mahan directed. Charlie leaned his quivering body forward and braced himself. He was in a high state of agitation and writhed in pain. Mahan quickly injected another ¼ grain of Morphine. A good portion of the top layer of skin had come off with Charlie's undershirt. He had first and second degree burns covering a good 30% of his body. I couldn't see any evidence of third degree burns but I couldn't be sure.

"OH LORD, OH LORD, OH LORD, OH LORD," he repeated over and over. I took a handfull of sterile four by fours and squirted Phisohex (liquid anti-bacterial soap) on the burned area and started scrubbing away the dead tissue. Once I had him cleaned up, Mahan covered the burned area with 4 X 4's soaked in Furacin Ointment. Charlie's blood pressure commenced to stabilize as the Morphine took effect.

"You're going to be okay, Charlie," I reassured him as we worked.

"Praise the Lord for you, John. Praise the Lord for you, Fred," he said between catches in his breath.

"I sure hope you can sleep on that big belly of yours, Charlie," I teased, hoping to bring a lighter moment to the situation.

"I just gonna stand up from now on," he grunted. We laughed with a sigh of relief. Putting him on his stomach wasn't that difficult. Making him comfortable was a whole other matter. Each morning, I would take off the old bandages and scrub the burned area until I could see healthy tissue shining through. The procedure was painful for him but he endured it with his usual good humor. In a few days, Charlie was back to his old self, laughing, talking and telling tales. A steady stream of officers and enlisted men came to sickbay to visit the fat man. The twelve days I had Charlie under my care were a rare pleasure. At night, when all was quiet, he would tell me of his experience in the old days before the Navy was integrated. His colorful vocabulary was laced with profanity and filled with laughter. Charlie had lived an eventful life. I was glad he recovered so quickly, but I missed him when he went back to full duty.

The Chao Phraya was a shallow river. The only two ships from the battle group that could navigate her waterway were the Belle Grove and the Carter Hall. Arriving in Bangkok, we anchored on the bank opposite the small boat landing that was the gateway into the city. The river was alive with small boats filled with people, produce, pigs, and chickens. The boats were long and narrow and built low in the water. They were sleek and fast but had an appearance of fragility. The screw was attached to a long movable pole that was operated from the back of the boat. It could be lifted out of the water and dropped at any angle. This enabled the boat to make precision right and left turns, seemingly on a dime. As we dropped anchor, I joined Catfish and Romero on the wing wall just outside their berthing compartment. We watched, fascinated.

"Look at them goddamn things," Catfish said nodding toward the myriad of craft that surrounded us.

"Think the Old Man will use our big launches to get us ashore?" Romero asked, looking at Catfish.

"Hell, yes. The Belle Grove's coxswains ought to be able to sink ten or twelve of them little boats and drown a couple of hundred people between here and the landing," answered Catfish with a chuckle.

"Yeah, that's one way to start an international incident," Romero answered sarcastically.

I am happy to report that the Captain decided to use commercial water taxis to get the crew ashore. The only incident we had was when EN2 Dixon decided to rock the boat to see if it would be easy to capsize. It was, and he had a nice swim with his shoes on.

I had duty the first night in Bangkok. It was just as well as I really didn't have a great deal of money to spend anyway. I was happy to get the marines and two thirds of the ship's company ashore. It was nice and peaceful aboard. I went to chow early in the evening and later on wandered back to sickbay to read a book. About 2130, I decided to stroll through the berthing compartments. I was walking through "S" Division's compartment when I heard a noise.

"Psst, Doc, come over here," someone summoned. I couldn't see very well, as there were several men standing in the dark against the far bulkhead. I knew something out of the ordinary was going on so I walked over to investigate.

"What's up?" I asked.

"You want a drink, Doc?" one of the men asked.

"What'cha got?" I asked.

He passed me a large bottle of something. I took it and held it up to the light. I saw a picture of a tiger on the label. I smelled of it.

"Damn! This shit's rotten," I commented.

"Take a drink, Doc," someone invited. I took a very small sip. It was, by far, the worst beverage I ever tasted.

"What the hell is that?" I asked and passed the bottle back to my benefactor.

"They fermented a thousand camel's assholes to make this shit, Doc," one of the men chuckled. Everyone joined in the laughter.

"Where did you get it?" I asked.

"Some old Poppason climbed up the anchor chain and was selling it," someone answered.

"I wouldn't drink that panther piss if I were you guys; it might make you sick. Who in the hell knows what it is, or where it came from, for that matter?" I cautioned.

It's strictly against Naval Regulations to drink alcohol aboard naval vessels without authorization. I certainly knew some old Poppason hadn't been authorized to shimmy up the anchor chain and sell booze to the duty section. But I didn't really give it a great deal of thought. Probably, I had become so accustomed to seeing Mahan drunk day in and day out that I had become desensitized to such matters. The group that I had encountered was made up of my friends and shipmates. It never once crossed my mind that I should report them to a higher authority.

We spent the next three weeks in Bangkok. My monthly earnings served to keep me out of trouble for the most part, but I did manage to get ashore on a couple of occasions. It was an enchanting city filled with fabulous Buddhist temples. Huge statues of the Lord Buddha stood in front of the magnificent structures. Inside these palaces of worship, were smaller Buddhas that were so dazzling that they would literally take my breath away. They were made of solid gold and covered in gems and other precious stones. Bronze, jewels, star sapphires and jade could be bought throughout the city at unheard of low prices. The cab driver who took me into the city had three wives. He informed me that you could have, by law, as many as you could support. I found that a novel idea.

"How do you keep them from fighting?" I asked.

"I don't; that's part of the fun," he said smiling at me in the rearview mirror.

Bangkok, due to its location, was geared more for the tourist's trade than the fleet. An air of sophistication permeated the ancient city that wasn't found in most Far Eastern cities of that era. Our mission had been to deliver the AMTRACS to Bangkok and off-load them. After three weeks of trying to disembark the big tractors, the marines determined it was too wet and muddy to navigate in the surrounding area. The majority of the crew had spent all their money by this time and we were happy to be on our way.

The second day at sea I went up to the XO's (Executive Officer) mailbox to deliver the sick list. There, much to my surprise, lined up outside his door was about twenty of my shipmates. I recognized DK2 Teutekin from disbursing.

"What's going on, Teut?"

"I'm not sure." I moved on down the line and came to Ridings.

"What's with all this, Ridings?" I asked. He shrugged his shoulders and smiled sheepishly but didn't answer.

"Move along, Doc," ordered the MAA that was controlling the line. I returned to sickbay feeling perplexed. I knew there was an investigation going on but I couldn't imagine why. I gave a quick examination of my conscience and concluded it had little to do with me. I had no more than dismissed the idea when a knock came on the door. I opened it up to see the duty MAA.

"The XO wants to talk to you, Messer,"

"What about?" I asked.

"You'll find out soon enough," he answered. I went up and joined the line with the others. No one seemed to know anything. As the men came out of the room they were ushered down the passageway in the opposite direction.

After an indefinite time, I was shown into Commander Anderson's stateroom. He had graduated from the Naval Academy and was every man's idea of a real Naval Officer. I could only speculate as to what fate had brought him to serve as Executive Officer on the Belle Grove.

"Have a seat, Messer," he ordered. I removed my cover and sat down.

"Are you familiar with your rights under article 131 of the Uniform Code of Military Justice?" he asked.

"Yes sir, more or less," I answered.

"Well, let me read it to you," he said and proceeded to advise me of my rights. He then closed the brown manila folder in front of him and looked up at me. His dark intelligent eyes searched my face. I held his gaze and tried not to waiver.

"Messer, you're one of the most respected men aboard this ship. I know you were drinking on board the night of April twenty-third. I have witnesses to that effect. You don't have to incriminate yourself but I would like to ask you a question."

"Yes, sir," I answered.

"Well, if you have such little regard for the regulations that govern this ship, I'm just wondering what the rest of this crew is capable of doing."

"Well, sir, I don't think they would kill anyone," I answered. He gave me a quizzical look filled with disbelief.

"I am just trying to understand. I would like to know at what point you folks would put duty before personality."

"Well sir, it's kind of like this. If someone is nuts and they don't do any harm to anyone, society doesn't lock them up. On the other hand, if someone is completely crazy, and they go around breaking out windows and causing a disturbance, they're put away. That's, more or less, the way it is with us. If there is some minor infraction and it doesn't cause any harm to our welfare, or threaten our mission, I think we're pretty tolerant of each other's behavior." I answered.

"So, rules and regulations don't mean a damn thing to this crew. Is that what you're telling me?" he asked. I sensed his disillusionment and decided not to answer. He looked sad. Maybe he regretted not having become a professor or an accountant. The words of Chief Causee from boot camp came back to me. "We won the Second World War. We quit the Korean War. God only help us in the next one." I squirmed uneasily in my seat. I thought maybe that I should tell him I only took a swallow and had told the others to be careful. But I knew he would think less of me if I didn't assume responsibility for my actions. He interrupted my thoughts.

"You can go now, Messer," he said. I stood up to leave. I wanted to apologize or do something to makeup for my behavior, but I knew it was too late. I felt dejected as I opened the door to leave.

"Send in the next man," he said in a tired voice. In the days that followed, we speculated about how the XO might feel about us but never about our possible punishment. The matter was dropped. Maybe the XO thought there were too many of us to punish, or perhaps he didn't want to worry the Captain. Whatever the reason, we would never know. We were left to stew in our own misery and to contemplate our evil ways.

We had no idea, at that time, the gravity of the problem that was brewing in Southeast Asia. Many of us would return here in a not-too-distant future to fight a war we were destined to lose. For the moment, we were just happy that for whatever reason, our mission had been canceled and we were on our way back to Long Beach. The voyage was long and boring back to Pearl Harbor where we off-loaded the AMTRAKS and their crews. We thought we were going to be gone only a few weeks, but instead it had turned into months. The night before arriving, many of us came down with that familiar malady called "channel fever." This is characterized by the inability to sleep in anticipation of soon being reunited with loved ones.

Peg had called ships information on a regular basis and knew the date we were arriving. She was waiting for me with Darrel, Terry, and new baby, Mary, on the Magnolia Street Landing. As the boat approached, I searched the crowd frantically. Peg had seen me long before I saw her. Once she became aware that I had found her, she switched the baby to her left arm and waved happily. Darrel was wrapped around her left leg sucking a blue bottle and Terry around her right with a pink one in her mouth. I leaped off the boat and fairly ran up the rickety old landing to greet them.

Coming from life aboard ship into the bosom of a family is always an adjustment. Meshing of the two ways of life can be stressful for everyone. Mom has been in charge and suddenly someone, almost a stranger, is giving orders. The dynamics of the family changes. Mom switches her attention from the children to this almost-stranger. They soon learn that crying and refusing to eat gets them attention. But nothing works like refusing to go to sleep. The first night I was home, Darrel and Terry fussed and cried the first two hours and Mary the rest of the night. The only unbroken sleep I had in those first two weeks back home was when I had the duty.

The Belle Grove was scheduled to go to Portland, Oregon for a Fleet Rehabilitation and Modernization Overhaul (FRAM) in late June. The crew was informed that this would take a minimum of six months. That would carry us into the latter part of 1961. We would then return to Long Beach for a month of underway training in January. If all went well, we would depart for our scheduled Western Pacific cruise around the fifteenth of February. There was one more little item that needed to be mentioned. The Navy wouldn't be paying for moving our dependents and household effects to Portland, as it was not considered a change of homeport. Well, it didn't take a lot of math to figure out that if you didn't bring your family, you'd be looking at a yearlong separation. This was not good news for the married men. Bitter resentment filled our hearts and cries of sorrow filled the passageways and berthing spaces.

In spite of the financial hardship, Peg and I decided she and the children would accompany me. We put our furniture in storage and packed a few essentials in a U-haul. On the second of June, we made our way up the Pacific Coast. After a long day of travel, we arrived at Portland in the early evening and rented a motel room for the night. While Peg was quieting the children down, I went to the corner and bought a local paper.

"I don't see any furnished apartments in here," I said to Peg after scanning the classifieds. All three of the children were still in diapers and sucking the bottle. The long hard day in the car, plus the disruption of their routine, had turned them into little demons.

"I sure hope we can find something soon," Peg lamented as she tried desperately to calm them down.

"We'll find something. What you look for, you find." I answered, trying to sound more confident than I was feeling.

The next morning, I went to the doughnut shop near the motel and bought a dozen doughnuts and a half-gallon of milk. After breakfast, we packed up the car and set out on our search. Since we had no real leads, we decided to drive around and look for rent signs. The month of June in Portland can be hot and humid. As the day dragged on it got hotter and hotter. Each "For Rent" sign we saw, I investigated, but they were all unfurnished. The children began to fuss and cry as we journeyed up and down the seemingly infinite number of streets. They sensed our anxiety, and often times, all three of them would be crying at once.

"Can't you do something with them?" I asked Peg, feeling agitated.

"What am I supposed to do?" she responded as she turned and tried to get bottles in as many mouths as possible. I looked over at her. I knew she was at her wit's end. I had noticed a sign in front of a little, white house with blue trimming that set well back off the street. I made the block and came back and parked. I went and rang the doorbell. A young woman of about thirty-five answered the door.

"Yes!"

"I saw your for rent sign."

"Oh, it was rented this morning. We should have taken the sign down," she said, and reached over and removed it.

"My ship is coming here to Portland for an overhaul and we had hoped to get a furnished place for a few months." She looked at Peg frantically trying to pacify the children.

"That's not going to be easy," she said, continuing to watch Peg. "Look why don't you bring your family in out of the heat for a little rest. You can use my phone to call around to a few of the local real estate offices." I looked back at Peg; her face glowed red from the afternoon heat.

"If you're sure you don't mind, I would appreciate it."

"Not at all," she said, opening the door, she walked out to the car. "I've invited your husband to use our phone to make a few calls. Won't you please come in for a little while?" she asked Peg in a tender voice filled with compassion.

Peg appeared embarrassed but accepted the invitation graciously. We were soon seated at the kitchen table drinking lemonade. Peg changed diapers around and I got on the phone. After a dozen or so calls, I had begun to think the situation was hopeless. I was contemplating us staying another night in a motel and then driving the family back down to Oakland the following morning. I decided to make one last call.

"Avalon Real Estate," a pleasant, middle-age male voice answered.

"My ship is coming to Portland for a few months and I need to rent a furnished apartment for me and my family," he listened, as I explained our situation.

"Just a minute," he said after a moment of hesitation. Peg noticed I was holding and looked at me hopefully. I shrugged my shoulders. In a short time he was back.

"We have a house that the owner has recently died. It's presently in probate and probably will be for a few months. The furniture is still in there. The attorney handling the case wants to rent it. If you're interested, I could show it to you in a half hour."

"Really!" I answered almost shocked.

"Yes, it's just over the South side of the B street bridge right next to the cemetery," he chuckled.

I took down the address and hung up. The sudden turn of events was almost unbelievable. I quickly explained to Peg and the lady of the house what had happened. We gathered up the children and loaded them into the car. It was impossible for us to express our gratitude to this kind lady. She had touched our lives in a profound way without wanting anything in return. We were powerless to repay her. She had truly been an angel in our hour of need.

We met with the real estate agent a few minutes later, paid him seventy-five dollars and moved into our new home. Our nearest neighbors lay quietly in the cemetery directly across the street. I think that must have been the only time while the kids were growing up that we didn't have any complaints about them being rowdy.

The Belle Grove arrived and had proceeded to the Willamette Iron Steel Shipyard where her overhaul was to take place. The overhaul was to be a complete modernization and it was going to be impossible for the crew to live on board. The Navy provided a barracks ship (APL-4) for the crew's berthing and messing. The majority of the work was to be done by the shipyard workers. But the Belle Grove sailors were to help and give technical assistance.

I am not sure exactly why, but the Belle Grove crew went absolutely wild. The shipyard had no gate security and we could come and go at will. Because we were living on the APL, it wasn't necessary to get permission to go ashore. The crew was scattered throughout both ships. It was next to impossible to account for the whereabouts of the crewmembers at any one time.

Portland wasn't a Navy seaport town and the city was ill-prepared to have three hundred and twenty-five healthy sailors show up on her streets. A pay phone was installed on the mess deck. It commenced to ring immediately and rang constantly for the next six months. Sailors that would have normally been ignored in Long Beach were suddenly very much in demand.

Mahan was due for transfer the latter part of July and had not brought his family with him. The second day after the BG arrived he disappeared. There was not a great deal for him to do as I was conducting sickcall and Meeker was taking care of supplies and consulting with the construction people. I knew Mahan was hanging out in a bar called the Green Lantern on Twenty-first Street. We really didn't need him and were happy to have him out of the way. A week had passed and I had just finished morning sickcall when the phone rang.

"Sickbay, HM3 Messer speaking sir."

"Messer, this is the XO. Could I please speak to HM1 Mahan?"

"I am sorry, sir. He took one of the men over to the Air Force Dispensary for a consultation," I lied.

"Very well! When he gets back, tell him the Captain would like to see him in his cabin."

"Yes, sir, I'll tell him." I rushed over to the small ward where Meeker was still sleeping and woke him up.

"Meeker, the Old Man wants to see Mahan. Do you have any idea where he might be?"

"No, but he'll be in the Green Lantern around one. Why don't you call them and tell them to have him check in with us," he suggested. With that, he pulled the cover over his head and went back to sleep.

Turning to leave, I saw someone in the bottom bunk. It was R.L. Hansen the cook. Chief Hudson had been looking for him earlier in the morning. "What the hell is he doing here?" I wondered and tried to wake him up. He reeked with alcohol. I shook him a few times, but it was useless. I went back to sickbay feeling a little hopeless. Catfish was standing in front of the door with his work dungarees on. His hands were shaking and I could see he had a hangover.

"What's up, Morrie," I asked.

"I'm shaking so damn bad I couldn't poop in a bath tub, Doc," he answered. I unlocked the door.

"Come on in," I invited. I took his pulse. It was racing at a hundred and twenty beats a minute.

"My heart is pounding like a baby robin's ass, Doc," he said.

"Little fast," I answered.

I then took his blood pressure. It wasn't too high considering his pulse. I had a drug by the name of Dexymal that was a mixture of Amphetamine and Phenobarbital. The idea was for the Amphetamine to pick you up and the Phenobarbital to calm you down. They were quite popular with the crew but I was reluctant to use them unless it was absolutely necessary.

"Doc, you have one of them little black and green mother fuckers that you could give me to help me get through the day?" he asked.

"Morrie, I'll give you one but I want you to stay on board tonight and get some rest. Deal?" I asked as I unlocked the working stock narcotic locker.

"Don't worry, I don't feel like going anywhere tonight." he agreed. I left a message at the Green Lantern for Mahan to call me around ten in the morning. At one in the afternoon, the phone rang.

"Yo ho," Mahan said and laughed hysterically.

"Goddamn it, Mahan! Are you drunk?"

"Yo ho, yo ho, yo ho, yo ho," he responded and laughed again, uncontrollably.

"Mahan, the Old Man wants to see you."

"Yo ho," came the response. I hung up, disgusted. The XO called back at three in the afternoon.

"Has Mahan returned from the Air Base?"

"No sir, not yet!"

"The Captain is going to be leaving in a few minutes. Be sure to tell Mahan to report to his cabin, first thing tomorrow morning, right after muster."

"Yes, sir," I answered and swore under my breath. Meeker stood nearby smirking. He knew I had lied to cover up for Mahan. He was thoroughly enjoying my predicament.

"Meeker, we got to get Mahan's dumb ass sobered up and get him up to see the Captain in the morning."

"Don't worry about it. I know where he crashes. I'll get him first thing tomorrow before he starts drinking."

True to his word, Meeker showed up with Mahan bright and early the next day. Mahan's face was cherry red. I knew the way that he was drinking put his life at risk but felt powerless to do anything about it. I wondered what the Captain would say when he saw Mahan.

"Oh, by the way!" Meeker said, looking at me.

"Yeah," I answered.

"What did you give your buddy, Catfish, yesterday?"

"Nothing! Why?"

"I saw him downtown this morning about two. He was walking around like a zombie. He didn't know which end his ass was on."

"Shit!" I knew I'd have to be more careful in the future about passing out narcotics. Prescribing them at sea was one thing, but Portland was a whole new ball game.

After a couple of weeks, more of the families joined their husbands. Some visited a short time and others took apartments to stay on for the duration of the overhaul. It was along about this time when a problem developed that I wasn't quite sure how to handle. Catfish had come down to sickbay just as I was getting ready to secure from sickcall. I had seen him hanging around outside the door and knew he was waiting to talk to me about a personal matter.

"Hey, Morrie, you look human today. Must have had the duty last night," I joked.

"Need to talk to you, Doc," he answered, appearing kind of grim.

"I'm listening, buddy. What's the matter?"

"Doc, one of the men in my division has a big problem."

"Jesus Christ, Morrie. What is it now? This morning PN1 Joe Moore told me that twenty-one men are AWOL? It's like everyone has lost their mind." The Catfish shrugged his shoulders and laughed.

"I know, Doc. We need to get this damn bunch back out to sea. We may not have a crew by the time this yard period is over the way things are going," he responded with a grin. "But, anyway, Doc, I'm going to need your help on this one."

"Let's hear it."

"One of the Latino kids that works with me thinks he has given his wife the clap."

"Oh, that's just goddamn great."

"Well, his wife just came up here this past weekend. He was here alone a few days and it seems he met some young woman and they got kind of friendly, If you know what I mean. Anyway, his dork is dripping like a sieve."

"Shit!"

"Look Doc, he's really shook up and he's bawling like a baby. He said if he told her what really happened she'd divorce him for sure and he'd never see the kids again. She's a hot-blooded Mexican and she might do more than just divorce his dumb ass. But more than anything else, I'm afraid of how this is going to affect him."

"Jesus, Morrie, I don't treat dependents," I remarked as I stood looking at him, feeling hopeless. I knew he expected me to do something. After a few minutes I said, "Hells bells, Morrie! Go get him and bring him up here while I think about this. I'll at least need to get him under treatment."

A few minutes later they were back. The Hispanic sailor's eyes were red and swollen from crying and his face was contorted with emotional pain. I had them come in and closed the door.

"Morrie has told me what happened. I'll need to do an examination to make sure you've really got something," I explained to my new patient. I soon had a confirmation that his worst fears were a reality. "I am going to call over to the Air Base and talk to Doctor Shoemaker. He seems like a pretty understanding guy. I'm going to ask him if he will tell your wife you've been exposed to meningitis and that she needs to have prophylactic treatment in order to protect her and your children." I stopped to let every thing I had said sink in. "If I can get him to go along with us, everything should be okay. I can't guarantee anything, but I'll give it my best shot," I continued.

I called Doctor Shoemaker and explained the situation and asked him for his help. At first, he seemed reluctant.

"Doctor, this is one of our best damage control technicians. He's young and healthy and has been separated from his wife a great deal over the past few months. He had a little too much to drink and made a mistake," I explained.

"I don't know," he said, hesitating. "We could all end up in big trouble if she ever gets wise. He's not the true confession type is he? Sometimes in cases like this, the guilty party wants to fess up in order to get rid of their own guilt."

"I assure you that won't happen," I answered. "It's within your power to save this marriage, Doctor Shoemaker." I pleaded in a servile voice. There was a long silence. I waited holding my breath.

"Alright! Send them both over here tomorrow morning at 0800. Tell him to come to the dependent's clinic and ask for me personally. He doesn't need to explain anything to anyone. What did you say his name was?" I breathed out his name with a sigh of relief. These were my friends and shipmates. I was duty bound to care for them, but this had taken me outside of the line. The look of relief on my patient's face, when I told him the details of our plan, made me feel a little better about our conspiracy.

Why this crew of people came together at this particular time to serve on the Belle Grove, I have no idea. Perhaps, it was destiny. I can tell you, that as time went on, almost nothing shocked me. In July, my friend Studenbordt had gone to Pennsylvania on leave. A couple of weeks had passed when a knock came at our door. I opened it to see Studenbordt and a beautiful, young, blackheaded woman of medium build standing before me. I invited them in.

"I'd like you to meet my wife, Betty, Doc," Studenbordt introduced as they stepped through the door.
"WIFE!" I exclaimed. "I didn't even know you were engaged," I said, trying not to show my surprise. Peg had come into the living room just in time to hear the last part of our conversation. We all took a seat.
"I know it's all a little sudden and I can't hardly believe it myself," Betty interjected. Studenbordt sat happily, listening, as his new bride explained the events of the past two weeks.
"Yeah, I was engaged to this guy for seven years and he kept postponing our wedding. I met Stu about ten days ago and we went out on a date. He asked me to marry him and the rest is history. That's really about all there is to it," she concluded.
"Well, Gees! That's quite a story. I can't help but wonder about your old fiancee."
"He had seven years to marry me and I was tired of waiting."
"Good enough! Let's drink to that," and so we did, far into the night. I figured they had about as good a chance at staying married as anyone else on the Belle Grove.

In July, Mahan was transferred to shore duty somewhere in the Great Lakes area. I had grown accustomed to him over the months and was sorry to bid him farewell. A short time later, a Hospital Corps Chief checked aboard as his replacement. He had spent sixteen years in the Navy Reserve. For whatever reason, he had put in a request to go Regular Navy and the Bureau of Naval Personnel had approved it. This was his first sea duty assignment and he was determined to prove himself worthy. The Belle Grove was in the middle of her FRAM and construction work was going on everywhere. Essential office spaces had temporarily been set up on the APL at varied locations and periodically moved from here to there. No one seemed to know what was going on or where anything was located. Mass confusion was the order of the day. The Chief found this to be unsettling and he soon became as elusive as Mahan had been.

The insanity continued on into December. The Navy had planned to have us out of the shipyard and back in Long Beach for the coming holidays. But first, they would need to send an Underway Readiness Inspection Team to see if the American taxpayer had got their money's worth. After a week, the Officer in charge of the team informed our Captain that we were nowhere near ready to take the Belle Grove to sea, much less to make a WESTPAC (Western Pacific) cruise. We would need to work around the clock if we were to meet our deadline.

I decided to move Peg and the children back to Oakland. They would be staying in the Pagendarm family home until I returned from WESTPAC. I had requested a weeks leave in order to complete the move and spend Christmas day with my family. The new Chief had informed me that all leaves had been canceled. Further more, regular working hours had been extended until the Belle Grove was operational ready.

"You can drive them down on a Saturday and catch a bus back on Sunday. That way, you can be ready to go to work here on Monday."

"That sounds like a bunch of bullshit to me. We've been screwing around here for six months and now everything is an emergency. Besides, sickbay was not involved in any major alterations. It's just a matter of moving our gear back on board."

"It's not up to me. It's the CO's orders. And don't be such a smart-ass. You're bordering on insubordination."

I made the trip down on the weekend of the nineteenth and returned on the twenty-first. We all knew, that in one way or another, we were responsible for the Belle Grove's dismal performance. We had played more than we had worked and now it was time to pay the fiddler. We had lost several of our old crewmembers due to expiration of their enlistments. The environment was hardly conducive for someone to want to reenlist. Dozens of brand new seaman and fireman, right out of boot camp, had checked aboard as replacements. These men would have to be trained and taught to work as a team if we were to successfully make the up coming cruise. Things became deadly serious. Resentment ran high that there would be no leave over the coming holiday period. The number of men AWOL went to a record high of thirty-two. This represented ten percent of our crew.

The career-minded, dedicated members of the crew put their shoulders to the wheel and we really went to work. The Chief volunteered Meeker and me to help the deck division paint the passageways. The second URI inspection we had was a little more positive. Now, it was time to go to sea and make sure all systems were functioning properly. The CO decided we would get underway on the twenty-third and try to make up for a little lost time. We could do a little target practice with our armament; God knew we needed it. This was not a popular decision. Nevertheless, Christmas Eve found us underway, traveling up the Willamette River. The Captain noticed a small growth of pine growing along the riverbank and he decided we needed a Christmas tree. He immediately dispatched a crew to cut one down. In very short order, a tree was retrieved, erected, and decorated. Late that afternoon we left the Willamette River and entered into the Columbia continuing on our voyage. The tree stood tall and straight in her designated spot on the mess deck. This was a constant reminder to the crew that it was Christmas and we were being denied the opportunity to spend it with our families.

Navy regulations require that, when underway, a report on conditions of readiness will be given to the Executive Officer at 2000 hours each evening. This procedure is referred to as the "eight o'clock report." We fell in formation, and one by one, each department reported anything of significance to the XO. When we had completed our reports, it was his turn to brief us.

"Tomorrow we'll be going to general quarters and do some gunnery practice."

"Sir!"

"Yes!"

"Some of the men have expressed a fear we might shoot Santa Claus down."

"I wouldn't be worried about this crew shooting anyone down. I'll be surprised if we can get a round out of the barrel," he replied sarcastically.

Sometime in the wee hours, of Christmas morning, some illustrious crewmember, or members, went to the mess deck to take a look at our precious little tree. Perhaps he, or they, became overcome with resentment at the sight of it. But what he, or they, did then was truly scandalous. He, or they, took the Captain's little tree and went up to the superstructure. There it was lashed on a lanyard upside down and ran up the yardarm for all to see.

Now, there are many, including myself, which can bear witness to this revolting act. The tree was quickly taken down in the early morning light and tossed over the side. I'm not sure if the Captain was ever informed of the final disposition of the pretty little pine. I do know that this put the crew in a mutinous mood. Perhaps, that's why the Catfish went down to where the OOD stood his watch when we were in port. There, he had access to the communication system throughout the whole ship. He had written a little poem and wanted to share it with the crew. These many years later he has confessed to the dastardly deed and here are the words as he remembers them:

"Good ship,
good crew,
Merry Christmas,
turn to."

The joy we received from these simple acts of rebellion seemed to boost our morale considerably. On the twenty-sixth, we pulled into Bangor, Washington and took on ammunition and on the twenty-seventh we refueled in Seattle. Finally, on the twenty-ninth, we arrived in Long Beach. I, for one, was glad to put the Portland ordeal behind us.

We were scheduled to sail for WESTPAC on the fifteenth of February, 1962. That gave us six weeks to do our underway training. We wasted no time; the first week of January, we commenced. Peg and the children were in Oakland, so it was of little consequence to me. Being at sea, after an extended yard period, was almost a pleasure. There were no bars or camp-following females to distract the more worldly among us. The fog of alcohol lifted and we commenced to function once again as a unit.

As personnel change, so do leadership dynamics. YN1 Padgett had left the Personnel Office and PN1 Joe Moore was now firmly in control. SK1 Doersch had become Leading Petty Officer in the Supply Department. R.L. Hansen had made first class and was now the lead cook in the Galley. A handsome, articulate, young sailor from Mississippi by the name of Powell had made second class machinist mate. He was growing into an influential leader in the Engineering Department. A young third class damage controlman by the name of Auman had recently reenlisted and reported on board. He was soon a big part of the colorful "R" division that Catfish and Romero were in. They resided just outside my sickbay door. SF1 McDermott was their Leading Petty Officer and mentor. He was squared away from head to toe and seemed almost out of character aboard the old BG. He was the only man that really understood the BG's complicated ballasting system. This was an essential function if we were to be successful in loading and off loading amphibious vehicles. He had been watching and waiting for someone that he felt he could train to his level of expertise and efficiency. A few weeks after the Catfish checked on board, he decided he had found his man. In a not too distant future, this would prove to have been a very important move.

The Fat Man "Miles" was still on board. Just seeing that big body and smile on his ebony face gave me a feeling of comfort. DK2 Teuetkin was seeing to it that we were paid on time. And I mustn't forget Fireman Boutwell who seemed to be the Catfish's shadow. He actually had more time in the Navy than the Catfish. Problem was, he just couldn't pass the exam for advancement to petty officer. Catfish was his mentor. During working hours, where you found one, you usually found the other. They prowled the passageways attending to their many tasks. I would often see them dipping their sounding rod in the seemingly infinite number of ballast tanks scattered throughout the ship. Boutwell would be wearing a contented smile as they moved about. It was obvious that he had a great admiration and respect for the Catfish. He seemed to be happy just to be in his presence. The interesting thing about Boutwell, was that even though he couldn't pass the rating exams, he could remember every trick played in a Pinochle game. He was a formidable opponent, and a great partner to have, in this unending contest that so many of us participated in when we were at sea.

The hours and hours of drills for fire, man overboard, and battle were getting to be tiresome. We had commenced to slow down in responding to the never-ending games. It was the end of the fifth week of our underway training and we were returning to Long Beach for the weekend. I had just secured sickcall and had sat down. Catfish and Boutwell had come into sickbay to get Boutwell a Band-Aid. I was examing his freshly cut index finger when I heard the 1-MC crackle.

"Not again!" I complained, expecting to hear an announcement for another drill. We stood waiting.

"FIRE! FIRE! FIRE IN THE PAINT LOCKER. THIS IS NOT A DRILL AND THAT AIN'T NO SHIT. AWAY THE DUTY FIRE AND RESCUE TEAM." The Catfish's chin dropped, his mouth fell open, and his eyes widened in a goofy grin.

"WHAT THE HELL?" he muttered and ran for the door.

A cigarette thrown in a trash can had started a small fire in the paint locker; it was soon under control. An hour later, we were gathered back in sickbay feeling relieved. We were speculating on the reaction of the OOD at the unprofessional way the Boatswains Mate had made his announcement.

"One thing about it, you sure can't deny he got our attention," the Catfish laughed. We all agreed on that one. It was time for chow and we joined our shipmates on the mess deck for more laughter. God help the poor Boatswains Mate, he'd have to live with this one for awhile. That reminded us of all the stupid things we'd heard over the 1-MC while serving aboard the Belle Grove.

"The one I like is, THERE'LL BE LIBERTY BUT NO BOATS," chuckled Boutwell.

"You have to be shitting us," someone exclaimed.

"No, that's the truth. One time, we were anchored about five miles out and it was too rough to put a boat in the water. It was 1600 and we were all lined up on the quarterdeck. I guess the OOD thought that was a good way to handle it." Romero rolled his eyes.

"My favorite is, NOW THE DUTY CHICKEN LAY DOWN TO THE GALLEY AND MAKE A SPEED RUN IN TODAY'S SOUP," added the Catfish, trying to look deadly serious.

"Let me out of here," Romero said, as he shook his head from side to side. Standing, he grabbed his tray and hurried toward the scullery. Catfish's eyes followed him, gleefully. He then turned to us, shrugged his shoulders, and chuckled. We all laughed.

On the fifteenth of February, we got underway for WESTPAC. Steaming at our maximum speed of 14 knots, we arrived at Pearl Harbor on the twentieth of the month. After a couple days of liberty, we proceeded on our voyage. Eleven days later, we arrived off White Beach in Okinawa where we were to take on a couple of AMTRAKS and their crews.

After almost two weeks at sea, the crew was chomping at the bit to go on liberty. I had drawn the duty and was the only medical person remaining on board. That was always a special time for me. Two thirds of the crew were ashore and it was peaceful and quiet. After dusting and swabbing the treatment room, I settled in for the evening. I knew the injured from the inevitable drinking, brawling, and fist fighting would soon be beating a path to my door.

My first patient showed up at about nine that evening. It was R.L. Hansen. I was writing a letter to Peg when he burst through the door. He was holding a blood soaked handkerchief on his right upper cheek. His dress blue blouse was soaked with blood and his eye swollen shut. I stood up and had him sit down.
"What happened, Robert?"
"Doc, I was in a cab coming back to the White Beach Landing. The driver had stopped at a red light in Village Three when this goddamn marine jerked the door open and said, 'Get out sailor; your ride is over.' I said, 'Fuck you, asshole.' And then the son-of-a-bitch hit me right in the face with this Nesbitt Orange Soda bottle."
"Damn, Robert. Here, let me take a look at that." I removed the handkerchief to see a mutilated cheek bone that looked very much like

ground up hamburger. I'd have to debris a good portion and suture the undamaged tissue. Thank goodness, he was inebriated and not feeling a great deal of pain. I cleaned the area and injected him with Novocain. As I worked, he continued to tell me his story.

"There were three of them, Doc. I couldn't do anything after he hit me. I was pretty well out after he cold cocked me like that. The bastards just dragged me out of the cab and dumped me alongside of the road."

"DAMN! What did the cab driver say?"

"Little nipper bastard didn't say anything. Those assholes got in the cab and he took off with them." I soon had him stitched up.

"It's going to be swollen for a couple of days, Robert. When you wash your face, be careful, and just pat it dry. Come on back down here in the morning and I'll take a look at it. Day after tomorrow, we'll take every other stitch out to take some of the pressure off. I put them pretty close together. If it doesn't get infected, you shouldn't have a scar."

"I'm not feeling well, Doc. Is it okay if I sleep here in sickbay tonight?" I knew his feelings had been hurt more than anything else.

"Sure! Take Mahan's old rack there by the door." The rest of the evening passed without a great deal of incident.

The next morning I had opened the door of the treatment room after having swabbed the deck. Catfish leaned his head in the door.

"You want to see something funny, Doc?" he asked.

"Sure! Wha'cha got?"

"Well, if we're lucky, the 0700 liberty boat is going to be coming bearing four barefoot sailors," he laughed.

"Are you serious?"

"Get your hat and let's go watch the fun," he answered. We were soon topside leaning on the lifeline, waiting. I heard the liberty launch make its approach. As it neared the BG, it made a wide swing to come alongside. The Coxswain cut the power and it came gliding by. Some movement drew my attention; it was Auman. His face was livid with rage and he was shaking his fist at us.

"I'm going to kick your ass, Catfish," he screamed. I looked over at the Catfish. He was laughing hysterically and looked quite pleased with himself. We watched as the four barefoot sailors climbed the ladder to the quarterdeck and requested permission to come on aboard.

Now, there was much explaining to McDermott and the "R" Division Officer about what had actually happened. Sailors being what they are, you can be sure the real truth was never told to their superiors. Later on in the morning, I was able to get the whole story from Romero. It seems that five of them had gone on liberty together. They drank the early part of the evening away and somehow ended up in this house where only young women live. They had all gathered in the reception area and the party continued. According to Romero, Catfish went into his nasty-man mode and started insulting one of the young ladies. Now, Auman had taken a special liking to this young woman and he took it on himself to defend her honor. A pushing contest broke out between the two and, in the process, Auman gave the Catfish a good pop. Romero got them separated and things quieted down. Auman went up stairs with his newfound love and the Catfish went into his opossum mode.

Now, When the Catfish roused from his stupor, he found himself all alone. As he sat there feeling neglected and unloved, he hit on a very ingenious plan for revenge. Japanese culture dictates that shoes be removed before entering living quarters of the house. Not more than eight feet away from the Catfish, lay his and the aggressors dress shoes. After going over the plan in his mind once again, he leaped into action. He quickly went to the vestibule and put on his shoes and gathered up the four remaining pairs. He made his way to the White Beach landing and caught a liberty boat. Halfway between the landing and the BG, he unloaded his troublesome cargo. This may not be exactly the way it happened, as I was not a witness to any of this. I can only relate the story as it was told to me. One thing I can assure you of, and that's four little barefoot sailors came tooling up the gangplank that bright early morning.

Over the next couple of months, the days proved to be long and arduous. We sailed between Taiwan and the Philippines and passed into the waters of the South China Sea. The days and nights droned on. Tempers were short. Things that would have normally been acceptable seemed intolerable.

The men who bore the heaviest burden were down in the hot engine room spaces. They were working four hours on and four off. One had to be resilient and tough to work down in the hole. They had their own code of conduct and tended to be clannish. Their berthing space was always dark except for the red night-lights. The odor of oil and sweat from their work clothes hung heavily in the air. Unless it was necessary, we avoided going into their berthing compartment so as not to disturb them.

It was along about this time when I had an unusual visit. It was on a Wednesday around 1230 in the afternoon and I was putting my laundry away. Meeker had gone to late chow and HMC Jones was in the Chief's Quarters. I heard the front door to sickbay open and the sound of several men come in. In a few seconds, I saw Machinist Mate Second Class Powell leading a group of three other petty officers toward me. I knew from the look on their faces that something was wrong.

"Hey, Powell! What's up?" I asked trying to sound as cheerful as possible.

"We need to talk to you, Doc." Powell answered in a business-like tone. The other men stood motionless a few inches behind him.

"Must be serious," I said, continuing to fold my clothes.

"It is, Doc. And someone could very well take a long swim if this gets out," Powell replied. I tensed at the insinuation.

"Go ahead, I'm listening."

"Doc, we hate to get you involved, but you're the logical one to turn to with this. We don't want to go to the Division Officer because, if we do, we won't be able to keep it quiet." I looked from one of the men to the other. Their eyes didn't waver and their mouths were set in firm lines of grim determination. My stomach began to feel tight.

"For Christ sake, Powell, what is it?"

"Well, there ain't no delicate way to put this, Doc. We got a couple of queers in our midst. And to make it worse, one of them has a brother on board." I stopped folding my clothes and looked at him.

"Damn, Powell, that's a pretty serious accusation."

"We know, Doc. But we are sick and tired of listening to these two assholes blowing each other all goddamn day and night while we're trying to get some sleep. The sorry mother fuckers even have the balls to turn off the night lights."

"Powell, this sounds more like a legal problem than a medical one. Why don't you take it up with your Chief?"

"He'll just start a goddamn on-board investigation and all hell will break loose. The one guy's brother is a good kid and we don't want to get him involved. Besides, he can be a mean little son-of-a-bitch. Someone could get killed over this, Doc."

"What do you want me to do, Powell?"

"We want you to talk to the XO and tell him what's going on. He can notify the Navy Investigative Service and they can come on board and march these turds off without anyone being the wiser."

"Goddamn it, Powell, you know the Chief is the Medical Department representative; you'll need to talk to him about this. He'll have my ass if I go over his head."

"We're not telling that fat-ass Chief anything, Doc. We've talked this over and we don't trust him. The XO respects you and he'll listen to you. You got to get these two creeps out of our berthing space or someone is going to disappear, Doc. We just can't take it anymore."

"Okay, look, let me give this some thought. Go on back to work and we'll talk a little later."

"Okay, Doc, but not a word to anyone but the XO, or by-god, we'll swear this conversation never took place. No offense, Doc, but that's the way it has to be."

I wasn't happy about being put in that kind of a situation. I was between a rock and a hard place. But I felt a great deal of satisfaction knowing they held me in such high regard. Chief Jones and Meeker had been at war for several weeks. The year and half I had been on board the crew had come to depend on me. The Chief had never said anything openly, but I knew he resented me. I really didn't want to agitate him anymore than was necessary. At 1300, I held regular sickcall and tried to get my mind off the problem for awhile. Shortly after I secured, I grabbed my hat and foul weather jacket and started out on my usual stroll. I had just come into the passageway alongside of the welldeck, just forward of the machine shop. I looked up to see the XO walking toward me. Without giving it a lot of thought, I looked him in the eye and stopped. He must have sensed my urgency.

"Someone die, Doc?" he asked jokingly.

"I need to talk to you Commander," I responded. I told him the whole story as succinctly as possible, without leaving out any details. When I finished he stood staring into space. His shoulders had slumped forward as I talked. He looked like he wished he were somewhere else.

"You'd think they would have said something long before now. These two men have been on board for over three years. Here we are short on watch standers in the middle of the South China Sea and...," his voice trailed off.

"Yes, sir, you'd think so, sir," I replied.

"Okay, go on back down to sickbay. I'll take care of it," he ordered. There was no need for me to explain how delicate this situation was. The Commander had been in the Navy for over sixteen years. A week later, we steamed into Hong Kong. Before the anchor had even hit the water, two men came aboard in civilian clothes. A short time later, PN1 Moore came to sickbay to retrieve the medical records of the two men in question.

"Where these two going?" Chief Jones asked PN1 Moore, as he flipped through the file cabinet looking for the records.

"I am not at liberty to say, Chief," he answered, as he put the records in a big manila envelope.

"What the hell was that all about?" Chief Jones asked after PN1 Moore had left. Meeker looked at me.

"Damned if I know," I answered and shrugged my shoulders.

The remaining brother was left on board to complete his enlistment. As far as I know, the incident was never mentioned again in the light of day.

By the end of the third month of our cruise, we had shuttled marines and their equipment between Subic Bay and Okinawa no less than seven times. At the end of May, we commenced Operation Tulungan. We would be operating with naval forces from several other countries. This required that we land marines on Mindoro Island in the Philippines. Once we reached our designated location, the crew worked around the clock for five days and four nights.

The Belle Grove and her crew had performed splendidly during the operation. The Captain wanted to do something special for his crew to show his appreciation. There not being a suitable place for us to go on liberty, he decided we would have a beach party. Beer and ice was procured from a nearby village. Hot dogs, hamburger meat, potato salad, chips, onions, tomatoes, pickles, canned baked beans and soft drinks came from the crew's mess. The ship's Special Services Department provided softball and volleyball equipment. The Captain wanted as many men as possible to attend the activity. Those that had the duty were to be relieved in the middle of the afternoon so that all hands would have an opportunity to participate.

We were all excited at the prospect of putting our feet on dry land and having a cold beer. The temperature was in excess of 105 degrees Fahrenheit. The hamburgers and hotdogs were cooked and washed down with bottle after bottle of San Miguel Beer. By 1700, the whole crew had spent at least some time on the beach. Some of the more fortunate had been there all afternoon. The fact that we hadn't had a drink in almost thirty days, linked with the heat, made us susceptible to the effects of alcohol. As the day turned into early evening, the beach became chaotic. Fist fights and general squabbling terminated the softball and volleyball games. Men started slipping away to the nearby Village of San Jose, which had been placed off-limits. Several piles of driftwood, six to eight feet high, had been set on fire. Yelling, screaming, and cursing of drunken sailors could be heard up and down the beach.

Romero and I had wandered off toward the Village. The Philippines had won their independence from Spain in 1948. Their language and customs still remained a strong influence in that part of the Philippines. We were having a great time with the natives as Romero chatted happily with them. Suddenly, a marine jeep showed up with two Military Police. The one opposite put a bullhorn up to his mouth.

"NOW, LISTEN UP, ALL HANDS FROM THE BELLE GROVE RETURN TO THE BEACH AREA IMMEDIATELY. THIS AREA IS OFF-LIMITS, I REPEAT, OFF-LIMITS." The jeep continued slowly down the street in front of the store where we were standing. Romero and I looked at each other. We still had enough presence of mind to fear the consequence of disobeying orders. We staggered back to find two big MAC boats loading up our shipmates to return to the Belle Grove. We clamored on board in the midst of the shoving and cursing. Upon our approach to the Belle Grove, I saw that the welldeck tailgate had been opened. The coxswain pulled the big boat up inside the welldeck and dropped the landing ramp and ordered us to disembark. We climbed off the boat into knee deep water and waded forward to the dry part of the welldeck.

"Is this anyway to treat our sorry asses?" questioned one of the men.

"Everyone is too goddamn drunk to climb up the ladder," someone answered.

"Hope we don't need to get underway in the next few hours," said another.

"We're going to be sailing in zigzags if we do," came the reply.

"NOW, HEAR THIS, ALL HANDS TO QUARTERS FOR MUSTER," blared the 1-MC. Several men had fallen into their racks with their clothes on. Others were showering or trying to change out of wet clothes. General pandemonium broke out down in the berthing spaces and profanity filled the air. Only about a fourth of our division had showed up as had been ordered.

"Chief Hudson, get the hell down there and get your division up here," commanded Lieutenant Frankeny.

"Yes, sir," the Chief replied.

An hour passed and finally a count was taken. Then another, and then another. Someone was missing. It was a fireman from engineering. A search party was formed and back to the beach went the big MAC boats. Hours passed with no word. It was just after reveille and I was on the mess deck surrounded by other crewmembers.

"They've found him."

"Where?"

"In twenty feet of water."

"Is he dead?"

"What do you think, asshole?"

Suddenly, everything became surreal; no one had a face or a name. One of our shipmates was dead.

"Who is he?"

"A Boiler Tender Striker from Arkansas. He just came aboard right out of boot camp a few weeks ago. He was only eighteen years old."

"What happened?"

"Someone hit him in the mouth and he went down the beach a little ways and passed out."

"But how did he drown?"

"Tide carried him out."

"Who hit him?"

"Don't know."

"Will there be an investigation?"

"Damn straight!"

"Messer, the Chief wants to see you!"

"Yeah, Chief! Wha'cha need?"

"You and Meeker get a body bag. They're bringing the corpse on board in a few minutes. You'll need to wash and clean him up."

"Where are we going to keep him, Chief?"

"We'll have to put him in the vegetable locker until the chopper arrives."

The boat crew hoisted the body to the main deck. I placed my hands under the shoulders of the deceased and lifted him up and onto a stretcher. As I lay him down, a loud noise erupted from his esophagus and a large amount of water ran out of his mouth and onto the deck. I looked down at the exposed cheekbone and ashen colored tissue. The fish had wasted no time in eating away a good portion of his face. I was overcome with nausea, but I had a job to do. The officers and crew were watching. If I was to keep their respect, I would need to maintain control over my emotions.

A short time later, the 1-MC blared. "Now all hands shift into the uniform of the day and report to quarters for mourning." We all gathered and stood at attention to render honors to a boy that we had failed to esteem in life. I felt we were all, at least in some small measure, responsible for his death. The men in his division wore one inch wide black mourning bands on their right arm between the elbow and shoulder. The Belle Grove was cloaked in a cloud of remorse and guilt. As the ship rocked to and fro, we stood swaying in an eerie silence. The sky was dark and the sea was black.

"I sure don't envy the assholes that have to escort his body home," someone whispered.

"SHUTUP, GODDAMN IT!" Chief Hudson commanded.

I got the results back on my exam for second class a few days later. I could put my second chevron on underneath my crow on the fifteenth. It didn't seem that important anymore. We'd be heading home in July. It couldn't be soon enough for me. Being in the Navy was sure one hell of a way to make a living.

Peg had driven down to Long Beach the latter part of June with her mother and the children. She rented a duplex in the same complex where we had lived before going to Portland. By the time the Belle Grove arrived, she had retrieved our furniture from storage and unpacked.

Although our reunion was a glorious one, it was short-lived. A US spy plane had photographed a Soviet-managed construction site in Cuba. There was an immediate suspicion that this area was being used to house ballistic missiles. At that time, it was all top secret and we had no idea what was taking place. We were ordered to Camp Pendleton to take on a marine expeditionary force and participate in a highly classified operation. It did seem a little strange that we would be operating so soon after completing a six-month cruise but we accepted it as a matter of course. We had been sailing in a southerly direction for five days when the news broke. Catfish stuck his head in.

"Doc, did you hear the news?"

"No, what is it?"

"Ol' Khrushchev may be building a missile site in Cuba."

"You got to be shitting me."

"Nope, I ain't shitting you a pound."

"Damn Soviets will be able to take out every one of our major cities if they do manage to get missiles in there."

"I got a pretty good idea we're on our way to make sure that doesn't happen, Doc."

"You think we are going to Cuba?"

"I'd bet on it. We'll shoot through the Panama Canal and out into the Caribbean. That way we'll be in a position to strike if we have to invade. The marines on board are ready to go."

"Damn, Morrie! Did you know the Belle Grove has been in Long Beach only twelve days in the past thirteen months?"

"Yeah, I know. And who in the hell knows how long we'll be gone this time. PN1 Moore told me the other day that him and Yeager calculated the percent of married men that have gotten a divorce since they came on board."

"Yeah, that ought to be an interesting number."

"Seventy-five!"

"Damn! That's pretty high. Can't blame the girls, though. Hell, they're better off single. After a couple of years on here, you're either a lunatic or an alcoholic. Who in the world wants to live with some crazy bastard like that?"

"Can't argue that point. I have to admit being a Belle Grove sailor is not conducive to being a good family man."

"That's for DAMN sure."

Morrie was right about our destination. We arrived at the Panama Canal a few days later along with dozens of other ships. It was fascinating to watch the big war ships pass through the locks. They would pump one full of water to elevate the ship and then it would proceed to the next level. This procedure was repeated over and over. Often times we would hit open waterways and steam a few miles before entering another set of locks. In a few hours we were floating peacefully in the Caribbean.

The following morning after sickcall, I walked out on the main deck to take a look around. The Caribbean was sky blue and the water smooth as glass. The gray line of warships that had come to do battle stretched out as far as the eye could see. The sight of such an awesome power sent a chill up my spine.

Over the next few weeks, the whole world held its breath. On the fourteenth of October, a ballistic missile was spotted at the site of construction. On the twenty-second, President Kennedy announced there would be a naval blockade. The word came down there was a Russian convoy on its way. President Kennedy requested that Khrushchev issue a recall. The ships stayed their course. We waited.

On the twenty-third, Kennedy was to make a major announcement to the country at 1400 hours. We were standing at the brink of the destruction of the civilized world. The Soviet ships were getting closer with each passing moment. We gathered around the television on the messdeck and waited to hear our Commander and Chief. Soon he appeared and made his way to the microphones. After a brief overview of the problem, he said, "I have given the following orders to the Commander of the Task Force that is responsible to enforce the Cuban Blockade. If the convoy, now headed to Cuba from the USSR, doesn't turn back, he's to fire one round over the bow of the lead ship. If she then doesn't turn about, he's to sink her." We reacted with whoops and war cries. We were pumped up and ready to go. Battle plans for the invasion of Cuba had been drawn up and we were waiting to implement them. The Belle Grove had been designated to receive causalities in her welldeck once the AMTRAKS were disembarked. Meeker and I cleaned and sterilized all the surgical equipment. We checked and double-checked the battle stations and stocked them with fresh medical supplies.

At about 1500 hours, on the afternoon of the twenty-fourth, someone knocked on the sickbay door. I opened it to see a young marine about twenty years old. He was leaning forward and holding his lower back with both hands.

"Can I help you?"

"I fell in the welldeck, Doc, and I'm really hurting."

"Come on in and have a seat. How in the hell did you fall in the welldeck?"

"We were just grabassing, Doc, and I lost my footing."

"Take off your blouse and let's have a look." His whole back was covered with big black and blue whelps.

"How far do you think you fell?"

"Oh, I'd say about twenty feet, Doc."

"Your bruises don't look like something you get with a fall. Do you know what you landed on?"

"On one of the big tractors, I think."

"I want you to pee in this bottle. I need to check it for blood. I think you're mostly just bruised but I want to make sure you don't have any kidney damage." I checked his urine and it was strongly positive for occult blood.

"Looks like you have a little internal bleeding. But I would expect that from the trauma. I want you to stay here in sickbay overnight so I can keep an eye on you. In all probability, it'll be cleared up by morning and I'll let you go back to duty."

"I appreciate it, Doc. To tell you the truth, I don't feel so hot." I got him in a pair of pajamas and put him to bed on the ward. The ship's standard operating procedure required that I fill out an accident report on all injuries. I went to the office and got the accident form and returned to the ward.

"Now, tell me exactly where you were and how this happened."

"I just slipped off the catwalk alongside that machine shop, Doc."

"You just slipped?"

"Well, you know we were scuffling a little. I don't want to get anyone in trouble."

It all seemed very vague. I went down to the area where he told me he had fallen and took a good look around. I came to the conclusion they must have been playing pretty rough if it, did in fact, happen like he said it did. I didn't give it a great deal more thought. I completed the report and put it in the XO's incoming mailbox.

After the evening meal, several marines came to visit my patient. I could hear them mumbling in a low, serious tone. I assumed they were getting their story straight so they could explain to their superiors what had happened. When they left, I heard the patient call me.

"DOC!" I went into the ward.

"Yeah, wha'cha need?"

"Doc, I lied to you about what happened. I want to change that accident report." I didn't like the sound of his voice. I hesitated a moment and studied him.

"Well, it's a little bit late, I already turned it in. What the hell you talking about anyway?"

"I was beat up, Doc."

"Beat up! What do you mean?"

"Just what I said, beat up."

"Who beat you up?"

"My First Sergeant and the company Gunny."

"You know you've kind of put me in a bind here lying to me like you did. I can't just go and start changing accident reports on a whim. If you want to bring this to someone's attention you'll need to take this up with your legal officer."

"What legal officer? Those dirty bastards are not going to let me talk to anyone in my command, Doc. Could you, maybe, ask the ship's Legal Officer to come down and talk to me?"

I thought of talking to the Chief about the matter but soon dismissed the idea. I knew he would probably just want to hush, hush the whole matter. My patient had obviously had the hell beat out of him by his superiors. My inclination to fight for the underdog had taken over. I decided to go and talk personally with our Legal Officer. The appointed Legal Officer was a full lieutenant that was also the gunnery officer. He was one of the busiest men aboard. After an hour-long search, I still hadn't located him. In my meandering, I ran into one of our aspiring young ensigns and explained a little of the problem I was facing.

"You go on back down to sickbay and I'll go to the bridge and have the word passed for him to lay to sickbay."

"That won't work. The Captain is going to hear the word being passed and he'll want to know what happened."

"I'll just have him to lay to my stateroom then."

"Well, okay, but, please, keep it low key." I returned to sickbay. The ensign went to the bridge and requested the OOD to have the Lieutenant report to his quarters. The OOD was a lieutenant junior grade by the name of D. Catron who was a mustang (previous enlisted man). There was no love lost between him and the young ensign. LTJG Catron informed him that it was against Navy Regulations to request a senior officer report to a junior. He then demanded to know what was going on. The ensign refused to answer anymore questions. "Just have the Lieutenant report to sickbay then," he demanded. I was sitting in the treatment room when I heard the word passed over the 1-MC.

"Oh, no," I said to myself and went out the back door of the ward to the mess deck. I got myself a cup of coffee, and sat down. I knew this was the worst possible scenario but there was nothing I could do but wait.

In a few minutes, the messenger of the watch located me and informed me the XO was waiting for me in sickbay. The Executive Officer had just recently relieved Commander Andersen and I had had very little dealings with him. I knew he was an Annapolis Graduate and the word was that he was a hard charger. My heart raced and I broke out in a cold sweat as I headed for sickbay. As I came in the backdoor of the ward, I could see the XO sitting in Meeker's favorite chair. He was talking to someone. When I got to the treatment room I saw that it was Chief Jones.

"You wanted to see me, sir?" The Chief had obviously heard the word passed for the Lieutenant to report to sickbay and came to investigate. I felt like a trapped rat between two cats.

"Will you excuse us, Chief?" The Chief gave me a questioning look as he left. The XO stood up, locked the door and resumed his seat.

"Messer, I want you to tell me what's going on and by-god if you lie to me, I'll have your ass. Do you understand?" The look in his eyes left no room for misunderstanding. I started at the beginning and explained in detail everything that had occurred. When I finished, he gave a big sigh.

"Damn! Messer! We were trying not to bother the Captain with all this nonsense. But, no doubt, he heard the word being passed. I'll have to tell him now, and all hell is going to break loose."

The XO didn't show any indication that he was in any hurry to leave. I waited anxiously to see what he was going to do.

"What happened, Messer, is that piece of shit you have here in sickbay refused to get up to relieve the watch last night. His Company Commander went to see the Captain and wanted to put him in the brig. The CO told him the BG wasn't equipped to hold prisoners and ordered him to wait and take it up with his superiors when he disembarked. These marines are getting ready to go into combat and they sure as hell don't want to take some shitball like that along. Anyway, from what I understand, the Company Commander told the First Shirt to take care of it. This is really going to piss the Old Man off, but I guess I better go brief him," he said.

"Yes, sir!" I answered. I knew I had handled the situation badly and really should have taken this up with the Chief. But it was too late; I'd have to live with the consequences of my decision. I was getting less popular with the Chief everyday.

On October the twenty-eighth, we got the word the Russian ships had turned around and headed back to Russia. The first week of November the Commanding General of the Marine Expeditionary Force sent over a formal investigation team to investigate the alleged beating incident. I was on the mess deck with several other men writing my statement for the Marine Captain in charge of the investigation. Suddenly, he turned toward us and said, "If this was one of my men I'd put a pack on his back and march the son-of-a-bitch until he fell dead." I got the distinct feeling this investigation was going to be short lived.

Little by little, the whole story came out. One of the eyewitnesses to the beating had been working in a storeroom holding inventory. During the investigation, one of them came to sickbay with a minor cut. As I cleaned and dressed his wound, we talked.

"Crutchfield, is it true that you saw what the marines did to that poor bastard?"

"Yeah, I did, Doc. Three of us were holding inventory down in one of them little out-of-the-way storerooms. They never knew we were there, but we saw the whole thing."

"You know, I treated the ol' boy here in sickbay and kind of unwittingly got involved. I'd like to know what really happened."

"Well, Doc, I don't think a dog ought to be treated like he was without some kind of a hearing. The First Sergeant and that Gunny took him below on the third deck where we were working. They thought there wouldn't be anyone way down there in the hole. They closed the hatches and stationed guards in front of them. They stripped him down buck-naked and took a piece of marlin line and tied it around his thumbs. Then they heisted his hands up over his head and secured him to a battle lantern. They had a little piece of rope about the size of a garden hose. I tell you, Doc, they beat his ass unmercifully. Every time they hit him they would ask, 'Do you love the Marine Corp?' That question must not have had an answer; no matter what he said, they'd hit him again. It went on for over an hour. I'm surprised they didn't kill the poor son-of-a-bitch."

"You were the senior man there. Why didn't you say something?"

"I don't know, Doc. It just kind of happened before we knew what was going on. We were in kind of a state of shock to tell you the truth. It was like watching something out of a horror movie."

"Yeah, I can see that. You probably did right by just keeping quiet. Not much you could have done anyway. Marines like to handle things their own way."

"You're right, Doc. But they shouldn't have went against the Old Man's orders and done it on the BG."

"I agree, but I don't think much is going to come of it,"

A few days later Khrushchev agreed to dismantle the missile site and allow inspections in exchange for a guarantee that the US wouldn't invade Cuba. President Kennedy and his administration concurred but weren't taking any chances. We were kept in the area until the inspection team satisfied themselves that the Russians had complied with their agreement.

It was the middle of December by the time we got back out into the Pacific. We were finally on our way home. I had delivered the sick list to the XO's mailbox and was walking down the passageway when I saw an IBM computer card lying on the deck. Reaching down and picking it up, I read the print across the top, it said: *HM2 John D. Messer 349 73 43 Laboratory and Blood Bank School, Oakland California.* My heart leaped with excitement. Was this what I thought it was? I bounded down the ladder and fairly ran to the Personnel Office.

"Joe, I found this in the passageway. Is this an advance notice of my orders?"

"Let me see…Where did you find this?"

"In the passageway."

"Someone must have dropped it. But, yeah, you're right. That's what it is. Looks like you're going to be leaving here in March."

We arrived in Long Beach on the fifteenth of December 1962. It was a joyous holiday knowing that we would soon be moving to the Bay Area where most of Peg's family lived. On the thirteenth of March, I packed my seabag and put on the dress blues with the dragons sewn inside the cuffs. Carrying my seabag to the treatment room, I set it down. Meeker was sitting in his favorite chair locked in his thousand-yard stare. Studenbordt was leaning against the sink in front of the mirror. The Chief was not to be seen. Catfish came to the door and leaned his head in. He looked at me sadly.

"Gonna miss you, Doc," he said.

"I'll miss all of you guys." I responded, and shook hands all around. "But I have to tell you the truth, I'm not a bit sorry to be leaving this old bucket of shit."

Everyone laughed.

"Come on, Doc. Seems like just yesterday I carried this damn thing on for you," commented Studenbordt, shouldering my bag. I followed him to the quarterdeck and requested permission to go ashore. As the liberty launch sped toward Magnolia Street Landing, I looked back at what had been my home for almost three years. Here, I had served with some of the best and worst men I had ever known. A sense of sadness, I hadn't expected, fell upon me. I turned my head into the wind and never looked back.

Clinical Laboratory and Blood Bank School

On the twenty-first of March, I arrived at the front gate of the Naval Hospital in Oakland, California. The morning was overcast and a light mist was peppering my windshield. I rolled down the window and held the big manila envelope up for the sentry to see. He slid the door to the gatehouse open but didn't step out.

"Checking in?"

"Yeah!"

"Follow the road down the hill and to your left. Keep looking left; you'll see the flagpole in front of the Administration Building. You'll need to check in there with the OOD."

"Do I need a pass or anything?"

"Nah! After you check in, we'll give you a parking permit and assign you to one of the parking lots near where you work. For now, park anywhere that's not marked reserved."

I wound my way down the hill and passed along, one-story building that had newspaper and Coke machines sitting out front. People, dressed in a mixed bag of pajamas and uniforms, were streaming out a double glass door. I assumed this was the Navy Exchange. Right after I passed the building, I looked left and saw the Administration Building. I made a quick left, circled the flagpole and scanned the parking lot. All the spaces were reserved. I drove around in circles for several minutes, extending my search until I was about a quarter mile away.

The compound was vast. I estimated it to be eighty or ninety acres. The familiar long, white-frame, temporary buildings of the Second World War era lined the hillsides and valleys. Oak Knoll, as the hospital was fondly called, was commissioned on July 1, 1942 as a five hundred-bed facility. As the war in the Pacific expanded, so did her bed capacity. At one time, she housed as many as eight thousand patients.

Peg and I had wasted no time in leaving Long Beach. We beat the moving van out of the driveway. We headed toward Highway Ninety-nine that would take us over the Grapevine and down into the San Joaquin Valley. I heard something hit the side of the car as I sped down the freeway.

"What the hell was that?" I asked.

"Darrel just dropped his bottle out the window," Peg replied, looking toward the rear window. "That's the only one he had."

"Well, I'm sure as hell not stopping on this freeway." Peg turned and gave Darrel a sympathetic look.

"You're a big boy. You don't need a bottle anymore do you, son?" she asked. I looked in the rearview mirror. He was standing in the seat with one hand on the half-opened window and the other on the back of the seat. His lower lip was turned down and had started to quiver as he whimpered softly. Big tears rolled down his cheeks. I glanced in the side view mirror and saw a small blue object far behind us bouncing along the side of the freeway. The whimpering soon turned into an ear splitting wail. Peg tried to comfort him as I fought our way through the Los Angeles traffic.

As the afternoon turned into early evening, we passed through Bakersfield, Fresno, Modesto, and on into Tracy. Nine hours after leaving Long Beach, we were in Oakland. Frances had invited us to stay with her until we could find a place of our own. That proved not to be an easy task. Fortunately, Peg growing up in the area gave us an advantage. We soon ruled out Oakland and adjoining San Leandro.

Peg widened her search to Castro Valley and over into Hayward. We were going to need a three-bedroom house or apartment. The glorious homecoming after the Cuban crisis had interfered with the rhythm plan of birth control that we had decided to rely on for family planning. We would be having another addition to the family in September.

After a couple of days, I became discouraged with what was available in our price range. Peg turned to her sister Marian, who was now called Lorraine, and asked that she intercede with the Lord. The whole Dominican Order of nuns must have bombarded heaven. In less than a week, we moved into a three-bedroom duplex on "B" street, in Hayward. It wasn't perfect but would serve our purpose. While Peg unpacked and organized our home, I drove to the Naval Hospital to check aboard.

By the time I checked into the various departments and delivered my pay, health and dental records, it was getting on toward 1600 hours. When I returned my check-in slip to the Personnel Office, they ordered me to return the following morning no later than 0800 and report to HM1 Bowers in the Laboratory. I would find it located directly in front of the Dental Clinic.

At 0745 the next morning, I arrived at the Laboratory. As I entered, I noticed ten or twelve people sitting just outside of a room that was located on my immediate left. Glancing up above the door, I noticed a little blue placard with gold letters that read "BLOOD DRAWING". A twenty-something HM2 came to the door and called out, "NUMBER 13." I hesitated; an older gentleman stood up and shuffled toward the door.
"Step this way, sir," the young corpsman invited.
"Commander, Commander Miller," the older man corrected him. The HM2 looked at me and then down at my rating badge.

"Bowers office?" I inquired.

"Straight up the hall as far as you can go," he replied, gesturing up the passageway. As I followed the brown-tiled deck forward between two pea-green-colored bulkheads, I couldn't help but notice the heavy, stale odor that permeated the air just outside one of the rooms. Looking up above the door, I noted it was the Bacteriology Department. I continued forward and soon saw three men clustered in front of a partitioned-off space. As I came closer, I could hear someone talking. I couldn't make out what he was saying but the admonishing tone was unmistakable. When I drew near, I saw the man doing the talking sitting behind a desk. He fixed his attention on me and his voice trailed off. The three men glanced in my direction and shifted around nervously. They looked grim.

"HM1 Bowers?" I asked.

"That's me," came the reply. He swiveled his chair around, opened a drawer of an old, upright, green file cabinet and placed a manila folder inside. "We'll take this up later," he said. The three men looked at one another; they seemed unsure of what they should do. In a few seconds, they drifted off in different directions.

"New student?" asked Bowers and closed a long, green logbook.

"Yes, sir."

"Next class won't be forming until May first. There'll be ten of you. The last man is not due to check in until the end of April." Standing up, he walked in front of me and indicated that I was to follow. "I'll assign you to the blood drawing booth for now," he remarked. I fell in behind him. I estimated him to be about thirty-five. I took a certain amount of pride in noting I towered over him a good six inches. His undress blues sported three hash marks with first class chevrons.

"You won't be standing any duties until your class starts. Enjoy it, because once you start, you're going to be on a four section watch," he cautioned with a smirk. I increased my gait to keep up with him as he strutted toward the blood drawing room. When we entered the room, everyone stopped what they were doing and looked at Bowers.

"New student checking in. He'll be working here until class starts," remarked Bowers. No one responded.

"Okay, Luke?" he asked, turning to a man that was about his height and dressed in civilian clothes. The gentleman looked up briefly and acknowledged with a nod that was barely discernible.

The young HM2 who had called the number a short time earlier stuck out his hand and smiled. "I'm HM2 Flink and this is HM2 Williams," he said nodding toward the Afro-American. HM2 Williams giggled and avoided eye contact as I reached for his hand.
"We're waiting for the next class, too," Flink volunteered.

The man Bowers had called Luke, retrieved his coffee cup and walked out the door. Flink and Williams were standing behind a booth that had been built specifically for blood drawing. Two patients sat watching the scenario unfold.
"Have you drawn any blood recently?" Flink asked, as he placed the tourniquet around his patient's upper arm.
"Not for a while," I admitted. Williams giggled again and scratched the front of his prematurely balding hairline. He placed a Band-Aid on the lady's arm and dismissed her.
"Ain't no time like the present to get started. Give Ol' Charlie here a break," suggested Flink. I took my position behind the drawing booth. Williams went to the door and called out the next number. The man Bowers had called "Luke" returned with his coffee and sat down in front of a small desk that faced the door.
"This is Mr. Sunde, Messer," introduced Flink. The man nodded his head at me and took a sip of his coffee.
"Luke's alright, just been here too long. He should've stayed in the Navy; he'd be retired by now," chided Flink. Luke gave a weak smile. The ambiance of the room was serene as we drew blood from an unending line of patients throughout the morning and into the late afternoon.

Over the next few days, HM2 Flink, whom I had begun to call Ron, and HM2 Williams, whom I was now referring to as Charlie, and I had started talking to the students and staff and gossiped endlessly about what we could expect in the coming months.

"Looks like they ain't but three ranks here," commented Ron.

"Yeah and what's that?" asked Charlie.

"Technician, senior and junior student," replied Ron.

"That's bullshit, I worked hard for my stripes. I'll do what they say professionally, but they gonna give me my respect," declared Charlie.

"You hung up your stripes when you accepted your orders to come here as a student, Charlie," chuckled Ron.

"We'll just see about all that," replied Charlie.

"One of these E-3's will have Ol' Messer here swabbing out the deck one of these days. They could give a shit that he was a big shot on some damn banana boat. This is a whole new ball game. The only thing that counts here is what you know about laboratory technique. And I'd venture a guess we know about as little as anyone. Yep, knowledge is king here, Charlie." Charlie scratched his head with indignation at the truth of our situation and cursed under his breath.

"Yeah, you're about as low as whale shit, Charlie. That second class crow you got on don't mean a damn thing," taunted Ron.

As the days passed, we realized a second class petty officer by the name of Charlie Stiles, who worked in Hematology, was our supervisor. He would look in the door from time to time, but for the most part, ignored us. We didn't know it at the time, but Stiles was destined to be one of the first casualties of the coming Vietnam War.

Luke's job was to do special blood clotting studies. When we weren't busy with patients, we would observe him as he skillfully performed his techniques with the mysterious machines that we didn't understand nor dare to touch.

I had been there a couple of weeks when HM2 Stiles, and a HM3 about Ron's age walked into the room. Stiles looked from one of us to the other through big, black, horned-rimmed glasses.

"Johnson needs some help in the morgue," he declared. Charlie and Ron made themselves busy. I made the mistake of looking at him.

"You!" he said as he pointed his finger at my chest. Ron and Charlie gave each other a knowing smile.

"You're the chosen one," gregariously laughed the one Stiles had referred to as Johnson. I stood and grabbed his hand that he had extended.

"I'm HM3 Johnson, one of the senior students. Get your cover," he instructed pleasantly. I got my white hat and fell in at his side and we headed in the direction of Bower's cubicle. About halfway down the passageway, we met a middle-aged female LCDR in a dress-blue uniform. "Morning, Commander," greeted Johnson. She acknowledged his greeting with a negligible head movement and continued on her way.

"That's Georgia Simpson, our Bacteriologist. If you want to graduate, my advice is not to fuck with Georgia Baby," he chuckled. The passageway doubled back left before we got to Bower's cubicle. We were passing the Pathology Department. A man dressed in civilian clothes was putting something in a big round glass machine sitting on the counter. He gave us a big smile and wagged his head from side to side like he knew something we couldn't possibly understand.

"Hey, Hal, what's up?" sang out Johnson.

"Everything's cool," came the response.

"That's Hal Seibert; he's alright. One of the few guys that really gives a shit about the students. Most everyone is burnt out with training a new bunch of assholes every few months," commented Johnson. We came to the door, turned back right and bounded down a set of stairs that led us out into the street.

"It's a short walk, Messer. I have to tell you it's not my favorite place."

"What are we going to do?"

"Not much! Stitch up a stiff. Won't take long. I almost dropped out of class because of the morgue." he explained as we walked along. "You know the school is fourteen months, but you only go to class in the morning for the first seven. You'll rotate through seven departments two times. One of the departments is Pathology. The only thing you'll do in there is assist the pathologist with postmortem exams (autopsy)."

"Is that why you almost dropped out?"

"I was scared to death of dead people, still am, but not like I was. Everyone knew I was having problems. Senior Chief Dodge, you'll meet him when you start to class, kept me out of Pathology for six months, but finally had to put me in there. Well, the very first day, a couple of the senior students told me there had been an airplane crash and the pilot had been killed and the body was all mangled up. They told me they wanted to give me support and offered to go with me to view the body."

Johnson and I had reached the wooden-framed building that housed the morgue. The old, white, faded paint was peeling and the windows had been tinted. I was unable to see inside. It seemed spooky and gave me an eerie feeling. Johnson turned the key in the lock, opened the door and we stepped inside. The smell of formaldehyde overwhelmed me and my eyes started to burn. What I saw shocked me. The nude body of a seventy something year old man lay on a stainless steel table that had been constructed over a sink. An incision had been made from each shoulder to the bottom of his sternum and down to his pelvis. His sternum had been cut away and his vital organs removed. We approached the cadaver as Johnson continued with his story.

"Well, we all came here to the morgue and they told me he was in the drawer over there in number seven," he said pointing toward one of the nine little doors that was built into the wall in front of us. We had approached the cadaver and he hesitated.

"We have to take the brain out," he remarked as he took a large stainless steel bucket which contained all of the intestines from our patient and poured them back into the body cavity. He then set the bloody bucket on the floor.

"Put the sternum back in place and sew him back together with this while I take the brain out," he said and handed me a needle and a big ball of twine.

"Do you know how to do a baseball stitch?"

"Like this?" I asked and pulled the abdominal cavity closed and took an overhand stitch."

"That's okay, it doesn't have to be fancy. Anyway, here we all were," he continued with his story. "So, I goes over to the door and slide it open, real slow." I watched Johnson as he took a scalpel and cut the skin on the scalp of our patient from ear to ear in a swift diagonal cut. He then rolled the skin down over the eyes, turning the skin inside out. Then repeated the process with the back part of the scalp, pulling the skin well down over the occipital. Taking a cast cutter, Johnson commenced to cut a wedge in the skull. The smell of burning bone and the noise from the cast cutter assaulted my sensibilities. Having completed his task, he lifted the bone out, exposing the brain. He then gently slid his hands under the brain, lifted it up, made a couple of snips where it was attached and gingerly lifted it out. I was amazed at how easy it came loose from the cranium wall. Turning the brain upside down, he slipped a piece of twine under the tissue that had connected the brain near the nasal cavity. He then suspended it in a large glass container of foramlin that was sitting on the surgical tray next to where we were working. I was feeling nauseous, but I sewed the cold flesh back into place.

"Is this okay?" I asked.

"Yeah, looks good. Anyway, as I was saying," continued Johnson. "I rolled the drawer out, expecting the worst. The body was covered of course. 'Open the sheet, Johnson,' one of them told me. So I reached down, undid the safety pin and pulled it back. All of a sudden, this son-of-a-bitch opened his eyes, raised his head up and said, 'BOO!' Well, it scared me so goddamn bad, I jumped this post table here, bounded out the door and ran all the way back to the Laboratory." Johnson had replaced the wedge of bone in the cranium and pulled the scalp back in place. I had finished closing the body cavity and was washing the blood off of the big sutures. Johnson reached for my needle and thread and started sewing the scalp back into its original position. "This is a sad case here," he said as he worked. This fellow was an old, retired Commander. They say he lived down on Thirty-second Street for over twenty years. 'He drank a bottle of vodka everyday since he retired,' his wife told the doctor. Help me lift him on here! Will you?" he asked as he rolled the drawer out of the wall. "The funeral home will be picking him up in a few hours. They'll get him fixed up." Turning on a spray hose he started washing the blood off the post-table and out of the sink where we had been working. "Yeah, Messer. I tell you I wanted to kill those bastards for doing that to me. I never roll one of these drawers out and pull that sheet back that I don't think about that," he laughed.

"I bet not," I replied. We soon were walking back to the Laboratory.

"That wasn't too bad now, was it?" Johnson asked as we strolled along. Little did he know that I was weak in the knees and struggling not to vomit.

The first of May, at 0700, found me and ten of my fellow students sitting at two long tables in our new classroom. We were a mixed group varying in age, color and pay grade. There were two E-3s: Hector Caudillo and Henry Carcache. Four E-4s: Norman Wilson, Larry Hoage, Richard Boll and Norman Peoples. Three E-5s: Ron Flink, Charlie Williams and myself. One E-6: Robert Norton. I had found the old, white, temporary buildings on the side of a hill. Most of my fellow students had already arrived. A tall, lean Senior Chief was sitting silently in front of the classroom. At 0701, the Chief looked down at his watch, stood up and walked to the blackboard, picked up a piece of chalk and wrote, RAY DODGE HMCS/USN. "I'm Senior Chief Dodge," he commented ceremoniously as he turned to us and dusted off his hands. We sat motionless waiting for him to continue. He cleared his throat. "Starting today you men will commence the curriculum to become Clinical Laboratory and Blood Bank Technicians. It's not going to be easy. The first six months you'll be in class every morning and in your assigned departments in the afternoon. Unfortunately, you won't always be working in the department that corresponds with the subject you'll be studying. Don't worry about it; it'll eventually all come together," he explained as he paced back and forth. "Each one of you will be assigned to one of the four duty sections that will be made up by you folks and the senior class. You'll be staffing the Laboratory from 1630 until 2200 on your duty days. There will only be one technician on watch and they'll be in the Blood Bank." He hesitated and looked down like he was trying to think of the best way to explain. We looked at each other nervously. The Chief walked over and put his foot on the seat of the chair he had been sitting in, leaned down on his knee, and continued. "Now, you'll sleep in the duty room upstairs by the Blood Bank. The following morning, you'll be going to the wards to draw blood from patients. The PM ward corpsmen drop off request forms on their way to evening chow. That gives the duty crew the opportunity to sort them out according to ward numbers and prepare the equipment needed. Reveille will be at 0430 to give you an opportunity to get squared away and be out on the wards by 0600."

We had heard all the war stories about the morning blood drawing rounds. The Chief sensed our uneasiness. He took his foot off the chair and walked back to the center of the room.

"You all requested to be here so I know you'll give it your best shot. I want to see all ten of you graduate from here next July. Don't worry, hundreds of technicians have completed this course and not one person has died from exhaustion," he chuckled lightly and let his words sink in. "This classroom material is going to come at you fast and furious. Standard Navy procedure requires that anyone falling below a seventy-percentile will be dropped. On your duty days, you'll have to study during your lunch hour and a couple of hours after you knock off. Okay, take ten while I go down and get your department assignments from Bowers."

We gathered on the front porch to smoke and chat. Destiny had drawn us together but we didn't all necessarily like each other. We started pairing off into small groups of two and three. Ron, Charlie and I had been thrown together in blood drawing for a few days and we felt a certain camaraderie. Charlie's anxiety was apparent and Ron didn't hesitate in exploiting him with some good-natured ribbing.

"They always put the black guys in pathology first, Charlie," he teased. Charlie giggled, scratched his head but didn't respond.

"Yeah, I hear they got three bodies down there they are going to post as soon as we get out of class," Ron continued. I had found Charlie's reaction so humorous I almost fell backwards off the banister where I was sitting. Ron caught my arm and pulled me back to safety. "Damn, Messer, no wonder you can't make first class," he remarked sarcastically.

The Chief was coming up the sidewalk; it was too late for a clever come back.

"Let's get you to your departments," the Chief commented, motioning us inside. Reassembling we listened as our names and corresponding departments were read off:

"Wilson…Serology
Williams…Hematology
Norton…Bacteriology
Messer…Parasitology
Carcache…Pathology

Peoples…Chemistry
Caudillo…Urinalysis
Hoage…Blood Donor center
Flink…Blood bank
Bolls…Blood collecting. Okay men, go get'em, and I'll see you back here in the morning at 0800."

We immediately departed for the Laboratory and reported to our respective departments. I found the Parasitology Department on the second floor above the main Lab. just down the hall from the Blood Bank. When I presented myself to Marie, the beautiful African-American lady who was in charge of the department, she gave me a warm smile.

"I'm so glad to meet you, Messer," she said graciously.

"Thanks," I replied and shook her hand.

"Let me show you around. We do the inoculation of the Tuberculosis Cultures here, too," she said, walking to the other end of the long room where a young redheaded corpsman was mixing some mysterious looking solution inside small specimen containers. "Gates, this is Messer, one of our new students," introduced Marie. Gates nodded and held up his hands indicating he couldn't shake with rubber gloves. We entered a small, back room just beyond where Gates was working. Two lone incubators stood against the wall full of TB cultures. "Not a lot to see here," she commented. After a quick glance around, we walked back to her desk. Laying down the pen she had held onto during our tour, she went to the refrigerator and opened it. The top shelf was stacked with little brown boxes with request slips wrapped around them and held in place with rubber bands. Marie started lifting them out and placed them on a long workbench against the wall opposite her desk. She gently removed the rubber bands and placed each box on top of the request form. A strong odor of feces rose up to greet us. I was a little taken back, but Marie seemed not to notice. When all the fecal specimens had been lined up in a neat row, she returned to the refrigerator and started taking urine specimens off the bottom shelf. I noticed they, too, had the request forms wrapped around them and a good number of them were wet. "We do the pregnancy tests here, too," she continued as she lined the bottles up on the opposite end of the bench near the sink. "Parasitology, in theory, is one of the most interesting things you'll study in clinical laboratory procedures. There are all kinds of parasites, of course, but what we are interested in here are intestinal parasites. I'm going to show you how we do a stool floatation and then you can get these all set up," she said. Taking a test tube and filling it with a solution. She then opened the first box in the neat little row, took two wooden applicators and stirred the feces briskly. Apparently satisfied she had a good mixture, she picked up a pea size particle of the feces and dropped it in the solution. She then picked up a slide and wiped the residue on to it. "We'll be doing an Iron Hematoxin stain on this later," she commented as she worked. "Not much to it, really," she added as she completed her task. I nodded my head in agreement. "Okay, you can get these all set up and then I'll show you how to do the pregnancy test," she added.

LCDR Simpson walked into the department. She glowered at us without speaking, went over to a big logbook that was laying on the desk, turned it toward herself and removed several request forms. Marie joined her. I was left to ponder what the hell it was that I was doing. The redheaded corpsman gave me a knowing glance, smiled, and turned back to his work.

I've always found going to the bathroom a very personal matter. Until one gets desensitized to such things, just to look at bottles of urine and boxes of feces, in the presence of the opposite gender can cause a certain degree of discomfort. I didn't understand my feeling of shame at the moment but, as I observed new students in the following months, I soon came to understand I was not unique.

Although I didn't know it at the time, I was putting feces in a heavy salt solution that would cause eggs from intestinal parasites to float to the top. Later, Marie would aspirate a small amount of the supernatant and examine it under the microscope. In the coming months, I would study the life cycles of these animals and call their names in my sleep. At the moment, I was just a new student mixing someone else's excrement in a test tube and feeling very humiliated. When I completed my task, Marie was ready to take me to the next procedure.

"You students are lucky today. Back when I went to Lab. school, we had to sacrifice a rabbit to do a pregnancy test."

"You're kidding?"

"No, I'm not. We'd inject them with urine from the patient and seventy-two hours later we'd kill them, dissect them, and inspect the bladder. The presence of a red discoloration, or lesion, on the bladder wall indicated a positive." Marie walked to the refrigerator, opened the bottom drawer and took out a large, green frog that weighed at least a quarter pound. "We buy these from South America in bunches of a dozen. I don't have to tell you they are expensive," she remarked. She laid the frog on the bench and took a two cc (cubic centimeter) syringe and aspirated a cc of urine from the first specimen, picked up our lethargic friend and injected half of it underneath his skin in the middle of his back. She then placed him in a round, glass container of sufficient size to hold him. "In two hours, we'll catheterize him and exam the urine under the microscope. Women produce a substance called hCG (human Chorionic Gonadotropin) when they are pregnant; that causes the frogs to produce sperm in their urine. That's about all there is to it," she explained. "Go ahead and get them set up," she instructed as she reached under the sink and took the round glass containers and sat one in front of each of the specimens.

Just before lunch, it was time to exam my friends for sperm. Marie sat at the microscope and I carried the glass containers to her. She would reach in and grab the frogs, which had become amazingly active, then hold their head and legs in such a manner that forced their butts to protrude. She would then smack their rears on a slide. More often than not, a moist place would appear; she would then quickly put a cover slip over the area and focus her microscope. Marie would dutifully show me the wiggley little sperm when she hit a positive; we quickly worked our way down the line. One fellow didn't care to give up his urine so easily. Marie quickly inserted a capillary tube up his rectum and expertly extracted a urine sample. It was time for lunch. I cleaned the area and returned the frogs to the refrigerator and sailed off to the cafeteria. I bumped into a couple of my fellow students and we exchanged war stories about our first day. They were as confused as I was, which made me feel better.

At 1300 in the afternoon, I was bounding up the stairs to my workspace. Marie was standing in front of the glass containers looking quite perplexed.

"Where are the frogs?"

"I put them back in the refrigerator."

"The positive ones, too?"

"Yeah, I thought that was what I was suppose to do." Marie went to the desk and sat down and looked around the room like she was in a state of shock.

"Georgia Baby is going to have a shit fit," commented Gates from the other end of the room and gave Marie a delightful smile as he shook his head from side to side. I felt a sinking feeling in my stomach.

"They produce sperm for a week or longer, Messer. You've mixed the positive back with the negative ones. We have no way of knowing, which is which. We'll have to discard them all," sighed Marie and sat staring off into space. "We're not due another shipment until the end of next week. Maybe Commander Simpson can call and put in a rush order. Anyway, I have to tell her," she said and reached for the phone.

"Can't we catheterize them and take out the positive ones?" I pleaded. Marie gave me an astonished look and shook her head from side to side. I assumed what I had said must have been stupid. I still don't know why that sounded so ludicrous.

In a matter of a few hours, everyone in the Laboratory, students and technicians alike were gleefully pointing me out to their coworkers. The rite of passage to become a technician had to be paid. Everyone, at one time or another, had experienced their own humiliation. For now, I was the butt of their jokes but tomorrow it would be one of my classmates. For the most part, everyone except one person soon forgot it.

Class started in earnest the following day. Each of the seven subjects would be studied for one month. Senior Chief Dodge reasoned that we should study the most important subjects first to qualify us as watch standers. Complete blood counts, urinalysis and chemistry made up the majority of the after-hours requests. We would start with hematology. The third day of class was my first duty day. Class started at 0800 and terminated at 1205. At 1300, I reported to Marie and at 1600, I reported to the Hematology Department to assume my duties.

My duty section was made up of three senior and two junior students. One of the senior students was assigned to chemistry and the rest of us covered the main Laboratory. The microscopic work of doing blood counts and urinalysis were months away for me and the other junior student. The majority of the work was simple mechanics that consisted of operating machines, dipping paper strips in solutions and recording colors. Simple procedures were explained and we worked our way through the evening until 2200. Request forms, by the dozens, were delivered to the Laboratory by the PM corpsmen on their way to chow and continued to arrive throughout the evening as new patients were admitted. Our section leader was a second class Filipino by the name of HM2 Idos. It was his first day as a senior student and he was determined not to end up in Bowers' office the following morning.

At 2200, we gathered in the blood drawing room and separated the requests according to wards. Idos assigned each one of us a fair portion of the request forms.

"Messer, you'll go with me to Pediatrics," he said quietly and started spreading the forms out on the drawing booth table. "We can't draw tubes of blood on the little ones, we'll have to do finger or heel sticks. We'll dilute the blood counts right on the ward," he continued as he gathered alcohol sponges, Band-Aids, small tubes, needles, lancets and dozens of vials of different colored solutions. He then took two blue boxes out from under the gurney that was sitting by the door. I noticed they had handles for carrying and looked very much like toolboxes without lids. He divided the request forms and supplies evenly and put them in the two boxes. "This one will be yours," he said and handed me one of the boxes and smiled pleasantly. "That's it until morning," he remarked and placed his box under the gurney and indicated I do the same. I followed him out the front door and we headed toward the stairs that led up to the duty room. "We'll get started a little early. We're not supposed to go on the ward until 0600 but if we wait that late we won't get done before it's time for you to go to class," he explained as we climbed the stairs.

We rose at 0430, showered, shaved and grabbed a candy bar out of the vending machine that stood in front of the Lab. The fog hung heavy in the early morning darkness and a chill was in the air. Retrieving our blood collection boxes, Idos led me across the street, up the side of a hill and down a ramp to the back door of one of the long, white buildings. We immediately entered into a long, brown-tiled corridor with glassed-in cubicles on each side. There was a light on in the first cubicle. I could see a corpswave standing in front of someone seated next to a bed. A closer look revealed a young woman holding the hand of a young boy who looked to be about five. His big blue eyes had a look of wonder as he watched and listened to us silently. I could see his hair was gone and his cheeks were a sallow color and swollen. Idos and I entered the room.

"We need a white count on this one," he said quietly as he placed his collection box on the green bedside table. The large blue, expressionless eyes followed his every move. The young woman smiled, moved her feet back to make room for Idos.

"Josh is a big boy. Aren't you, son?" she commented. Idos took the boy's finger, straightened it out, wiped it off with an alcohol sponge and jabbed him quickly with the lancet. He didn't flinch. Pale, anemic-looking blood ran out the end of his finger. Idos inserted a small rubber tube in his mouth that held a small pipette on the end. He carefully sucked the blood up to the graduated mark, wiped the excess off the outside, stuck it in one of the specimen vials and blew it into the container. He rinsed the pipette in the solution several times. The blue eyes watched as though he was detached and merely an observer.

"Why don't you find the rooms on your requests and get started?" asked Idos as he picked up the next request form.

The name of the patient, and number of the cubicle and bed, were on the requisitions. I soon found my first patient. He was a newborn not more than a week old. He had been born with a high concentration of bile in his blood. I would have to fill one of the giant capillary tubes Idos had put in my tray. He was sleeping peaceful on his stomach with his little butt up in the air. I pulled the blanket up from the bottom. He moved uneasily in his sleep as I grasped the little warm foot and pulled it toward me. I could see his heel was black and blue from all of the previous lancet cuts. I prepared his heel and stabbed him. A small amount of blood trickled out. I sucked it into the pipette; there wasn't a sufficient amount to reach the graduated mark. I squeezed his heel for more blood; the wound soon clotted. The baby began to cry and fret.

Idos had moved from one of the other rooms and had stopped to watch me through the glass. Noting my frustration, he entered the room silently and walked to the bed. He took a lancet and stuck the baby's heel, giving it a vicious twist as he exited. Blood poured out of the wound. The baby screamed in pain. The lights came on in the corridor. I looked at my watch, it was 0600. We had been on the ward a half-hour. I broke out in a cold sweat. At this rate, we would be here until noon. Idos indicated with his head for me to continue on.

My next patient was a three-year-old male. The lights had wakened him and he wasn't happy. He had never seen me before, but he had had experiences with other men, dressed in white, that carried toolboxes containing instruments of torture. When I approached his bed, he started kicking his feet and commenced to cry. I tried to restrain him and pull his hand out to get to his finger with my left hand while wielding the lancet in my right. The pipette was attached to a rubber sucking tube that hung out of my mouth. We were in a battle of wills. In my determination to complete my task, I had lost sight of the fact I was dealing with a three-year-old. In his attempt to escape, he kicked my collection box off the bedside stand and onto the floor. Solutions, pipettes, lancets, Band-Aids and tubes went flying across the room. He had wakened his roommates and they set up a hue and cry that could have been heard in the Admiral's quarters. A corpsman came running into the room and tried to restore order. Idos soon joined us. He looked at the disaster, seemingly unruffled, "Maybe we better get one of the interns to get this one," he commented to the corpsman and handed him the request form. The corpsman, being too busy to argue, accepted it. We both knew the requisition would go back to the Lab. in the evening and someone else would be back in the morning. It would then be their problem but I was too frustrated to care. I had lost the battle.

The morning continued. Idos finished his collections and came to my aid. We returned to the Lab. at 0830. Half of the requests still remained in my box. I looked at my collection box of bloody, broken half-empty vials and was overwhelmed with despair. Herman, the civilian technologist in charge of Hematology, gave me a look of contempt.

By the time I got to the classroom, it was 0900. I took my seat, feeling exhausted. Senior Chief Dodge gave me a quizzical look. "Been frog hunting, Messer?" he quipped. Everyone laughed.

I had missed an hour of notes and hadn't gone over the ones from the day before. Lunchtime found me in the duty room with Flink's notes scribbling furiously. At 1300, I was back in Parasitology for a long weary afternoon. I was tidying up the counter when Zeke Norton (Robert) stuck his head in the door.
"Want to get a cool one?" he asked.
"I could sure as hell use one," I replied. I had left home the day before at 0700. I had sat in class for seven hours, worked eighteen, and slept for five. I was wound tighter than a guitar string and completely fatigued. We climbed the hill to the enlisted men's club.

Meanwhile, Peg had been alone for two days with three kids in diapers. Being five months pregnant didn't help. She had prepared dinner and listened expectantly for the sound of the car. At 2300, she heard me drive into the driveway. I got out of the car and staggered up the sidewalk. She didn't meet me at the front door, as was her custom. The light was on in the kitchen and I could see the cold food still sitting on the dining room table. I found Peg in the living room sitting in the semi-darkness.
"Where have you been?" she demanded. "I've been worried sick with visions of you lying dead in the street somewhere." I could see the pained look in her face.

"I'm sorry, babe. It's been a hell'va two days," I stammered. Slowly her pain turned to sympathy as I explained the night away. She cradled me in her arms and listened as I poured out my tale of woe and frustration.

"Please, just call me if you're going to stay out and drink."

"But I didn't intend to stay so long. One thing led to another and the next thing I knew it was after 2200."

"Dick, I know how you are with your buddies. If you'll just call me, I promise you, I won't be mad. I just don't want to sit here and worry about you all night."

"I'll call. It's a promise."

Had Peg said to me that night, if you ever do this again I am going to take the kids and leave, our lives might have been different. But it wasn't her way. A pattern of behavior was established over the next few months that would continue for many, many years to come. Perhaps, I had inherited the seeds of alcoholism, perhaps not. But they were there. I had watered them sufficiently on the Belle Grove that they had become budding plants. By the time I graduated from Lab. School, they were in full bloom. Later on in life, I would learn there are people who should never drink and I was one of them and give it up. But that was a few years off.

Bacteriology and Parasitology were considered to be one Department. After completing two weeks with Marie, I rotated downstairs to Bacteriology. Hours were spent preparing the stool floatations so that Marie could examine them under the microscope for a few minutes. It was no different in Bacteriology than it was in the other departments; eighty percent of the work required menial labor. Junior students made up the labor pool for these long, tedious, monotonous procedures. My job in Bacteriology was to inoculate the specimens onto enrichment media in order to cultivate the bacteria. Only senior students were allowed to work with the microbiologist and technicians to identify the microbes.

Duty days were another matter. We trained under fire. Senior Chief Dodge concentrated on teaching us how to identify the five different white cells on a peripheral blood slide. This was the technical part of the complete blood count. Within a week, out of absolute necessity, we were doing things while standing duty that would have been frowned on during the regular workday. Looking at spun urine and determining if it contained red cells, white cells, trichomonas, yeast, or bacteria was something that had to be learned immediately if we were to be effective as watch standers.

Senior Chief Dodge pounded us daily with his philosophy. "Intellectual honesty is required to be a good Lab. Technician. No one knows what you're looking at down that microscope. You have the ability to do mankind a great service or a lot of harm. It all has to do with how capable you are of telling the truth about what you see or don't see, or what you know and don't know. If you're sloppy and don't care, sooner or later it'll catch up to you. As time passes, your true character will show through," he repeated day after day. In the years that followed, I came to understand the wisdom of his words.

My second department was Chemistry. I was happy to have escaped Pathology another month but was filled with trepidation. Chemistry, by far, was one of the most labor-intensive departments. There were four civilian and three military technicians, two senior and four junior students, a Secretary, and a Biochemist working there. The senior enlisted man was an HM1 by the name of Bradford. He greeted me warmly and showed me through the department.

"We have a ton of dishware that the students are responsible to wash. We're too busy to do this during regular working hours. Unfortunately, it has to be done after 1630," he said and led me into this large room with flasks, tubes, and other miscellaneous paraphernalia that was piled to the ceiling. I'm going to put you on filtrates," he commented and led me back to a counter in the main part of the Department. Chemicals stood along the wall and on the shelves. Reaching into a drawer, he pulled out three four-by-eight inch cards covered with plastic protectors. "Here are the procedure cards," he informed me. I looked at him in wonder.

"Is anyone going to go through the procedure with me first?" I asked.

"I'll be giving you a hand as you need it," he said and dropped about twenty-five request forms in front of me. "Take these! You'll notice there is a number on the requisition here marked with a grease pencil. There'll be a corresponding number on the test tube of the specimen that you'll be performing the procedure on," he said, leading me to the front of the room where there stood row upon row of tubes filled with blood. Several people were gathered in the area, selecting specimens. Everyone seemed to be oblivious to each other as they frantically selected specimens. They would need to work as fast as was humanly possible, if the hundreds of chemistry tests that had been ordered were to be completed. "Grab three of those wire racks over there and we'll get the specimens we need," instructed Bradford, pointing to a huge pile of wire racks under a stainless steel hood.

The procedures for the three different filtrates were to precipitate the protein from the plasma with a weak solution of acid and pipette the clear supernate into a clean tube sitting directly behind the specimen tube. Chemicals would be added and the supernate would change into various colors depending on the test. After waiting a specified time, their density would be measured on a photometer and their concentration calculated by using a known standard. I was working with three dozen different specimens, putting in minuscule amounts of different chemicals. Time passed quickly as I raced against the clock. A few minutes before 1600, I was ready to do my measurements and calculations. Bradford had been observing my technique and checking the time. Seeing I was finally ready, he came to my workbench. "I'll give you a hand with this," he said and we moved to the Coleman photometer. He took a tube from the middle of the rack. "Let's check your control first," he said and decanted the solution into the Phototube. The needle swung wildly on the scale. Bradford pursed his lip. "Looks like something is not quite right," he commented dryly and looked toward the clock. "You'll have to repeat these tomorrow. It's too late to start over today. Go ahead and get started on the glassware," he ordered and walked over and dumped the test tubes in a big stainless steel bucket that sat in the sink near where I had been working. "Take this bucket back with you," he said, lifting the big bucket toward me.

I felt totally defeated. Three hours of intense work, following the directions of procedure cards, having absolutely no idea of what I was doing, had been overwhelming. The hour of 1830 found me and three of my fellow students wiping down the stainless steel counters in the glassware room. Peg was waiting for me to come home or call. I decided on the latter and several of us climbed the hill to the EM Club. Peg would spend another long evening at home alone.

When I reflect on those days and think about what the military demanded of us, I try to identify what it was about certain men that made them good or poor leaders. I remember the old military training manual described leadership as the ability to exercise one's will over another. How one goes about doing that wasn't quite made clear. In 1966, when I was serving in 3rd battalion, 26th Marines at Camp Pendlleton, California General Krulak came and gave us a pep talk.

"A staff non-commissioned officer's relationship with his men should be that of father and son. Our system of warfare is such that old men take young men to war. Officers and staff non-commissioned officers have a grave responsibility."

Considering the average age of the men who fought the First, Second, Korean and the Vietnam War, I would certainly have to agree with him. I have seen poor, fair, good, excellent and outstanding leaders. The exact characteristic that makes up one's ability to push men to their highest capability doesn't seem to be any one particular thing that I can identify. I do know that we're more transparent to those around us than we realize. When a designated leader is more concerned with himself and his ambition than he is for his men it is quite obvious and he's destined to fail as a leader and ultimately in his mission. That doesn't necessarily mean he won't be promoted or be placed in charge.

The two men I knew in my military career who I admired and considered to be outstanding leaders were CAPT. D.B. Rulon and HMCM John Tuomala. The question of course is, "why?" The answer is simple. They inspired me and others around them. Were these ordinary men with human frailties? Yes, but they put professional duty, love of their men, and dedication to country above their own selfish desires. I knew when I did my best, even when my performance fell short; they would go to the wall for me on matters of principal. No cowardly, self-seeking individual can prevail against such men. Giving them my loyalty also empowered me. I would have gladly followed them to the ends of the earth. Today, when I glimpse others that inspire those same feelings in young men who will be led into harms way, the hair on the back of my neck stands up. I suspect that all men long for a just cause that they can dedicate themselves to. In the following paragraph, you will meet CAPT. Rulon and if you're still with me when I go to Vietnam you will briefly meet HMCM John Tuomala.

After Chemistry, I was assigned to Pathology. I waited fearfully for my first postmortem. It wasn't long in coming. The second day, a middle-aged woman died of an unknown etiology. I was to assist with the autopsy. The senior student working in Pathology went to the morgue with me and helped take the body from the long drawer and place it onto the postmortem table. He soon departed and I was left to ponder my surroundings and the cadaver before me. A short time later, I heard the door to the morgue open. I turned to see CAPT. Rulon enter. He was a big middle-aged man, standing over six-foot, three-inches. He nodded.

"How are you doing, Messer?" he asked in a quiet voice as he neared the table. "Nervous?"

"Yes, sir, a little."

"Let's cover her face with this towel," he said picking up one of the medicine towels from the stack on the cart next to the table. He covered her gently. "We have to treat the dead with the same dignity as the living," he commented quietly as he searched my face.

"You okay?"

"Yes, sir," I answered. Strangely, I had started to relax.

"We'll do this in a professional manner like any other medical procedure. We're here to try to determine the cause of death. In the process, you'll have the opportunity to learn things about anatomy you couldn't possibly learn anywhere else." He had opened the chest and abdominal cavity and commenced to remove the vital organs. I watched as he weighed and recorded them. Small pieces of tissue were removed and put into specimen jars. Finally he came to the bile duct. His professionalism was so overpowering that I had become absorbed in our work. "What's this?" he asked and followed the four to six inch bile duct to the gall bladder. "Looks like this duct was plugged," he commented and removed it. "Surgery might have saved her life," he continued and looked across the table at me. I nodded. "What you and I do here today may very well save someone else's life in the future," he spoke slowly and deliberately. "We'll report our findings and her case will be discussed with present and future surgeons. Hopefully, the next time it will help them make a timely diagnosis." I nodded again, hypnotized by this big man's quiet dignity. He looked deep into my eyes. I sensed he was seeing more than I would have cared for him to. "I hear you're one of our better students, Messer," he commented.

"I'm trying, sir."

"I'll be teaching you Blood Banking personally. That's the one area we can't afford to make mistakes. I want to assure myself, before any of you set up a crossmatch, you know exactly what you're doing and the theory behind it." He removed his rubber gloves. "You going to be alright here by yourself cleaning up?" he asked.

"Yes, sir," I answered. He looked at me closely again. "I'll be fine, sir," I assured him. I wanted somehow to communicate to him what a profound affect he had on me. The anatomy lesson may have been important, the cause of death certainly was. But for me, the most important thing I had learned was very simple. A good man with the right character can bring dignity to any task, even working with the dead.

Days turned into weeks and the months passed. It was the beginning of September and our new baby was due. It was a difficult time for Peg as she struggled with her pregnancy and our three young children. But, as it so often has been in our marriage, she was more concerned for me than for herself. I was under enormous stress and found it impossible to give her more than token emotional support. Rotating through the departments before we had studied the subject matter was overwhelming. It made absolutely no sense to me. I felt we were nothing more than lackeys. The thirty-six-hour shift every fourth day, linked with my studies, seemed an impossible task. A good portion of the time I wasn't sure I could keep up the pace and at others, I wasn't sure I wanted to. I talked with Peg about throwing in the towel. Each time I seriously considered it, she would plead for me to think about it another day before making a final decision.

"After all, this was your reason for reenlisting in the first place," she reminded me. "Besides, I have promised Saint Thomas of Aquinas that I would name this baby after him if he would intercede with the Lord to help get you through this course."

Not having been raised up in the Catholic faith, praying to saints was a foreign concept to me. Peg, on the other hand, was not above cutting a deal. After all, I would never have made third class had she not promised to name our daughter "Mary" after the Blessed Mother of Jesus. I was left to ponder how non-Catholics ever made rank.

The first name of our next son was non-negotiable; however, I could pick his middle one. I had always liked Joey. But we couldn't very well put that with a sophisticated name like Thomas. It would have to be Joseph. That was fine with me. I hadn't made any promises to any saints living or dead. I was going to call him "Joey" no matter what we put on his birth certificate. This all seems a little strange to me today, considering we had no idea what sex our new addition was going to be.

Due to the fact I was spending so much time at the Naval Hospital and leaving Peg and the children alone, Frances insisted we move into her house until the baby arrived. It was a welcome invitation. We accepted and moved into her house on the fifth of September.

The tenth was my duty day. I had attended classes in the morning and had reported to urinalysis at 1300. HM2 Oscar Willis was the technician in charge. For some reason, I was the only student working in the department that day. Rows and rows of urine specimens awaited my arrival. My responsibility was to take the specific gravity, check for protein, record the acid base pH, etc…and spin the urine down in a centrifuge. HM2 Willis would then decant the supernate and do the microscopic exam. At 1330, the phone rang.

"It's for you, Messer."
"Hello!"
"HM2 Messer?"
"Yes!"
"Your wife, Margaret, has been admitted to the labor deck."
"Is she alright?"

"Yes, she's fine. She's not dilated yet, but we think she's in early labor. We'll call you if there is any change. Don't worry she'll be okay."

"Thanks! Please call me when she goes into the delivery room."

"We will."

Although we were busy, the afternoon passed slowly. Every five minutes, I looked at my watch. I tried not to think about what pain Peg might be having but it was hard to keep my mind on anything else. At 1600, my section took over the watch. There were only three of us working and, as always, we were inundated with emergency requests. I didn't want to abandon my shipmates until it was necessary. I would wait until they called to tell me she was in the delivery room before going to see her. Around 1800, a tube of blood with a lavender top and urine specimen was handed to me. I unwrapped the request form to log in the name. My heart skipped a beat as I read Margaret A. Messer. I handed the tube of blood to Idos.

"Let me know the results of this when you get done? It's my wife; she's in labor," I remarked, trying to stay calm. He nodded politely and inverted the tube a couple of times and started preparing the dilution for the white and red blood cell count. I would do the urine myself. I had spun it down and sat down to do the micro exam when the phone rang. I grabbed it. I knew it would be for me.

"HM2 Messer! Can I help you?"

"Yes, Messer, your wife just had a big boy."

"I thought you were going to call me when she went into the delivery room."

"We didn't have time; she went very fast. Sorry!"

"Were there any complications?"

"No, she is fine, but she had a hard labor. The baby was quite large."

"How much did he weigh?"

"Eleven pounds!" I rushed to the OB Department. I found Peg lying on a gurney in the hall waiting to be moved to an empty bed. I took her hand, leaned over and kissed her. She smiled weakly through the fog of the medication.

"Did you see him?" she slurred.

"Not yet, they're still cleaning him up."

The nurses soon came and took Peg to her room. I knew they needed me in the Lab. but I waited at the nursery window, hoping to get a look at my new son. In what seemed like an eternity, a young lady dressed in a green scrub gown appeared pushing a bassinet in front of her. She saw me waiting, smiled and pointed down to the baby, indicating he was mine. She lined him up in the row with the other eight newborn infants. He was so much bigger than the others were that he looked out of place. The comic book character Baby Huey came to mind. I smiled to myself.

The next morning, I was assigned my portion of patients to draw blood from and class convened at 0800. At noon, I hurried to the maternity ward. I found Peg sitting up with her lunch tray in front of her. When I entered, she gave me a big smile.

"The Admiral came to see me," she chirped.

"Really! What did he want?"

"Nothing! He said he just wanted to see the mother of that big boy." We both laughed.

I was delighted when, finally, my assignment to Blood Bank and the Donor center corresponded with my class room instructions. CAPT. Rulon, true to his word, taught the class. My admiration for him motivated me to give my studies a little extra effort. It paid off and I completed the course with 90.7%, the highest grade in the class. I was feeling pretty good about myself along about this time.

At the end of seven months, we completed the theoretical phase of the course. The senior students had graduated and we had a brand new class of junior students. It seemed we had completed some kind of metamorphous. Magically, we had become somebody and were allowed to perform more sophisticated procedures that required the technical training we had been given in the classroom.

Zeke, Flink, Charlie and I were in charge of the four duty sections. After hours, we were the last word and ultimate authority in the Lab. As graduation drew near, we became cocky and full of confidence to almost the point of arrogance. I was about to have a very rude awakening.

I was rotating through Bacteriology for the second time. The junior students were in class and I was stuck with inoculating the new specimens onto the enrichment media. They continued to flow into the Laboratory as the morning passed. I had my back to the door as I diligently performed my mundane assignment. Hearing a knock, I turned to see a young man dressed in the typical blue pajamas and robe of a hospital inpatient. He was holding a small plastic container in his hand.

"Where do I put this?" he asked.

"Let's see what you got," I answered and undid the rubber band and removed the request form. I could see it was a sputum specimen. I unscrewed the lid and looked inside. There was a small amount of sputum that looked so innocuous that I wondered why a sputum specimen had even been ordered. I had become somewhat adjusted to the new interns ordering what I considered unnecessary tests. For the most part, I considered a good portion of what we did a waste of time, energy and technology.

"Is it okay?" the young man asked. Being bored and looking for an excuse to have some interaction, I took the opportunity to play the part of a learned scientist.

"Looks like cancer to me," I remarked, nonchalantly.

"You think it could be?" he asked, looking somewhat alarmed. I assumed he was feigning fear and going along with the joke. You could've never convinced me that there was anyone in the whole US Navy that could possibly think someone could just eyeball a specimen of sputum and diagnose cancer.

"I am sure of it," I replied and turned back to my workbench. Less than a half-hour passed. I heard heavy footsteps coming down the hall. CAPT. Rulon looked in the door. A young Medical Officer and the patient, who had delivered the sputum specimen, accompanied him.

"Who took the sputum specimen from this patient?" asked CAPT. Rulon, nodding toward my young friend.

"I did, sir," I answered.

"Did you tell him it was positive for cancer?" he asked.

The young Medical Officer was glaring at me with utter contempt. The young patient looked petrified. I stood motionless, not really knowing how to respond. I knew I had broken every rule of etiquette and really had no excuse for my behavior.

"It was something I said off the cuff just kidding around, sir" I answered feeling hopelessly inadequate to give any kind of reasonable explanation.

"This man shouldn't be in contact with patients. I want him out of the Laboratory," the Medical Officer demanded.

"I'll take care of it," replied CAPT. Rulon and led them back to his office. I watched them go inside and close the door. My self-importance had turned to shame in less than a minute.

CAPT. Rulon never mentioned the incident to me again. Had he told LCDR Simpson, I doubt if I would have been allowed to graduate. Certainly she would have given me a failing grade in Bacteriology. The tremendous respect and admiration I had for CAPT. Rulon added to my humiliation. It was a lesson I would not soon forget.

The middle of June 1964, I received my orders. I would be going to the Naval Hospital at Camp Pendleton, California. I had hoped to stay in the Bay Area but it was not to be. I resigned myself to the fact I would be leaving. Peg and I looked forward to my graduation day with joyous anticipation.

Much to my surprise, HMCS Dodge informed the class that there were three of us within a half a point of each other at the head of the class. All the grades were in except Bacteriology and Parasitology. LCDR Simpson's practical grade would determine who would graduate with honors. We waited impatiently. Finally, the last week of school we were advised to pick up our evaluation sheets from Microbiology. I found LCDR Simpson in her office sitting stiffly at her desk. She was writing in one of the many logbooks stacked in front of her. I knocked on the door.

"Yes!"

"Commander, I understand you have the practical grades completed." Without looking up, she sifted through a stack of papers and handed one of them to me.

"For me, Messer, you'll always be the man that mixed up my frogs," she commented dryly. I looked down at the 75% marked in big red letters at the top of the form. The title "Honor Man" would go to HM3 Bolls.

At 0900, on graduation day we assembled in one of the many conference rooms on the second floor of the Administration Building. A short time later, CAPT. Rulon came through the back door and walked to the podium and laid the manila folder he'd been carrying down. He looked at each one of us individually.

"I could stand up here a half an hour and tell you how proud I am of you, but I'm not going to do that. I want you to leave here with just one thought." He hesitated and made sure he had our attention. "Always remember that medical care does not revolve around the Laboratory but the other way around. You're one of the satellites that are responsible to contribute to the over all good of patient care. So many times we get so puffed up with pride we forget that. If you'll always keep that in mind, I promise you'll be a success and a credit to the Navy's Medical Department. Fair winds and smooth sailing to you all," he concluded with a nod and strolled out of the room.

I know today that he saw in each one of us the potential for both failure and success. His desire was to challenge us to be more than ordinary. It's the only graduation speech I ever heard that I have remembered. We were all better men for having known him. I'm proud to have trained under his tutelage. Although my personal contact with him was brief, he had a profound effect on my life and how I performed my tasks in the years that followed.

Naval Hospital Camp Pendleton, California

The last week of June 1964, Peg and I with the four children, departed for the Naval Hospital, Camp Pendleton, California. I had passed the base several times over the past few years and knew it was adjacent to Oceanside, a city that was located between San Diego and Long Beach.

Camp Pendleton, as we know it today, came into existence on the twenty-fifth of September 1942, when Franklin D. Roosevelt named the 125,000-acre purchase in honor of Major General Joseph H. Pendleton. It became one of the largest amphibious bases in the world. Here, the marines had initially trained for the invasion of the Japanese-held islands in the Pacific and continue to train there down to the present day.

The west side of the base starts at Oceanside and runs twenty miles north to the city of San Clemente and extends some seventeen miles east to the city of Fallbrook. The Naval Hospital is approximately nine miles from the front gate at Oceanside and is located on the north side of Vandergrift Boulevard near Lake O'Neil.

Upon our arrival in North San Diego County, Peg and I commenced our search for adequate housing. Oceanside was obviously a marine town and being a navy family we decided to go to Fallbrook. It didn't take us long to check out the two real estate offices and the newspaper ads there. The property owners weren't interested in leasing to a military family with four children under the age of five. We were soon back on Highway76, headed for Oceanside. On our return trip, we took a wrong turn at the Bonsal Bridge and ended up on a street named Vista Way. We soon saw a sign telling us how many miles to Oceanside and continued on our way. Suddenly, I saw a small business district coming into view.

"Peg, look on the map and see what's the name of this little berg."

"I don't see any town on this map."

"That old map is the one we got back in Virginia for our trip out west."

"Yeah, it's pretty old."

"Looks like we're still on Vista Way and that cross street coming up is Escondido Boulevard."

"Hey, there's a real estate office there on the right and it looks like they have a house for rent." I made the block and came back to the parking lot. The front door to the small office building was open. As I stepped inside, a middle-aged man with a slight paunch stood up, smiled and stuck out his hand.

"I'm Clyde Brown," he said and we shook hands.

"John Messer." I felt the presence of someone else in the room. I looked behind me and saw a heavyset, sixty something looking gentlemen. He tilted his head back, peered through his bifocals at his newspaper and slowly turned the page and pretended to be ignoring me. "The sign says you have a house for rent."

"We sure do. A three bedroom," replied Mr. Brown looking toward the station wagon where Peg and the kids sat waiting. "Would you like to take a look at it?"

"We'd appreciate that very much. Is this part of Oceanside?"

"No," he chuckled and reached in his desk and pulled out a set of keys. We headed for the door. "This is Vista," he continued.

"We didn't see anything on the map indicating a town between Fallbrook and Oceanside."

"Vista has only been incorporated a few months. We're probably not on the map yet. Follow me; the house is only a few blocks from here," he said and climbed into an old, rickety, gray Chevrolet.

"It's still for rent," I commented to Peg as I hurried to follow the old car.

We sped down the almost empty street a few blocks and made a right on Santa Fe. In less than five minutes, we came to a street called Buna Place. The old gray car turned right, went to the end of the short street and pulled into a driveway. By the time I got parked, Mr. Brown had exited his car and opened the front door.

"This house belongs to a Marine on a three year assignment in Germany. He won't be coming back until late in 1966. The rent is $110.00 a month and I'll need $50.00 cleaning deposit, if you decide you want it."

Darrel, Terry, and Mary were romping though the house, glad to finally be out of the car. Peg put Joe down on his fat, wobbly legs and he waddled down the hall. "Cute girl," commented Mr. Brown. Peg gave me an accusing look. I had refused to let her cut his curly blond, shoulder length hair and it had become a matter of contention.

"Yes, he is," I answered.

"Oh, I'm sorry," he said.

"My husband won't let me cut his hair," Peg explained.

"I can see why. It's rather becoming on him. John, you're in the military, right?"

"Yeah!"

"How long you been in?"

"Eight years!"

"What's your rank?"

"E-5."

"You know, John, I can get you in a house of your own for around a hundred a month. We can get a VA loan with no money down. All you'll need is about seven hundred and fifty for closing costs. How does that sound?"

Peg and I looked at each other.

"We'll take this place for now but, when I reenlist, I'd like to talk to you more about it."

"Good, let's get back to the office and have you sign a few papers."

"John, Vista is the perfect place for you and Peg to raise your family. We're twelve miles from the beach, forty-five from San Diego, fifty-five from the Mexican border, sixty-five from Disneyland, twenty from Palomar Mountain and it's only thirty to the desert. If you want to go to Las Vegas, it's about a four-hour drive and Palm Springs is about two and a half. You're in a vacation wonderland."

"Really! What's the population of Vista?"

"Just over ten thousand. The Chamber of Commerce claims the sun shines here 350 days out of the year. At one time, it was nothing more than a desert. But with them bringing water in from the Colorado River for irrigation it has become, literally, a paradise on earth."

The first house in Vista that we lived in was at 127 Buna Place. I went there this morning to refresh my memory of those long ago days. I hardly recognized the old neighborhood. The end of the street now opens up into a new housing project. I parked the car and got out to look around. Five or six Hispanic children between eight and ten years old were playing in the street. They eyed me suspiciously as I exited my car.

"I used to live in that house," I said nodding toward the house in front of us, hoping to alleviate their suspicions. Two of them rode their skateboards over to where I was standing and the others followed.

"I don't ever remember seeing you here," one of the skate boarders said.

"Yeah, well, that was thirty eight years ago."

"WOW! That's how old my Papi is," one of them exclaimed. Smiling olive faces with almond brown eyes watched me in wonder.

"I am writing a book about how things were back in those days."
"Was it a better place then?" They all waited for my answer.
"Maybe not better, but different."
"A stout, middle-aged Hispanic lady walked toward her car parked directly in front of me; two teenage girls followed close behind her.
"Buenos Dias, Senõr," the lady greeted me.
"Buenos Dias, Señora."
"Mom, he's writing a book about this place," one of the boys called out to her cheerfully.
"Verdad!" she answered eyeing me curiously. I could see she was nervous having me in the neighborhood.
"Tenga un buen dia Señora," I said and got into my car.
"Igualmente!" she replied, and hesitated, making sure I was leaving.

On the second day of July, 1964, I went to the Naval Hospital and checked aboard. It was seven miles to the back gate of Camp Pendleton from Vista and another six to the Naval Hospital. I took Vandegrift Boulevard northwest for five miles to a curve in the road and followed it down the declining hill. Looking northwest, I saw long, white, temporary buildings with green roofs, constructed on the edge of a ten-acre lake. I could see the early morning sun shimmering off the water as I continued on my journey. Soon, I came to the road that led a quarter mile back north to the compound. At the entrance, I turned east and followed the row of eucalyptus trees that lined the edge of the water. I could see the flag flapping in the early morning breeze. As at all commands, I knew that would be the Administration Building. The OOD logged me in and directed me to the Personnel Office. Two days later, I reported to Chief Jett in the Laboratory. He was an energetic forty-year-old who would be retiring in a few weeks. He informed me his relief, "Chief Boor," would be responsible for my indoctrination and assigning me to a duty section. He quickly showed me through the Laboratory and assigned me to Chemistry. There were four of us in the department and I would be the senior man. At Oaknoll, there had been a Biochemist and civilian technicians with years of experience working in Chemistry. Considering my limited knowledge and training, I found the fact that I would be in charge of the department down right chilling.

I met the second class in charge of Hematology by the name of Roy Armstrong when Chief Jett had hurriedly showed me through the departments. He gave me a warm handshake and seemed genuinely happy to meet me. I figured I was going to need a friend and had remembered his name. At lunchtime, I found him in the blood donor waiting room eating lunch with a half dozen other technicians. I got a candy bar and a soda out of the vending machines and sat down. I knew they would be sizing me up so I stayed cool.

"So, Messer where did you go to school?" asked Armstrong.

"Oaknoll!"

"Damn! You should have stayed there where they have students to do the shit work. Here E5's and below are little more than slaves. I guess old sorry ass Boor hasn't told you yet, but we are on a four section watch."

"Really!"

"Yeah! E-6 and above stand Chief of The Day duty at the OOD's desk. In case you haven't noticed there are four chiefs and four first class out of a sixteen man crew." That, indeed, was bad news. I listened intently as the others added their comments.

"Leaves only eight of us, and we have to have two technicians on watch at all times."

"Hell man, we'd be better off riding around in the security truck. Those clowns are on an eight section watch."

"Yeah, so much for being a scientist."

"Ain't that the damn truth."

"Laboratory, X-Ray, Pharmacy and Operating Room technicians bust their asses at these little hospitals where they don't have students."

"Yeah, every fourth day you work from 0800 until 1630 the following afternoon."

"Your ass is wound up so tight when you finally get off you have to get drunk to stand it and then the next day you're sick with a hangover."

"Really, you only have one descent day out of four." Everyone laughed. Somehow I didn't find it at all funny, but I figured it was better for them to see me laugh than cry so I tried to smile. 1630 found several of us at the club. Someone was retiring and the tap was open. I called Peg and told her I would be a little late.

Over the next few weeks I came to understand that the men had not exaggerated their horrendous working conditions. Armstrong and I were the two senior men that stood the duty in the Laboratory. We became allies in our struggle for justice against the system and consummate drinking buddies. His frustration and anger was equivalent to mine but I was more open and vocal. It seemed to have a tranquil effect on him to incite me into a profane discourse on the injustice of the situation and he did so at every opportunity. We seemed to have hit on a method of relating that gave us both a great deal of satisfaction. Every conceivable idea was presented to HMC Boor in an effort to alleviate our intolerable situation. We recommended putting four men on the evening shift. It would increase the daily workload but would at least bring some normalcy to our lives. The first class and chief petty officers objected to this idea. After all, they had paid their dues before they made their rank and it would require a greater work effort on their part during the day. They pointed out we would reap the rewards for our hard work later on when we were promoted. According to them, they were protecting our future.

On the second of August, 1964 I heard the first sound of the war drums roll. The USS Maddox penetrated into Communist North Vietnamese waters, known as the Gulf of Tonkin, and was immediately fired on by patrol boats. On August fourth it was reported the USS Turner Joy was attacked. President Johnson took this opportunity to bomb North Vietnam for the first time. Johnson took his case to the American public. Shortly thereafter, the Congress overwhelming passed the Gulf of Tonkin resolution effectively giving him full war powers until such time peace and security could be established in Vietnam. A later investigation would cast doubt on the Turner Joy ever being attacked. I was too caught up in the day to day grind at work to pay much attention. I assumed it was another minor international incident that would soon be resolved.

On a Saturday morning in late October of 1964 after a late Friday night drinking binge, Peg came into the bedroom and started cleaning. I was tired, hung over and depressed. I listened as she rustled noisily around in the room. I knew she was upset about my staying out late and suspected this was her way of getting back at me. When I opened one eye to look at her she was watching me.

"I'm sorry babe," I started to explain. She sighed and sat down on the side of the bed and reached over and took my hand.

"It's okay, I understand why you don't want to come home."

"It's not that. I'm just so damn up tight…"

"I said it's okay. But I need to talk to you about something else."

"Don't tell me your Mom is coming to visit?"

"No, it's nothing like that." I knew something wasn't right and I started feeling uneasy. I sat up on the edge of the bed. My heart raced and my head throbbed.

"Just tell me, please. I'm not in the mood for twenty questions."

"Well, I know you're not going to like this but…I'm pregnant again." I collapsed back on the bed feigning a heart attack. I don't know which one of us I felt the most sympathy for at that moment. Peg was caring for four children under school age with very little emotional support from me. I, on the other hand, was dealing with unimaginable pressure at work. The responsibility took so much out of me I had very little left to offer her. We were in crisis. Alcohol became my great escape and comforter.

Mr. Brown had stayed in touch and had found us a home in one of two housing tracks in Vista.

"You're going to love this place," Mr. Brown said as he drove us to see the house. These houses were financed with a five-year balloon payment and a lot of them are on the market. This one I'm going to show you is on the market for fourteen thousand. I think we can get it for thirteen-seven-fifty. With a VA loan, your payment would be less than a hundred a month."

"Look, all the streets are named after birds," commented Peg. I looked at the next street sign. Sure enough, it read Blackbird.

"Yeah, they call this project, "Birdland"," chuckled Mr. Brown as he turned into a cul-de-sac. Five houses framed the neat little circle. They all looked exactly alike, except for their color. In February of 1965, Peg and I moved into the yellow one at 522 Cockatoo Circle.

That same month, the North Vietnamese Communists attacked, killed eight Americans, and wounded a hundred and twenty-six others in Pleiku, South Vietnam. A short time later, they attacked Qui Nhon and killed twenty-three Americans and wounded twenty-one. President Johnson retaliated by bombing Hanoi and ordered thirty-five hundred United States Advisors to the area. In April, he bumped up the number to fifty-six thousand. In June he increased it to seventy-four thousand. I wasn't really worried. According to the news, North Vietnam was a small country and with that many troops I expected the conflict to be resolved very quickly. I had been assigned a normal tour of shore duty, which was thirty-six months. I saw no reason to think that it would still be going on when the time came for me to rotate back to sea duty.

Through the month of February we settled into our new home at Cockatoo Circle. In spite of the hardships at work, life took on a happy rhythm. Peg enjoyed having a home of her own for her growing family. We looked forward to the arrival of our new addition with joyful anticipation. I made a concentrated effort to spend less time at the club. As the delivery date drew nigh, we talked about how best to deal with the children during Peg's postpartum convalescence.

"You know, honey, I hate to ask Mom to come and help out again with another baby. She's getting old and it's so hard on her."

"I've been thinking, babe. Why don't I just take leave for a few days? I can watch the kids while you're in the hospital and help out a week or so after you get home."

"You think you can manage these guys by yourself?"

"Sure! Joe is seventeen months now and the others are big enough to play outside."

"Yeah, but you'll have to really watch them. Even though we're away from street traffic, they can wander off. And you'd be surprised what they can get into. Do you know how many kids are living here in this circle?"

"Not really, I know there's a bunch."

"Nineteen! And the five and seven-year-old boys next door are little hellions. You have to keep an eye on them every minute. The other day I came in the kitchen and the little one was up in the cabinets."

"You're kidding!"

"No! He'd found a package of strawberry koolaide and was eating it like sugar."

"Jesus!"

"It's not that bad. They're sweet, really. But you can't sit around on the couch and drink beer and ignore them. And I wish you'd have waited before you got that damn pup. I spend as much time chasing him as I do the kids. I don't know why we can't tie him up during the day when you're gone?"

"Oh Jesus! I told you it breaks a dog's spirit when you keep them tied."

"Well, I just can't watch four kids and that damn dog. I sure won't be able to handle him and a new baby. You either get a fence up or the dog has to go and I mean it, Dick."

"We'll get it up. You know it's always been my dream to have an AKC German Shepherd."

"I know, I just wish you could have waited until after this baby is born."

"Did you talk to Ed Schnoblen's wife about watching the kids if you go into labor and I'm not here?"

"Yes, she's so nice. She said she'd be happy to. She said her and Eddie are thinking about adopting since they can't have children."

"I hope there won't be a problem."

"Why should there be?"

"You know, her being Japanese."

"It won't. This isn't Arkansas. People are a little more accepting here in California."

Peg's due date was the third of April. I had requested ten days leave to commence on the first. On the evening of the twenty-eighth of March, Peg didn't look like she felt well.

"You okay, Hon? You're not going to go into early labor on me are you?"

"I have a few cramps, but I'll be okay. After dinner, I'll lay down on the couch while you bathe the kids. It's normal to have false labor a few days ahead of delivery. Don't worry, I'll let you know." The evening progressed and we went to bed early. Peg seemed preoccupied and was quiet. I felt uneasy, but didn't bother her. About four in the morning, she woke me up.

"Dick!"

"Yeah! What! You okay?"

"I think you better call Betty Schnoblen to come and watch the kids." A few minutes later, I retrieved her packed bag from the top shelf of our closet and we raced toward Camp Pendleton. Upon arrival and a quick evaluation, Peg was admitted to the delivery room. Richard was born at 0520 that morning. I went to the Laboratory and initiated my leave shortly thereafter and returned home to take charge of my four wards.

These were happy days for me. Even though the responsibility of my family weighed heavy on my shoulders, I adored my children. As we waited for Mummy to come home, I tried to make them happy by preparing their favorite meals. It seemed my efforts fell short of their expectations and mealtime became a disaster. I burned the hamburger and put too much water in the macaroni and cheese. No one would eat the vegetables because they tasted yucky. Glasses of milk were turned over and plates of food, seemingly accidentally, were dropped onto the floor. By the end of the first day, I had had it.

"That's it you guys. There will be no TV tonight. And Terry you and Mary are going to wash the dishes. Mom can't possibly do all there is to do around here by herself when she gets back. It's time you learned how to start doing things."

"But, we're too little. We can't even reach the sink," complained Terry.

"No matter! Here, I'm going to put a chair here on this side of the sink for you. Mary can stand on the other side and dry. And you two better not break anything."

I must say, in looking back, they did amazingly well and it became a chore they didn't easily escape. Trying to get them down for the night was a whole other ordeal. Fighting and wrangling with them to bathe and trying to find clean pajamas exhausted me. The wailing of being scared and "I want my mummy" echoed through the house. Finally, I hit on a plan.

"Okay, all of us are going to sleep in my bed. Joe, I want you and Mary up here with me. Terry, you and Darrel at the foot," so went the long restless night. It wasn't something I ever repeated.

The following day one of the neighbors agreed to mix her brood with mine and try to keep them from killing each other while I visited with Peg. Our new baby "Richard Kevin" was the most beautifully formed child I had ever seen. It's very hard to understand, and even more difficult to explain, what happens to a parent the first time they see their own child. Something magical takes place. It happens in a few seconds and you're hardly even aware of it. Once I laid eyes on him, I became eager to take him and Peg home. But that was not to be. Over the next few hours a problem developed. He had become jaundiced and his bilirubin reading went up to twenty-four milligrams. Anything over twenty would cause permanent brain damage if it persisted more than five days. There was a chance it would come down in a day or two. We'd have to wait and see. If it didn't, they'd have to do a complete blood exchange.

The third day, I took Peg home. It was the first time she had gone to the hospital to have a baby and went home empty handed. As I drove into the driveway, the kids rushed out of the house to see their mummy.
"Where is our new brother?" asked Terry, looking confused.
"He'll be coming home in a couple of days." Peg answered, trying her best to be cheerful. They all started talking at once. I lifted the bag out of the car and stole a look at Peg's face. The children continued to chatter and she moved her attention from one to the other. I knew her empty arms ached for our new baby but for the moment she had others that needed her attention.

Richard's life hung in the delicate balance between life and death. The bilirubin was stubborn; it hung in at twenty plus until the fourth day. Finally, it dropped and we went to the hospital and brought him home. That night, I watched as Peg happily cradled and cooed Richard, refusing to put him down. The other four lay out on the floor watching television. A feeling of peaceful contentment permeated our home. Little did I know how elusive those rare moments would prove to be in a not-too-distant future.

Over the next couple of months, we lost three of our chief petty officers from the Laboratory. Chief Boor was now our senior enlisted man. His primary function was to order supplies and make out a watch list. He had been a technician the major part of his career and his leadership skills were minimal. Although he was of little help in resolving problems he stayed out of our way and left the departments to the senior petty officers.

In the late spring, an Ensign in the Medical Service Corps checked aboard. It was said he had a degree in an allied science. He had previously been an enlisted man but at the end of his first enlistment had left the navy and attended the University of Kentucky. He talked slow with a southern twang and appeared to be a likable, unassuming man. Chief Boor, being from California, made the mistake of presupposing that because he talked slow, his mind functioned in the same manner. Based on this erroneous assumption, he either ignored or treated the young Ensign as a nonentity. That proved to be a major mistake.

Over the next few weeks, the young officer proved to be as sly as a fox and guile as a serpent. I had come to work early on a Monday morning when I heard loud voices coming from the administrative office.

"From now on, when you address me, you'll call me by my rank. The first and last word I want to hear coming out of your mouth is Sir. Is that understood?" As I passed the office, I saw Chief Boor standing stooped over with a look of shock on his face. The Ensign was standing toe to toe with him and his eyes were blazing.

"I don't give a damn how long you've been in the Navy. I'm your superior officer and, by god you're going to treat me with respect or you won't be a Chief Petty Officer much longer."

I was astonished to see the role reversal. The Ensign had done little to earn our respect in his short stay. I had always admired the rank of Chief Petty Officer and felt embarrassed to see Chief Boor humiliated. I also was disappointed that he had allowed his arrogance to put him in that position. Later on that morning, he went to the Personnel Office and requested a transfer out of the Lab. By 1300, he had been assigned to the Special Services Department.

A couple of weeks later, a new Chief Petty Officer reported to the Laboratory. Chief Boor's problem was no secret and apparently the new chief was determined not to make the same mistake. The young Ensign had some ideas about leadership he wanted implemented. The new chief, apparently, was in complete accord and they became a formidable team.

The winds of war continued to blow. The Marines had built an air base in Da Nang, Vietnam. It had to be protected and the build up of forces continued. Without notice, my friend, HM2 Armstrong, had his shore duty cut short and was ordered to join the Fleet Marine Force. This sent a shock wave through the Laboratory. If this could happened to him there was a good probability it would happen to others.

For the reader who is not familiar with the complex relationship between the Navy Medical Department and the Marine Corps, I'll briefly try to explain. The Marine Corps was established on November 10, 1775 as a separate branch of service but was put directly under the authority of the Secretary of the Navy. This remains so down to the present day. Funds were never appropriated to form a separate Medical Corp. It became a common practice to utilize the navy's medical personnel and facilities. Medical Field Service Schools were established to teach infantry tactics and field medicine to the medical personnel that would be directly assigned to combat units. It can sometimes be a shock to a young sailor, who has joined the navy to escape the army, to find himself in a marine infantry battalion.

The Green Machine, as we often called the Marine Corps, had sucked us down to nine technicians. Barely one man for each department remained. A four-section watch became three. The demand to keep pace with the workload intensified with each passing day. We were literally putting out thousands of test results daily. The fresh blood we were required to draw and ship to the war effort added another burden to an already-strained workload.

HM1 Willie Carbum was our technician in charge of Bacteriology. Without notice, he was transferred, leaving the department unmanned. Most Naval Hospitals have a Bacteriologist. But Camp Pendleton was only a hundred-bed facility and the precious few the navy had were needed in the larger hospitals. The Pathologist was desperate to find someone to take charge of the department. I was working in Chemistry when the Ensign and LT. Hitman, the Pathologist, came into Chemistry.

"How's your bacteriology, Messer?" the Pathologist inquired.

"Not that great, sir." I answered, trying to avoid eye contact.

"Let's go to the office. We need to talk to you a minute," he replied. I left my rack of blood tubes and followed them to the office. The Pathologist sat down behind his desk and nervously moved a couple of papers around. The Ensign had sat down in the one chair next to the wall. I stood silently waiting for LT. Hitman to speak. "Messer, I have to have someone to work Bacteriology. I know you don't have a strong background in Microbiology but neither does anyone else. Your last fitness report states you're the best technician in the Laboratory. I figure if anyone can do it, you can." I had feared this would happen. I knew the Bacteriology Department was in a shambles and we'd been shipping the specimens to Balboa in San Diego. "These doctors aren't going to put up with waiting five days to get back a culture and sensitivity much longer. I'd like for you to just go in there and give it your best shot. I know it's going to be a lot of work, but you can do it. Can I count on you?" I knew I didn't have the option to refuse. Any protest would only have put me in a bad light. I decided to try to be gracious.

"When do I start, Sir?"

"This morning," he laughed and stood up. The meeting was over. The next few weeks became the most challenging of my career as I struggled to be competent in a department I knew very little about.

The Ensign and the new Chief had agreed that because of the war in Vietnam we all needed to improve on our personal appearance and start being more military. Instead of reporting directly to our departments in the mornings, we would be having a formal formation and inspection. A murmur of protest went up from the crew but little heed was paid to the grumbling. Precious time was wasted in the morning quibbling over trivia. Morale plummeted right along with the proficiency of the technicians. Rarely had I seen a more downcast crew of men. I became truly concerned about the results we were putting out and decided to go talk to the Pathologist.

"Sir, the men are really busting butt trying to keep up with the workload. Do you think that we could get the Chief and the Ensign to at least recognize the men's efforts and give them a little pep talk to let them know they're appreciated?"

"I don't see why not, Messer. You guys are performing splendidly. I'll speak to the Ensign about it."

I knew the Pathologist would say something to the Ensign and the Chief. They would at least know he was aware of our efforts. I waited eagerly for the outcome of our conversation. It wasn't long in coming, the next morning both of our would be leaders showed up at formal muster. Once roll call was over and a quick check for clean uniforms and haircuts was performed the Chief walked to the front of the formation. The Ensign stood to one side listening.

"Finally," I said to myself, expecting to hear some glowing praise.

"It has come to our attention that some of you have been complaining about doing a little work. Well, there will be no more of that. If you'll take a look on the lower right hand side of your check you'll see written in big blue letters, U.S. Navy. As long as you're accepting that check, your ass belongs to us. Now, get to your work stations and I don't want to hear about anyone else sniveling to the Pathologist."

The Ensign looked at me with a smirk of satisfaction. To say I was shocked, would have been an understatement. My facial expression must have shown my contempt for these two so called, "Leaders". They neither assisted nor inspired us, but at every opportunity added to our already impossible burden. Rarely have I loathed two men more. From that moment on, I made very little effort to conceal my contempt for them both.

A few days later, I had the duty with one of my shipmates and we had worked until one in the morning. There were no beds for the watch section and we were forced to sleep on the blood donor bunks. We had gone into the drawing salon to lay down when I became aware that music was being piped in through the 1-MC system.

"What the hell is that?"

"Those two fucks left the radio on in the administrative office when they left."

"Is there anyway to turn the damn thing off?"

"No, they won't give anyone a key, so we're stuck with it."

"No, we aren't," I said and took a pair of bandage scissors off the bedside locker and cut the wire to the speaker. The next morning right after formation I had a visitor.

"Messer, they said you cut the wire to the speaker in the donor room last night. Is that right?" twanged the Ensign in his slow southern drawl. I continued to work and didn't give him the satisfaction of making eye contact.

"Yes, sir, I couldn't get into the office to turn off the radio. It was one-thirty in the morning and we'd worked seventeen straight hours and needed to rest."

"You're about an arrogant prick aren't you? How'd you like to explain this to the Commanding Officer?" I stopped working and looked him straight in the eye.

"That will be fine with me, Sir. I'd welcome the opportunity to explain to him why I found it necessary to do what I did."

"Well, we'll just see about that." Not surprisingly, I never heard anymore about it and, as far as I know, the radio was never left on again. It seemed in spite of my efforts I had gone from being the best technician in the Laboratory to one of the worst and it was duly noted on my quarterly evaluation of my performance.

As unbelievable as it seemed to us, Peg and I found out in September that she was pregnant again. We were devastated. Our lives seemed to be out of control on all fronts. I wanted desperately to restore some kind of stability in our lives. Six children in a three-bedroom, track home was unimaginable. I had agreed to allow Peg to practice her Catholic faith when we were married and had converted to Catholicism. But I knew having so many children one after the other was destroying our lives and our marriage. My military duties were all consuming and our finances strained. I was at a loss as how to handle the situation. Peg was convinced we would go to hell if we used any method of artificial birth control. I wasn't convinced, but I felt honor bound to keep my pledge. I could only hope and pray for a solution.

The only possible alleviation to our financial woes was for me to get promoted. I had been an E-5 for four years. I decided to throw everything I had into preparing for the coming exam, another sixty dollars a month wouldn't solve our problem but it would sure help. The last rating period, there hadn't been one man promoted to E-6 aboard Camp Pendleton. But I knew, if the United States continued to expand her roll in Vietnam, that would all change and I wanted to be prepared when it did. The navy gives all hospital corpsmen the same exam for promotion regardless of one's specialty. The fact I had spent fourteen months studying laboratory procedures would be of little value on the test for advancement. I threw myself relentlessly into studying the advance training courses of the Hospital Corps.

By the end of 1965, I had become the one eyed-man among the blind in the Bacteriology Department. I struggled daily in my efforts to do a competent job, while the Chief and the Ensign struggled to keep me under control. In a last ditch effort to render me powerless, the Ensign assigned the Chief to Bacteriology to oversee the department. The effort I had put into learning the theory and practical procedures of clinical bacteriology had empowered me. The Chief hadn't worked in Microbiology for years. If he ever knew anything, he must have forgotten it. I showed him no mercy; in short order, he became so intimidated he left. The Ensign continued his unceasing effort to bring me under the heel of his boot. It seemed perverse to be in a war that I could only lose but principal drove me to continue the fight.

Bacteriology specimens have to be inoculated onto media and incubated. The first reading is done at the end of the first twenty-four hours. Providing there's growth of a pathogen, it's identified by biochemical studies and a drug susceptibility study is performed. My policy was to go through the new cultures first thing in the morning. Anything I found out of the ordinary would be called to the ward immediately. There wasn't anything heroic or unusual about this procedure. It was what LCDR Georgia Simpson had taught us as students and I was running my department according to her instructions.

One morning in early December, I noticed a heavy growth of a gram-negative rod on a specimen from a newborn that had been diagnosed as having Pneumonia. A closer look at the request form showed the newborn was being treated with Penicillin, which is the drug of choice for Pneumonia. Problem being, gram-neg. rods are resistant to Penicillin. I notified the ward and didn't give it any more thought. Around eleven that morning, the Medical Officer from Pediatrics came into Bacteriology with the Pathologist, followed by the Chief and the Ensign.

"Messer?" asked the Medical Officer. I stopped what I was doing, fearing the worst.

"Yes, sir?"

"Dr. Mitsunaga," the Medical Officer said, offering me his hand.

"I wanted to come down and thank you personally for calling in the results on that newborn this morning. I had him on penicillin and he would have been dead before I got the results back through regular channels. I can unequivocally say you were instrumental in saving his life." Turning, he looked at the Pathologist and his entourage and added, "It would be a better Laboratory if everyone was conscientious as Messer."

A half-hour passed and I was basking in the glory of my recognition when I sensed someone's presence. Turning, I saw the Ensign come strolling into the department. He meandered up to my workbench. He watched me work without saying anything for a few minutes.

"Messer, you really got Ol' Mitsunaga fooled ain't ye?" he twanged. I didn't answer. "Well, you ain't got me fooled and I'm the one that gives you your fitness report. I'm going to see to it that you never make first class. We'll see what Ol' Mitsunaga can do about your career." We both knew that the need for me in Bacteriology insulated me for the moment. We also knew he could ruin my career and was committed to do so at the first opportunity. There was little I could do to change the situation so I hardened my stance. I became a true prima donna. I wouldn't give the bastards the satisfaction of being anything else.

In February of 1966, I took the written examination for E-6. Fortunately, the quarterly marks for my last evaluation were not reflected on my multiple for promotion.

President Johnson had continued his buildup of military forces in Vietnam. In March of 1966, there were in excess of two hundred thousand and climbing. On the tenth of March, I was ordered to Field Medical Service School at Camp Del Mar aboard Camp Pendleton for seven weeks of training. That dashed any hope Peg and I may have had that I wouldn't be going to Vietnam. The crisis in my nation, career, and family was full blown. Peg and I now walked in the valley of tears and our future seemed uncertain. In the midst of these tears, Martha Louise Messer was born to us on 26 March 1966 at 0735 in the morning.

On the fifteenth of April, I was promoted to First Class from the February exam. On the first of June I was the first medical person to be assigned to 3rd Battalion, 26th Marines of the recently activated old 5th Marine Division. We were to mount out for Vietnam as soon as possible. I was on my way to war.

The Vietnam Saga

From all indications, nothing in the history of man has been studied more than the art of how to successfully wage war. The saying, "War is the supreme contest among men," has been attributed to General George S. Patton. However, it seems the concept is universal. Although modern man professes to loathe war, there seems to be an instinct in us that craves blood and longs to hear the sounds and see the sights of battle. It would appear Homosapiens think there is something sacred in the idea of sacrificing one's life for a virtuous cause. Providing we believe that we are fighting against evil and injustice, it seems reasonable to think that God would receive us as one of His own. Our sins would surely be forgiven and we would be welcomed into heaven as saints. It's little wonder that political leaders often use this theme in promoting their causes.

As foolish as all this may seem to the intellectual, I must confess, even as a child, I found the idea of going into battle exhilarating. The wearing of the uniform, for me, was more than a job; it was a calling. I consider military service a noble and honorable thing. I hold no other profession in such high regard. We live in a world where others would surely enslave us if they could. For this reason, we owe our freedom and way of life to men who have been willing to lay down their lives on the field of battle. But we must keep in mind too, that there have been men who have died in vain for no rational reason that we can discern and, in some cases, their cause has been deemed an injustice. We should remember that war is the end result of a political situation that can't otherwise be resolved. The men who have fought our wars have had little to do with the decisions that led to their untimely deaths. I would ask you, are these men who gave their lives in so-called "Unjust Wars" any less heroic than their counterparts?

My lifetime desire to fight in a great campaign for the betterment of humanity has been frustrated by serving in a war that we ultimately lost and eventually was deemed a horrible mistake by most historians in today's civilized society.

In the coming pages, I will try to pay tribute to all the brave and courageous men who served with me in Vietnam. We believed we were in a life and death struggle for the survival of our country and way of life. Our efforts were lost in a world of confusion and we returned to a country that despised us and spit on us and called us baby killers. The majority of us have recovered and sought our own solace in this matter. Some are alcoholics; others have committed suicide; many have died or gone insane. None of us are as we once were. There have been volumes written about Vietnam. I can add nothing new to this unfortunate time in our history. But here is my story and what happened to me.

On the first day of June in 1966, I reported to the headquarters building in the Thirteen area aboard Camp Pendleton, California. Although I had been in the Navy for ten years and was a First Class Petty Officer, this was the beginning of a whole new way of life. I had come aboard Camp Pendleton almost everyday for the past twenty-three months but today was much different. I was wearing the Marine Corps tropical khaki uniform with an E-6 navy-rating badge on my left arm.

I soon found the Detailing Office of the newly activated 5th Marine Division. A thirtysome-year-old Chief Petty Officer was sitting quietly at his desk in front of a big plastic TO (table of organization) chart. I handed him my records and noted his nametag read HMC Curry. He greeted me cordially and turned to the TO chart and studied it for a moment then turned back to me.

"First and Second Battalion are up to compliment. You'll be the first corpsman in the Third," he commented dryly. Taking my service record, he turned to page 601-5 (Rev, 12-60) and stamped the following entry:

> H&SCO, 3dBN Rlt26 FrsTps
> FMFPac, MCB, CAMPEN, CA
> Sea Duty Commenced: June, 66

He then handed me back my record, picked up a red colored grease pencil, walked to the chart and printed my name in a blank space.

"You'll find them at Las Pulgas in the Forty-three area. Do you know where that is?"

"Not exactly, Chief."

"Just follow Vandergrift and make the first right before the commissary then follow the road until you see a sign. You can't miss it."

Half an hour and ten miles later, I found myself in the office of Headquarters and Service Company of the Third Battalion, Twenty-sixth Marines. The First Sergeant had seen me enter but made no attempt to assist me.

I was to learn very quickly that wearing a marine uniform did not make me a marine nor did it give me automatic acceptance into their club. There is as much difference in the way the Marine Corps and the Navy relate to their men as there is between daylight and dark. There is an unbelievable bone-deep rivalry between the two services that's hard to overcome. The Marine Corps Boot Camp is a right of passage and, unless you've completed it, you're never going to be thought of as a marine. The most one can hope for is acceptance. That will come only with time by proving you can run as far, march as long, carry as much and be ready to move when you hear the words, "corpsman up." At this point, I had done none of those things and the First Sergeant was intent on making sure I understood that. Until he acknowledged my presence, none of the other men dared say anything. After a two-hour wait, I became exasperated.

"Who do I have to see to get checked in?" I finally asked one of the young sergeants. He didn't answer me but looked at the First Sergeant. I turned my attention to him.

"First Sergeant, could I pleased get checked in?" I asked politely.

"I'll be with you in a minute," he answered. Another hour passed before he came and took my record. Flipping though it hurriedly, he handed it back to me.

"The Navy takes care of their own records," he informed me and gave me a look that indicated he thought there was a possibility I might be retarded.

"So, where do I go?" I asked feeling irritated with his attitude.

"You're the first one that has checked aboard. Just have a seat, I'll ask the S-1 when I have a chance," he said flippantly and walked away. I knew he was messing with me but there wasn't anything I could do about it.

At about 1100 hours, a Chief Corpsman walked in carrying his records. He was about my height but tended to the lean side. I noticed a Korean Combat Service Medal, with a Marine Corps emblem, in the middle of his three rows of campaign ribbons. I couldn't help but think he looked like a recruiting poster. He looked me up and down, smiled and stuck out his hand.

"Chief Retzloff! Been here long?"

"Yes, sir, Chief, since about eight thirty this morning. They say we're to take care of our own records. I'm waiting to find out what building we are supposed to go to." He turned and looked at the First Sergeant.

"First shirt, could I see you a minute?" The First Sergeant looked in our direction and acknowledged he had heard him with a quick upward nod of his head but didn't move. The Chief's face grew serious.

"I'D APPRECIATE IT IF YOU'D GIVE ME A MINUTE OF YOUR VALUABLE TIME THERE, FIRST SERGEANT. WE'VE BEEN ASSIGNED TO GIVE MEDICAL SUPPORT TO THIS BATTALION NOT TO COME HERE AND BE JERKED AROUND. NOW, if you don't know where we're to be billeted at, I suggest you get on the phone and ask someone who does." The typewriters had stopped and you could have heard a pin drop. All eyes were on the First Sergeant. He walked over to where we were standing, taking in the Chief's demeanor and uniform. His eyes found the Marine Corps emblem on the combat ribbon.

"Sorry, Chief, I am waiting for S-1 to come back from a staff meeting. I have no idea at this point what building you'll be billeted in. Why don't you go to lunch and maybe by 1300 I'll know something?"

"I've got a better idea. What do you say you get your marines to bring me a desk up here by the door? I want to meet my men as they check in. I don't want to leave them standing around cooling their heels if there is nothing for them to do." One of the sergeants had been listening to the conversation. The First Sergeant looked at him and nodded his head slightly. The Sergeant stood up quickly and motioned to a Corporal sitting near by. They soon had a desk and chair at the front of the office and the Chief took his seat.

"Corporal, give the health records we've been holding to the Chief," ordered the First Sergeant. In the commotion of moving the desk another corpsman had come into the building.

"Over here, Doc," the Chief called. The new arrival walked over and handed the Chief his records. "I'll see you boys back here in the morning at 0700," the Chief said as he accepted his record. We looked at each other rather surprised but didn't wait for him to say it again.

From that day on, I accepted the fact the marines were not there to baby us or to do us any special favors. We had a job to do and they expected us to do it. Being timid was not the Marine Corps way. If we were weak and allowed ourselves to be walked on, that was our problem. Once the Chief demonstrated he was going to take charge of his department and care for his men they gave him the respect he deserved. It was a lesson I was to never forget.

A couple of days later found us in a Quonset hut. The lust for blood was all around us and highly contagious. Everything we did and every oath we swore was with the idea that we would soon be in the business of killing the enemy. This was not a place for schoolboys or Sunday school teachers. The military values that had been instilled in me during boot camp and fostered on the Helena had awakened. I was fulfilling my destiny as a warrior and had never been happier. I was thrilled to be free from the rows and rows of tubes of blood with names that had no faces. Finally, I was liberated from the demand of tedious technical skills that consumed my life and drained my energy.

It was fascinating to watch a battalion being built from the ground up. Four men formed a fire team. Three fire teams and a leader, normally a sergeant E-5, made a squad. Four squads made a platoon. Four platoons made a company. Four letter companies, designated India, Kilo, Lima and Mike, and Headquarters and Service Company made up 3/26 (Third Battalion Twenty-sixth Marines). Formed respectively, in the same manner, were 1/26 and 2/26 with the letter companies having different designations, starting with Apha, Bravo, etc. The three Battalions made up the RLT (Regimental Landing Team).

Each Battalion was to form, train and prepare to go to Vietnam. The Table of Organization for medical personnel called for fifty-two hospital corpsmen and two doctors. Each letter company required eight hospital corpsmen with a second class petty officer (E-5) as the senior corpsman. The remaining twenty hospital corpsmen, along with myself, were attached to the Battalion Aid Station, which was part of the Headquarters and Service Company. Our primary mission was to give support to the letter companies.

Chief Retzloff initially assigned me to sickcall. At that point, we had not been assigned a doctor nor had we received any medical supplies. My duties consisted of treating minor problems and referring the more complicated cases to Regimental Aid where they would see a doctor. A week later we received on board our Battalion Surgeon. Not having any supplies, he was not a great deal more effective than I had been. A couple of days passed and the Chief called me into his office.
"Messer, have you ever worked supply?"
"No, sir, I haven't!" He handed me a list of several items.
"Well, there's not a billet for a laboratory technician in the grunts but I need a good supply man so you're it. See what you can do about getting some of those things. According to FLSG (Fleet Landing Support Group) we don't exist and there isn't any method for us to officially draw any gear. The Doctor is putting pressure on me to get him, at least, enough supplies to render basic first aid in case of an emergency. Go around to the different dispensaries here on base and see what you can do."
"I'll take care of it, Chief." Then he reached in his desk and took out a long computer printout.
"In a few days, we're going to start receiving our mount out block. Here is a copy of everything we'll be issued. It's all going to have to be packed into 4.2 cubic boxes, weighed and tactically marked. The Battalion Cargo Officer will need to know the number of boxes and the other information in order to calculate the space we'll need when we go aboard ship. Also we have to be set up so we can break into an Alpha and Bravo command group. That means you'll need to divide and pack everything into two separate blocks and maintain two sets of 508 cards. That way if, and when, the command splits, each group will have it's own supplies and records. I'm going to assign four men to help you. But for now, see what you can do about procuring what's on that list."

"Gotcha, Chief." Over the next few days, I made the rounds to the different dispensaries. The corpsmen knew we were on our way to Vietnam and they could very well be joining us shortly. My shopping list was filled sooner than I had expected.

The Chief assigned HM2 Hays to give me a hand a couple of days later. He was an Afro-American from North Carolina and had been in the Navy for over sixteen years. He was one of those rare individuals who had learned to make being a minority work to his advantage. He never threatened anyone or refused an order but had a quiet mannerism and a ready smile. If things weren't exactly as they should've been, he pointed it out in a way that made you wonder if he was keeping notes. HM2 Ely joined us next. He looked and talked like a Gary Cooper with red hair. He worked and played hard and was often sleep-deprived. Ely's difficult efforts at staying awake seemed to delight Hays and he soon worked out a system where one of them was always missing. When I questioned them about their whereabouts they always seemed to have the right answer: "Been to a dental appointment" or "Had to pick up emergency gear at some far off, unknown place," were their standard alibis.

Once the gear started arriving, we were assigned to work in a Butler Building about a mile from the BAS (Battalion Aid Station). The work was getting done and we'd be deployed soon enough. I figured now was a good time for them to take some slack so I feigned just enough irritation to keep them on their toes. Along about the middle of June, a nineteen-year-old Afro-American by the name of Washington was assigned to work with us. Hays took him under his wing, and soon he was as corrupt and delightful as the other two.

Over the next month, the Battalion Aid Station came up to full complement. We had two chiefs, four first-class, six second-class, five third-class and five hospitalmen. The second chief assigned to us was junior to Chief Retzloff. Having two chiefs, with one assisting the other, is never an ideal situation. The junior chief, even though outranking fifty-two other corpsmen, actually was supervising fewer people than the senior corpsmen in the letter companies. Chief Volmer soon found his niche by putting himself in charge of our physical fitness program. This consisted mainly of getting as many men as possible together every afternoon at 1600 and running up and down in front of the Command Post. The Chief was making us the laughing stock of the Battalion and our fellow marine staff non-commissioned officers were having a field day laughing at us. I was disgusted and embarrassed by the whole affair. I knew this was going to make it harder for all of us to earn the marines' respect.

Down the road heading south a few miles, in the 33 area known as "Margarita", 2/26 was getting ready to deploy. The word came down one of the first-class had been hospitalized. He had been in charge of supply and the Chief in charge of the BAS wanted to see me. His name was Clifford Bassett. I knew him from my old Laboratory School days at Oaknoll. He had been shot in the head by a jealous husband and had almost died when I was a senior student. I was working in the Blood Bank when the ambulance brought him into the Emergency Room. I had drawn his blood for the cross-match, which ultimately was part of the team effort that saved his life. He was well aware of the roll I had played and never missed an opportunity to show me his appreciation. I made my way to the BAS at Margarita. The place was in total disarray and the corpsmen were packing everything not tied down into the familiar 4.2 cube boxes.

"Where is Chief Basset?" I asked.

"On the loading dock," someone answered. I found my way out to the dock. The Chief was helping one of his men cover a four-foot-high pallet of medical equipment with a big, green tarp.

"Hey, Chief Bassett."

"Messer, you Ol' Son-Of-A-Bitch. Go get your gear and come on down here man. I need you."

"What the hell for?"

"To work supply for me, man. They told me you know this system from the ground up. I've asked regiment to assign you to us if it won't put a hardship on you and your family. It's going to be up to you but if you do agree to it, you're it, dude. Hey, Oscar, here's Ol' Mess. He's going to go with us to shoot people in the head and shit." I looked up and saw Oscar Willis walking toward me. Big, pearly-white teeth smiled out of his handsome, ebony face. He grabbed my hand.

"Damn! Good to see you man. I heard Ol' Chief Volver has you guys running up and down in front of the Command Post trying to impress the CO." he laughed.

"I'm afraid you heard right."

"That silly Son-Of-A-Bitch. I knew him when he was a third-class. He was crazy as a shit-house rat then and don't look like he be changed none."

"We have a good Battalion here, man; the CO is great, a good Sergeant Major, a couple of good Battalion Surgeons and a great bunch of corpsmen. You'll be leaving a little sooner than you planned. But what the hell man, you got to go anyway, and that'll put you home that much quicker. Besides that, you'll be with us. You know we'll take care of you." I looked at Chief Bassett and he gave me the same smile that, no doubt, contributed to getting him shot. These men were my friends and I felt comfortable with them. The next day I joined 2/26.

Shortly after I got to Vietnam, I wrote about the day of our departure as I remembered it at that time. I don't think I can improve on how I described it so here it is, word for word:

I don't think I will ever forget that morning of 27 July 1966, when the full impact that my departure to the war zone of Vietnam had finally arrived. I was leaving my loving wife Margaret and my six children for a thirteen-month-tour in a far off, unknown land. As I looked into their uncomprehending faces, the realization of how much I loved each one of them slammed into my heart like a bullet. I leaned over and kissed each one gently as they twisted and turned on Peg's skirt, each reacting differently in their own individual way. Peg struggled to hang on to baby Martha as she kicked and screamed. I stood erect and looked into Peg's eyes. The anguish and sorrow on her loving face was more than I could bear. I fought back the tears that welled up in my eyes. I kissed her quickly on the lips and walked hurriedly to the car that was waiting. I glanced back for one last look. Peg and the children standing there waving goodbye is forever burned into my memory. Peg retreated into the house to spare me the pain of seeing her cry. The tears streamed down my cheeks and dropped silently on the uniform that she had so lovingly pressed for me just a few moments before.

I was distraught with utter despair and an empty feeling of loneliness overwhelmed me. The trip to the base was like moving in another world, outside of consciousness.

I soon joined my comrades in arms. Eighteen hundred men with their own farewells fresh in their minds forced me to act much braver than I was feeling. New gear and freshly-cleaned weapons gleamed in the early morning sunlight. I occupied my mind with the task at hand. We broke camp, did last minute packing and prepared to load the waiting buses that were to haul us to the big, gray, warship in San Diego.

Having completed last minute details, I took refuge on the back loading dock to be alone for a few minutes and to collect my thoughts. The four letter companies commenced to assemble in formation a few meters from where I was sitting. They came together in the traditional no nonsense Marine Corps fashion. They moved and flowed as though they were liquid and quickly formed into a single entity. I became aware that I was looking at the pride of our nation and the Marine

Corps. Men who were tough, cocky, well-trained, and could react instantly like a precision machine. The bark of the Sergeant's voice cut through the morning air like a sharp knife and the letter companies commenced to move down the street like a beautiful, powerful animal, muscles rippling. I was caught up in the moment and my chest swelled with pride to be a part of such a glorious war machine. At that moment, I had the feeling that I was fulfilling my destiny. This was what I had been born to do and, though it could be my death, I was meant to be here. A few moments later, gear was loaded onto buses and I was caught up in the final preparation.

Upon arrival in San Diego, the bus pulled alongside the big naval vessel that wallowed, in and out, alongside of the pier. Gear and personnel came rolling out of the buses and off the trucks in all directions. Wooden footlockers bounced as though they were made from rubber and collected into a huge pile along with the officers' and staff noncommissioned officers' Val packs. We soon formed ranks in full seven-eighty-two (pack containing haversack, shelter half and entrenching tool) gear with helmets on and our TO (authorized) weapons at our side. The hot sun beat down on us as we waited for the Navy to invite us to come on aboard. We stood quietly listening to the jingling of the cranes and the cursing of the crew. They were reluctantly preparing to receive the bastards who would crowd them out of their living and work spaces, triple the length of the chow line and double their workload for the next thirty some days. It's little wonder we were unwelcome guests.

Hours later, we went tumbling into hot, humid troop berthing spaces far below deck. Body odor hung heavy in the air as we struggled to find the bunks that would be our homes for the next several weeks. The chain-suspended bunks creaked and groaned under the weight of the gear as it was dumped on top of them. We all rushed, trying to stake ourselves out a suitable claim. I finally ended up on a floating piece of canvas three bunks high on the inside; it had long since stopped fitting snugly into the holding stanchion and promised to plummet onto the deck at any minute.

That wasn't the most important thing at hand. The ship was to deploy the next morning. This was our last chance to call home, get a cold beer, or do whatever that would help us in dealing with our departure. It was something none of us were willing to miss out on. No time for showers, the hell with it, shake a leg, we're out of here.

The Fifties music never sounded so good; steak and french-fries never tasted so sweet. We drank toasts and slapped each other on the back. Always, we assured ourselves that we would come home again to take up where we left off, even if we had to kick Old Satan's ass himself. No doubt about it, the war would soon be over after we got there.

The next morning, I was awakened by the sound of the Boatswain Mate's pipe and his loud voice, "Now, set the special sea and anchor detail." I felt the ship jerk to life as she twisted and rolled and heard the sound of the strained steel as it creaked and moaned. I opened my eyes and looked around in the semi-darkness. The smell of body odor and stale alcohol hung in the lifeless air. The man on my right moaned. My head hurt and I felt nauseous. I closed my eyes and fell back to sleep. When I woke up, the lights were on and a few men were moving around on the deck. I lay quietly listening to them talk.

"Somebody has shit or they have piped in an elephant fart?"
"What the fuck is this?"
"Goddamn! Some son-of-a-bitch has puked here."
"Fucking air conditioner ain't working."
"We'll die on this bucket of shit before we get to Vietnam."

When we boarded, E-6 and above had been directed to the SNCO berthing. In the melee that followed, we wandered around like sheep until we had found this berthing space. There were no lockers. Seabags were strapped to our individual bunks and footlockers littered the deck. I was the only corpsman in the compartment. I knew some of the marines on sight but didn't know anyone personally. I lay listening to them talk.

"Did you know the USS Henrico landed troops at Normandy during the Second World War?"

"The hell you say!"

"Yeah, one of my uncles served as a crew member on here. I remember, as a kid, Mom had a photo of her hanging on the wall and right across the bow painted in big, white letters was PA 43."

"Life's weird as hell ain't it, man?"

"Can be!" I got up, showered and made my way to sickbay. There, I encountered Chief Bassett.

"Hey, Mess!"

"What's up, Chief?"

"Not a hell of a lot. The Chief on here has agreed to let us use one of their storerooms to hold sick call for the marines. They don't want the grunts stinking up the place anyway. It'll give us something to do and a place to get together."

"Great idea!"

"Come back up after chow and we'll see what they have in mind." Days passed and fifty of us corpsmen standing around in one small storeroom got to be more of a hassle than staying in the berthing compartment. My source of entertainment was reading anything I could get my hands on.

"Doc, you ought'a read this book when I get done with it."

"What's it about, Gunny?"

"Vietnam! I'd venture a guess most of us don't know shit about that place, except what the damn government has told us and you can bet your ass most of that's propaganda."

"I just know they have a communist government in the north that wants to take over the country."

"Communist ass! What the hell does that mean?" Four men were playing cards on top a footlocker and a couple of others were watching the action. They had been listening and were anxious to express their own opinions.

"You know Ol' Ho Chi Minh helped us whip the Japs. They say the US Government had made him a special OSS agent (US security agency that was replaced by the present day CIA)."

"Yeah, Ol' Ho wanted Vietnam to be independent from the damn French after the war; even wrote Truman a letter. The Government wouldn't have it, of course, after us being allies with them during the big one."

"Seems like we're always kissing the French's ass."

"Yeah, or saving it."

"Hell, the French plundered Cambodia, Laos, and Vietnam from way back in 1880."

"The hell you say?"

"Shit, man! Why do you think they called that part of the world French Indochina?"

"Quick as the war was over they came steaming back in to reclaim their empire. They convinced us Ol' Ho was a communist puppet for the USSR. According to this book, we even used US war ships to ferry some of France's crack troops in there."

"The battle of Dien Bien Phu in 1954 put an end to that shit."

"Yeah, them little nipper shits beat the fuck out of the goddamn French with bamboo poles." Everyone laughed.

"French might be great lovers but they ain't for shit when it comes to soldiering."

"Did you know after the French pulled out they drew up an accord in Geneva guaranteeing Vietnam free elections to be held in 1956?"

"Yeah, but the US wouldn't sign it."

"There was no way in hell we were going to let the damn communists take over that part of the world."

"Ol' Ho held his election anyway, and won."

"Yeah, that's true, but the US had put Ol' Ngo Dinh Diem as head of the anti-communist regime down there in Saigon. At our insistence, he refused to participate in the national election and held his own. They said they counted two hundred thousand more votes than there were people living in Saigon.

"That figures, should've known we'd be backing some sorry bastard like that."

"Well, anyway, he declared South Vietnam to be an independent nation after the election and we've been backing the South ever since."

"It's a damn good thing or the Russians would be running things there by now."

"I don't know about all of that. Didn't do Ol' Diem much good as it turned out. Did you know JFK gave the CIA the go ahead with a coup and they ended up killing the son-of-a-bitch?"

"What the hell did they do that for, man?"

"Ol' Diem's brother was head of the army and things weren't going too good. Looked like the whole South Vietnamese Government was going belly up. The CIA picked out and backed a Buddhist to put in power so the majority wouldn't go communist. Ol' Diem and his bunch were Catholics you know."

"They said Kennedy didn't know they were going to kill him and he almost shit a brick when they told him."

"Well, boys, none of it makes a damn bit of difference now. Johnson is committed to win this war even if it kills us."

"And it probably will, at least some of us."

"There goes that goddamn air conditioner again. We're going to die of heat exhaustion before we get to Vietnam."

"Yeah, this is really great. I always wanted to die down in the hole of a fucking troop transport, in the middle of hell, going nowhere."

"Well, they didn't promise you no rose garden."

"Shut the fuck up, will you?" Everyone laughed. I went back to my book. I was beginning to like these crazy bastards.

We had spent a couple days liberty in Pearl Harbor after a five-day voyage and had been at sea again for eight more. I was lethargic from sleeping so much, constipated from overeating, and bored beyond endurance. The constant speculation as to where we were going and what we would be doing was the topic of every conversation. I had read every magazine and book that I could beg, bum, borrow, or steal. The heat in the hole was stifling. Topside, hundreds of men lounged on the steel deck trying to escape the heat. They were constantly being herded from one area to another as the sailors painted, swabbed, scrubbed, accused, threatened and cursed the idle marines.

I decided that I would go up to the supply room, where we were attempting to hold sickcall, and try to break the monotony. Half a dozen corpsmen were sitting, a few were standing, while others squatted in the little cubbyhole. A big six-foot, two hundred and twenty-pound HM1 by the name of Dan Hahn had become the unofficial leader of the group. Dan had a big resentment about being assigned to the Marine Corps and didn't make any bones about it when he was talking to the marines. He hadn't made a lot of points with them but had endeared himself to some of the more rebellious corpsmen. We had been in the same training company in FMF School and got along pretty well but I didn't share his antagonistic attitude toward the Marine Corps. He was hard to miss so he was the first man I saw on my approach. He was sitting on a wooden box with his elbows propped on his knees watching me as I drew near. He had taken his blouse off in the sweltering heat and big beads of perspiration stood out on his forehead.

"Hey John, you see the Chief?" he asked.

"No, is he looking for me?"

"He just got back from a staff meeting and it looks like the CO found out where we're going."

"Where?"

"We're relieving 3/3 in place just outside of Da Nang. They are sending in an advance party." As we were talking, Chief Bassett and HM1 Kirkpatrick walked up to the door. Kirkpatrick was the senior PO1 and was Chief Basset's assistant. He had been in the Navy longer than Bassett but had never made chief. That bothered him more than a little and he had kind of a chip on his shoulder. He figured he'd been around long enough he didn't have to take BS from anyone and let everyone know it. I kind of liked him in spite of him being obnoxious and overbearing. It was obvious Chief Bassett depended on him for counseling and guidance and looked up to him like a big brother.

Chief Bassett looked from Dan to myself, "We have to send in a PO1 on the advance party. I don't want to designate anyone if someone wants to volunteer. Dan, you or John interested?"

"Not me!" Dan replied and looked at me expectantly. I was thinking about the hot compartment and the miserable living conditions that we would be suffering for the next few days on the Henrico.

"What would be my responsibility?" I asked.

"Just get orientated to Service Record entries, where to draw supplies, and check out the area's sanitation conditions. You'll be flying in on a C-130 and 3/3 will send a six-by for you. There will be about fifty SNCO and Officers in all. Want to go, Mess?" It sounded a lot easier than off loading with eighteen hundred green troops in Da Nang. The more I thought about it, the better I liked the idea.

"Yeah, I'll go."

"Okay, get your shit together. You'll be leaving as soon as we get into Okey."

The sound of the engines from the C-130 filled the cabin. Fifty, or so, of us sat motionless against the wall of the fuselage in green, cloth seats made from parachute rigging. Our seven-eighty-two gear lay at our feet. A huge pile of military equipment was tied down in front of us. The cool air from the overhead vents formed a misty vapor as it entered the hot cargo bay. We had all come from different units and sat as strangers among each other, staring up at the white cloud as it formed and dissolved into nothingness. I could read no emotion on the expressionless faces of the men around me. The smell of freshly-issued combat gear permeated my nostrils. The flak jacket I was wearing felt burdensome and the helmet on my lap, awkward. The plane droned on for what seemed like an eternity. Suddenly, a red light flashed over the door leading into the cockpit. A young Airman moved among us and gave an unintelligible order. We looked from one to the other. One man put on his helmet and we imitated him. The engines were cut back and we seemed to gain speed. I heard the sound of the tires hit the runway and felt a jolt; the reverberation at the increased sound from the motors made my ears pop. The vapor stopped and we watched as the huge tailgate at the back of the cargo bay slowly opened. I could hear forklifts running on the tarmac.

"Us go, us go marines, get your asses off here," commanded the big six foot, three inch Marine Sergeant as he bounded onto the plane. He moved as lithe as a panther, with a sense of urgency. We unbuckled our seat belts and started gathering up our gear. "Who's in charge here?" asked the Sergeant.

"I am," responded one of the Captains.

"I gonna ax you not to bunch up here on de runway. The slope-heads blow this muderfucker away bout every udder night," shouted the Sergeant. We carried our gear off the plane into the darkness. The scream of a fighter jet deafened us as it streaked overhead so near the ground we ducked our heads. Sounds of artillery pounded in the distance.

"3/3 is supposed to be sending a six-by for us," replied the Captain.

"Ain't nobody be coming fer ya tonight. The VC (Viet Cong) rules everything outside de wire by night; we rules everything by day. Dats de way it is Capn. Head ye men on down dat away a piece and you come to some empty hooches. Make ye-self to home. Tomor you can talk to the command post and they can gi'em a call fer ye."

"Let's go. Don't worry about falling in formation," the Captain ordered and we headed south like lost children.

The night was hot and humid. The sound of thumping propellers from a helicopter passing overhead accompanied us on our labored march. The jets roared off the runway one after the other in rapid succession. In the distance, air illumination lit up the sky. I recognized the thump of a mortar as it came out of the tube, followed a few minutes later by the sound of semi-automatic weapons fire. We soon came to a long row of dark shadows shaped like huts. We found the opening and a half dozen of us pushed our way inside. Someone lit a cigarette lighter. I could see about ten empty cots scattered about. The Captain dumped his gear on top of the one nearest the door and turned towards us, "Looks like all the tents in this row are empty so find yourself a cot. Let's try to stay in the confines of these first five. We'll muster here in front of this tent at first light."

I lay on the cot in the darkness and listened to the sounds made by the activity of making war. I wondered if tonight would be the night the mortars would rain down. Someone lit a cigarette in the darkness. My thoughts flew quietly through space to my home at 522 Cockatoo Circle. There, I went inside and looked at all my children sleeping in their beds. I found Peg in the darkness and kissed her so gently she never knew I was there. Sometime early the next morning, I found myself back in Vietnam. Rousing from my dreams, I heard someone talking.

"First Sergeant, see if you can find a place to shower and where the chow hall is located. I'm going to find the CP (Command Post) and give a call out to 3/3," the Captain commented.

"Aye, aye, sir" responded the short, chubby, Irish-looking First Sergeant.

I had taken off my utilities the night before in an effort to beat the heat and laid them on top of my seven-eighty-two gear. I sat up on the edge of my cot and reached for my blouse; it felt wet. The man in front of me had lit a cigarette and sat watching me.

"Damn humidity is something ain't it?" he asked.

"It's unbelievable," I replied and slipped the damp blouse over my shoulders. We found the shower and the chow hall in short order and had collected back in the hooch by 0700. The Captain was nowhere to be seen. Finally, around 0800, he returned, looking a little irritated.

"The Engineers have to mine sweep the roads before any traffic is allowed to travel," he informed us nervously. "May as well relax; it'll be at least 0900 before we get out of here."

As the sun climbed, so did the temperature. Our uniforms became soaked in perspiration as we lounged on the cots and waited. What seemed like hours later, the sound of a rapid moving vehicle approached our tent and came to a screeching stop. I looked toward the street and saw a young corporal bound out of a jeep and head toward the door. A few seconds later, a big six-by truck ground to a halt.

"Is this 2/26 forward party?" he asked.

"That's us, Corporal. Why two vehicles?"

"Division orders! Can't go anywhere outside a secured area with one. If you're by yourself, you have to wait and catch a ride." We had already started to gather up our gear.

"Doc, you're with me in the jeep," the Captain ordered.

The young driver looked to be around twenty. I noticed his faded uniform was made out of a light weight, shiny material with huge pockets in front, both on the blouse and trousers, in a matter of days our whole Battalion would be issued these so called "jungle utilities." The bronze chevrons on his collar, unlike ours, had long ago given up their black color. His unzipped flak jacket was faded from wear and hung limply around his shoulders. He had removed his helmet when he started talking to the Captain.

"Okay, Captain! Have your men put on their helmets and button down their flak jackets. We're going to be going through Indian country. You can bet your ass the VC knows you're here. They may just try to get off a few rounds to let you know you're not welcome."

We didn't have to be told. We had heard the young corporal and had put on our helmets and were snapping closed the heavy vest. The First Sergeant climbed into the back of the jeep and I followed. The Captain then got into the seat opposite the driver. The young rifleman who had been riding shotgun climbed behind us and sat down on top of the back seat, cradling his M-14 in the crook of his arms. The driver had started the motor before we were completely seated and we roared off toward the entrance to the airfield. After a slight pause at the gate, we headed off in what I thought to be a southerly direction.

The gravel roadside was lined with short, slender-built men and women dressed in black pajamas and straw cone hats. Some were balancing a five-foot piece of lightweight wood across their shoulders with huge loads attached to each end. They bounced in rhythm with their burden, taking a step when the weight floated up. Half-naked kids stood along the road, hands extended. Making a sudden stop at a cross street we were surrounded by beggars.

"DEE DEE MOTHERFUCKERS," yelled the rifleman, waving them away from the jeep. The driver ignored them, and we were off like a shot. Shortly, we entered a quarter-mile-long shantytown filled with lean-tos, booths, and small buildings. Most had been constructed from bamboo, thatch, and military packing crates that still bore the tactical markings. Laughing children darted in and out of the busy booths, bumping into the marines who milled about. I watched a young marine laugh and smile back at his waiting companions as he followed a young girl into one of the huts.

"Everyone calls this Vil, Dogpatch," chuckled the driver.

"Fits!" smiled the Captain.

Soon, we came to another checkpoint that was joined on both sides of the guard shack by rolls of barbed wire. The sentry waved us through; the rifleman sitting behind us locked and loaded his weapon. The jeep driver accelerated and the big six-by followed close on our tail. Soon, we were exceeding sixty-five miles an hour.

"Anytime you go outside the wire you can be hit. Daytime is usually pretty safe. The only real danger is hitting a mine," the driver explained. We nodded. "The engineers sweep the roads every morning but you never know when the Dinks are gonna come back and re-mine. Notice, I stay in the middle of the road. The minesweepers have been known to miss a few on the edge. Another thing to be aware of, the VC retrieve five hundred pound bombs and bury them alongside the road; when someone passes by, they electrically detonate them. A convoy came down through here the other day. They saw some kids standing alongside the road with their hands over their ears. The point stopped but it was too late; they blew hell out of two six-bys." he continued.

"Kill anyone?" asked the Captain.

"Driver and his shotgun. Lucky they weren't loaded like we are." I heard an automatic weapon off in the distance. I stole a look at the driver; he hadn't flinched. I relaxed. We came to a bend in the road surrounded by heavy growth and the rifleman scooted down on the seat between the First Sergeant and me. Once around the curve, he resumed his previous seat.

On both sides of the road were rice paddies filled with stooped black forms crowned with straw colored cones. Big, gray, water buffalo, followed by workers dressed in black, pulled primitive plows through the wet, muddy fields. I noticed a small boy riding on the back of one of the giant animals, waving a small plant as if shooing away flies.

"See that lone tree on the side of that hill up ahead?" the rifleman asked.

"Yeah," answered the First Sergeant.

"Right below there is where 3/3's garrisoned." We came speeding up to the entrance of the encampment and made a sudden stop. The young marine standing post walked over to the jeep.

"Any problems?" he asked.

"Nah," responded the driver.

"Did you hear they hit CAC 13 last night?"

"No! Kill anyone?"

"The PF's (Popular Forces) blew some fuck away. They found him this morning and come to find out he'd been cutting hair over at regiment."

"Son-Of-A-Bitches are working among us during the day and trying to kill us at night." The rifleman cleared (removed live round from the barrel) his weapon. The six-by honked its horn behind us.

"Move it," the driver of the big truck yelled. The driver dropped the jeep in low and we sped up the dirt road.

A city of GP (general-purpose) tents filled the camp, lining both sides of the road for a quarter of a mile, stretching up the incline of a small hill. The compound was a beehive of activity. Trucks, jeeps and six-bys were being gunned down the dusty roads. The ubiquitous noise of the generator that supplied electricity to the camp droned in the background. Half-naked men on both sides of the road were busy filling sandbags. One tent had the side rolled up and I could see men moving among tactical marked boxes. A squad of marines, armed to the teeth, with helmets and flak jackets came marching up the path toward us. A group of four or five dogs ran past them and headed in our direction.

"BE CAREFUL, THEM MOTHERFUCKING VIET CONG DOGS," one of the young marines yelled. Laughter filled the air and the dogs barked as if they were in on the joke. I watched the marines as they neared the perimeter. The reckless swagger suddenly took on an air of dead seriousness. They spaced themselves well apart as they prepared to leave the safety of the camp. We past a mule (flat motorized vehicle for transporting small loads) hauling four marines with a stack of barrels cut in half. My eye followed their movement. The rifleman noted my curiosity.

"That's the shit fry," he laughed.

"The what?"

"The ground is too sandy for regular four-hole latrines here in Vietnam," he said, pointing to a small, square building made out of plywood. The backside was up and a couple of marines were pulling out half barrels. "We put about four inches of diesel in the bottom of the barrels so we can have a cookout," he joked, nodding his head toward a roaring fire under a pyramid stack of half barrels.

We had stopped in front of a small CP tent and the Captain went inside. As we sat waiting, I noticed, across the street, an open-air structure a little larger than a GP tent with a tin roof and a plywood floor. A rich aroma of meat frying floated through the hot, humid air. Twelve or so Vietnamese were hunkered down on the side of the hut scrubbing pots and pans. Their melodious chatter of bong, bong, bing, bing, bong, bounced back and forth between them like a ping-pong ball. They laughed among themselves and eyed us suspiciously. I watched, horrified, as they scooped up handfuls of dirt and used it to scrub the grease from the big GI pots and pans.

The Captain came back in a few minutes and walked over to the six-by.

"Listen up! You men climb on down and standby here at the CP. There'll be a man from each respective department coming by for you in a few minutes," he informed us. I grabbed my gear and hopped down out of the jeep. A few minutes later, a PO1 Hospital Corpsman approached us. I recognized him by his navy insignia and the caduceus on his collar. I started gathering up my gear. He had spied my movement and came toward me.

"HM1 Felts. Welcome to Nam, Doc," he said, reaching out his hand.

"HM1 Messer," I responded and grabbed his hand. I felt elation at seeing a colleague. Even though I had never met Felts before, I felt like I had just been reunited with a family member. I had functioned almost in total silence the past twenty-four hours and it was nice to be able to talk to one of my own kind.

"This way," he said and we headed north up the incline.

"So, how long you been here, Felts?"

"Got here last December. Hundred twenty-one days and a wake up and I'm out of here."

"Been rough on you, huh?"

"Not that bad. It's tough to get used to but after awhile, it's like anything else, you just do what you gotta do."

"Been in the grunts the whole time?"

"Yeah, I came in country with 3/3 and I don't really want to leave until it's time to rotate. Division says they try to transfer you out of the grunts after six months. But you know how it is with that damn bunch of political shitheads. They are too busy looking out for their own asses to give a damn about anyone else. Besides, I figure you're safer surrounded by twelve hundred grunts than you are anywhere else anyway. It's the nineteen-year-olds sitting out there on ambush who are paying the price. We've lost a lot of kids and we're losing more of them everyday."

The path to the BAS led us past a barrel sticking up out of the ground that was surrounded waist-high on three sides with material from an old tent. Two marines walked into the pyramid shaped area. The strong smell of urine radiated up from the ground.

"That Urinol (barrel set over a rock bed to leech urine into the soil) needs to be relocated. I been kind of saving that for you guys since I knew you'd be relieving us in a few days," Felts said, and smiled over at me. I nodded and smiled back as we continued up the incline. A short distance ahead, I saw a few men lined up outside of a tent where a jeep ambulance was parked. We passed the men and Felts led me up a couple of wooden steps into a hardback tent (tent with hardwood floors made out of plywood). The hot, lifeless air inside washed over me. A couple of corpsmen were busy treating marines in the front portion of the tent. Felts led me back to the right a few steps to a small corner where boxes of records were stacked. A couple of men sat at a long makeshift desk made out of packing crates typing on field typewriters. If they were aware we had entered, they didn't acknowledge it. Behind them, at a smaller desk, sat an older-looking, balding man with a slight paunch, reading a magazine. He looked so out of place, I couldn't help but wonder what he was doing there. No one was wearing a blouse so I was unsure of his rank, but assumed he was the ranking petty officer.

"Chief Carbum, this is HM1 Messer from 2/26's advance party," introduced Felts. The Chief seemed indifferent to the whole affair and glanced up briefly.

"Get him settled in the staff tent," he commented dryly and turned back to his reading.

We found our way out the back of the BAS, walked about a hundred more feet up the incline and went inside another hardback tent. The sides had been rolled up and a hot, gentle breeze was blowing though the tent. We located a cot at the very back. "This should be okay for you," commented Felts. I dropped my gear on the cot. "Why don't you get yourself squared away and come on back up to the BAS. It's about time for chow. And don't pay any attention to Chief Carbum. He went Asiatic years ago. He married an Okinawan and has been in the Orient for the past nine years. I think he's been over here so long he's forgot how to act, but he's a harmless old fart," chuckled Felts.

I unpacked a few toilet items and took out some dirty clothes that I wanted to wash later on in the evening. I rummaged around in my seven-eighty-two gear and found my rubber lady (air mattress), inflated it, and covered it with my blanket. I heard small arms fire in the distance. I could see men just outside the tent and they weren't scurrying around so I figured it was friendly fire, probably target practice I thought. I got as comfortable as was possible and hurried back down to the BAS.

I noticed a young HM3 in faded jungle utilities who seemed to be aimlessly wandering around. He had smiled warmly at me when I entered but we didn't speak. He seemed confident and had an air about him that was unusual. Curiosity motivated me to engage him in conversation.

"I'm HM1 Messer," I said and offered my hand.

"HM3 Harris," he replied warmly and took my hand.

"Been in country long, Harris?"

"Came in with 3/3 nine months ago."

"I just pulled Harris in out of the field," interrupted Felts. I knew Felts had something he wanted to tell me so I waited. "He just got his second Purple Heart and has been recommended for a Silver Star. I want him to live long enough to receive it," explained Felts. Harris smiled with an air of confidence but didn't say anything. Even though he was only an E-4, he was treated almost reverently. I was to learn he had earned that honor by putting the lives of others before his own in the heat of a deadly battle. It's a valor few men have and sets one well apart from his peers. Although he was young in years, it was obvious he had completed the right of passage to manhood.

"Lost one of my best buddies on the last operation," he said quietly. I waited, hoping he would continue without me asking him what happened. He looked at me for a moment before continuing and I thought he was going to cry. "He came in on a MEDEVAC under fire. We threw the wounded on the chopper and ran back to cover. I had my head down but I saw the chopper when it got a few feet off the ground. It banked right and then it just exploded in a ball of fire…It was the most hopeless damn feeling," he said with an air of melancholy and his voice trailed off. I didn't pursue the subject any further.

At noon, Felts and I went to chow. On our way back, we stopped by supply and got me a couple of sets of jungle utilities and a pair of jungle boots. The top part of the boots was made from linen but a piece of metal was built into the rubber sole to protect from pungy sticks (sharp piece of bamboo hidden in the ground, usually covered with feces). It felt good to be dressed in a lightweight uniform like everyone else.

Besides being the Battalion's Medical Department Representative with the forward group, Chief Bassett had directed me to learn where and how to requisition supplies, to get a copy of the combat entry from a page thirteen and to learn as much about sanitation as was possible. Felts made me a copy of the division's supply requisition and of a page thirteen. Having that out of the way, our conversation turned to sanitation requirements.
"Messer, Preventive Medicine will be coming around when your Battalion gets in country. They are going to be aggravating you about a whole bunch of shit that doesn't make a lot of sense."
"Like what?"
"Like how much oil to put in the barrels for the shit fry, relocating Urinols and things any damn fool would know. But the biggest pain in the ass is they are always harping about getting the slopes to work inside the screened-in garbage room and to get them physical examinations. Hell, I've never seen the same people show up two days in a row since we've been here. The division has contracted to employ so many of the little fuckers and we can't even fire them."
"I noticed they were using dirt for scouring the pots this morning."

"Ain't that some shit. I tried to talk to the motherfuckers through an interpreter and I thought I had it straightened out. I went back the next day and they were back at it."

"You ever check them for tuberculosis or intestinal parasites?"

"I'll let you do that, Messer. You know they come with the camp and you're fresh with ideas. I'm worn out with these assholes. Maybe you'll have better luck. Listen, let me tell you what's really important. Teach your marines if they get dog bit not to shoot the goddamn thing in the head. The brain has to be examined for rabies. Unless we get a negative result, we have to give them the whole rabies series. Make damn sure your line corpsmen keep snakebite kits and know how to use them. Stay in touch with your senior corpsmen in the field and make sure they don't run out of malaria tablets. There are all kinds of pests here in country we're not accustomed to seeing. You can bet your ass the first week you're going to be treating someone for a spider or snakebite. One kid had an anaphylactic shock from some kind of an insect and he damn near died. Your young corpsmen will have to be brought up to speed in a hurry. They are going to be treating a lot more maladies like that than they are bullet wounds."

"How about food service?"

"Keep it simple. Train the stew burners to never, ever, keep any kind of leftovers in the field. If it's not eaten, throw it out. If you can get them to go along with that, you won't have to worry. Nothing will take a battalion out of action faster than a good case of food poisoning. Marines aren't stupid; they know when you're shitting them and when something's serious. Hell, they don't want any problems anymore than you do."

"What's the venereal disease rate like?"

"Well, you know how it is. You get a company out in the field and the girls set up business alongside the road. We don't have any jurisdiction over them so we have to concentrate on educating the troops on prevention. We have a lot of gonorrhea; sometimes one hooker will infect a whole damn squad. We've had a couple of cases we've had to transfer out of country. The corpsmen in the field are your best line of defense. Give them a lot of support. Don't just drop them out there and forget they exist."

Felts taught me a lot of things and I was grateful. I talked to as many of the younger men as I could and they, too, gave me a lot of great information. I was impressed with how mature some of them were. They had developed a jargon of their own and how well one used it was a good indication of how long they had been in country. I noticed that their swagger was sometimes directly related to how faded their utilities and chevrons were. The term, "Yeah, he's hard." indicated that one was a good trooper and highly esteemed.

A young Afro-American who everyone called Ozzie stands out in my memory. My second day with 3/3, Ozzie came in out of the field to spend the night and pick up some supplies. He was highly respected by everyone and a great deal of joking was directed toward him. He was probably twenty or twenty-one, on the short side and tended to be stocky. It was obvious he loved being a corpsman and I was drawn to his enthusiasm. We all gathered out in front of the tent that evening for a bull session. Since I was the new man on the block, it was a great opportunity for them to educate me.

"Problem here in Vietnam is we don't hold enough territory. Last figures I heard, we control about fifteen percent."

"Yeah, that's about right, man."

"The marines go patrolling down through the Vil kicking ass trying to get some old papason to tell them where the VC are. They get their info and go on back to camp. That night the VC come into the Vil and kill the old bastard for talking."

"Would you tell the marines anything if it was going to get you and your family killed?"

"Why don't we just extend the perimeter? Hell, once they knew they were safe they'd be on our side."

"That's right! They don't give a damn who's in power. Shit, they don't even know what the word communist means."

"Hell, a good corporal could do a better job than the generals we got running this damn war."

"Shit, man, Johnson is running it from Washington."

"One of them ass-kissing generals ought to tell him he's fucked up."

"Don't make no damn sense to me."

"Now, Ozzie, he's out there in one of them CAC units and that makes a little more sense. But hell, we only set up these units where we know it's safe."

"What's a CAC unit?"

"You tell him, Oz."

"Well, a squad of marines and one corpsman go into a friendly Vil and live with the locals. The marines help the PFs protect the Vil and the corpsman provides medical services. It's all part of Johnson's MEDCAP program."

"PFs?"

"Popular Forces, young men in the Vil not old enough for the regular army. They kind of act as a home guard."

"And what's MEDCAP?"

"Medical Civil Action Program. All the battalions go out on MEDCAPS. Sometimes, it's just for a few hours."

"You'll be out there pretty soon too, man."

"Not a hell of a lot you can do for some old blind fart with cataracts. Lot's of tuberculosis, hepatitis, and parasitic infections. All the kids got some kind of creeping crud from poor hygiene. They live in it man, so what can you do? Sometimes you can treat them for a fresh cut or a burn and feel like you're doing something. But most of the time it's just shit you can't do anything about."

"If it's hopeless and you don't know what to do, give them some cough syrup. They love the sweet taste."

"Give 'em soap, man. They love that shit,"

"Make sure you cut the bar in half or they'll sell it on the black market."

"Yeah, and another thing, don't ever do a MEDCAP in the same place more than twice. The VC are mixed right in with everyone else and if they think you'll be coming back you can bet they'll booby trap your ass." A grenade went off near the perimeter followed by automatic weapon fire.

"MOTHERFUCKER," someone yelled from off in the distance. Ozzie rolled his eyes and the others smiled.

"Fucking grunts are all crazy."

"Some of the corpsmen are just as bad or worse, trying to prove they are hard."

"How about that corpsman from 2/3 that shot that old man because he was acting weird."

"Yeah, come to find out he was just a fucking retard."

"I knew the Doc that did that from FMF School. He always wanted to be bad."

"He'll be bad when he gets out of Leavenworth in about twenty years."

"Probably would have gotten away with it if he hadn't put the old man in that hooch and set it on fire."

"The old man's family was happy. I hear the spooks gave them enough money to buy three water buffalo."

"This a crazy mother fucking place, man. I'll be glad to get back to the world."

"Me too, but I rather not go in a body bag."

"You got that shit right."

I sensed that was everyone's fear as they all nodded in agreement. I was beginning to realize this was indeed a crazy place. All the things these men knew from their experiences would have to be learned by the corpsmen in 2/26. I shuddered at the thought.

On a bright and early morning a few days later, 3/3 nailed the lids on their tactical boxes and stood by, ready to move out. About midmorning, big six-bys started arriving with men from 2/26. Their brand new gear and regular issue utilities were a sharp contrast to 3/3's weathered equipment and jungle uniforms. The men from 2/26 had barely cleared the vehicles before 3/3 commenced to load. I was out in front of the BAS when a big six-by came grinding up the incline. As it made its approach, faces started materializing. HM1 Willis smiled and waved over the top of the cab of the lead truck. From the look on his face, I thought he must have made a very anxious trip. The truck came to an abrupt stop and Chief Bassett and HM1 Kirkpatrick dumped their gear out the back of the truck and hopped down. Another big truck followed and more familiar faces appeared. I saw big Dan Hahn come down off the second truck. His face was red. He was carrying his gear slung over his shoulder like a book-bag with one hand and his helmet was in the other.

"Stupid motherfuckers," he raved and threw his gear on the ground in a rage.

"Dan's a little upset; we took our first causality getting off the boat."

"What happened, sniper?" I asked.

"No, one of the men from Echo Company didn't clear his weapon like he was supposed to. He tripped coming down the gangplank, knocked it off safety and blew the back of the head off of the marine in front of him."

"I'd like to see how the lying bastards explain that to his mother," HM1 Hahn ranted. The corpsmen from 3/3 were already climbing in the back of the trucks.

"Good luck, Messer," Felts said and reached for my hand as he prepared to climb up on the back of the six-by.

"Hey, thanks!" I responded and grabbed his hand.

"Your boy got all the information you'll need," remarked Chief Carbum to Chief Bassett and reached to pull himself up in the truck. The old Chief tottered for a second, Felts gave him a little boost, and the old man pulled himself up. I couldn't help but think that was the most I'd seen him move. I had to give him "E" for effort; he was trying like hell to fulfill his duties. Felts winked at me as he clamored up behind him. Once Chief Carbum was on solid footing, he pulled himself up with great dignity and walked toward the cab of the vehicle. The younger men made way for the old warrior. I smiled to myself and looked at Kirkpatrick. He shook his head from side to side and we walked up the steps and into the BAS.

All day long trucks arrived with men and gear. A lot of speculation about the VC knowing we were green troops and the possibility of us being hit the first night ran rampant through the camp. The line companies quickly took up positions in the already fortified bunkers that surrounded the camp. The medical supplies, health and service records arrived late in the morning and, by 1600, we were ready for business. Leaving a couple of HM3s in the BAS, we retired to the hooch for the evening. The messing facility wouldn't be up and running for a couple of days so we made ourselves content with C-rations. Twelve different rations came in each case and their contents varied. Ham and lima beans were the most unpopular because of the fat content and were referred to as ham and motherfuckers. Why that came to be, I have no idea, but it stuck.

By 1700, the engineers had the field showers functioning and word went out to the troops. The facility had been installed just a few meters up from where we were quartered. We had been the first to hit the showers and were lounging leisurely. Suddenly, a pop and a whoom, whoom, whoom sound came over our tent.

"INCOMING, HIT THE DECK," someone yelled. We sprawled out on the floor. Another whoom, whoom, whoom. I had only been in country for nine days but I knew when a unit was hit that within two minutes there was some kind of return fire from artillery. I was beginning to wonder what was going on. I lifted my head and looked out the front of the tent. The Gunnery Sergeant from mortars was standing with a towel wrapped around his mid-section looking in at us. He caught my eye.

"What'cha pecker checkers doing in there?" he asked.

"Get down Gunny, we're being hit," replied HM1 Willis. Another WHOOM, WHOOM, WHOOM, went over. "You mean that?" the Gunny asked incredulously and started to laugh. "That's the canister that comes off the air illumination we're using to line up the mortars, you damn fools." We all looked at each other sheepishly and got up off the deck. The gunny shook his head and went on his way to the shower.

"Give him something to talk about at the SNCO Club when he gets back to the States," commented Chief Bassett in a defensive tone. We all had a good laugh at ourselves that day and the battalion enjoyed ribbing us for several weeks.

That night the men on the line were nervous. Automatic weapon fire could be heard spasmodically. A couple of grenades went off and men yelled at one another in the pitch-black darkness. I held my hand up in front of me and couldn't even see an outline; it was that dark. The anxiety and restlessness of my comrades kept me awake until the wee hours of the morning.

The next day, we continued with straightening up and getting things in order. We curtained off one section and put a field stretcher on a couple of wooden horses to use as an examination table. Later in the afternoon, I set up the Field Laboratory to enable us to do simple blood counts, urinalysis and smears for gonorrhea. It was getting on toward 1700 when I heard a grenade go off. I didn't give it a lot of thought at first, as I knew the troops were overly excited. Then I heard someone running out the front door of the BAS. I had been cleaning the microscope and left it where it was and went to investigate. Only

HM3 Hunter and myself remained in the BAS. We looked out the front door and saw several men clustered around a bunker.

"Someone is hurt," said Hunter and took off running toward the cluster of people. Last thing we needed was a group of people massed in the same area in case of an attack. I stayed where I was. Suddenly, I saw HN Farmer running toward the BAS.

"They blew Jones up with a mine," he cried as soon as he got within hearing distance.

"Shit!"

"The Gunny said get a couple of garbage bags from you. We're going to try to pick up the pieces of his body."

"What happened?"

"This old man feigned he was hurt and Jones ran out to him to help; he hit a mine and blew his ass to kingdom come." I had found the bags and handed them to him. "I got to go," he exclaimed and ran out the door. A half-hour later, I saw HM1 Hahn coming up the incline with two marines carrying someone on a stretcher. It was an old Vietnamese man about sixty-five or seventy years old. They carried him into the BAS and placed him on the stretcher we had set up. The marines had tied his hands down.

"S-3 is going to want to talk to this sorry motherfucker when the Doc gets done checking him over," one of the marines said and they left. Dan's eyes blazed with anger and he paced up and down the tent. Suddenly, he took his pistol out, rushed over and jammed it against the old man's temple. The old man was talking out of his head and rolling his eyes. It was obvious he was either insane or retarded.

"I'm going to kill this son-of-a-bitch," Dan said and looked at me.

"Don't do it, Dan. The old man is tied down and isn't a threat to anyone. Besides, I think he's nuts."

"I don't give a fuck. He killed Jones and by-god he's gonna die."

"Okay, go ahead and kill him if you want to. But, it'll be murder; we're not exactly in a fire fight here." His hands commenced to tremble. I wasn't sure if he was going to pull the trigger or not. Big tears rolled down his cheeks. He continued to hold the weapon against the old man's head.

"Put the pistol away, Dan" I pleaded. I heard someone coming into the BAS. It was Doctor Steinman. Dan turned and stomped out the back door. A couple of corpsmen joined the doctor in his examination. I followed Dan into the hooch. It was a sad night for us all. I think for the first time we realized that this was no game we were playing. Jones should never have left the confines of the compound without the area being secured first. It was a bitter lesson that wouldn't soon be forgotten.

I had joined 2/26 so near its departure date that I hadn't got to know the Medical Officers very well. Once we were in country, I worked in close proximity to them both. LT. Miller MC USNR spent most of his time just out the back door of the BAS painting. His ambition had been to become a surgeon but the draft had forced him to put that on hold for a while. He was somewhat withdrawn and seemed to prefer being alone.

LT. Ted Steinman MC USNR was another personality altogether. He had played professional football for the Green Bay Packers before deciding to become a doctor. Ted was athletic, competitive and friendly, and not the least bit intimidated by the Marine Officers in the Battalion. He was vibrant, extroverted and delighted in being with his corpsmen. He joined in the long evenings of beer drinking, tall tales and pinochle games that became a part of our daily routine. Almost everyone received care packages periodically, but Dr. Steinman received, almost daily, huge packs of kosher foods and pumpernickel bread that we consumed with utter gusto. During the day he worked diligently with the corpsmen at sickcall while Doctor Miller painted his seascapes.

I had gotten the Laboratory somewhat functional and managed to get out CBCs (complete blood counts) and urinalyses without a great deal of effort. This brought LT. Steinman and me into a close working relationship. He was enthusiastic about everything he did and everyone around him. He had a way of smiling when he talked that made you wonder if he was going to break into laughter at any minute.

One evening, Dr. Steinman showed up with a five-gallon container of popcorn, two or three pounds of salami and two loaves of his black, pumpernickel bread. The card game was well underway when the conversation turned to our Vietnamese friends working at the mess hall.

"The Colonel asked me about the Vietnamese food service workers today," commented Dr. Steinman.

"Yeah, what did he want to know?"

"Basically, if I thought it was safe for them to be handling food."

"Well, I think we all know the answer to that."

"John, you're in charge of sanitation. Why don't you check them out for TB and see what kind of intestinal parasites are causing their bellies to swell up?"

"Maybe I could get enough serum from Da Nang to do PPDs on them," I replied.

"That would at least get rid of the ones with TB."

"Doctor, why don't we just go ahead and worm them all?" I asked. "Hell. I know they're all wormy."

"Do we have any Tetarachlorethylene Hydrochloride in our mount out gear?"

"Yeah, I'm pretty sure we do."

"Okay, break it out and we'll do it first thing in the morning."

"Done deal! I need to go into Da Nang tomorrow for some supplies. I'll run by Preventive Medicine and see if I can get enough serum so we can do the PPDs day after tomorrow."

"I'll go with you, Messer. Got a couple of buddies in the Medical Battalion (Field Hospital) I've been wanting to see."

"I'll go along too," commented Chief Basset.

The following morning we sent for the Battalion Interpreter and had him accompany the thirteen Vietnamese workers to sickbay. There, according to their size and weight, I administered the proper dose of antihelmintic (class of drugs used to treat internal parasites). A short time later Doctor Steinman, Chief Bassett and I went to Da Nang. We had lunch, talked to old friends, drank a few beers, picked up a few supplies and in general had a modified holiday. We returned to the Battalion Compound around 1430.

What I saw when I entered the BAS shocked me. Sickbay's deck was covered with Vietnamese lying on stretchers. The air was filled with a foul odor mixed with loud moans and groans. I heard someone gagging and then vomit.

"Oh, no, this one has shit himself," one of the young corpsmen said. Kirkpatrick came walking out from behind the screen where the examination table was located. He gave me a disgusted look.

"Messer, you sorry SOB. Why did you give them worm medication then leave? About an hour after you left they all got sick as dogs. They were puking and shitting worms all over this fucking compound. This ain't anything now compared to what it was around noon. I really thought a couple of these poor bastards were going to die."

"Damn, Kirk, I didn't know,"

"That's the goddamn problem, you don't know shit, you dumb fuck. Next time you get a bright idea about giving someone medication you don't know anything about, I hope you go to the trouble of finding out what the side effects are. You can take over in here now and get this shit-house cleaned up."

One by one, I got them back on their feet and sent them home. The next day I went by the garbage shack where they were working. They all pointed at me and started chattering excitedly among themselves.

I'm sure they must have wondered why I would take them up to sickbay and give them something that made them sick. I wasn't going to try to explain it. I waved at them but they ignored me.

Over the next few days, we grappled desperately trying to understand what was happening around us.

"Lost two more marines last night."

"What happened?"

"No one knows, they found them floating in the river this morning. Platoon Sergeant thinks they slipped off to the Vil and got bushwhacked."

"Damn! That's four men we've lost, all due to stupidity."

"I know, Dan. I know."

Ten days later:

"Hear about Master Sergeant Frankeny from communication?"

"NO! Now what?"

"Blown away this morning by a Bouncing Betty."

"SHIT!"

"He was in the field with some young troops. He was showing them how he learned to jerk the radio wire to blow the booby traps on his first tour. The slopes got smart. They put one where it would blow when he jerked the wire and then another, off to the side about six feet. He'd blown one and they went out to check on it. He stepped on a trip wire and it bounced up about four feet and went off. Killed him dead and wounded a couple of others."

"Did you hear what happened in Golf Company yesterday?"

"No, haven't heard anything."

"Little kid, about eight years old, delivered the laundry to the troops on line. They started going through it and found a grenade on the bottom with the pin pulled."

"Anyone hurt?"

"No, they grabbed it before it went off."

"Little bastards,"

"This ain't no regular war, man. Guerrilla shit! They don't have the equipment, aircraft or support to fight a conventional war this far south. They just pick us off one at a time."

"Yeah, demoralize us."

"They got North Vietnamese regular up along the DMZ around Dong Ha."

"Ninth Marines getting the shit kicked out of them up there."

"I heard we'll be moving up there next?"

"Yeah, they're just waiting for us to get a little of this green wore off."

One of the most interesting things about being in combat is the way different men react to situations. There are those who seem like ideal military men under garrison conditions, but in combat prove to be useless or, at times, even a burden. On the other hand, there are those who seem always to be problem children, or in trouble, under normal conditions but become your best troops when they are in the field. Predicting how men will react is an iffy business. A good sense of humor and an optimistic attitude has little to do with military bearing but it can be more valuable than gold to those who share in the combatant's daily life. A funny occurrence can not only lighten the day, but also be therapeutic for weeks to come as the story is told and retold and embellished.

We had several probes on the north side of the camp and upon investigation discovered underground bunkers only a few meters outside our perimeter. This made us all a little nervous and the slightest provocation would send us scurrying to our bunkers. One evening, in late August, as we were preparing to turn in, a grenade went off followed by several rounds of automatic weapon fire. It persisted and another grenade detonated. The alarm went through the camp and we took to our bunkers, or at least most of us did. It was pitch black and our greatest fear was we'd be overrun. Weapons inside the camp were to be kept cleared until it was absolutely certain there was a need to lock and load. Corpsmen are considered non-combatants in accordance with the Geneva Convention and only carry side arms. I would have to say, under normal conditions, they are of very little danger to anyone other than themselves. A fire team from Kilo Company had piled into the bunker on our right. In front, and a little to the right of us, was a supply tent. As we sat staring off into the darkness, we heard footsteps.

"Halt, who goes there," one of the marines from Kilo Company challenged. No one answered and things became very quiet. After a moment, the sound of someone moving could be heard again.

"Advance and be recognized," the marine challenged. Still no answer! I could see a silhouette against the background of the supply tent. KLAK, KLAK, KLAK, KLAK went the sound of the M-14'S as the bolts slid back and the rounds were chambered into the barrel.

"Hold it, muderfucker, you'se en Garrison! It's me, Sergeant Graham over here woking in supply. I can't be running and jumping in no goddamn hole every time some crazy muderfucker thinks he be hearing sompin. I gots work to do over here."

"You best identify yourself next time you're challenged asshole or they'll be shipping your ass home in a bodybag," came the reply. Laughter rang out and floated through the darkness. Maybe, it was the relief that we weren't being overrun or perhaps we thought it poetic justice that someone who took the danger so lightly was put in his place. For whatever reason, it was hysterical to us. Thereafter when someone became overly excited about something he would be chided with, "Hold it, muderfucker, you'se en Garrison."

Chief Bassett probably should never have been returned to full duty after the shooting incident and most certainly not assigned to an Infantry battalion in Vietnam. Headaches plagued him from the plastic plate that replaced part of his cranium. To wear a helmet was sheer torture. I shouldn't have been shocked when one day I went into the hooch and he was packing his gear. Kirkpatrick was sitting on the end of his cot a few feet away.

"Hey, Chief, going somewhere?" I asked. He didn't answer.

"He's being transferred to Medical Battalion," volunteered Kirkpatrick. His voice was a little shaky and he looked like someone had just told him his best friend had died. Several of the corpsmen had already been transferred to other units that had been hit hard and I felt like a child whose family was breaking up. I sat down in the silence and watched him pack. I was so overwhelmed I hadn't noticed a new Chief, a few cots up from me, arranging his gear. He struggled trying to assemble his recently issued seven-eighty-two gear into a pack. I needed to direct my thoughts away from the moment.

"Let me help you with that, Chief," I offered.

"Thanks! Last time I rolled up a shelter half like this was in Korea."

Chief Bassett had collected his gear. He walked to the door and set it down, then turned and went to where Kirkapatrick was sitting. Kirk stood up quickly, almost formal, and grabbed his hand. The emotion that flooded the hooch was so overpowering, I had to turn away to hold back the tears. I busied myself with the new Chief's gear.

"See you, Mess," Chief Bassett called as he picked up his gear and headed out the door. I couldn't speak but nodded my head. Chief Bassett was loved by all of the corpsmen and it was going to be a tough job for someone to replace him. This new Chief was going to need all the help he could get.

"Sorry, Chief, I'm HM1 Messer."

"HMC Clements. You all come here together?"

"Yeah we did, Chief."

"Well, you know, it's good to break things up sometimes. Otherwise you get clicks going and the new men coming in don't get treated fairly."

Kirk was watching our new boss and I could see he wasn't impressed. Chief Clements was a big man, well over six-foot and weighing around two-twenty. His wrists were as big around as my ankles. His powerful jaws were set in rigid determination. His front teeth were spaced wide apart causing him to spit when he spoke in his heavy Southern accent.

"Yeah, I've kind of made it a career of breaking up clicks. You might say it's a hobby of mine," he said.

"I don't think we have a click here, Chief, it's just we've all been together a long time." I explained. He had taken his dress uniform out of his Val pack and hung it up on a nail behind his cot. I saw he had four rows of campaign ribbons, one of which was a Silver Star.

"You know I was in Korea and learned a couple of things I hope I can put to use. I'm not out to get anyone. It's just that I have an understanding of how things are under combat conditions. You know the guys below E-5, here in the BAS, sooner or later are going to end up in a line company. They sweat it out until the time comes and then they find out that the fear was worse than the reality of being there. My policy will be to assign them there right away and not let them hang around in the BAS and get soft. If they survive the first six months, I'll pull them in and they can enjoy the rest of their tour. They'll be motivated more to help the men in the field, too, because they've been there."

"I agree with your line of thinking Chief, but that would have been hard for us to do as we all came here at the same time. I see you were awarded the Silver Star, Chief."

"Well, I'm no hero, Messer. I was with an outfit in Korea when the Chinese overran us. It looked like we were all goners. I ran and jumped on the back of a jeep where the machine gunner had been killed and took over his position; I just started mowing them down. They said I killed seventeen. It was more an act of self defense than heroism." He had finished stowing his gear and apparently that was all the explanation I was going to get for the moment. I knew it would be awhile before the men would warm to Chief Clements. But I had the feeling that wasn't going to bother him too much.

"Come on, let's go get some chow, Chief," I invited and we strolled toward the messing facility.

Over the next couple of weeks, I got to know Chief Clements and came to appreciate his personality. He was a great storyteller and had lived a very colorful life. He seemed to enjoy telling me his tales as much as I loved hearing them. We often worked together on the supply records and laughed as much of the day away as was possible. It was in those first few days of Chief Clements arrival when HM1 Hahn came rushing into the hooch where we were busy making out requisitions.

"Chief, one of the Staff Sergeants in Golf Company hit HM3 Maas in the mouth with his helmet." The Chief's mouth went in a straight line and his eyes narrowed.

"Where is Maas?"

"The Doctor is working on him right now."

"Send him up here as quick as he gets fixed up," Dan left. The Chief became quiet and pensive and I waited for him to break the silence.

"John, did I ever tell you about the time I had my picture in Life magazine during the Korean Conflict?"

"No, Chief you haven't."

"Yeah, well, we were way up in the mountains sloshing around on a seek and destroy operation. I was always lugging all this heavy ass medical gear around on my back. One day this damn Zipperhead came along with this old donkey. I asked him if he was for sale. He said, 'Sure, for five dollars US.' I bought him on the spot. He was one sorry ass looking old burro but it didn't matter. I rigged up a pack for the Ol' Boy, and for awhile he carried my gear. Some reporter from Life heard about it and came up there and took our picture."

"You're kidding?"

"No, full page photo of me and that old mule came out the next month in one of their weekly issues. We were kind of famous for awhile."

"What happened to him, Chief?"

"Got hit by a mortar one night." I saw HM1 Hahn and HM3 Maas coming toward the hooch. I'd have to wait to hear the rest of the story.

Maas came in first and HM1 Hahn followed a few steps behind him. His mouth was swollen and he had a couple of stitches in his lip. Maas was a blond-headed, blue-eyed kid about five foot, ten inches and weighed around a hundred and fifty pounds.

"Want to see me, Chief?" he asked.

"Sit down, Maas. I'd like to talk to you a few minutes," the Chief replied. Maas sat down on the cot opposite the Chief. He took his helmet off and set it down between his feet. HM1 Hahn sat down in the chair next to where I was sitting.

"So, what the hell happened out there, Maas?" the Chief began.

"It wasn't anything, Chief. Really, wasn't nothing." We sat in silence for a full moment. Chief Clements seemed to be studying Maas' face. "I just want to go back out to my company, Chief." The Chief's face grew dark and the lines around his mouth hardened.

"Why don't you humor me a little, Maas, and tell me what happened." Maas looked at HM1 Hahn and then back at the Chief.

"Well, Chief, we were being transported from one position to another in the back of a six-by. I took my helmet off for a minute and the platoon Sergeant told me to put it on. I made a smart remark and didn't put it on fast enough to suit him, so he jerked it out of my hand and smacked me in the mouth with it. That's all there was to it and, to tell you the truth, I think I probably deserved it."

"Maas, you may think it's alright for the marines to be knocking the shit out of you, but I sure as hell don't. If I let them get away with slapping you around, I won't be able to protect any of our corpsmen. Now, I want you to go get your gear and come on back up here to the BAS.

I'm going to assign someone else to Golf Company until I find out what went on out there."

"But, Chief!" Chief Clements' cold stare stopped Maas in mid sentence. He gave HM1 Hahn a hopeless look. HM1 Hahn stood up.

"Come on, Maas, let's go get your gear," he said.

The afternoon past into early evening. We were lounging in the hooch when the First Sergeant from Golf Company came to the door.

"Chief Clements in here?"

"Yo," answered the Chief.

"Could I talk to you a minute in private, Chief?" The Chief reached for his soft cover and joined the First Sergeant. A few minute's later I heard loud voices. I recognized Chief Clements' Southern accent.

"YOU MAY RUN GOLF COMPANY, FIRST SERGEANT, BUT I'M IN CHARGE OF THE HOSPITAL CORPSMEN IN THIS BATTALION. I'LL TELL YOU WHO YOU CAN HAVE AND WHO YOU CAN'T. IF YOU THINK YOUR PLATOON SERGEANTS CAN BEAT MY CORPSMEN AROUND, YOU GOT ANOTHER THINK COMING. I WON'T HAVE IT."

"I'LL GO SEE THE BATTALION COMMANDER IF I HAVE TO, CHIEF."

"YOU GO SEE WHOEVER THE HELL YOU WANT TO. BUT I WANT YOU TO SEND THAT PLATOON SERGEANT'S ASS UP HERE TO SEE ME. WE'll SEE HOW HE DOES KNOCKING A MAN AROUND INSTEAD OF SOME KID. I'LL KICK HIS MARINE ASS ALL OVER THIS FUCKING COMPOUND AND YOURS TOO BY-GOD IF YOU FUCK WITH ME.

"COME ON DOWN TO THE COMPANY OFFICE WITH ME, CHIEF."

I feared for the Chief but I stayed in the hooch. We all looked at one another. "He can take care of himself," commented Kirk. The loud voices trailed off into the night. Several hours later, the Chief stumbled into the hooch. Apparently, the Chief and the First Sergeant had solved their problem over a few beers. I heard him fumbling around in the dark for several minutes before he lay down.

The next morning Chief Clements sent for Maas.
"Maas, you sure you want to go back to Golf Company?"
"Yes, sir, Chief."
"Okay, get your gear and go on back down there. But remember, you work for me. And if they give you anymore shit, you let me know."
"Will do, Chief."
"One other thing. If you're told to do something, do it and keep your smart-ass trap SHUT. Got it?"
"Yes, sir."

The word buzzed through the Battalion about the run in between the Chief and First Sergeant. It seemed we had gained a whole new respectability. From that day on, no one in the Battalion questioned Chief Clements authority. Ironically, HM3 Maas was to later be recommended for a Bronze Star for heroic action under fire by the same Platoon Sergeant that hit him in the mouth.

In July of 1967, the Third Marine Division moved north to the Province of Quang Tri in an effort to stem the ever-increasing flow of the North Vietnamese Regular Army into the area. The American forces now exceeded five hundred thousand and, on average, American KIAs (Killed in Action) were exceeding over a hundred a week. We had relieved 3/3 in order for them to make the move north. We knew it was just a matter of time until we would be joining the rest of the Division.

In mid September, the word came down. We were to strike camp. We would be airlifted into the Phu Bai area via C-130's and our mount out gear would follow by truck. From there, we would receive further orders.

Upon our arrival at the air terminal in Phu Bai, the Battalion formed up in ranks in front of the control tower. As we stood waiting, a helicopter landed across the street in front of a large complex of tin top, plywood structures that were screened in. A closer look revealed drop linen clothes rolled up near the top of the screen that could be let down during foul weather. We saw a half dozen men running to the chopper. Four big jeep ambulances with red crosses painted on their sides sat next to the landing zone. Fifteen or so Vietnamese women, dressed in their black pajamas and straw-colored cone hats, were squatting just to the right of the opening of the first tent. The familiar sound of, "Bink, bink, bonk, bonk, bink," floated through the air as the constant stream of rice flew into their mouths from the end of their chopsticks. They seemed to be oblivious to the helicopter.

"Looks like Third Med. Battalion over there where the chopper landed."

"Helicopters have sure changed how battlefield causalities are handled."

"Yeah, the wounded go straight to the operating room in minutes."

"During the Second World War, the wounded were transported by stretcher from the field, to the BAS, to Regimental Aid and then on to the Field Hospital."

"Lot of them died from shock and the loss of blood that would've been saved today."

"I wouldn't want to be part of a MEDEVAC crew. One minute you're sipping coffee and playing cards and the next you can be taking hostile fire in a LZ (landing zone)."

"See that chopper running over there? They keep them ready to go twenty-four hours a day."

"I got a buddy in MEDBAT (Medical Battalion), he says the duty crew sleeps on there."

"You have to be shitting me. How in the hell could you go to sleep?"
"I guess you get used to it. Some guys get off on that shit."
"Maybe they have a death wish."
"Who in the hell knows? But you gotta give'em credit. They're brave bastards."

Once all the C-130s had landed, the whole Battalion came together and we marched a couple of miles out onto the flat, desolate, treeless terrain.

"Drop your traces and stand at ease," the Sergeant Major ordered. We dropped our seven-eighty-two gear and took a good look around at the area. It appeared Headquarters Area stretched about four or five miles in both directions. We could see newly-constructed, plywood structures clumped in different areas within the confines of the Garrison. A jeep appeared and the Battalion Commander was whisked off in the direction of what we thought to be the Commanding General's Office. We were put at ease while we waited for his return.

"What do you think the temperature is?"
"Jesus, has to be a hundred."
"With this flak gear and helmet on we're going to die."
"We need to get out of the direct sun."
"I don't see a bush big enough for a dog to piss on." An hour or so later, the jeep returned with our Battalion Commander. The Executive Officer and Sergeant Major surrounded him. A few minutes later the Sergeant Major called us to attention.

"Now, listen up. We have our orders. We're going to be billeted here in Phu Bai for a few weeks as part of the palace guard that protects the perimeter. Within the confines of the compound, are the Airport Terminal, Medical Battalion, Seabees Construction Battalion, the Air Force's Top Security Compound and the Commanding General and his Headquarters Staff. Besides ourselves, the compound is protected by artillery and helicopter gun ships, plus we have the Navy and Air

Force giving us air support. Looks like we're in for some soft living so saddle up, we're in for a little hike."

We marched west for half an hour and came into a complex of hooches that resembled the structures at the Medical Battalion. We settled in and drew C-rations for noon and evening meals. It would be a couple of days before our gear arrived and the stew burners could get the field kitchen up and running. The camp was almost modern, compared to what we had been used to, but there wasn't any fortification. The next three days were spent filling sandbags and building bunkers in front of the structures. The Medical Battalion was a short distance away and had a SNCO Club where hard liquor and cold beer were being served from noon until 2200. Life in Headquarters and Service Company of 2/26 was pretty plush for the moment. The line companies were dispatched to the perimeter and assigned various other tasks. CAC units were formed and sent into nearby villages that were dotted along Highway One, which ran south along the South China Sea Coast toward Da Nang. North of us, about thirteen miles, was Hue City. From there, it was about sixty miles to Dong Hoa, which was located near the border of North Vietnam. That was the Third Marine Division's farthest outpost. Frequent exchanges of artillery barrages between the North and the South were a common occurrence.

Daily, intelligence reported that thousands of North Vietnamese troops were flowing into South Vietnam. The Third Marines were fighting fierce battles in places like Khe Sanh, Vinh Linh, and Le Thuy. Ground would be taken at tremendous sacrifice only to be abandoned a few days later. The philosophy that body count over terrain prevailed. The Bad Luck Ninth Marines, as we had now started to call them, were strung out along the DMZ (demarcation line, of 1954, that declared the area between the North and South as the demilitarized zone). Their thirst for replacements gobbled up our young troops. A good number of times, young marines who had been in 2/26's supply or support units would be sent to the Ninth Marines and, within a matter of days, sometimes hours, it would be reported they were killed in action.

One day, an old truck showed up with a young Vietnamese woman at the steering wheel and two young male helpers. They contracted to pick up the garbage every Thursday afternoon for salvage rights. We soon dubbed her with the dubious title, "Garbage Girty and the Shit Truck." Over the next few weeks we became accustomed to seeing the old truck meandering up and down between the row of hooches picking up garbage.

September past into October and the weather began to cool. As we entered November, it became cloudy and overcast and the Monsoon rains commenced to fall. We weren't engaged in the major battles that were being fought along the DMZ but were taking causalities on seek and destroy operations and from the eternal booby traps and land mines. As the weather worsened, enemy activity increased in the surrounding area.

I had become accustomed to the sounds of mortars as they were tossed back and forth between the VC and our troops. I knew the VC had no heavy artillery or aircraft in the area so our only real danger was mortars. My helmet and flak jacket were my constant companions and were never more than an arm's reach away from me.

It was 0200 and we were fast asleep. I heard the mortar go out of the end of the tube with the distinct "THUMP." I heard it as clearly as I would've had I been awake. I leaped from my cot, gathered my helmet and flak jacket all in one motion, and flew to the end of the hooch and out the door into the sandbag bunker, yelling as I went, "IN COMING, IN COMING." I hit the bunker about the time the first mortar exploded. Sand and gravel hit the top of the tin roof, and within seconds ten men had piled in on top of me. The mortars were being spaced about a hundred meters apart and walked through the compound much like a giant would take steps. As they would move away from us, we relaxed. But as they were adjusted to walk back through the same area with only a minor adjustment of a few meters, much like you would walk up and down rows of corn, the tension and fear would return. Provided you kept your head down, unless you got a direct hit in your fighting hole, you would be safe. My mind was constantly calculating the location of the incoming rounds. WHOOM! I heard debris flying through the air. Someone's scream pierced the darkness. I felt Kirkpatrick go tense and raise up. I pulled him back down.

"Wait, you don't even know where he is." I said. He was peering over the top of the sandbags. The mortars moved away from us.

"Damn, here they come again." This time closer and the sand and debris banged down on the roofs of the surrounding hooches. Then, I heard the artillery going to work. The choppers were up. I knew it was over. We had been under attack less than two minutes.

"Sorry motherfuckers sure have a strange way of saying good morning."

"Think those were 60 millimeters or 81's?"

"They were 81's! They got about a two mile range, which means they're right outside the wire."

"Little dinkey fucks can blow us away before we can get a fix on them."

"They know it takes about two minutes, so by the time we react they're back in their tunnels."

"Artillery is sure blowing hell out of something."

"Damn fools!"

In the morning light we assessed our damage and were amazed at the pinpoint accuracy with which the mortars had taken out some of the buildings where weapons and supplies had been stored. The thing that disturbed most of us, more than anything else, was our missing chow hall. The only thing that remained after the attack was the cement slab it had been built on. S-2 was taking a serious look at the Vietnamese that frequented our camp. Garbage Girty was definitely under suspicion as she was familiar with every aspect of our camp. The Battalion Commander thought it might be a better idea for the ARVNS (South Vietnamese Soldiers) to interrogate her rather than our marines. Her being a woman made for a potential public relations disaster and that was the one thing we didn't need.

A few days after the attack HM1 Kirkpatrick and I had gone to one of the forward line companies a few miles outside the wire to deliver some supplies and take a look at the camp's sanitary conditions. We made our return trip that afternoon about 1600; a slow drizzle was falling. About five hundred meters out from the checkpoint, we saw a large number of people collected in the middle of the road.

"What the hell is that up there?" Kirkpatrick asked.

"Something's hanging out over the road that's tied to that old tree."

"Damn! It's a naked woman; looks like she's dead." Seven or eight vehicles were honking for the people to move out of the road. We slowly made our approach.

"It's Ol' Garbage Girty."

"They got a sign around her neck." We were directly opposite the grotesque site as our jeep moved slowly through the crowd.

"Jesus H. Christ, they've cut both of her tits off and stuck a bamboo pole up her ass." I saw an ARVN standing with two marines looking up at the sign.

"WHAT DOES THE SIGN SAY?" I yelled.

"I WAS AN INFORMER FOR THE VC," one of the marines called back. Kirk and I sat in stone silence as the jeep plowed through the evening mist toward the BAS. Our sensibilities had been so shocked we were unable to speak.

Shortly after the Garbage Girty incident, one dreary afternoon, Kirk, Dan and I were in the BAS talking about the Medical Battalion personnel being lucky to have a nice, well-stocked SNCO Club. All the corpsmen in the division had a standing invitation to frequent the facility and it was a fun place to gather and tell war stories. Our problem, however, was a matter of transportation and timing. The Club opened at 1600, but in order to get there we needed a vehicle to get us past the three checkpoints between the two compounds. The jeep assigned to the BAS could only be used after-hours for emergencies. Doctor Steinman had overheard our conversation and sauntered over and joined us.

"Hey, listen, you guys, the Captain in charge of transportation sleeps in my hooch. He told me I could have a jeep anytime I wanted it. Why don't I check one out and let's tool on over there this evening and get a couple of cool ones?" We all agreed that would be a great idea and decided around six that evening would be a perfect time. Right on schedule, our favorite doctor came driving up. We all piled in and headed over to the Medical Battalion with the good physician driving and returning salutes to the marines at the checkpoints in a most military like manner. We found the Club, went inside and reveled in drink, singing of songs and telling of bawdy stories until 2200, at which time we were invited to leave. We proceeded to our jeep in the same festive spirit and commenced our noisy journey back to our Battalion Compound. Upon arrival, much to our surprise, LT. Ted Steinman MC/USNR wheeled the jeep in front of the chain that barred entry to the Motor T. Area and jumped out.

"RUN EVERYONE," he laughed and dashed into the darkness. All this activity hadn't been wasted on the sentry posted in the area and he came hurrying toward us un-slinging his weapon.

"Halt!" he yelled. Well, it didn't take long for us to figure out what had happened and we took off in opposite directions. I reached the darkened hooch to find Kirk already lying on his cot covered up with a blanket. I followed his example and thirty seconds later Dan entered and leaped under his cover. In less than two minutes, a Marine Captain stepped into the hooch and snapped on the lights.

"Turn the goddamn lights off," Chief Clements ordered. After a brief look, apparently to ensure all the bunks were full, the Captain turned the lights off and left. We lay listening to the foot steps disappear in the darkness. Once he was out of hearing range we started laughing.

"That damn Ted. He's going to get us all court-martialed," commented Dan dryly. For some reason we found that very hilarious and everyone in the hooch cracked up. We never found out what happened between the Captain and Doctor Steinman but it was rumored there were some very loud voices coming from their hooch later on that night.

The last week of November, one late afternoon, Chief Clements opened the front door of the hooch where I was making out requisitions.

"John, come go with me," he ordered as a jeep came to an abrupt stop in front of the BAS. I grabbed my flak gear and helmet. Chief Clements had already climbed in the front seat and I piled over the top of him. A few seconds later a PC (personnel carrier) came roaring up with four riflemen in the back.

"Ready!" called the man behind the wheel in the PC.

"Waiting!" answered our driver.

"What happened, Chief?" I asked as the jeep hurtled forward.

"One of our corpsmen in Hotel Company has been accidentally shot," he said and fell into thoughtful silence.

The next forty-five minutes we traveled at breakneck speed through the falling rain. Finally, off to my right, and up a small incline, I saw a large number of two man tents and a couple of CP (Command post) tents. A large group of men were gathered in front of the first CP tent. The low, gray, dark clouds and heavy fog hung over the camp like a dismal blanket. We came to a sudden halt and bailed out of the jeep. The Chief and I pushed our way through the crowd. The body lay on the ground in front of the tent rolled up in a poncho. A young HM3 was down on his knees rocking back and forth whining like a wounded animal.

"I didn't mean to do it, I didn't mean to do it," he cried in a mournful wail over and over. The Chief knelt and did a quick examination of the corpse. The bullet had entered the temple on the left side, and exited on the right, taking with it a good portion of the brain and skull. Once the Chief saw the corpsman was dead, he pulled the young HM3 up and looked at the Company Commander.

"Let's get him back to base camp," the Chief directed.

"Fog has us socked in, already tried to get a chopper out. He won't fit in the Jeep?" asked the Company Commander.

"We need to keep the body laid out straight if we can."

"How about the PC?"

"I hate to crowd him up in there with the men if we can avoid it. Do you have a six-by we can use?" The Company Commander yelled at someone; unintelligible words floated through the air. A few minutes later the six-by appeared. I watched it stop and start backing toward where we were standing. As I stood listening to the mournful sound of the transmission grinding, I was overcome with a feeling of hopeless desperation. The vehicle stopped and four marines picked the body up and lifted it toward the truck. Blood ran out of the poncho and dripped into a small puddle of water under the tailgate of the truck. I watched as it turned to a brilliant pink. The young HM3 broke away from the Chief, ran, and threw himself back on his knees and started beating his head up and down on the ground.

"Oh, God, no! Please, no," he prayed. The big six-by bounced over the rutty road leaving in its wake a trail of bright red blood. The Chief and I climbed back into the jeep. Our driver fell in behind the six-by and we traveled in a sorrowful silence.

The following morning the Chief had us fall in formation. "Yesterday, we had a tragedy. One of our corpsmen from Hotel Company came off patrol and didn't clear his forty-five. He took the clip out but forgot to clear it. He went to clean his weapon and snapped the trigger. The round in the barrel went off and it was at such an angle, it killed the man sitting on the cot next to him. One life has been lost and another destroyed over a stupid mistake. I want to remind you that when you come into garrison you're to take that clip out and snap the weapon to make sure there's not a round in the chamber. And, like I've said a thousand times, always assume your weapon is loaded. Never, ever point a weapon at anyone unless you're planning on using it. Okay, that's it. Let's get to work."

By the first week of December, the monsoon rains had flooded out the low lands. Many of the rivers that carried the run-off passed under the bridges on Highway One that came north from Da Nang. A good percentage of the supplies needed in the war effort were trucked north over this route and it was essential to keep it open. Once the rivers had crested, the water often ran either over the bridge or within a few feet of the surface. The VC would put depth charges on rafts, or in old boats, and float them down the river and in an attempt to take out the bridges. The fog and low hanging clouds very often prevented the helicopters from being able to patrol the rivers safely. It was determined 2/26 would build bunkers on each side of the bridges and man them with a fire team from the letter companies. In addition, they would make search and destroy patrols and set up ambushes in the surrounding area. In order to accomplish this, the Alpha Command group would move thirty miles south from Phu Bai and set up along Highway One to give tactical support. As always, the order to move came at the last minute when we least expected it.

"Dan, I want you and John to pick out three good men and get ready to go with Doctor Steinman and the Alpha Command group on a forward operation a few miles out," ordered Chief Clements. The rain was pouring in torrents on top of the tin roof of BAS. I looked at Dan and I could see he was about as thrilled as I was about the upcoming ordeal.

"Why us, Chief? There are three other First Class here in the BAS," Dan challenged.

"Dan, I can send someone else in your place, but I want you to give this some thought. How would you feel if someone got themselves killed doing what I had asked you to do? My philosophy has always been not to ask for volunteers to do anything foolish. But, at the same time, I think everyone should do their duty when it's their turn."

I'm not sure that Chief Clements would have designated anyone else had Dan continued to protest. He had appealed to our sense of honor and fair play. We gave him the names of the three men we wanted to go with us and started gathering up our seven-eighty-two gear. The Chief looked down at the list.

"Good choices, I'll go tell them in what high regard you hold them," he chuckled.

"Jesus, John, it's almost dark. How in the hell we going to decide what gear to take?" asked Dan.

"The mount out is set up to split into two command groups, but hell man, five of us can't go lugging fifty 4.2 cube boxes around. They'd take up a whole six-by themselves," I answered. Two of the men we requested had joined us under the supply tent. They didn't look too happy. A few seconds later, Doctor Steinman came in with our last selectee. "Let's just grab four Beach Bags and the Dispensatory Set and we'll make out a list of things we need when we get settled," I suggested.

"Sounds good to me," answered Dan. We started pulling the gear off the pallets and putting it in a big pile next to our seven-eighty-two gear. I heard the big six-by pull up in front of the BAS.

"I hope everyone knows I'm scheduled to go to Hawaii on RR (relaxation and recreation) and meet Carol on the twenty-eighth of

December. They may have to stop this war for a week but you can bet I'm going," proclaimed our surgeon. I looked from him to Dan, and then at the three other men standing in the semi-darkness. They looked strange and out of place. Water streaked off their helmets and dripped down onto their ponchos. As I listened to the rain falling on the canvas the thought we were lost souls wondering in an unknown world entered my mind. The horn on the big six-by blared. We hesitated, dreading to leave the safety of the dry tent.

"Let's go." someone yelled.

"Ain't this some shit," one of the men said and we started gathering up the gear and headed for the waiting truck.

The convoy journeyed through the early evening. Soon, we came to the first bridge and stopped. I looked out over the cab of the open-air truck. I could see marines standing in the rain on the other side. They were pointing up the river.

"Hold up a minute! Something's coming this way," one of them yelled. I saw what looked like a treetop and a couple of logs floating rapidly down the river. The marines opened fire on the floating mass. Twigs and pieces of wood flew into the air. It disappeared quietly under the bridge. We lurched forward and the big truck groaned and grumbled as we made our way on through the night. The next bridge, I didn't bother with the commotion but stayed seated in the bed of the truck trying to stay warm and dry. Two and a half-hours later, we ground to a stop.

A general-purpose tent weighs just less than five hundred pounds when it's dry. I can only guess at the weight we struggled with in the darkness. Dan and I had both been squad leaders in Field Medical School and we had cursed the class on erecting a GP in the dark. Our past bitterness turned to gratitude as we struggled in the ink black night. Once the tent was up, we hauled our gear inside and erected our cots under the light of a Coleman lantern. The sound of the rain on the canvas gave us a feeling of accomplishment. The light from the sputtering Coleman danced on the foot-and-a half high weeds in our new home. Suddenly, the flap of our tent was pulled aside and the fiftish-looking Protestant Chaplain stuck his head in.

"Would you corpsmen give my assistant a hand with our CP (Command Post Tent)," he asked in a whiny tone and withdrew.

"That fuck! Don't we have enough shit to do without coddling that old fart?" Dan asked as we staggered through the darkness. I laughed out loud at his annoyance. It somehow made me feel better to think he was just a little more miserable than I was.

The morning light seeped under the edge of the GP tent. Hunger had awakened me. Dan was sitting on the edge of his cot with a look of disgust on his face. Seeing I was awake, he turned his attention to the front tent pole leaning at about a fifteen-degree angle.

"It's a wonder the goddamn thing didn't fall on top of us," he commented.

"Let's draw some rations and, after breakfast, we'll straighten it up."

"We're going to have to figure out what kind of field latrine we're going to use, John."

"We'll just dig a soakage pit and stick a shell casing in it for a urinal. I don't see worrying about trying to transport a urinol out here from Battalion. We'll dig a six-foot hole and put the old standard four-holer over it for a shitter. We don't have that many people here in the command area anyway."

"Sounds good to me. Let's get some chow." I opened the flap of the tent and we went outside. The rain had stopped and the sun was peering through a small hole in the cloud cover. From the hilltop where we had camped, we could look down on the South China Sea.

"Jesus, what a beautiful country. Look at that," commented Dan. We stood transfixed, our eyes drinking in the natural beauty of the sea extending out to infinity.

"Doc, pick up your C's over here if you want to eat. I'm not running a catering service," called out Gunny Sanchez. We walked over and started helping him unload the two dozen or so cartons of C-rations onto the ground. "The Top Kick Stew Burner is going to be coming out today and set up a field mess so we can have B-rations (large bulk cans of foods). It won't be like home cooking but at least it'll be hot," the Gunny informed us.

In a couple of days, we had pulled all the weeds in the tent and set up for sickcall. The items in the Beach Bags and the Dispensatory Set were designed for treating emergencies under combat conditions and inadequate for regular sickcall.

"Dan, let's sit down and try to think of every conceivable condition we might treat out here. Then, we'll make a list of what we would need to treat it and one of us will go to Battalion and pick it up."

"Great! You know, I've been thinking. We're not going to have a field shower set up out here," commented Dan and walked over and picked up two field litters and stood them on end. "Why don't we take the wood out of an ammo box and lay it across the top to hold these two together. Then we'll take a number ten can (about a gallon container) and punch holes in it and put on top. Then we can heat water in one of these five-gallon cans and take turns pouring for each other so we can shower. We can put it over there next to that big rock so we can stand on it to pour." The other corpsmen suddenly became interested. In a very short time, we had a pretty fair makeshift shower.

The following day, the Top showed up with his field kitchen. That evening, the big six-bys hauled us down the hill to the field galley where we feasted on hot pork and beans, canned Vienna Sausage and green Kool-Aide.

"You know, I like the idea of junior men eating first in the field," I said to Dan as we made our way through the line in front of the officers.

"They say it's a tradition that goes back to Genghis Khan."

"Really! Well, I don't know about that but if the Field Commander is the last to eat I have a pretty good idea the troops have a better chance of being fed."

The Battalion was strung up and down Highway One for several miles. The letter companies ran search and destroy missions and routinely sat on all-night ambushes. The Ninth Marines along the DMZ continued to be pounded and their need for replacements was like a plague to the whole Division. The line companies fell below complement and many times our young corpsmen would sit on all night ambushes with one squad and take a patrol with another squad the following morning. Nineteen and twenty-year-olds coming from the States oftentimes found themselves in the middle of horrendous conditions hours after they arrived in country. If there are any true heroes from the Vietnam War, it must surely be those young sailors and marines who served so valiantly.

A few days after we arrived, we were sitting inside the BAS playing cards. Suddenly, we heard several loud explosions. We had become accustomed to the sounds of war and normally paid them little heed. Then, I heard people running and yelling and the motor of the big six-bys come to life. We looked at each other and waited expectantly. Seconds later, the flap of the tent was jerked open.

"Echo is being hit. Couple of you corpsmen come with us," ordered the Sergeant Major. Dan and I jumped up and both of us grabbed a Beach Bag and we bailed for the trucks. They weren't waiting on anyone and were barreling down the hill. Dan had run ahead of me and jumped in the back of the last truck and reached back to catch my hand to pull me up. I got halfway up when my foot slipped and I fell backwards. The truck was going about twenty miles an hour by this time. I felt the impact of the road hit the back of my steel helmet, stunning me momentarily. Dan, thinking I was seriously hurt, jumped out of the truck and ran to my aid. The truck had accelerated and was traveling at high speed toward Echo Company.

"YOU ALRIGHT?" Dan asked when he saw I was able to move.

"Yeah, I'm okay," I said looking after the truck.

"Goddamn, we'll have to hump it," he said and we took off down Highway One toward Echo Company, some mile and a half away. Suddenly, out from the side of the road came seven young Vietnamese males. Any South Vietnamese, armed with weapons, who wasn't in an ARVN uniform was considered to be VC. Where these men had come from, I wasn't sure. They looked toward the trucks in the distance and turned their attention to us. There was no doubt in my mind they were VC and were calculating the possibility of overpowering us. As they approached, I sensed danger and saw the anger in their faces.

"Dan, these bastards are VC." I said.

"Probably are," he answered. I dropped my Beach Bag and took out my forty-five and chambered a round. Dan did likewise.

"Don't come any closer," Dan ordered when they were within a few feet of us and leveled his gun at the lead man and started pointing, indicating for them to go around. They walked a wide circle, talking aggressively and jeering at us.

We finished our hike to Echo Company. They had received over twenty-five rounds of sixty-millimeter mortars but had not taken any casualties. One mortar had landed just outside of their mess tent and blown it to smithereens. A young L/Cpl had been heating up B-rations inside the tent. He was white as a sheet and shaking from the adrenaline rush. He had missed being killed by a hair.

"I tell you the truth, Doc. I dived in my hole just as the round hit, but before it exploded. Now, you explain that shit to me."

"I can't, Red, but someone is looking out for your country ass," I said and walked over and took out my knife and pried a piece of shrapnel out of one of the field ranges. I could see the marines beating the bushes on the side of the hill about three thousand meters away. They didn't find anyone. Charley was long gone. Wasn't any doubt in my mind that Dan and I had past him on the road.

Christmas was just around the corner. One of our corpsmen had found a little scrub cedar growing on the side of the hill between our camp and the highway. He had cut it down and brought it into the tent. A fourth grade teacher in the middle of Wisconsin had gotten our address from somewhere and had her students send us Christmas cards with notes of gratitude for our sacrifices. We divided the cards up among ourselves and answered each one of them individually. When we finished addressing the envelopes we took some suture thread and tied the cards on our little tree. Several colorfully-wrapped gifts from home had arrived and, of course, Dr. Steinman's huge monthly package of goodies. They looked quite nice under our little tree. One of the men had received a tape of Christmas music and the familiar sounds floated through the tent. We were trying our best to celebrate Christmas in the traditional style.

It was around nine in the evening. We were playing cards and trying to amuse ourselves. Without any warning, the Battalion Commander's aide came rushing into our tent. This was not a good sign and we waited for the bad news.

"One of our Aircraft saw some VC with Mortar Tubes hiking about twenty miles south of here. He circled around, came in low and discharged a whole payload of five hundred-pound bombs. He was off-center a little and they landed right in the middle of a Vil. The damn place is on fire and there are casualties everywhere. We're the closest unit that has a doctor. Division has ordered us to get down there without delay and give medical support." We started gathering up the Beach Bags and our Unit Ones (field first aid kits).

"How many troops will be giving us support?" Doctor Steienman asked.

"One rifleman will be in the Colonel's jeep with the driver and there will be a fire team in the PC with the rest of you."

"We're going twenty miles into Indian Country to a bombed out village with one fire team?" questioned Dan.

"We're going to try to get you some air cover," the young marine officer answered as he turned and left the BAS. A vehicle had stopped in front of the tent and was waiting. We piled in as quickly as we could and took off down the road hell bent for leather. We soon approached a bridge over a river manned by the marines. The usual screaming and yelling took place and we were allowed to pass over after identifying ourselves.

After what seemed like an eternity, we pulled off to the side of the road. The PC was covered with a tarp and we hadn't been able to see the fire raging in the village. Once out of the vehicle and on the ground, we could see the flames licking the ink black sky about a quarter of a mile away. The sound of the mourning villagers floated across the rice field.

"Where is the goddamn road leading in there?" asked Dan.

"Don't see one," answered the driver of the Command Jeep. We could hear him talking on the radio to Battalion. The radio crackled and we heard the Old Man's voice.

"Don't be bullshitting around looking for a road. They'll have to hump in. Got a MEDEVAC Chopper on its way. Tell the Doc the first thing he'll need to do is to set up a LZ."

"Fucking lovely."

"Can't believe this shit." We climbed over the dike and into knee deep water of the rice paddy and started the long hike to the Vil. Upon our approach, the heat from the burning two dozen, or so, thatch huts threatened to overwhelm us. The first hut we came to had rice three to four inches deep lying on the floor. Then I looked at the walls and realized the Vietnamese had packed the rice inside, probably to hide it from the VC. An old woman was sitting on a grass mat at an eight-inch high table inside the hut. Her hand was wrapped in a death grip around her teacup. A piece of shrapnel had hit her in the forehead. She was probably killed instantly and never knew what hit her. The Village Chief, or someone of importance, ran up and started trying to talk to Doctor Steinman. We formed a triage area and, with sign language, Doctor Steinman was able to communicate to him to bring all the injured to the area. Suddenly, a helicopter dropped air illumination and the night sky lit up like day. We were directly under the bright light and could be seen from a mile away. I felt eyes watching us. I had little doubt that we were being observed.

"Dan, if we live through the night, we'll live forever," I commented.

"This is some scary shit, man," he responded. A young Vietnamese man ran up to Dan with a two or three-year-old child and started screaming. The child's cheek was laid open to the bone with a three-inch laceration. Dan was tense and in no mood to be patient. He shoved the young man backwards, grabbing the baby away from him. The man yelled and lunged at Dan trying to retrieve the child. A group of Vietnamese surrounded us.

"Dan, goddamn it, give him back the baby. Just treat the motherfuckers and let's get out of here." I pleaded.

The MEDEVAC arrived within the hour; the crew from the chopper piled off and had the injured on board in seconds.

"YOU GUYS GET THE HELL OUT OF HERE," one of them yelled as the chopper lifted off. The tension in the Vil was growing. Dark, angry eyes watched us from the shadows.

"Let's go," said Doctor Steinman and we headed for the lights of the jeep in the far distance. Upon arrival, we could hear the driver on the radio talking to a chopper in the air.

"ROGER THAT, THERE'S ENEMY ACTIVITY THROUGHOUT THE AREA. YOU'RE PROBABLY GOING TO GET HIT ON THE WAY BACK. WE'RE GOING TO GIVE YOU AIR COVER TO THE BATTALION. WE'RE GOING TO WORK

OUT A FEW OF THESE HEDGE ROWS"…static and then something I didn't understand.

"ROGER OUT," said the driver.

"That was the helicopter gun ship you hear overhead. He's going to give us cover. Load up," ordered the driver.

The gun ship was a Huey Helicopter with a Gatling Gun that fairly rained down fire from the sky. The sound it made was a BUREEE, BUREEE rather than an explosion when it fired. Every third bullet was a tracer and it literally looked like a stream of fire from heaven. Of all our weapons, this may have been the most feared by small VC units.

The twenty miles back to Camp was made in an eerie silence. Each man was dealing with his fear and the possibility of an immediate death in his own way. For myself, I was thinking of my family and how tragic it would be for my children to grow up without a father. I was thinking of how Peg would react when she received the news. The jeep came up the incline and stopped in front of the BAS. We jumped out and ran inside. I shook myself from side to side just to make sure I was really safe. The big thirty-gallon GI can buried in the ground up to its lip was full of cold beer. There was a lot less of it the following morning.

A few days later, I found myself bending over a Vietnamese woman lying on the ground. I touched the side of her temple and moved the pieces of crushed bone. I could see part of her brain exposed.

"Is she dead?" the Battalion Commander asked.

"Yes, sir," I replied.

"Are you absolutely sure?" What I really wanted to say was, "Can't you see her fucking brain sticking out of her goddamn head? How fucking smart you got to be to know that she's dead? Even a dumb-ass mother fucking grunt like you should be able to figure that out," but I held my peace.

"I'm sure, sir." One of the six-bys had come barreling over the bridge that crossed the river near our camp. It hadn't swerved sufficiently to miss the old blue bus that was crowded with Vietnamese civilians, pigs and chickens that was waiting to cross. I thought it strange that there was only one casualty, considering the damage to the old bus. One old woman was desperately trying to hang on to a thirty-or-so-pound pig she had tied with an old piece of rope. His loud squealing as the old woman tugged at him, mixed with the clucking of the chickens, made the moment seem surreal.

"We'll MEDEVAC her to division and try to find out where she's from. Some compensation will have to be made to the family. Doc, you stay here until the chopper comes," ordered the Battalion Commander.

I was within a stone's throw of the camp and had been left alone with the Vietnamese. After several moments, a middle-aged woman walked to where the body lay and gently covered her face with a white lace handkerchief. I was embarrassed that I hadn't thought to do that myself.

The chevrons on my collar had lost their paint and my tropical utilities were faded from the months of wear. I had learned to harden my heart and numb my brain with alcohol in an effort to maintain my sanity in the midst of the cruelty brought on by the war. I was becoming a different person and I didn't like the feeling. I reflected on some of the more disturbing events of the past couple of weeks. A few days earlier, Dan and I had gone to Battalion Headquarters in Phu Bai to pick up supplies. We had caught a ride with a big six-by whose crew was in the process of exchanging the old M-14 for the newer M-16. We had come upon a small Vil a few miles out where a CAC detail was stationed. I stood up to stretch my legs and looked down in the midst of the gathering. Propped up against a small building directly in front of me was a dead Vietnamese. He had been stripped naked and was propped up in a manner that his genitals were exposed in a grotesque manner. The driver was talking from the cab of the truck to one of the marines near the corpse.

"What's with the naked Zip?"

"ARVN killed his ugly ass last night."

"What do you have him out there like that for?"

"Had quite a few probes on the perimeter past few days. We thought it would be a good idea if the VC see what will happen to them if they fuck with us." I felt the presence of evil and the hair stood up on the back of my neck. The ARVNS killing Garbage Girty was one thing. But the idea that American Marines would have such little regard for another human being was incomprehensible to me. There was something inherently wrong here and I was ashamed. I was too meek and cowardly to voice my opposition. A few days before, one of the Staff Sergeants from the sniper section had come to the BAS.

"Doc, I think I need to talk to someone."

"What's troubling you, Sarg?"

"I been in the mother fucking Bush too long."

"How long you been out there, Sarg?"

"Ever since we got in country." He was built like a football player and his voice was quiet and controlled but beads of sweat stood out on his handsome, black face.

"Sit down, Sarg." He took a seat.

"Tell me what's going on."

"You know I go out and live in the mother fucking trees and shit with my BAR (Browing Automatic Rifle). I take all the stuff I need with me and just make myself comfortable. I spend my days scanning the area with my scope. If I see someone who looks like a VC, I blow their ass away. The other day I was watching this Vietnamese come across the patty. A couple of six-bys were passing and all of a sudden he acts like he's hoeing rice. I zoomed in on him and his hoe was an AK-47. I dropped him right on the spot."

"Damn! That has to be tough."

"Doc, what's happening is, I'm beginning to get off on this shit. I love that look of surprise on their face when that round hits them right between the eyes. It ain't normal what I'm feeling, Doc. Something bad is happening to me."

"Sarg, let's get you back to the Medical Battalion to talk to someone." The Sergeant hadn't returned. Maybe they admitted him or transferred him out of country. The noise of the chopper brought me back to the moment. The war was changing all of us. The thought crossed my mind maybe we should all get blown away. How could we ever go back and live a normal family life after all of this?

It was the evening of December 23rd. We were pretty pleased that the United States and North Vietnam had agreed to a cease-fire over the Christmas Holiday and the coming 1967 New Year. The sound of the bombs being dropped by the high flying B-52s had ceased. The Top Stew Burner had promised us turkey with all the trimmings on the 25th. The heavy monsoon rain beating down on the tent gave us a cozy feeling. We had broken up our card game around 2300. I had just dozed off. The sound of someone talking loud startled me awake; then I heard the motor of a jeep start. I didn't hear anything that really alarmed me so, after assuring myself all was well, I closed my eyes again.

"Doc!" someone yelled through the flap of the tent.

"Yeah!" I answered. The Sergeant Major pushed the flap of the tent aside and stuck his head in.

"Strike your tent, we're breaking camp," he said and immediately left.

"What the hell?" complained Dan and he sat up on the edge of his cot and lit the Coleman lantern. Doctor Steinman came into the tent.

"3/26 took four hundred rounds of 180-millimeter mortars last night somewhere up near the DMZ. We've been ordered to go give them support."

"I thought they weren't supposed to be any major troop movements," whined Dan, as he reached for his utilities.

The camp was alive in the darkness. We knew it was useless to offer any resistance, orders were orders. We got dressed and rolled up our seven-eighty-two gear with our personal items. Most of the medical gear was still packed in the tactical boxes. We quickly nailed the lids shut and closed the metal container that held the Dispensatory Set. We, then, carried it all outside and set it in front of the tent. I looked toward the sound of the throbbing engines of the big six-bys. I could see the rain falling in torrents in the headlight beams.

"WE'LL TAKE IT DOWN LIKE IT WENT UP," yelled Dan and started kicking the pegs that held the guidelines down in the soft earth. We dropped the big, wet tent in the red clay and rolled it into a regulation fold. The normal four-hundred-and eighty-pound tent had at least doubled its weight. When our truck, arrived we attempted, in vain, to load it ourselves. No one else was having it any easier with their wet burdens. We joined forces, even the Chaplain helped and, little by little, we rolled the massive canvases on one of the six-bys.

We were already soaked to the bone and the rain pelted our faces as we climbed in the back of the open-air truck. We got as close as we could against the cab and hunkered down. My teeth chattered and my body shook as the truck lurched forward into the night. We huddled together under our ponchos trying to share each other's body heat. Three hours later, we arrived at the Phu Bai Airport and were taken to the hangars where the Marine Helicopters were housed. We disembarked and fell into formation. At first light, we were to be airlifted. We waited silently in the driving, cold rain. Lights came on in the hooches where the Airwing's crews worked. I could see them lighting their little "Gook Stoves" and placing them on their desks. The hangars rolling open were a welcome sight. I expected they would invite us in out of the cold rain. A half-hour past.

"Fuckers don't want us dripping in there and rust out the grating," someone said. I looked at Dan. His face was purple and contorted with rage. My own anger was so great I think it must have served to keep me from going into complete hypothermia. I'm still not crazy about the Airwing to this day.

The fog had the airfield completely cloaked. We stood waiting until 1400. Finally, the word came down that there was a possibility the choppers couldn't get up. They ordered us back on the trucks. Three hours later, we arrived somewhere on the other side of Hue City, right at dusk.

"No time for a permanent camp. We're going to move off the road a few meters and I want you to dig yourselves a fighting hole," ordered the Battalion Commander. We hiked about a quarter of a mile and came to the crest of a little rise.

"Spread out and dig in," someone yelled. We dropped our gear and retrieved our entrenching tools. Dan hit the ground with his.

"This ground is as hard as hammered hell," he complained. I figured he was exaggerating and took a good swing.

"Damn," I said, as my teeth jarred from hitting the hard earth. Doctor Steinman hit the earth a couple of times.

"I'm sleeping right here on top of the ground," he said and unfurled his rubber lady and sat down. "John, did you pour the last bit of that scotch in your canteen?" he asked.

"Yes, sir," I answered and unscrewed the cap of my canteen and passed it to him. He took a couple of nice jolts and handed it to Dan.

"Well, you damn fools can do what you want to. But I'm digging me a hole," I informed my comrades and started to dig. The other corpsmen had started to shovel out spoonfuls of dirt from the hard earth.

"We'll share a hole, John," Dan said and walked over to where I was working. It was well after dark when we had the hole deep enough to where we could lie down and nothing vital would show above ground.

Two inches of water had accumulated during our excavation. Dr. Steinman looked quite content on his rubber lady covered up with his poncho. I had an idea we were going to have company if the mortars started flying. We passed the canteen around one more time and Dan and I climbed in our hole.

We hadn't slept at all the previous night. I soon fell into a fitful sleep filled with nightmares. When I moved my legs, I could feel the water squishing between my thighs. It was a very long night and I was happy to see the break of dawn. It was Christmas day. One of the marine drivers had drained some oil from the crankcase of his big truck. He poured it on an old towel and set it on fire. We gathered around the flickering blaze.

"Aren't you glad you ain't on some old rusty ass ship, Doc?" one of the marines joked with Dan.

"You're about a dumb fuck, aren't you?" he answered dryly.

"Let's move down range," came the order from the Battalion Commander. We packed up and humped down the hill a few hundred meters. Doctor Steinman was called away to a staff meeting. He returned within the hour and directed us where to set up the GP. We knew that if the choppers couldn't get in we might very well have our hands full if we started receiving casualties.

"First, we'll dig fighting holes for ourselves. Then we'll put up the GP tent," he instructed us.

The ground was softer in the new area and we made good headway. In a short time, we had a hole about five feet long and two feet wide. Dan was down in the hole digging, and I had climbed out to give him room to work. The sun had peeped out and he had taken his shirt off. Suddenly, he looked up at me and threw his entrenching tool down and stood looking off in the distance. I thought he was going to cry.

"I've never been so disgusted in my life," he said. It struck me as comical and I had to suppress the urge to laugh.

"Don't worry, Dan. We're going to get out of here," I reassured him with a smile. C-rations had been delivered and we took a rest to eat. Doctor Steinman had found the turkey ration.

"Looks like I'll have Christmas dinner after all," he chuckled. The Shore Party had moved into the area with a couple of bulldozers. Doctor Steinman sat watching them work. "Why don't we get one of them dozers over here and have them excavate the side of that hill over there. We'll put the tent in it and will only have to fill enough sandbags to fortify the front." he suggested. We all agreed it was a great idea.

Dan made his way over to one of the drivers and a few minutes later we were putting up the tent well back inside the hill. It had started to rain again. "Mail Call," someone yelled and came down the hill carrying several letters and a few packages. One of the packages was for me. I went into the tent and got my cot set up, sat down and opened my package. It was a pair of boxer shorts with a big red Santa Claus on the front with him driving his reindeer. At the top of his sleigh were two little silver bells. I was soaked to the bone; there wasn't one dry rag in my seven-eighty-two gear. I went to one of the blanket sets and took out a new blanket. It had been wrapped in waterproof canvas. The pungent smell of mothballs floated up to me. I held the heavy, wool garment to my nose and took a good whiff. I stripped down and put on my new shorts and rolled up in the blanket. A short time later I fell into a deep sleep. I kept my Santa shorts for many years. What Peg sent me as a gag, became one of my most memorable gifts.

The next morning I let my arm fall off the cot and felt it hit water. I opened one eye and looked down and saw a shower shoe floating by. Then I heard a swish, swish and looked toward the end of my cot where the sound had come from. Doctor Steinman had his utility pants legs rolled up to his knees and was wading through a foot and a half of water. We had neglected to put in drainage furrows around the tent.

"I've got to get someone out here to relieve me if I'm going to make it out to Hawaii tomorrow," Doctor Stieneman informed no one in particular as he sloshed through the water gathering up his floating toilet articles. Frankly, I didn't think he had a snowball chance in hell of getting back to the Battalion area that day. I underestimated his resolve. I was surprised a short time later when I heard him on the field phone. "YEAH, TODAY," he yelled into the receiver. Then he stopped and looked at me. "John, you want me to get someone out to relieve you and Dan?" he asked.

"Hell, yes," I answered. There were other first class petty officers in the Battalion that hadn't been on a forward operation since we had arrived in country. I figured they were due. About four hours later, trucks arrived bearing the poor devils that were to relieve us. We helped them carry their gear into the muddy tent that we had just drained the water from. The look of shock on their faces at seeing what horrendous conditions they had come to was disconcerting to me. There wasn't anyway that we could make it any easier for them. They'd have to make their own way.

"We'd like to stay and help you guys but we have to go if we're going to catch that truck out of here," explained Dan as we hoisted our seven-eighty-two-gear on our backs and headed for the six-by that sat idling a few meters away.

The trucks arrived in Phu Bai just as it was getting dark. We stopped and disembarked in front of the Command Post. Dan and I recovered our gear and started walking up between the rows of hooches toward the BAS.

"Looks like smoke coming from our hooch," commented Dan. I looked, and sure enough, smoke was rolling out of a black stovepipe that was sticking up out of the roof.

"I don't see any pipes coming from the others." I replied. We climbed up the three steps and entered the hooch. A warm toasty feeling permeated our living quarters. Chief Clements was sitting in a chair next to his cot reading the New Testament. Upon seeing us, he laid it on his cot.

"Been expecting you," he said and pointed to two empty cots at the far end of the hooch. The flame from the oil burner twinkled and cast a shadow across the floor in the semidarkness. A couple of new men I hadn't met were watching us in silence. I dumped my gear on the cot.

"How in the hell you get a stove?" I asked turning back to the Chief.

"Half of Hotel Company came down with trench foot. The doctor said we needed to bring them into Garrison and get them out of their wet boots. I was able to get a couple of these old oil burners from division so I decided to put us up one," the Chief explained.

"S-4 about shit his pants when he saw the Chief up there sawing a hole in the roof. He came running over here and told him we weren't authorized to alter these buildings," laughed Kirkpatrick as he started helping me unpack my wet utilities from my haversack.

"I told him since the hole was already cut I couldn't do nothing about it, and I sure was sorry, but we may as well go ahead and put up a stove," grinned the Chief.

"Silly fucking marines rather freeze than do anything that makes sense," commented Dan.

It was good to be warm and feel safe. We had missed the big turkey feed but New Years was coming and Dan and I were getting ready. We had made a hike to the Medical Battalion cutting through the back of the camp on the thirtieth.

"John, we can follow this path and go to the big blow out at MEDBAT tomorrow night."

"Yeah, great idea, Dan. You think we can find our way back in the dark?"

"Who gives a shit? Can't get lost here in Phu Bai anyway." The next evening found us in the packed club. Marines and corpsmen from every part of the division had managed, in one way or another, to get to the club. Men dressed in jungle utilities wearing their weapons jostled and joked with each other and told their war stories. The club had a strange custom, which I had never seen before, nor have I witnessed since.

"LISTEN UP! LISTEN UP!" one of the men in the forward part of the club called out and things quieted down. "LET'S DO A HYMN FOR SENIOR CHIEF WILLIAMS," he continued. He then held his glass up, pointing toward a ruddy looking old Chief sitting at the table with him. Everyone raised their glasses and, in unison, sang out, "HIM, HIM, HIM, FUCK HIM," followed by loud boisterous laughing that could surely have been heard by the VC on the outskirts of the perimeter. The Chief didn't join in the toast but it must have been great fun for him as he gave a wide smile to all the participants. Apparently no one was exempt from this special honor as it was drank to almost everyone in the club that evening.

About eight, the party turned sour for Dan and didn't do much for me either. In the middle of the festivities, Dan looked around the crowded room at the different people in attendance.

"You know how many of these sorry motherfuckers haven't ever been outside the goddamn perimeter?" he asked me. I took a good look around. A large number of people who worked in the Administration Section of the Division Surgeon's Office were in attendance.

"Don't worry about it, Dan," I said and shrugged it off.

"No, by-god. These sorry son-of-a-bitches will get their tickets punched for promotion and are going to be wearing the same campaign ribbons as the people who have served in the bush. You can bet your ass we're going to have to listen to these sorry fucks tell about how they won the war the rest of our careers."

"Probably," I laughed.

"You know the same pricks that ain't worth a fuck here in country are the same ones that are going to be getting disability for combat fatigue." The Chief who detailed corpsmen to the various units and worked out of the Division Surgeon's Office was seated a few feet away. Dan had a special dislike for him. He kept eyeing him with hatred as we continued to drink.

"I think I'm just going to shoot that sorry motherfucker," he commented glaring at the Chief. "It's the closest he's ever going to get to seeing combat," he raved. I knew he wasn't really serious, but I also knew the slightest thing could set him off. The memory of sleeping in a wet foxhole was too fresh in his mind.

"Come on, Dan. It's getting close to lights out," I urged and, a short time later, we left the club and staggered drunkenly toward the compound. Arriving at the barbed wire that we had moved aside the day before, we found it had been put back into place. As we kicked it aside and cursed the sharp barbs, a young marine appeared in the darkness.

"Halt, who goes there?" he challenged.

"Who in the fuck wants to know?" answered Dan as we continued on our way.

"Advance and be recognized," he ordered.

"You'se en Garrison mudder fucker, you'se en Garrison," laughed Dan hysterically and we kept walking.

"Assholes," muttered the young marine.

A few days after the first of the year, I was under the supply fly tent (open-air tent) with the senior corpsman from Golf Company, getting him some things together to take out to the field. I looked up and saw Doctor Steinman walking toward me. He had completed his six months in the infantry and had been transferred to the Medical Battalion shortly after his return from R&R to Hawaii. He had a wide smile on his face and I was happy to see him. 2/26 had changed a lot from the first days of our arrival at Lone Tree Hill in Da Nang.

"Get all the Vietnamese wormed yet, John?" he joked and grabbed my hand.

"Still working on it," I laughed.

"John, they've sent out a flyer to all the units looking for someone skilled in Bacteriology. The Divisions Preventive Medicine Section has a whole bacteriological laboratory and no one knows how to set it up. I talked to the officer in charge over there and I told him you had been the Senior Petty Officer in charge of the Bacteriology Department at Camp Pendleton Naval Hospital. He wants you to come over there this morning and talk to him and Senior Chief Middleman." I tacked the lid back on the tactical box as I listened.

"I think I may just be their man," I chuckled. Ted slapped me on the shoulder and smiled laughingly.

"I'll tell them you're coming," he said.

I stood watching him walk back toward the Medical Battalion. He had come on foot to tell me. Destiny had tied the boy from Rural Arkansas and the Doctor, who would later teach Medicine at Harvard and do some of the country's most important research, together for a short while. He and I would be the only two medical people from 2/26 who stayed in touch in the following years.

On the 24th of January, 1967, I checked into 3rd Medical Battalion. That same day Dan went to see the Chief in charge of detail at the Division Surgeons Office to demand he be transferred out of the infantry. A few days later, he was transferred to an Artillery Battery at Dong Ha within artillery range of North Vietnam. My life was about to change for the better and Dan's for the worst. I wouldn't see him again until we boarded the same plane on our return trip back to the States.

The First Class in charge of personnel at the Medical Battalion was one of my old acquaintances from my Lab. School days by the name of Art Conger.

"Damn, Messer, good to see you," he greeted and took my records. Turning to the field phone that set on the desk just behind him, he gave the lever a couple of turns. "Goggins, can you come by and pickup one of our new First Class and get him set up over there in your hooch?" he asked, hung up, then turned back to me. "You're going to love the hell out of this place after where you've been. No patrols, no operations, just finish your thirteen months and wait for your flight number," he smiled.

A First Class, about five-feet, six-inches shuffled into the office. He was of a slight build and his drooped over shoulders gave the impression that the weight of the cigarette in his mouth was pulling him forward. Ignoring Conger, he looked at me.

"Ready?" he asked flippantly like we could have been old friends or never met. I got the impression it wouldn't have made any difference to Goggins.

"Yeah," I answered and I reached for my gear.

"Let me give you a hand," he said and grabbed my seven-eighty-two gear and slung it over his back like it was a cotton blanket.

"Thanks, Goggins," called out Conger as we were leaving.

"See you at "him" singing tonight," he replied over his shoulder. Goggins led me between a couple of wooden structures and on passed the chow hall to a row of five hooches. We went up the steps of the first one and I followed him back to an empty cot. There was a Vietnamese woman, about forty years old, sweeping the floor. She was wearing the standard black pajamas and white blouse. Her cone hat hung down the back of her neck, held in place with a white string chinstrap. "BOOM, BOOM, BOOM, BOOM," chanted Goggins and the little woman smiled and slid across the floor away from him, seemingly never taking her feet off the floor. "FUCKING ZIPPER HEAD," he teased as he dropped my gear on the cot. "That's Missy BOOM, one of the VC's forward observers and our house mouse. You'll know you've been in country too long when she starts looking good," he jokingly added.

"Bonk, bonk, bink, bink," went our Missy BOOM.

"FUCK YOU," replied Goggins.

"VC come get you tonight," Missy BOOM threatened.

"Here, I got this for you to sleep in; it gets cold as hell in here at night," commented Goggins as he rolled a heavy, fur lined sleeping bag out on my cot. I looked around and saw that all the occupants in my new home had one. "I work in supply," explained Goggins.

"Thanks, Goggins," I said. I was beginning to like him.

The Preventive Medicine Section did indeed have a Bacteriological Laboratory Kit. Unfortunately, it was still in a box somewhere back in Da Nang. But not to worry they were still in the process of moving and it would be coming up a little later. In the meanwhile, I would be working with HM1 Jake Jacobson and HM1 Andy Damian to build the countertops and shelving space for the coming laboratory. But, the priority for the moment was to build a storage shed for the many pesticides we were receiving on a daily basis. The three of us were the junior men in the Preventive Medicine Section and its only real work force. We also had mosquito control, which included cold fogging with Malathion out of the back of a big PC every evening, and rodent control.

Jake was about six-foot-four and thin as a rail. He was the nervous type and very intense. When he went somewhere, he walked very fast, leaning slightly forward, like he was in a hurry to take the next step; he talked pretty much the same way. When he tried to make a point, and it wasn't understood right away, he would start to stutter. Andy, on the other hand, was a calm Filipino who had been a Lieutenant in the Filipino Army some twenty-five years earlier during the Second World War. Andy was used to not being understood and spoke only when it was absolutely necessary. His quick smile and willingness to agree on almost anything more than compensated for any lack of communication skills he might have had. That is to say, with everyone except Jake. Jake, being senior to us in time in grade, felt we needed to match his tempo and get excited when he did, which was pretty much all the time. The calmer Andy would appear, the more upset Jake would become. He would then talk a little faster to try to make his point, which in turn caused him to stutter.

Finally after a month of arguing, cursing and fighting amongst ourselves, I had a laboratory. The kit had come down and I was surprised at how complete it was. In a very short time, I was equipped to identify most routine bacteriological pathogens and perform Ova and Parasite studies (examine feces for internal worms). And, oh, yes, Jake decided I would be assigned to rodent control within the compound. After all, he and Andy had commenced to do routine sanitary inspections in the confines of Division Headquarters and didn't have time for this very important function.

"Now, John you got to put these twenty live rat traps out around the compound and run them every morning before the Vietnamese workers come on board. If you don't, they'll rob the damn things and kill the rats and take them home. They consider it a delicacy," Jake explained.

"You have to be shitting me," I answered.

"No, I'm not. The problem is, the fleas jump off the dead rat onto people within a few minutes after they die. That's how people get Plague.

"Great! How in the hell do I keep from getting it?"

"We got this big metal box here that's air tight," he reached up on one of our recently-constructed shelves where we had stored the unpacked mount out gear and grabbed a big metal container, laid it on the floor and opened the lid.

"We pour a bunch of Chloroform on an old rag and throw it in here with the rats. The fumes kill the rats and the fleas along with them. We then comb out the rat's hair to recover the fleas so we can identify the species of the flea. The only one that carries the disease is *Xenopsylla cheopis*." Jake had gotten down on his knees to demonstrate how this combing procedure would be done. I gave Andy an incredulous look. He laughed silently as he watched the demonstration. I was thinking that maybe I should have stayed in 2/26. Jake was serious about doing his part in winning the war and taking a few rats and fleas out was one sure way of doing it.

"Okay, so what do I use for bait?" I asked, picking up one of the live traps. Jake took the trap out of my hand.

"Peanut butter wrapped in a 4X4 inch gauze. Just tie it on this trigger right here," he said, flipping the wire-trigger that was hanging down. That afternoon, I put out my traps in strategic locations and my safari commenced. I was quite successful right away and, in no time at all, Jake was happily combing his dead rats in search of the dreaded *Xenopsylla cheopis*.

The Vietnamese rats must have been more intelligent than your average ol' rat, as they would often outsmart me and steal my bait. I had prepared for these unfortunate losses in advance by making a large number of peanut butter baits to take with me to replace the stolen ones. Being moist, and not wanting them to dry out, I hit on the ingenious plan of carrying them in one of the brown cups that was used to collect stool specimens.

I had been attempting to do fecal studies for internal parasites on all the Vietnamese ladies that worked inside the compound for the past couple of weeks. I would dutifully perform the procedure and report my findings of whipworm, hookworm and roundworm to the Examining Center. I would, of course, then warn against worming them. Now, the ladies must have found it rather strange that an American Boxey (Vietnamese for doctor) somewhere had such an interest in their doo-doo. They were, of course, very familiar with the container that they had used to transport their excrement. Misey BOOM and her friends, of course, had no idea that I was the one who took such a personal interest in such things.

As fate would have it, one morning, I was late in running my traps. Around 1000, I had recovered a nice fat rat that I had managed to outsmart and went by the hooch to pick up a pack of cigarettes. Now, it was break time for Missy BOOM and her companions. When I entered, a half dozen of them were squatted down having a snack and, no doubt, discussing current events. I walked to my cot and set the trap on the floor and the container of bait on top of it. The chatter immediately picked up and the laughter began to roll. Now, the Vietnamese are very curious people and I could see right away they were trying to put together why I was carrying a box of doo doo around in one hand and a live trapped rat in the other. One of the bolder ladies came over to where I was opening my footlocker and flipped up the lid to my bait box. Seeing the little round balls of brown stuff she glanced over at the others and clapped her hand over her mouth; they all screamed with glee.

"Don't fuck with that trap," I warned as she moved the lever up and down jabbering all the while to the others. I was busy and didn't think she would have the audacity to push the lever down to open the trap door. I was very mistaken. She had not only pushed it open but had locked it in that position. I looked down to see the rat cowering in the corner. I reached to close the door. Alas, too late, he darted out. "GODDAM IT," the Boxey who trapped rats with doo doo screamed. The tent came alive with activity. The ladies grabbed their thatch brooms and they set off in hot pursuit of the escaped animal. Through the hooch they ran, beating the rodent in the head with their brooms. Cots went flying in one-direction, footlockers and blankets and rubber ladies in the other; around and around they went. I stood watching the action absolutely astonished. One of the ladies had hit him a good one upside the head and fractured his skull. His skull bone protruded on one side and his jawbone on the other and he had begun to bleed; the pursuit raged on. Finally, in his efforts to escape he ran back in the trap. I quickly closed the door; a cry of victory went up from the ladies. I grabbed my doo doo box and poor wounded rat and fled by the rear door, leaving the women in hysterical laughter. One of the Chiefs was passing the hooch and had stopped at hearing the commotion.

"What the hell is going on in there?" he asked.

"You wouldn't believe it if I told you, Chief," I answered and kept walking.

There was a road that passed between our hooch and the grave registration tent. Helicopters brought in the dead and the wounded all hours of the day and night. The sound of the moving of the previous KIAs to be airlifted to the States, mixed with arrival of new casualties, were constant reminders that the war raged on. The Phu Bai Airport in front of the MEDBAT was a favorite target of the VC's Mortarmen when the fog had us socked in. Occasionally, they would drop a few rounds into Medical Battalion just to keep us rattled.

The philosophy that the lower ranks be put at greater risk might seem cruel, and perhaps it is, to those that have not studied the art of war. But the fact remains, the higher rank one has obtained, the more skill and experience that individual has in his or her field. This, obviously, makes them more valuable to their unit. If SNCO, Senior Petty Officers and Officers were put in harms way in the same numbers as junior troops, an Army at war would quickly lose its leaders. Chief Petty Officers that were required to send nineteen and twenty-year-olds to their deaths, while not taking any real risk of their own, often times became guilt ridden to the point of it influencing their judgment.

The Chief in charge of the MEDEVACS had taken it on himself to take turns with his corpsmen to fly into hot spots. He was well known in the MEDBAT for two reasons. One, when he came to the club he wore two bandoleers of ammunition; one strapped over each shoulder. The second, he was the brother of the then-well-known actor, Tab Hunter. On one occasion there was a firefight and a call for a MEDEVAC. The Chief took the flight and upon their arrival at the LZ, he left the chopper to retrieve a wounded man. In the process, he was killed. There is no question of his bravery, but the loss of his leadership to his unit was a great tragedy. I believe the advice, "Don't do anything stupid to get yourself killed but always do your duty," given to me by Chief Clements was very sound, and I adhered to it.

The mortar attacks surrounding Phu Bai never lasted more than two minutes. I never jumped out of my hole and dashed off into the dark looking for someone who had started screaming, nor did I encourage others to do so. I felt it was better to wait until the mortars had stopped falling and the lights were on. I never saw anyone do anything during that short period of time that made a big enough impression on me that I changed my mind.

I don't have to tell you how tuned-in we were to the sound of mortars. Like everyone else, we had our share of pranksters and just damn fools. One old, gray headed Chief by the name of Sam McCain loved to wake us up at five thirty in the morning by throwing a baseball size rock on our tin roof a couple of times a week. All the cursing, pleading and threats only encouraged him. We finally formed a committee and went and complained to the senior man in his hooch. Two days later, "WHAM" in the middle of the night. That was the final straw. The next evening we went to the club and plotted our revenge. Ramondo, a big Filipino who was somewhat psychotic, red-headed Rogers, who loved a good fight, a big, overbearing Staff Sergeant from the Biological Detection Team, Goggins and myself made up the war council.

"I think we ought to set their mother fucking hooch on fire," suggested Ramondo. We all laughed. "I'm serious," he responded, indignantly.

"No, we can't destroy any government property or do anything they can use to bring charges against us," commented Rogers. We continued to drink and look for a suitable plan for revenge. With each drink, our ideas became more outlandish. It was 2130, only a half-hour to lights out when we finally hit on a strategy.

"Listen, let's go get a trash can and fill it with rocks and when they're sleeping good, we'll throw the whole shit and caboodle on their hut," suggested the Staff Sergeant.

"Great idea, but why don't we pour about a ½ gallon of lighter fluid on top of the rocks and light them off before we throw 'em?" asked Goggins.

"HELL, YEAH," clamored Ramondo. It sounded good to me and in a short time we had gathered up several containers of lighter fluid, thirty or so baseball size rocks and put them in a regular desk size GI can. We stood poised between the club and the club's storeroom. At 2230, we decided the time had come.

"I'll pour in the fluid," volunteered Goggins and started pouring the cans of lighter fluid onto the rocks.

"I'll light the motherfuckers," replied Ramondo and lit his lighter.

WHOOFFF! The can went, sending a flame of fire into the air three or four feet.

"THERE YOU GO," shrilled Goggins and shoved the can in my hand. I grabbed it and ran about halfway to the enemy's stronghold and let it fly, can and all. I darted between two hooches and was nearly to the other street when I heard it hit with an earth shattering, BANG! I looked back to see a stream of flaming stones rolling off the roof in every direction. The excess fluid was burning and six feet of flame cascaded to the earth. Men came flying out both ends of the hooch and dived into their fighting holes. They must've thought Old Ho Chi Minh himself had arrived.

I quickly found my hooch and jumped into my sleeping bag. Lights had come on all along hooch row and a tremendous hue and cry went up. The men who had come under attack had by now figured out, more or less, what had happened. Had we been thinking straight, we would have gotten up and turned our lights on too. Our plan hadn't gone that far so we had to settle for pretending to be asleep. My heart was pumping adrenaline to my brain along with the alcohol as I lay and waited for what I knew was surely to come. The Ranking Petty Officer from the enemy's camp soon appeared at our door.

"Turn on the goddamn lights and get your asses out here," he yelled. Goggins got up and snapped the lights on and pretended to be surprised. I got up out of my sleeping bag and sat on the edge of my cot. The Chief had stepped up on the first step and opened the door to our living quarters. I sprang to the door.

"Don't come in here, Chief," I proclaimed and stationed myself firmly in the doorway with my hands on the 2 X 4 door facings. I was standing about three feet higher than he was. I was ready to kick him in the face if he took one more step. He hesitated. Ramondo grabbed his forty-five out of his footlocker, chambered a round and ran to my side.

Meanwhile, a huge crowd had gathered outside our door. In a few minutes, the OOD (Officer of the Day) appeared. He walked up the steps and I stood aside to let him in.

"What's going on in here?" he asked and marched up the center of our berthing quarters.

No one answered. The seriousness of the situation had begun to dawn on us. Ramondo had put his pistol away and lay down without saying anything. The rest of us followed his example. The OOD turned off the lights. "There will be a full log entry on this incident and you can explain it to the XO (Executive Officer)," he said after a moment of silence. I heard the screen door slam shut as he walked down the steps. "Back to your huts," he ordered the grumbling men in the street.

"ASSHOLES," someone yelled over their shoulder as they strolled back to their hooch.

"That's just a taste of what's coming if you throw another fucking rock over here, McCann," called back Ramondo.

Fortunately for us, there had been an international incident in the Officer's Club the night before and the XO was too busy to worry about something over in hooch row. Seems one of the Marine Corps Lieutenants took offense at an entertainment troop of three men and three ladies from Australia. He informed them that dancing around half naked with their lovers in front of a bunch of sex-starved combatants was nothing less than cruel. He suggested if they wanted to really do some good, they should fuck everybody in camp and let their boyfriends watch. A fight ensued in the Officer's Club and the entertainers ended up having to be protected by a squad of marines.

McCann's throwing arm must have gone out, as he never threw another rock again until the morning he left for the States. Rest in peace, Sam. You had the last word after all.

Although I made light of identifying disease vectors a little earlier, one should not underestimate its importance to the mission of an Army in the field. General McArthur lost more men to malaria during the Second War World than he did to the Imperial Japanese Army. The flea that Jake was so conscientiously wanting to destroy was responsible for the plague in Europe during the fourteenth century. According to some reports, it killed more than eighty percent of the population in some areas. I was not unaware of these things, and although I found some of my tasks in Preventive Medicine mundane, I knew they were important.

I had the distinction of being the only man in the Third Medical Battalion who had the expertise to isolate, identify and do a drug susceptibility test on disease-producing pathogens. I had gained these skills through my suffering under the tutelage of LCDR Georgia Simpson and the awesome responsibility the pathologist had placed on me at Camp Pendleton. I was now reaping the rewards of my labor and enjoying the prestige from both enlisted and officer alike.

Although it was common knowledge Vietnam was endemic to Bubonic Plague, the American Forces had never been able to culture the organism. The big support activity in Da Nang was clamoring for someone to get them the live pathogen. Unbeknownst to me, our Commanding Officer had a keen interest in the Third Medical Battalion being the first to isolate the infamous Yersinia pestie. He had advised the Division Surgeons Office to put the word out to the surrounding CAC units if any of the local Vietnamese died with swelling in the groin area he was to be notified. It is little wonder, that one Saturday morning after a late Friday of binge drinking, he sent for me. Arriving at his private quarters with my flushed face and throbbing head, I knocked on the door.

"Come in!" he called.

"It's me, sir, Messer from the Preventive Medicine section. You wanted to see me?" He came to the door and looked at me.

"Are you the HM1 that does the Bacteriology?"

"Yes, sir, I am."

"A woman has died in a Village a few miles from here. It looks like she may have had Bubonic Plague. I want to go there and see if we can establish the cause of death. If she did die from plague, I'd like to try to culture the organism. How could we do that?" I was wondering if he was going to go personally.

"Well, sir, if she has a bubo in the inguinal area we could just inject it with normal saline and aspirate it. If there are any live organisms present we should be able to recover them. I'll take a tube of Thioglycolate Enrichment Broth with us and we can inoculate the broth on site."

"Do you think you can isolate the organism if she was infected?"

"It'll be a new experience for me, sir, but, I don't see why not."

"How much equipment will we need to take with us?"

"Thirty cc's of saline, a 10cc syringe and a tube of media."

"Is that all, you think?"

"Yes, sir, I'll do the rest in the Laboratory when we get back."

"Very well! Go get what you'll need and meet me in front of S-1 in a half hour."

When I got to S-1, a PC and jeep sat waiting with their drivers ready to go. In less than a minute, the Commanding Officer arrived in full flak gear wearing his pistol. He motioned me into the back of the jeep and we sped off to the perimeter and Highway One with the PC trailing close behind. A half-mile out, we came to a civilian truck that had run over a mine. The engine had been blown completely out of the vehicle. It had made a hole the size of a Volkswagen in the middle of the road and was still smoking. A squad of marines came rushing across the rice paddy toward us. They were being led by a Second Lieutenant the size of a giant. Upon seeing the eagle on the Commanding Officer's collar, he walked over to the jeep and took his helmet off (Commissioned Officers weren't saluted in the field for obvious reasons). I saw a string of human ears hanging off of his belt. He looked to me like he was having the time of his life. As the squad drew near, I couldn't help but notice how animated they all were. I knew from my own experience, that this kind of enthusiasm came from holding one's leader in very high regard. The whole squad had got my attention. I studied the big man to see if I could identify the quality about him that so motivated his men.

"Lots of activity around here, sir. Maybe you should turn back," commented the Lieutenant.

"Just going a few miles to one of the CAC units," explained the CO, indicating for the driver to proceed around the hole in the road.

"Good luck, sir," the Lieutenant called after us as we sped away. After a few minutes, I looked back at the squad. They had left the road and were halfway across the rice paddy. It looked to me like they were spaced a perfect hundred meters apart. The sight inspired me. I couldn't help but smile.

A few miles farther down the road, we came to a village with a corpsman and a marine waiting on the outskirts. The jeep came to a halt in front of them.

"The body is in the fourth house up on the left, Captain" explained the Corpsman and started walking alongside our jeep. As we approached, I noticed, unlike the other houses, it had a thatched roof. A good habitat for rodents, I thought to myself. Coming to a stop in front of the house, we all got together and went inside. Six or eight of the village women were gathered in the one-room house. A young woman in her early twenties was crying softly and one of the older women was comforting her. The corpse had been laid on a four-foot-high table in preparation for burial.

"How long has she been dead?" asked the CO.

"Died early last evening, sir," answered the Corpsman. The CO then moved her pajamas down exposing the inguinal area and felt of her groin.

"Yes, the lymph gland is swollen," he commented and looked at me. I took the syringe from the sterile package and filled it with 5cc of saline and passed it to him. He injected the swollen groin and aspirated a couple of ccs. I undid the tube, flamed the mouth of it with my cigarette lighter and held it over in front of him. He squirted the cloudy substance into the tube. Offering our condolences through an interpreter, and thanking them for their cooperation, we made our departure.

On returning to the Laboratory, I put the inoculated tube of enrichment broth in the incubator. There was nothing more I could do but wait and hope. The following morning I hurried to the Bacteriological Department. The tube was cloudy with growth and bubbling with gas. I sub-cultured it onto a Blood Agar Plate and waited another twenty-four hours. Everyone in Preventive Medicine was excited about the possibility of us isolating the organism. We held our breath.

The following day was Monday. I got up at six in the morning and rushed to the Lab. I took the culture out of the incubator and removed the top. It was lit up like a Christmas Tree. I did a quick Gram Stain and took a look at it under the microscope. I'd never seen Yersinia pestie before but it fit the description. I immediately notified the Preventive Medicine Officer. He, in turn, notified the CO. I was directed to pack the specimen for shipment immediately and it was flown to Da Nang that afternoon. I was famous for a few days and then it was forgotten. I have kept the Letter of Commendation to remind me that I did, indeed, have my fifteen minutes of fame. But, what I remember most about the whole incident, is that big, gregarious Lieutenant with all those ears dangling from his belt.

Horrible tragedies mixed with stupidity and things that were just downright funny were everyday occurrences. Some of the characters I served with during the Vietnam era are absolutely unforgettable. The main force of the Third Medical Battalion was in Phu Bai but there was a detachment in the encampment at Dong Ha along the DMZ. Preventive Medicine had detailed a team of Technicians to the area to support the on going operations. Different Chief Petty Officers headed up the team from time to time but the two First Class Petty Officers who were assigned to the team while I was there were Ed Durante and his sidekick Bernie Ellis. Ed had a New England accent that fairly twanged when he talked. He tended to the short side and although he wasn't heavy, looked like some of his ancestors might have donated some fat cells to his gene pool. He was blond-headed, blue-eyed and wore thick, navy-issue, black, horned rim glasses. Ed was a complete extrovert and his life's mission, it seemed, was to look for humor in the midst of tragedy and to share it with others. Bernie Ellis was taller, thinner and an introvert. They seemed to be inseparable and I never saw one without the other. Ed would tell his humorous stories and Bernie would laugh as though he hadn't heard them all twenty times before. They would often catch an aircraft down to Phu Bai, stay overnight and get drunk. It was always a delight for me to see them and I would spend as much time with them as was possible.

One evening, we were at the club and Ed was in rare form and full of beer.

"Now, that Herby Jackson, he's what you call a front line, behind the lines, kind of a Chief Petty Officer, don't you see." We all sat listening intently to the New England twang, waiting for Ed to tell us his perception of our notorious friend.

"What that means is, you volunteer to go to the front. That gets you all kind of attention, don't you see. Now, you take all of your gear and a couple of schmucks like Bernie and me with you and when you get there, you immediately get on the next plane and head to the rear of the rear. For example, in Herby's case, he's supposed to be in Dong Ha but he's really in Da Nang, don't you see." Bernie laughed and shook his head from side to side.

"Now, the Preventive Medicine Officer thinks he's out there risking his ass to save his, but the only thing Herby is risking is catching the clap, don't you see."

"Tell 'em what he did to you, Ed," insisted Bernie. Ed pushed his glasses back on his nose, looked down for a moment to collect his thoughts, then moved up on the edge of his chair and told us the following tale.

"Well, what happened was, one time this silly motherfucker tells me, 'Durante, we need to go to the Da Nang Naval Support Activity and get some supplies and drink a couple of beers.' I thought it was a great idea so he didn't have to suggest it twice. Well, we gets down to Da Nang and caught a ride on the back of a big six-by with some grunt and right in the middle of downtown, Herby says to the driver, 'Let us off on the corner. We have to inspect that restaurant over there.' Now, any damn fool knows we're not authorized to inspect food service facilities in downtown Da Nang because everything is off limits to the marines. But this damn grunt, he don't give a shit what we do, so

Herby and I bail out, don't you see. We're walking down this side street when suddenly, Herby grabs me by the arm and jumps into the lobby of this hotel, dragging me with him, don't you see."

Ed had stood up and was demonstrating how Herby had surprised him by jerking him into the lobby so unexpected. We're all down on the floor rolling around with laughter. This encourages Ed to go on and he became more animated with his tale.

"Well, he rents us this suite and we go upstairs to this luxurious room decorated with some of the finest furniture I've ever seen. The two double beds have canopies and are covered with magnificent French linens. Once we are inside, Herby takes a radio out of his AWOL bag, puts it on the bedside stand and plugs it in. He then takes a bottle of scotch out of his bag and sets it on the dresser. Well, that surprised me but when he pulls out a blue smoking jacket, hemmed in golden lace, you know, like the ones you get in Hong Kong, and laid it on the bed, I just about shit. I mean he came prepared for a party, don't you see. Before I can recover from my shock he says, 'I'm going to take a shower, Ed,' and looks me up and down like I'm some kind of a shit and adds, 'You know, Ed, you really need to start trying to show some class. Just because we're in this shit hole don't mean you can't have a little style'."

Ed has us now and is giving a performance you couldn't pay to see in Las Vegas. We are literally doubling over with laughter as Ed continues with his yarn.

"So we start drinking and Herby gets on the horn and asked if they can send him up a hooker. Now, mind you, I didn't have any money with me. I didn't want to ask for a loan. I wouldn't have been able to bear listening to him lecture me on the need to keep a few bucks on me at all times so I could show a little dash. So, anyway, I decided to make the best of it and started hammering the scotch, don't you see. Well, a little later, this really foxy broad shows up and Herby sends me out to wait in the hall. I stayed out there for what I thought was a respectful amount. But, finally, I did knock, and he yells, 'Not yet, Ed.' This goes on a half a dozen times over a two-hour period. Now, I'm really beginning to feel like he's just fucking me around, don't you see. Well, after awhile, I look in and they are both asleep. So I tip toe over to the dresser where Herby's wallet is and take out this big roll of bills that would've choked a horse. I then get down on my hands and knees and crawl over to the bed and reach up and shake Herby's girl."

Ed had gotten down on the floor and showed us how he crawled to the bed.

"I heard her come awake so I say, I'll give you twenty-five dollars to come over to my bed. And right away she says, 'No, no, I have boyfriend…go way.' I waited a little while and counted Herby's money and then said, I'll give you fifty dollars to come to my bed. This time she didn't answer right away and I knew she was thinking about it. I waited for what seemed like a half-hour but finally, she did answer. 'No,…no, I got boyfriend already.' Now, I really want to get even with this, fuck, don't you see. So I say, I'll give you a hundred dollars. This time there was a short pause and I heard her moving around getting ready to get up. I guess Herby figured he was about to lose his girlfriend, as he says, 'Get the fuck outta here, Eddie'."

Maybe it was the place or maybe you needed to know Herby Jackson. But it was one of the funniest stories I ever heard. We almost burst our guts laughing. The evening rolled on as we drank round after around and listened to Ed's humorous way of looking at life.

"Now, you guys know you have to be real smart, and do smart things, to get picked up for senior chief. I'll give you an example." We all nodded in agreement. "Everyone knows the Ninth Marines are getting the shit kicked out of them along the DMZ every goddamn day. I don't know anyone that's in one of those battalions that wouldn't kiss the Division Surgeon's ass in front of the flagpole for a transfer. But you can believe this shit or not. There's a Senior Chief by the name of John Tuomala that's TRYING TO GET INTO ONE OF THE BATTALIONS. Says he wants his own battalion in combat. You go figure that shit. He'll probably be picked up for Master Chief as smart as he is," laughed Ed.

And so it went until the club closed and then to the hooch and on into the early morning. It was people like Ed and Herby who made our life tolerable. Although, I must admit, I wasn't happy when Herby stole a generator from the Seabees, manifested it on a C-130 and had it flown to one of his buddies in a grunt battalion. The Seabees were holding inventory for their rotation to the States when they discovered it missing. They tracked it to Preventive Medicine and threatened to hold up everyone's flight date in the section if we didn't come up with it. I was glad they didn't stay mad when Herby gave it back. The Seabees seemed to be understanding about marines stealing from them. They had almost everything and the poor old marines hardly had anything. The VC had blown 2/3's generator away somewhere up around the DMZ and, according to Herby, the Seabees had two or three they didn't even need. "Besides, I just borrowed it for a few weeks," he said. Now that I think about it, Ol' Herby was a regular Robin Hood and, from time to time he did, indeed, show a little style.

A couple of days later, a Senior Chief came in the back door of Preventive Medicine. I was pouring Media and Andy was working on a logbook. The Chief was in full battle dress. He wasn't a big man but he looked powerful with broad shoulders. His face was set in rigid determination. He stopped at the sink across from where we were working, turned on the faucet and filled his canteen. I waited for him to speak, but he never looked in our direction. He hesitated long enough to screw the cap back on his canteen and strolled on into the Preventive Medicine Office. Andy looked at me.

"Senior Chief Tuomala," he remarked.

"About a friendly shit," I replied. Andy laughed silently and returned to his work. I wouldn't see Senior Chief Tuomala for another two years.

A short time after that, I was going to chow around 1140 in the morning when I saw dozens of bodies stacked in front of Graves Registration. One of the young marines came out and was checking the name on a dog tag of one of the KIAs.

"Who's been hit?" I asked.

"2/26 walked into an L shape ambush along the DMZ. Over four hundred WIAs and thirty nine KIAs," he answered. My heart jumped and I hurried to the triage area. Choppers were continuing to pour in. I looked for a familiar face among the wounded. The face of 2/26 had changed.

"Mes," someone called in a high-pitched voice. I turned to see Hospitalman Farmer, one of the old original crewmembers, being carried into the ward. He had a bandage around his chest and his flak jacket and helmet were riding on the stretcher with him. I ran and grabbed the handle of the stretcher to free up the attendant and he ran back to triage.

"What happened out there, Farmer?" I asked. His voice trembled with excitement.

"They shot the hell out of us and we couldn't figure out where it was coming from. The fighting was so close I dropped my flak jacket to work on someone, and then I was hit. Sometime during the melee one of the VC scooped up my flak jacket. I guess one of the marines must have blowed his ass away, as when I got on the MEDEVAC chopper this Dink had my flak gear on. Can you believe that shit, Mes?"

"Damn, that's close as it gets buddy." We had come to the ward and the Senior Corpsman directed us to a cot near the front entrance. He had taken the admission sheet and was reading it. I helped Farmer from the stretcher onto the cot.

"Chest wound," commented the Senior Corpsman.

"A month to go, and I get hit," complained Farmer.

"You're on your way to Yokosuka, Japan in a few hours and, if you got less than a month to do, you won't be coming back," commented the Senior Corpsman.

"You did good, Farmer," I said and gave him a pat on his leg.

The wounded and the dead came in all afternoon. I went back to Preventive Medicine with a heavy heart. That evening, I went back to see Farmer but he was gone. I went to the prisoner of war ward to see the benefactor of his flak jacket. He was lying with a blood-soaked bandage wrapped around his stomach. I looked into the dark eyes of a kid who appeared to be no more than seventeen years old. He was scared and in great pain. I went there to hate him, but instead, came away sickened at the senseless killing of kids on both sides.

The same men who could be heroes under fire could do unimaginable acts of debauchery when they were left idle. The influence of alcohol, mixed with boredom and lack of purpose, created a kind of insanity in the Medical Battalion. The Commanding General had issued an order that we were to consume only two beers a day. I sincerely tried to keep my consumption down to six a day through the week and twelve on Saturday and Sunday. When I think about it today, I realize that, within itself, was kind of an insanity.

In June, we had a cot come open and within a couple of days we received what I can only describe as a crazy man. I won't give his name out of respect for his family, but I sincerely believe he should have been locked up somewhere in a psychiatric ward. He was a hummer and hummed constantly both day and night. He had been assigned to one of the companies within the Battalion, but as far as I know, he never went to work and spent most days lying on his cot humming to himself. Occasionally, he would get up, growl like an angry bear, wander around and take care of his personal needs. His pinups were of a German Shepherd dog and Medusa (female from Greek legend with snakes for hair).

As time went on, I learned he had been the Chief in charge of the medical personnel in one of the battalions. The Battalion had been sent out of country to Okinawa to re-supply their mount out block. The Chief had spent his time on liberty getting drunk, instead of paying attention to business. When the Battalion came back to Vietnam all the medical gear was missing. That linked with the fact his wife had divorced him just before he was shipped out had apparently driven him over the edge.

He was a source of irritation to all of us with his constant complaining about us making too much noise for him to sleep. Never mind it was daytime, and he was driving us nuts with his infernal humming. The men who worked for Goggins were always looking for him for one thing or another. They would come into the hooch at various times of the day and ask his whereabouts. This did little to endear the Chief to Goggins, as this further disturbed his all-day siestas. Over a short period of time, the two came to detest each other. It's little wonder, that in our boredom, we contemplated daily how we might be able to add to the Chief's misery.

One Saturday night, as we sat drinking, Goggins hit on an idea.
"Do you guys remember that old joke about calling someone up and asking for someone three times and then the person calls and asks if anyone has left them a messages?" Yes, we all remembered that. And from the idea Goggins had conceived we hatched out a plan. "Messer,

you go down to the hooch first and ask the Chief if he knows where I am." A couple of more beers and away I went to play my part.

"Chief, do you know where Goggins is at?"

"NO, I DON'T KNOW WHERE THAT SKINNY MOTHER-FUCKER IS NOR DO I WANT TO." I went back to the club and gave my report of the Chief's irate behavior. About fifteen minutes past and it was the Staff Sergeant's turn. This was going to be fun so we all sneaked down to listen.

"Chief, have you seen Goggins in the past half hour?"

"I HAVEN'T SEEN THE SON-OF-A-BITCH. NOW, LEAVE ME THE FUCK ALONE." Back to the club we went and laughed ourselves into a frenzy, thoroughly enjoying our new game. Two beers later, it was Romando's turn. We were all crouched down behind the sandbags trying to be quiet. Romando let us all get settled down. He then entered the front screen door and let it bang shut. We heard the Chief grunt with annoyance.

"Cheap, yu sea Goggins tonight?"

"GET OUT, GET OUT, GET OUT, GET OUT, GET OUT," he screamed over and over as he sat up on the edge of his cot. It was so hysterical we had to rush back to the club in order to let go of our laughter lest the Chief suspect something.

Finally, it was time to send Goggins in for the kill. We took our positions up once again behind the sandbags. Goggins came quietly in the back door near where his cot was located and went over and unlocked his footlocker. The Chief sat morosely on his bunk, giving him the evil eye. Goggins turned and looked at the Chief. I think he would have liked to have forgotten the whole matter, but he knew we were all waiting and listening.

"Anyone been looking for me, Chief?" he asked, meekly. The Chief leaped off of his cot, rushed to his footlocker and grabbed his forty-five.

"YOU CRAZY COCKSUCKER," he screamed jacking a round in the chamber. Goggins took one look at the Chief and took off out the back door like a bat out of hell. The Chief was dead on his tail waving his pistol in the air.

"I'M GOING TO KILL ALL YOU BASTARDS," he screamed. We all took off running in different directions. We figured he was just crazy enough he might do it. Finding ourselves a safe place, we laughed and sipped beer until around mid-night. Sneaking back to the hooch, we found the Chief's cot empty. Later, we learned he had sought refuge in "B" Company's Administrative Office. The next morning I heard him come in the back door and go to his cot. "URGGHH, URGGHH," he growled.

The Vietnam War was different than other wars. It was about body count and not taking territory. Time in country determined when you would go home and not when the war was over. The insanity of this philosophy will, no doubt, be discussed as long as the United States remains a nation and beyond. But, my war was coming to an end.

The government had contracted with civilian airlines to fly its military personnel out of Vietnam. Headquarters Third Marine Division counted the number of men who would be rotating home each month and issued each of them a number. If you were given number one, you'd be the first man out and etc. The airlines would advise Headquarters how many seats were available each day and the date of your departure could be calculated by knowing your flight number.

It was the first day of August, 1967. My flight number was 1437. I would be leaving Phu Bai on the fourteenth of August. My tour of duty had started when the USS Henrico set sail with 2/26. I was jubilant from the day I received my number. I could finally let myself think about being with my family once again. Andy's and my flight numbers were so close we would be leaving Phu Bai on the same plane to go to

Da Nang to catch the big bird to the world. To say we had a short timer's attitude, would be an understatement. "Thirteen days and a wake up, don't start no long conversations with me, tell someone that gives a shit," was in our mouths day and night.

We had a not-so-subtle reminder that we hadn't quite made it when a planeload of homebound marines and corpsmen went down on a C-123 between Phu Bai and Da Nang. CPL Scott from Motor Transport had checked out the PC to me every morning for the past six months. He had escaped the heat of battle but the war claimed his life anyway. I had seen him the day before and we congratulated each other on having successfully completed our tours in the Nam. I just couldn't believe he was gone. They had not found the plane or the wreckage when I left Phu Bai. I don't know to this day if they ever did. The war had given me one last reminder of its cost in human tragedy.

On the night of the twelfth, Andy and I packed as we drank the evening away. The next morning we went to the airport across the street. Andy had filled his canteen with bourbon and would take a little sip when time and conditions permitted. As we waited in line, he continued to nip it along.

"Hey, you!" the Flight Attendant called to Andy. Andy ignored him and smiled his silent laugh. The Sergeant was not to be dismissed so easily and approached where we were waiting. "You were warned not to show up drunk," he proclaimed loudly.

"Who's drunk?" asked Andy.

"Let me see your canteen," ordered the Sergeant. I left Andy arguing with the Sergeant. I had no intention of missing my flight for Andy or anyone else. Andy caught up with me a few hours later. He had sobered considerably and I'm happy to report he stayed that way the next twenty-four hours.

The Da Nang SNCO club was like old home week the night of the thirteenth. Kirkpatrick, Dan, Oscar Willis and half a dozen others sat with me as we sipped our beer and told war stories. I couldn't help but notice the wrinkles around Dan's eyes. He tried to smile but the hard, sad look never left his face.

"So, tell us about being in the Artillery, Dan," someone asked. He didn't answer right away. We all waited respectfully as he collected his thoughts.

"The worst mistake of my life was leaving 2/26. They flew me in there on a chopper. We came in low and fast, taking rounds all the way. I knew then, I had stepped in shit. The marines were living in holes like ground hogs. We got hit every goddamn day I was there. One night they hit us so hard they blew the tires off the 105s. We were out there turning them by hand to return fire. I was so scared, I cried all night like a baby. The next day I sobbed like when I was a kid and had cried too long.

"Damn, buddy," I commented. He looked at me and I felt guilty for having had it so good the past six months. Kirk picked up his drink in the embarrassed silence that followed. Then Dan chuckled. "You want to hear something funny?" he asked. We all waited. "The next morning after the attack…when they blew the tires off…the General from Division came in on his chopper. He looked around and said, 'I can see you boys have got them on the run now,' and someone asked, 'How's that General?' 'Look how far these rounds are spaced apart,' he answered. Can you believe that shit? You couldn't take one step without putting your foot in a hole. It was like being a one legged man out there walking around. They'll never get my ass back over here. Ho Chi Minh can have this fucking place as far as I'm concerned." We ordered another round.

"Well, unless they mortar our sorry asses tonight we'll be leaving this shit hole tomorrow."

"I'll drink to that."

The next day we stood in formation watching the big orange and white Boeing 707 come in for a landing. Once it touched down, the hatch was opened and the ramp was lowered. A few minutes later, marines appeared in the door of the plane. The Marine Flight Attendant called us to attention and we started our march forward. A few meters from the plane we passed the men who were relieving us. Their green utilities looked liked they had just been issued. The black paint was still on their chevrons. A reverent silence encompassed us. We knew a lot of these men wouldn't be making the return trip home. We were the lucky ones. No one knew better than we did that this was nothing to jeer about. Thirteen months can be longer than a lifetime in a place like Vietnam. I felt only compassion for these warriors.

Soon, we were seated on the beautiful air-conditioned plane. We were a sorry looking lot in our faded clothes and colorless boots. Most of us were twenty pounds lighter than we were when we arrived. I looked around at the hard eyes and weather-beaten faces. Oscar Willis sat just across from where I was. He had a big smile on his ebony face as he shook his head up and down and repeated over and over, "Yes, sir. Yes, sir." The pretty stewardesses in their mini skirts walked up and down the aisles joking with us. The plane lurched and moved forward, turned and taxied down the runway. The stewardesses working the forward part of the plane walked to the front, sat down on their little jump seats, fastened their seatbelts and smiled out at us. The sound in the cabin changed as the big plane lifted off and I knew we were airborne. Suddenly, without warning, a spontaneous yell went up and hats went flying from one end of the plane to the other. "Yes, sir. Yes, sir," repeated Oscar as he looked out the window and down at the rice paddies.

We were finally going home. Little did we know that our sacrifices would be acknowledged with jeers, curses and accusations of being baby killers. The wounds inflicted on us by our countrymen would be a lot longer in healing then the ones we received from our enemies.

End of the Story

On the ninth of March 1969, I was sitting in the Preventive Medicine Department located in the old, now defunct, Thirteen-area Dispensary. I had just completed an inspection of the Twenty-four area's SNCO Club and was filling out my report. The two desks in the office had been shoved together and HM1 Ray Rangel sat opposite me.

"So, John. How did you find that shit hole this morning?"

"Filthy, as usual!"

"Did you pass them?"

"Not this time, I closed the club."

"You did what?"

"I got a hold of the manager and showed him some of the discrepancies. He said, 'Well, the working party didn't show up so I can't do anything about it. If you have any suggestions, I wish you'd tell me'. I said, 'I think I can help you out, Gunny.' I then reached across the desk, picked up the phone and called the Sergeant Major of Headquarters and requested permission to close the club until further notice."

"No shit! What did he say?"

"He said, 'Do what you need to do, Doc. Call us when you think it's ready to be opened. I'll ask the Colonel to accompany you, the Senior Chief, and the Preventive Medicine Officer on the final inspection'."

"What did the boss say when you told him?"

"I called and talked to Senior Chief Tuomala before I notified the Sergeant Major. He talked to Willie Victor for a minute, came back on, and told me to close it if I thought that was what I needed to do."

"What did Ol' Tom say to that?" chuckled Ray.

"He said, 'Now, I know why you're the most hated man aboard Camp Pendleton. You can't just go around messing up other people's careers like this'."

"Damn, Doc, that's serious."

"Ray, they haven't been paying a damn bit of attention to our recommendations. In fact, they think we're a joke. I think it's time we let them know we got the Base Commander on our side. When working with marines, you can't let them intimidate you. May as well stay home if you do. They respect authority if you got the balls to use it. One thing I learned in the grunts, and that's they'll exploit the hell out of you if they think you're weak. If he gets the place up to anywhere near a reasonable level, we'll open it back up for the noon meal."

Master Chief Tuomala had walked across from his and CWO4 W.V. Parkin's Office.

"Bad John, you best be getting yourself a new Chief's uniform." That was the last thing I was expecting to hear and I didn't quite comprehend what he had said.

The time requirement between First Class (E-6) and Chief Petty Officer (E-7) was three years. I had been promoted to First Class on the sixteenth of April 1966. Due to the fact I would have three years in grade for the next rating period, I had been allowed to take the exam for advancement in November of 1968. In Vietnam, I had seen marines in 2/26 promoted from E-6 to E-7 in one year. I didn't begrudge their promotions but felt it was unfair that we weren't extended the same consideration. After all, we had all served under the same arduous conditions.

My heart skipped a beat as the significance of what he had said dawned on me. I wondered if I had heard him correctly.

When I left Vietnam, Senior Chief Middleman had insisted I should request Preventive Medicine School. "With your background in Bacteriology and Preventive Medicine School behind you, you'll be able to go to work for any health department in the country," he assured me. I wasn't too hot on going back to the Clinical Laboratory, so I took his advice. I completed PMT (Preventive Medicine Technician) School in June of 1968 and was assigned to Marine Corps Base, Camp Pendleton, California. Much to my surprise, Senior Chief Tuomala was the senior enlisted man in Preventive Medicine.

"Why do I need to be worried about a Chief's uniform, Senior Chief? The results of the exams aren't even back."

"Division just called. They received the latest promotion list in this morning's mail. Navy Personnel is promoting three hundred and fifty new Chief Hospital Corpsmen this rating period. They are doing it in increments of fifty over the next seven months. You're on the first list and will be putting the hat on this coming Friday." His lower lip trembled as he studied my reaction. Only someone who has had the experience of waiting and studying for years can understand what it means for a sailor to hear those words. I stood up, weak-kneed.

"Congratulations, John," he said as he clasped my hand and gave me a big bear hug.

On the 21St of February 1969, I received orders to the Marine Air Group 36 in Okinawa, Japan where I served twelve months. Upon leaving there, I returned to Marine Corps Air Station in El Torro, California and was assigned to the Third Marine Air Wing to complete my sea duty. On the 9th of August 1973 I was transferred to the Naval Regional Medical Center, Camp Pendleton California.

On the 6th of November 1975, at 1000 in the morning, I stood in the Commanding Officer's office at Camp Pendleton, California. HMCM John Tuomala USN, now retired, stood a few feet from me in civilian clothes. He had come to pay me the honor of being at my side the last hour of my active duty. His eyes were misty as we gathered to hear Capt. R. Milnes read me my final orders.

A few days earlier, we had gathered at the club to drink and talk of days gone by.

"John, you may do a lot of things in the future but this is the acme of your life's work. No doubt, you'll earn more money and have other titles. But you will never again feel like you do when you get up in the morning and put that Chief's hat on your head." I remember wondering if this could possibly be true. In the years since, I have come to understand there is no sound sweeter than that of, "Hey, Chief," on the ears of a thirty-five-year old man, in the fullness of his strength, doing what he loves most.

Captain Milnes stood up, looked at me and smiled.

"Stand over here, Chief," he said and directed me to the front of his desk. I moved to my appointed place. The men in attendance came to attention and he commenced to read:

"*To all these who shall see the presents. Know ye that on the occasion of the United States Navy's two hundred year of service, commemorating the date in 1775 that the Continental Congress first ordered outfitting of a Naval Vessel, that Chief Hospital Corpsman John Dell Messer, USN, 403 46 6721 was on active Duty and serving in support of his country against all enemies at a significant moment in our nations history. On this 6th day of November he is hereby ordered to be transferred to the Fleet reserve.* Congratulations, Chief!"

I shook hands with everyone in the room and came to John last. The realization that our days together in service to our country had now come to an end brought with it a sweet sting of sorrow. He shook my hand and quickly turned away. I walked out the back door of the Naval Hospital and passed between the row of Chief Petty Officers that stood at attention rendering me a hand salute. I returned their courtesy and walked into another world.

My Naval career, like these humble pages, had finally come to:

The End

0-595-25687-2

Made in the USA
Las Vegas, NV
08 January 2023